MAHLER IN C

Mahler in Context explores the institutions, artists, thinkers, cultural movements, sociopolitical conditions, and personal relationships that shaped Mahler's creative output. Focusing on the contexts surrounding the artist, the collection provides a sense of the complex cross-currents against which Mahler was reacting as conductor, composer, and human being. Topics explored include his youth and training, performing career, creative activity, spiritual and philosophical influences, and reception after his death. Together, this collection of specially commissioned essays offers a wide-ranging investigation of the ecology surrounding Mahler as a composer and a fuller appreciation of the topics that occupied his mind as he conceived his works. Readers will benefit from engagement with lesser known dimensions of Mahler's life. Through this broader contextual approach, this book will serve as a valuable and unique resource for students, scholars, and a general readership.

CHARLES YOUMANS, Professor of Musicology at Penn State University, is the author of *Richard Strauss's Orchestral Music and the German Intellectual Tradition* (2005) and *Mahler and Strauss: In Dialogue* (2016). He is editor of *The Cambridge Companion to Richard Strauss* (2010) and has written nine chapters on Strauss's tone poems for the *Richard Strauss-Handbuch* (Metzler/Bärenreiter, 2014).

COMPOSERS IN CONTEXT

Understanding and appreciation of musical works is greatly enhanced by knowledge of the context within which their composers lived and worked. Each of these volumes focusses on an individual composer, offering lively, accessible and concise essays by leading scholars on the many contexts – professional, political, intellectual, social and cultural – that have a bearing on his or her work. Biographical and musical influences, performance and publishing history and the creative afterlife of each composer's work are also addressed, providing readers with a multi-faceted view of how the composers' output and careers were shaped by the world around them.

Titles forthcoming in the series

Beethoven in Context
edited by GLENN STANLEY and JOHN D. WILSON

Liszt in Context
edited by JOANNE CORMAC

Richard Strauss in Context
edited by MORTEN KRISTIANSEN and JOSEPH E. JONES

Stravinsky in Context
edited by GRAHAM GRIFFITHS

MAHLER IN CONTEXT

EDITED BY

CHARLES YOUMANS

Pennsylvania State University

CAMBRIDGE
UNIVERSITY PRESS

Shaftesbury Road, Cambridge CB2 8EA, United Kingdom

One Liberty Plaza, 20th Floor, New York, NY 10006, USA

477 Williamstown Road, Port Melbourne, VIC 3207, Australia

314–321, 3rd Floor, Plot 3, Splendor Forum, Jasola District Centre, New Delhi – 110025, India

103 Penang Road, #05–06/07, Visioncrest Commercial, Singapore 238467

Cambridge University Press is part of Cambridge University Press & Assessment,
a department of the University of Cambridge.

We share the University's mission to contribute to society through the pursuit of
education, learning and research at the highest international levels of excellence.

www.cambridge.org
Information on this title: www.cambridge.org/9781108438353

DOI: 10.1017/9781108529365

First published 2021
First paperback edition 2022

A catalogue record for this publication is available from the British Library

Library of Congress Cataloging-in-Publication data
NAMES: Youmans, Charles Dowell, 1964- editor.
TITLE: Mahler in context / edited by Charles Youmans.
DESCRIPTION: [1.] | New York : Cambridge University Press, 2020. | Series: Composers in context |
Includes bibliographical references and index.
IDENTIFIERS: LCCN 2020018637 (print) | LCCN 2020018638 (ebook) | ISBN 9781108423779
(hardback) | ISBN 9781108438353 (paperback) | ISBN 9781108529365 (epub)
SUBJECTS: LCSH: Mahler, Gustav, 1860-1911. | Mahler, Gustav, 1860-1911–Criticism
and interpretation. | Mahler, Gustav, 1860-1911–Influence. | Mahler, Gustav,
1860-1911–Appreciation. | Composers–Austria–Biography.
CLASSIFICATION: LCC ML410.M23 MI63 2020 (print) | LCC ML410.M23 (ebook) | DDC 780.92–dc23
LC record available at https://lccn.loc.gov/2020018637
LC ebook record available at https://lccn.loc.gov/2020018638

ISBN   978-1-108-42377-9   Hardback
ISBN   978-1-108-43835-3   Paperback

In memory of James Marquez (1932–2013)

Contents

Figures

Music Examples

Notes on Contributors

ROGER ALLEN is Emeritus Fellow in Music of St. Peter's College, University of Oxford. His most recent publications include extended contributions to *The Cambridge Wagner Encyclopedia* (2013), *Richard Wagner's Beethoven (1870): A New Translation* (Boydell and Brewer, 2014), and *Wilhelm Furtwängler: Art, Politics and the Unpolitical* (Boydell and Brewer, 2018). He is a member of the editorial board of *The Wagner Journal*. His current research includes issues of harmony and musical syntax in the music of Wagner and Bruckner and an investigation into the idea of the organic metaphor as a means of understanding musical process.

JEREMY BARHAM is Professor of Music at the University of Surrey. He researches in Mahler and modernism, screen music, and jazz. His publications include *Rethinking Mahler* (Oxford University Press, 2017), *The Cambridge Companion to Mahler* (2007), *Perspectives on Gustav Mahler* (Ashgate, 2005), and the *Nineteenth-Century Music Review* issue "Mahler: Centenary Commentaries on Musical Meaning." He is currently completing a monograph on Mahler and musical meaning for Indiana University Press, and an edited volume on early global film music for Routledge. He is director of the Institute of Austrian and German Music Research at the University of Surrey.

ANNA HARWELL CELENZA is the Thomas E. Caestecker Professor of Music at Georgetown University and the author of several books, including *Jazz Italian Style, from Its Origins in New Orleans to Fascist Italy and Sinatra* (2017), which won the Bridge Book Prize, and *The Cambridge Companion to Gershwin* (2019). She has also published numerous articles on a range of composers, from Franz Liszt and Gustav Mahler to Duke Ellington and Billy Strayhorn, and eight award-winning children's books.

LESLEY CHAMBERLAIN is a London-based writer and independent scholar of German literature and philosophy. Her books include *Nietzsche in Turin* (Quartet Books, 1996) and *A Shoe Story* (Harbour Books, 2014), a study of the controversy aroused by Heidegger's essay "The Origin of the Work of Art" in postwar America. She is also a literary journalist and frequent contributor to the British and American press.

STEPHEN DOWNES is Professor of Music at Royal Holloway, University of London. His recent books include *Music and Decadence in European Modernism: The Case of Central and Eastern Europe* (Cambridge University Press, 2010), *After Mahler: Britten, Weill, Henze and Romantic Redemption* (Cambridge University Press, 2013), and the edited collections *Aesthetics of Music: Musicological Perspectives* (Cambridge University Press, 2014) and *The Szymanowski Companion* (Ashgate, 2014). He is a coeditor of *Music & Letters*. He was awarded the Wilk Prize for Research in Polish Music (University of Southern California) and is a recipient of the Karol Szymanowski Memorial Medal.

CONSTANTIN FLOROS, Emeritus Professor of Musicology at the University of Hamburg, deciphered the oldest Byzantine and Slavic notations, demonstrated the Byzantine origin of Gregorian notation, and developed a method of semantic musical analysis that he applied to numerous works by various composers. His research focuses on culture and music of the Middle Ages and the eighteenth, nineteenth, and twentieth centuries. Among his thirty-five published books is a three-volume work on Gustav Mahler. In March 2010, the International Gustav Mahler Society awarded him the Golden Gustav Mahler Medal in recognition of his services to Mahler research. More about the author can be found at www.floros.de.

PETER FRANKLIN retired from the University of Oxford as a Professor of Music in 2014 and is an Emeritus Fellow of St. Catherine's College. He writes on late nineteenth-century musical culture in Europe, on post-Wagnerian opera, and on film music. Publications include *Mahler Symphony No. 3* (Cambridge University Press, 1991), *The Life of Mahler* (Cambridge University Press, 1997), and *Seeing through Music: Gender and Modernism in Classic Hollywood Film Scores* (Oxford University Press, 2011). His 2010 Bloch Lectures at the University of California at Berkeley were revised and published in 2014 as *Reclaiming Late-Romantic Music: Singing Devils and Distant Sounds* (University of California Press, 2014).

TIMOTHY FREEZE currently holds the Pocock Family Distinguished Visiting Professorship at the College of Wooster. His research on the music of Gustav Mahler, George Gershwin, and Aaron Copland has been published by Cambridge University, Oxford University, Böhlau, and Transkript presses. He is also editor of the forthcoming critical editions of Gershwin's Concerto in F and *"I Got Rhythm" Variations* (Schott).

EVA GILOI is Associate Professor at Rutgers University-Newark, with a PhD from Princeton University that received the Fritz Stern Prize (German Historical Institute). Currently at the Institute for Advanced Study in Princeton, she is working on the book *Authors and Epigones: Navigating Modernity in Nineteenth-Century Germany*. Her books include *Monarchy, Myth, and Material Culture in Germany, 1750–1950* (Cambridge University Press, 2011) and *Constructing Charisma: Celebrity, Fame, and Power in Nineteenth-Century Europe* (Berghahn, 2010). She has also written essays on material culture, visual culture, museums, socialization and childhood, copyright and photography, charisma in the urban space, and other topics in urban geography.

MICHAEL HEIDELBERGER, Professor Emeritus of Philosophy at the University of Tübingen, is the author of numerous works on the philosophy of science. His books include *Nature from Within: Gustav Fechner's Psychophysical Worldview* (University of Pittsburgh Press, 2004).

JOSEPH HOROWITZ, author of ten books dealing with the American musical experience, is the central authority on the institutional history of classical music in America. He writes about Mahler in New York in *Classical Music in America: A History of Its Rise and Fall* (2005), among other books. His book in progress is a fictionalized treatment of Mahler's New York sojourn. A former *New York Times* music critic, he has also served as Executive Director of the Brooklyn Philharmonic Orchestra, and Director of Music Unwound, an NEH initiative that produced cross-disciplinary festivals linking orchestras with institutions of higher learning. Since 2002 he has been Executive Director of an experimental chamber orchestra, PostClassical Ensemble, in Washington, DC, dedicated to curating the musical past. His website is www.josephhorowitz .com; his blog is www.artsjournal.com/uq.

KEVIN C. KARNES is Professor of Music and Vice Provost for the Arts at Emory University. His work includes *A Kingdom Not of This World: Wagner, the Arts, and Utopian Visions in Fin-de-Siècle Vienna* (Oxford University Press, 2013), *Arvo Pärt's Tabula Rasa* (Oxford University

Press, 2017), and the forthcoming *Sounds Beyond: Arvo Pärt and the 1970s Soviet Underground*. His newest research focuses on new wave music and culture.

CAROLINE A. KITA is an Associate Professor in the Department of Germanic Languages and Literatures at Washington University in St. Louis. Her scholarship examines German and Austrian culture in the nineteenth and twentieth centuries, focusing particularly on the intersections of music and literature. She is the author of *Jewish Difference and the Arts in Vienna: Composing Compassion in Music and Biblical Theater* (Indiana University Press, 2019) and has published on the philosophical and literary influences on Mahler's symphonic works, and on Mahler's friendship and intellectual collaborations with the poet Siegfried Lipiner.

REINHOLD KUBIK was born in Vienna, where he received his musical education. After ten years as an operatic conductor (Dortmund, Düsseldorf/Duisburg) he studied musicology, art history, and theater studies at Nuremberg/Erlangen, earning a doctorate with a thesis on Handel's *Rinaldo*. He also worked as a pianist, song accompanist, and composer. Editor of some 200 musical works, he has authored scholarly publications on Bach, Handel, Schubert, and Mahler, and on performance practice and scenic realization of the baroque opera. He edited the project BACH 2000 by J. E. Gardiner and won the 2004 prize from the German Music Publishing Association for his edition of Dvořák's *Stabat Mater*. As curator he produced the 2005 exhibition "Mahleriana" in the Jewish Museum Vienna, "Gustav Mahler in Vienna" in 2010 at the Austrian Theater Museum, and "Gustav Mahler in Vienna and Munich" in 2011 at the Deutsches Theatermuseum Munich.

DAVID LARKIN is a Senior Lecturer in Musicology at the University of Sydney. His scholarly writings have appeared in *The Cambridge Companion to Richard Strauss*, the journals *19th-Century Music*, *The Musical Quarterly*, and *Music and the Moving Image*, and various essay collections. At present he is working on a study of progressive composers and their audiences in the nineteenth century. He is also a regular pre-concert speaker at the Sydney Opera House and other local venues and is active as a music critic.

STEPHEN MCCLATCHIE is a Full Professor at Huron University College at Western University (London, Ontario) and served until 2016 as its sixteenth Principal. He is the author of *Analyzing Wagner's Operas:*

Alfred Lorenz and German Nationalist Ideologies (University of Rochester Press, 1998) and various studies of aspects of Austro-German music and culture between 1850 and 1945. His translation and edition of *The Family Letters of Gustav Mahler* was published in both German (Weidle Verlag) and English (Oxford University Press) in 2006.

MARILYN L. MCCOY teaches music history at Columbia University and Barnard College. A popular pre-concert lecturer, she has presented at the Amsterdam "Mahler Festival 2020," Carnegie Hall, Lincoln Center, and Disney Hall. She also served as annual pre-concert lecturer at the MahlerFest in Boulder, Colorado, from 2002 to 2016. Recent publications include *Schoenberg's Letters to Alma Mahler* (Oxford University Press, 2019), coedited with Elizabeth L. Keathley. She appeared as a commentator in the film *Mahler's Titan: The Romance, Death and Triumph of a Young Musician* (2019) and collaborates with Aaron Cohen on the podcast "Embracing Everything: The Symphonies of Gustav Mahler."

VERA MICZNIK is a retired faculty member from the musicology division of the University of British Columbia in Vancouver, Canada, where she taught for twenty-five years. She has published articles on Gustav Mahler, aesthetics and analysis of program music of Berlioz and Liszt, and applications of literary theory to music, such as narrativity in Mahler's music, semiotics, and intertextuality. Her publications have appeared in various collections on Mahler and other composers, as well as in journals such as *Nineteenth-Century Music*, *Music and Letters*, the *Journal of the Royal Music Association*, and the *Journal of Musicology*. Currently, she is working on a project entitled "Schumann's and Mahler's *Faust* as Documents in the History of *Faust*'s Reception."

CARL NIEKERK is Professor of German, Comparative and World Literature, and Jewish Studies at the University of Illinois/Urbana-Champaign. He is the author of *Reading Mahler: German Culture and Jewish Identity in Fin-de-Siècle Vienna* (Camden House, 2010). He is currently the editor of *The German Quarterly* and the *Lessing Yearbook*. Together with Caroline Kita and Francien Markx, he coedited "Music and German Culture," a special issue of *The German Quarterly* (91/4 [Fall 2018]).

MARGARET NOTLEY, Professor of Music at the University of North Texas, is the author of a recently published monograph, *"Taken by the Devil": The Censorship of Frank Wedekind and Alban Berg's "Lulu,"* and an earlier monograph, *Lateness and Brahms: Music and Culture in the Twilight of Viennese Liberalism* (2007), as well as a number of journal articles and chapters in multi-author volumes. A wish to understand why particular music sounds beautiful to her is her usual motivation for exploring a topic.

KAREN PAINTER, on the faculty of the University of Minnesota's School of Music, writes on music and politics in Germany and Austria. Visiting scholar at Harvard's Center for European Studies (2015–16) and the École des Hautes Etudes en Sciences Sociales (2010), she is also past recipient of the Humboldt fellowship and Berlin Prize. Her current research involves music and memory in the world wars. Author of *Symphonic Aspirations: German Music and Politics, 1900–1945* (Harvard University Press, 2007), she has also edited *Late Thoughts: Reflections on Artists and Composers at Work* (with Thomas Crow; Getty Research Institute, 2006) and *Mahler and His World* (Princeton University Press, 2002).

THOMAS PEATTIE is Associate Professor of Music at the University of Mississippi. He is the recipient of fellowships from the Social Sciences and Humanities Research Council of Canada, the Paul Sacher Foundation, and the Italian Academy for Advanced Studies in America at Columbia University. His articles and reviews have appeared in *Acta musicologica, Contemporary Music Review, Journal of the Royal Musical Association, Music and Letters*, and *Nineteenth-Century Music Review*. He is the author of *Gustav Mahler's Symphonic Landscapes* (Cambridge University Press, 2015) and is currently preparing a monograph on the transcribing practice of Luciano Berio.

MARTINA PIPPAL is Professor of Art History at the University of Vienna. She has served as guest professor at the Hebrew University of Jerusalem (2007) and the University of Zaragoza (2003) and has given lectures in Be'er Sheva, Beijing, Chicago, Frankfurt am Main, Haifa, Jerusalem, London, Lucerne, Moscow, Munich, New York, Rome, Shanghai, Trieste, Veszprém, Zaragoza, and elsewhere. Her scholarly focus is cultural studies, iconology, and stylistic analysis in the tradition of the Vienna School of Art History. She has particular interests in late antiquity, the early middle ages, and the twentieth century and has explored the implementation of kinesthetic learning in research and teaching.

WOLFGANG RATHERT is Professor of Historical Musicology at the Ludwig-Maximilians-Universität München with a focus on music from the twentieth century to the present. After completing a church music exam, he studied at the Free University of Berlin from 1980 to 1987 and received his doctorate with a dissertation under the direction of Rudolf Stephan on the work of Charles Ives, winning the Joachim Tiburtius Prize of the State of Berlin in 1988. From 1991 to 2002 he directed the Music and Theater Library of the Berlin University of the Arts. His habilitation followed in 1999 at the Humboldt University in Berlin. He is a member of the Board of Trustees of the Géza Anda Foundation Zurich and the Paul Sacher Foundation Basel.

PETER REVERS is Professor of History at the University of Music and Performing Arts in Graz (Austria) and has been president of the Austrian Musicological Society (2001–9). He studied musicology and composition in Salzburg and Vienna. From 1981 to 1996 he taught at the University of Music and Dramatic Arts in Vienna and completed his habilitation in 1993. In 1988–89 he was fellow of the Alexander von Humboldt Foundation and became full professor in Graz in 1996. His publications include volumes on Mahler (*Mahlers Lieder* [Munich, 2000]; *Gustav Mahler – Interpretationen seiner Werke* [ed.], [Laaber, 2011]), the European reception of Far Eastern music (*Das Fremde und das Vertraute: Studien zur musiktheoretischen und musikdramatischen Ostasienrezeption* [Stuttgart, 1997]), and more than 120 published articles.

MORTEN SOLVIK, a native of Norway, received his education at Cornell University and the University of Pennsylvania before moving to Austria, where he currently resides. Solvik's research focuses on the connections between music and culture, especially with regard to Gustav Mahler. He is active as an author, book editor, speaker, and contributor to productions for radio and television. He is the cofounder and Artistic Director of the Gustav Mahler Festival in Steinbach am Attersee and Board Director and Vice President of the Mahler Foundation. Solvik serves as Center Director of IES Abroad Vienna, a study abroad program for US university students, where he also teaches music history.

RENATE STARK-VOIT was born and raised in Munich, then pursued graduate work in musicology, German studies, and Romance studies at universities in Munich, Graz, and Vienna, earning a PhD in 1988 (then as Hilmar-Voit) in Vienna with a dissertation on Mahler entitled

"In the Wunderhorn-Ton." She has conducted independent research on Schubert, Schumann, Webern, and Mahler, producing various essays and lectures, and has served as a freelancer at Universal Edition, Vienna. Her work includes collaboration with interpreters, especially Kammersänger Thomas Hampson on various projects and publications. For the Neue Kritische Gesamtausgabe of Gustav Mahler (NKG), she has edited songs from *Des Knaben Wunderhorn* with piano and orchestral accompaniment (Universal Edition Wien, 2008 and 2011), the Second Symphony (UE/Kaplan Foundation, 2010), and the Fourth Symphony (forthcoming, 2019).

ANNA STOLL KNECHT holds a four-year research grant "Ambizione" from the Swiss National Science Foundation for a project entitled "Music and Clowning in Europe, 20th–21st Centuries" (Accademia Teatro Dimitri). Previously a British Academy postdoctoral fellow at the University of Oxford (Jesus College), she has engaged in research on Gustav Mahler's interpretation of Richard Wagner, both as a conductor and as a composer. Her recent publications include a monograph on Mahler's Seventh Symphony (Oxford University Press, 2019), book chapters in *Wagner in Context* (Cambridge University Press, forthcoming) and *Rethinking Mahler* (Oxford University Press, 2017), and an article for *The Wagner Journal* (2017).

RICHARD WATTENBARGER teaches in the Music Studies Department at Temple University. He has served as a freelance program annotator and has written on Theodor Adorno, Richard Strauss, music historiography, and the history of musicology as an academic discipline.

MATTHEW WERLEY (DPhil, Oxford) is a lecturer in Musicology and Dance Studies at the Mozarteum and the University of Salzburg, Austria. He has held appointments at the Universities of Cambridge and East Anglia and has been awarded several fellowships from the German Academic Exchange Service (DAAD) and the Gerda Henkel Stiftung for his research into Richard Strauss and Stefan Zweig. His research focuses on German literature, opera studies, performance history, and modern dance. Recent work has focused on Mahler's interaction with Alfred Roller and the ballerina-turned-modern dancer Grete Wiesenthal. Currently, he serves as editor of the peer-reviewed *Richard Strauss-Jahrbuch* (Hollitzer Verlag). Further information can be found at www.matthew-werley.com.

CHARLES YOUMANS, Professor of Musicology at Penn State University, is the author of *Richard Strauss's Orchestral Music and the German Intellectual Tradition* (Indiana University Press, 2005) and *Mahler and Strauss: In Dialogue* (Indiana University Press, 2016) and the editor of *The Cambridge Companion to Richard Strauss* (2010). He has published articles in *19th-Century Music*, *The Musical Quarterly*, the *Journal of Musicology*, and elsewhere. In 2014 he contributed nine chapters on Strauss's tone poems to the *Richard Strauss-Handbuch*, ed. Walter Werbeck (Metzler/Bärenreiter, 2014).

JAMES L. ZYCHOWICZ, PhD, has published on various aspects of Mahler's music, including *Mahler's Fourth Symphony* (Oxford University Press, 2000), a study of the composer's compositional process. His critical edition of *Die drei Pintos* (A-R Editions, 2000) has been performed in various venues, including Lincoln Center. His article on Mahler's legacy at the composer's recent centenary won the Richard Hill Award from the Music Library Association in 2011. He is active in the American Musicological Society and other professional organizations and works for A-R Editions.

Preface and Acknowledgments

Placing a composer in context is a Mahlerian idea. Contemplating himself, Mahler found that external conditions determined his identity. "I am thrice homeless: a Bohemian among Austrians, an Austrian among Germans, and a Jew throughout the world" (*ML*, 109). Performing other people's music, he turned the tables; now he was the context, imposing a bold interpretive vision and even reorchestrating classics (most famously Beethoven's Ninth). And in his own works Mahler thematized the interaction of text and context, through a widely noted (and often criticized) fondness for quotation, allusion, reminiscence, homage, transformation, modernization, and strong reception, which paradoxically made him at once derivative and forward-thinking.

He came by these tendencies honestly. A gymnasium education – completed with substantial effort two years *after* he left Iglau for the Vienna Conservatory – attuned him to the complexities of interpretation. On one hand, the humanistic tradition directed his mind forcefully toward the past, that is, to classical culture, revered authority figures, and ostensibly stable meanings. On the other, the rousing chaos of incipient modernism encouraged young thinkers to question anything and everything, with transformative results that became apparent as a generation of iconoclasts reached maturity. "And ancestors, long to their graves confined / Are yet as close to me as my own hair," Hofmannsthal would write in 1895.[1] Innovation and tradition were two sides of the same coin in fin-de-siècle Europe.

Perhaps this symbiosis explains why Bach and Goethe were the only artists represented in the tiny libraries of Mahler's composing huts. Bach created music by putting old materials into new contexts. The cantatas,

---

[1] Hugo von Hofmannsthal, "On Mutability," *Stanzas in Terza Rima*, in J. D. McClatchy, *The Whole Difference: Selected Writings of Hugo von Hofmannsthal* (Princeton: Princeton University Press, 2008), 26.

which Mahler came to know through his subscription to the Bach Gesell-schaft edition, revealed the power of assertive reinterpretation: of a Lutheran chorale, a stylized dance, a form devised by Vivaldi. Fresh settings lent these artifacts deeper significance and, with it, richer identities.

Goethe, Mahler's lodestar, spent his life in close observation of anything and everything, in the belief that value, and therefore meaning, depended on the observer's interest. This individual responsibility to strive, to realize oneself through fresh experiences and continuous becoming, would define Mahler's worldview. Emblematically, Natalie Bauer-Lechner recalled that her first conversation with Mahler, during his student years, concerned *Wilhelm Meister's Apprenticeship*. What did they discuss? We cannot know, but one way or another they pondered the individual's struggle to make sense of the world, a theme that pervades the book. The problem is summed up toward the novel's end by the Abbé, who, representing the conservatism of Mahler's educational background, anticipates bitterly but perceptively the future of "meaning" as an idea:

> Nowadays most people treat finished works of art as if they were soft clay. The finished marble shall modify its shape according to their inclinations, their opinions and whims, the firmly established building expand or con-tract . . . [E]verything is relative, they say, and so the only things that are not relative are nonsense and bad taste, which, in the end, predominate as absolutes.[2]

Contingency, styled here as a symptom of decay, would over the next century become an inescapable fact. Yet already in 1795 Goethe recog-nized that the boundary between work and reader might be an illusion.

If Mahler did not fully grasp the emergent critique of absolute truth – though the presence of Kant's writings in the hut, as the only non-art, suggests that he did – the situation would soon be spelled out for him by Nietzsche. The philosopher's attacks on the idealist pantheon (Plato, Jesus, Schopenhauer, and Wagner) cannot but have troubled the composer of the "Resurrection" Symphony and Part II of Goethe's *Faust*. Indeed, aside from his setting of the "Midnight Song" from *Also sprach Zarathustra* (in the Third Symphony), Mahler remained conspicuously silent on the philosopher's rift with Wagner and the antimetaphysical texts it precipi-tated. But any experienced listener knows that his apotheoses are balanced

---

[2] Johann Wolfgang von Goethe, *Wilhelm Meister's Apprenticeship*, ed. and trans. Eric A. Blackall, in cooperation with Victor Lange (Princeton: Princeton University Press, 1989), 351 (translation emended).

by scenes of resignation: after the Fifth Symphony comes the Sixth; after the Eighth, *Das Lied von der Erde*. In his creative work, the eternal and the secure are fantasies. And that conviction, disguised though it often was by magnificently staged hopes, made him a faithful witness of his moment in intellectual history.

All of this is to say that the only Mahler is a Mahler in context. "There is no outside-text," Derrida famously observed. Text and context are one; people, like works, must be read through the conditions in which they exist. Mahler's music regularly embodies this idea – for example, in passages to be played "in the far distance" or "like a sound of nature," where the object blends with the experience of perceiving it. Likewise, his infamous predilection for referentiality asks listeners to notice their contribution to the process of interpretation, as when Alma remarked of the Fourth, "I think Haydn has done that better." The judgment surely stung, but the comparative impulse honored the composer's invitation to draw meaning from an encounter.

We can study his life in the same way. The five parts of this book represent experiments in that sort of thinking: broad themes that loosely organize a variety of perspectives. The categories of inquiry are straightforward enough. In Mahler's world, what factors shaped a musician's development? How was music realized practically? To what ends, and by what means, did creation take place? What significance did art have physically, intellectually, and psychologically? To whom did this music and its creator matter in the end? Within each part, the choice of topics is meant to provide a diversity of viewpoints, though of course other choices are conceivable and deserve to be explored.

The range of scholarly approaches is likewise as broad as could be managed. With an international roster of contributors, differences are to be expected in methodology, writing style, organization, and so on, and I have not smoothed those over. An alternate and equally viable book could have been produced by distributing these topics differently among the same scholars, who stand at the forefront of current research on Mahler. In some cases, the reader will notice divergent opinions on certain works, individuals, and issues; here again I have left the heterogeneity in place rather than imposing a simplistic conformity.

My first word of thanks must go to the contributors, thirty-one in all, a splendid group of scholars representing seven countries and a diverse range of institutions and approaches. A book of this sort would not be possible without the enthusiastic participation of relevant experts, and a host of the world's leading Mahler specialists are here, along with some intrepid authorities from outside the subdiscipline who embraced the challenge of writing on a vitally important composer tangentially related to their own work. I am deeply grateful to everyone involved. The intellectual expertise, collaborative spirit, and determined efficiency that these colleagues brought to the project was nothing less than inspiring.

All of us owe a debt to Henry-Louis de La Grange, Donald Mitchell, and Stephen E. Hefling, whose work paved the way for the current happy state of Mahler research. International cooperation and good will, a hallmark of the Mahlerian scholarly community, was facilitated in this volume by Juliane Schicker, whose sensitive, readable translations are a model of that demanding art. I am extraordinarily thankful as well for the editorial assistance of my graduate advisee Celeste Belknap, whose keen intellect and careful attention to detail improved every chapter.

In the spring of 2019, I taught a course in which early versions of many chapters served as the text, and I wish to acknowledge the useful and candid feedback of those students: Sarah Adsit, Charlie Alves, Dylan Crosson, Michael Divino, Sarah Files, Nick Kazmierczak, Gage Kroljic, Sarah Neff, Maggie Nostrand, Caroline Senko, Victoria Senko, Jenny Tokarek, Sean Toso, and Kristen Zak. The Penn State School of Music, now under the capable stewardship of Director David Frego, continues to be a pleasant and fruitful environment in which to work; this is due above all to my dear colleagues in music history and theory. For the kind favor of permission to use copyrighted images, I would like to thank Universal Edition and the Sony Corporation. Paul Sommerfeld, Music Reference Specialist at the Library of Conference, kindly provided information about the Music Division's Arnold Schoenberg Collection. For the invitation to edit this volume, I want express my genuine gratitude to the brilliantly able and unfailingly genial Kate Brett, who with her assistant Eilidh Burrett made the process easier than I could have imagined possible. My heartfelt thanks go also to Stephanie Sakson, a skillful and perceptive copyeditor, and to Niranjana Harikrishnan, who managed the project with welcome efficiency. And finally, I want to close, as always, by thanking Nancy, Frances, and Hannah, whose love and support mean everything.

Abbreviations

GMB2   *Gustav Mahler Briefe*, 2nd ed., ed. Herta Blaukopf (Vienna: Zsolnay, 1996)

HLG1   Henry-Louis de La Grange, *Gustav Mahler*, vol. 1 (Garden City, NY: Doubleday, 1973)

HLG2   Henry-Louis de La Grange, *Gustav Mahler, vol. 2: Vienna: The Years of Challenge (1897–1904)* (Oxford: Oxford University Press, 1995)

HLG3   Henry-Louis de La Grange, *Gustav Mahler, vol. 3: Vienna: Triumph and Disillusion (1904–1907)* (Oxford: Oxford University Press, 1999)

HLG4   Henry-Louis de La Grange, *Gustav Mahler, vol. 4: A New Life Cut Short (1907–1911)* (Oxford: Oxford University Press, 2008)

ML   Alma Mahler, *Gustav Mahler: Memories and Letters*, ed. Donald Mitchell and Knud Martner, trans. Basil Creighton (London: Cardinal, 1990)

NBLE   Natalie Bauer-Lechner, *Recollections of Gustav Mahler*, ed. Peter Franklin, trans. Dika Newlin (Cambridge: Cambridge University Press, 1980)

SLGM   Alma Mahler and Knud Martner, eds., *Selected Letters of Gustav Mahler*, trans. Eithne Wilkins, Ernst Kaiser, and Bill Hopkins (London: Faber and Faber, 1979). For each quotation from Mahler's correspondence, both *GMB2* and *SLGM* are cited. Some translations have been amended.

PART I

Formation

CHAPTER I

Family Life

Stephen McClatchie

The well-known peroration of Theodor Adorno's magisterial *Mahler: A Musical Physiognomy* calls attention to Mahler's family life and its influence on his subsequent development as a human being and as an artist: "Mahler's music holds fast to Utopia in the memory traces from childhood, which appear as if it were only for their sake that it would be worth living. But no less authentic for him is the consciousness that this happiness is lost, and only in being lost becomes the happiness it itself never was" (*Adorno*, 145). Adorno's gnomic comment resonates with Mahler's 1886 remark to Friedrich Löhr that his "whole life is one great homesickness" (*SLGM*, 101/*GMB2*, 78). Mahler was indelibly marked by the circumstances of his childhood: the physical, social, and psychological conditions in which he was raised. Adorno's observation, initially poignant but trending toward hope, and Mahler's own, with its sense of loss and longing, encapsulate the effect of these things on the composer's life. The first two conditions are primarily external and comprise such matters as his physical surroundings, the economic circumstances of the family, and their social position and religious engagement as part of the first generation of emancipated Jews in the Habsburg empire. From these circumstances emerge the emotional and psychological conditions unique to Mahler's family: ill-matched parents and frequent conflict, the illness and death of half of his siblings, and the outsized presence of Mahler's raw talent within these family dynamics.

Three months after Mahler's birth in Kalischt, the family moved to the Moravian town of Iglau (population ca. 17,000). They were among the first Jews to settle in the town after the removal of legal impediments to living there and purchasing property; by the end of the decade, there were 1,090, comprising 5.4 percent of the population. A school was established in 1860, the *Gemeinde* (congregation) in 1862, and a synagogue and cemetery consecrated in 1863 and 1869, respectively. The physical world of Mahler's childhood Iglau included military barracks, a theater, a hall owned by the men's *Gesangsverein,* a post office, a Catholic church, and a railway station, which from 1871 offered a direct connection to Vienna.

Bernard Mahler (1827–89) originally had a four-year residency permit, subsequently renewed, and the family lived until 1872 in a rented dwelling on the Pirnitzergasse (now Zmojemská Ulice 6). That year, Bernard purchased the three-story house next door from the widowed mother of Gustav's music teacher and in 1873 renovated the property to make the ground floor into a shop where he distilled and sold spirits (initially, he had rented a small pub and distillery nearby); the top floor was rented out. Thus established, Bernard became a citizen of Iglau in 1873.

While most biographers have emphasized the Mahlers' participation in a wider trend of Jewish assimilation and secularization, Michael Haber has recently shown just how connected they remained to their Jewish faith.[1] Bernard was a close friend of the cantor in the synagogue, who served as Justine Mahler's godfather in 1868. In 1878, Bernard was elected to the education committee of the *Gemeinde,* a sign of growing status in the community. His social and political involvement likely extended into local religious life, and, indeed, one unpublished portion of Natalie Bauer-Lechner's *Erinnerungen* records a visit to the synagogue when Gustav was three – surely not a one-off visit.[2] To some extent, then, Mahler was brought up and educated as a Jew, underwent the rituals of Judaism (circumcision and bar mitzvah), and attended synagogue at least on holy days. He also studied religion privately with the rabbi, J. J. Unger, and received an attestation to that effect at the time of his *Abitur* (gymnasium exit examination). Evidence from the family letters and elsewhere supports Haber's contention that the composer's mother, Marie (1837–89), may have been the most observant member of the family.[3] These links to the Jewish faith bear emphasizing, although the Mahler family was certainly well along on the continuum of Jewish assimilation; Bernard was ambitious to get ahead in socioeconomic terms, and to better himself and his family by embracing the German (and hence Christian) notion of *Bildung,* that is, character formation. Thus, the Mahler family celebrated Christmas (at least to the extent of exchanging gifts): an external acceptance of a tradition, reflecting an internal desire to belong to Christian society.[4]

---

[1] Michael Haber, *Das jüdische bei Gustav Mahler* (Frankfurt am Main: Peter Lang, 2009).

[2] The excerpt was first published by Norman Lebrecht in *Mahler Remembered* (London: Faber & Faber, 1987), 10.

[3] See Haber, *Das jüdische bei Gustav Mahler,* 23–34, and Donald Mitchell, *Gustav Mahler: The Early Years* (Berkeley: University of California Press, 1980), 270–73.

[4] Haber, *Das jüdische bei Gustav Mahler,* 53–54.

There is no surviving evidence that anti-Semitic prejudice or discrimination affected Mahler's childhood, although he cannot have escaped the myriad microaggressions directed at children who are different in some way. In his memoirs, Guido Adler celebrated tolerance as the "highest principle of the humanistic education" that he received in Iglau at the hands of Catholic priests and the rabbi.[5] Mahler was rather an indifferent student, yet under his father's influence he developed a love of reading that he maintained all his life.

Accounts vary with respect to the family's economic circumstances. Alma Mahler wrote that Gustav did "not come of a poor home, merely from one of soul-destroying narrowness" (*ML*, 63). Richard Specht noted that Mahler's parents "never had to let their children go hungry" and Paul Stefan even called them "well-to-do."[6] While his relatives were certainly affected by anti-Jewish legislation (both parents were born of illegal Jewish marriages and thus deemed illegitimate until their parents could be civilly married), his paternal great-grandfather Abraham Bondy was a prosperous merchant in Kalischt, and his maternal grandfather, Abraham Hermann, was a wealthy soap manufacturer. Bernard and Marie, therefore, both came from families of some means.

Additional evidence of the family's relative prosperity comes from the fact that Mahler had music lessons from a young age and was even sent to Prague for a year of school (presumably, for its better musical possibilities). However, he did apply for (and receive) financial aid from the Vienna Conservatory about 1876 because his father was not in a position to support him. On balance, Donald Mitchell's conjecture rings true that the family "at best, never achieved more than a pinched, lower middle-class status," given that much of their resources would have been tied up in the business. Mahler's parents' estate was valued at 28,000 fl. at a time when an annual salary of 750–800 fl. would have been significant.[7]

While the physical, social, and economic conditions of Mahler's childhood certainly shaped his character, the emotional and psychological circumstances of his family life undoubtedly were decisive. In Stuart Feder's assessment, the family letters – the most significant source of biographical information before the mid-1890s – show a devoted family,

[5] Guido Adler, *Wollen und Wirken: Aus dem Leben eines Musikhistorikers* (Vienna: Universal 1935), 3; in *Mahler: His Life, Work, and World*, compiled and ed. Kurt Blaukopf and Herta Blaukopf with contributions by Zoltan Roman (London: Thames & Hudson, 1991), 20.

[6] Mitchell, *The Early Years*, 17–18, 274.

[7] Ibid., 18; see Tomáš Cvrček, "Wages, Prices, and Living Standards in the Habsburg Empire, 1827–1910," *Journal of Economic History* 73 (2013): 1–37.

one reflecting "traditional values of caring and mutual responsibility despite internal conflicts and, at least amongst Marie, Gustav, and Justine, a tendency towards guilt and self-punishment."[8]

Understanding these dynamics begins with Mahler's own description of his parents to Natalie Bauer-Lechner:

> My father (whose mother had previously supported the family as a pedlar of drapery) had the most diverse phases of making a livelihood behind him and, with his usual energy, had more and more worked himself up [the social scale]. At first he had been a waggoner, and, while he was driving his horse and cart, had studied and read all sorts of books – he had even learnt a bit of French, which earned him the nickname of a "waggon scholar" [*Kutschbockgelehrter*, "car-seat scholar"]. Later he was employed in various factories [i.e., distilleries], and subsequently he became a private coach [*Hauslehrer*]. On the strength of the little estate in Kalischt, he eventually married my mother – the daughter of a soap manufacturer from Leddetsch – who did not love him, hardly knew him prior to the wedding, and would have preferred to marry another man of whom she was fond. But her parents and my father knew how to bend her will and to assert his. They were as ill-matched as fire and water. He was obstinacy itself, she all gentleness. (*NBLE*, 69)

Alma, too, records Bernard's ambition to better himself personally, socially, and culturally. His ambition extended to his family and particularly to his talented son, whom he sent off alone to Vienna at the age of fifteen. Surviving letters demonstrate that Mahler's father was temperamentally difficult, domineering, and occasionally ruthless and that this often led to conflict with others.

Mahler's mother was ten years younger than her husband and, according to Alma, "lame from birth" (*ML*, 6). The match was in all likelihood an arranged one, Marie bringing a dowry of 3,500 gulden as well as material goods from her prosperous parents. In any case, Gustav was deeply attached to her. Löhr characterized her as "a woman richly endowed with the virtues of her sex, one whose tenderness and gentleness, kindliness and warm receptiveness, are an abiding memory of any of those who knew her" (note to an undated letter from Mahler to Löhr of September 1889; *SLGM*, 403/*GMB2*, 438). Alma rather maliciously records that she was sometimes called the "duchess" because of her "superior refinement." Alma's unflattering portrayal of Mahler's family – Marie's "unending

[8] Stuart Feder, *Gustav Mahler: A Life in Crisis* (New Haven: Yale University Press, 2004), 20. For a concise overview of Mahler's family history and the significance of these letters, see Stephen McClatchie, ed., *The Mahler Family Letters* (New York: Oxford University Press, 2006), 3–16.

tortures," the "brutality of her husband, who ran after every servant, domineered over his delicate wife and flogged the children" (*ML*, 7) – nevertheless found confirmation in Mahler's 1910 conversation with Freud, who told Marie Bonaparte that Mahler's "father, [was] apparently a brutal person, treated his wife very badly."[9]

While some of the details may be controverted, Mahler clearly did not grow up in a stable family unit; as Feder notes, an early life overshadowed by conflict and death and where his nuclear family was not a shelter from the outside world surely had an impact on him. Mahler rarely spoke of his father; Bernard, in turn, may have been ambivalent about a potential rival for the family's love and admiration. Gustav's close identification with and attachment to his mother could not have helped, since she clearly favored him even over her husband. Freud himself diagnosed a "Holy Mary complex" and "mother fixation" (*Marienkomplex – Mutterbindung*), and Mitchell suggests that Mahler's famous "jerking" foot may be an unconscious echo of his mother's lameness, part of a broader youthful identification with her tendency toward martyrdom. Over twenty-one years, Marie Mahler bore fourteen children, eight of whom died of childhood diseases, including her first-born, Isidore (1858–59). "Born in the shadow of death," he was particularly close to his younger brother, Ernst (1862–75), whose passing from a congenital heart condition brought his "first sorrow" and in Feder's view colored all of his adult relationships with women.[10]

Amid these tensions and likely contributing to them was the omnipresence of Mahler's talent, which made him the "admired idol of the family."[11] Stories of his family listening secretly to his piano playing and promoting him in the wider community confirm that he was admired and adored by them and that, in some sense, he acquired a special status rivalling his dominating father; such dynamics certainly colored his subsequent relationship with his less-talented musical brother, Otto (1873–95). A natural dreamer, Mahler could withdraw from his

---

[9] Mitchell, *The Early Years*, 7.
[10] Feder, *Gustav Mahler*, 9–29, 24; in addition to Alma Mahler's account (*ML*, 175), information about Mahler's session with Freud comes from notes made by Marie Bonaparte in 1925 and from Freud's account to Theodor Reik in 1935, as detailed in Feder, *Gustav Mahler*, 206–42; Mitchell, *The Early Years*, 13; Feder, *Gustav Mahler*, 15, 23.
[11] Letter of February 1917 from Natalie Bauer-Lechner to Hans Riehl; see Morten Solvik and Stephen E. Hefling, "Natalie Bauer-Lechner on Mahler and Women: A Newly Discovered Document," *Musical Quarterly* 97 (2014): 12–65; here 40.

surroundings at will, and his extraordinary power of concentration was noted by many.

Minor conflicts within the family increased over the years as Mahler's parents' illnesses and debilities worsened. By the mid-1880s, both were ailing: Bernard from congestive heart failure and diabetes (which doubtless contributed to his irritability) and Marie from asthma and a weak heart (not to mention the rigors of almost ceaseless childbearing). Mahler's eldest sister remaining at home, Justine (1868–1938), compromised her own physical and mental health in nursing their parents.

These stressors weighed on Mahler, the "golden boy" and eldest child, whose letters describe frequent visits to doctors and consultations with professors. Increasingly, he took on a quasi-parental role, sending money home, insisting that it be used for their pleasure, and arranging deliveries of treats like sardines, preserves, graham bread, and cakes. He wrote frequently to Justine, to encourage her to be tolerant of their sick father and to alleviate their mother's suffering,[12] and he often unburdened himself to Löhr. Depressed after a visit home in July 1883, he wrote how "wretched and gloomy" it was: "I myself, so hard and cruel to them – and yet I can't help it, and torment them to distraction" (*SLGM*, 73–74/*GMB2*, 47). Feelings of frustration and helplessness mounted as he "watch[ed] the clouds gather over them without being able to do a thing," even as he remained committed to help his family in any way possible (*SLGM*, 101/*GMB2*, 78). A palpable need to control emerges in these letters as he tried to manage the situation from afar.

At his father's death in February 1889, Mahler became the male head of the family at the age of twenty-nine and took this responsibility seriously. His eldest sister, Leopoldine (1863–89), was married and living in Vienna; brother Alois (1867–1931) was in the military; and Otto was at the Conservatory in Vienna. Only his ailing mother, along with Justine and his youngest sibling, Emma (1875–1933), remained at home. By fall, things were grim. Leopoldine was ill (and died only a few weeks before their mother), Marie was terminal, and Justine was almost prostrate with exhaustion and worry. Despite its inevitability, Mahler's mother's death was extremely painful and disorienting for him, breaking as it did this last tie to his youth.

In the years to come, Mahler remained devoted to his family, and his letters – admittedly often demanding, critical, and even biting in tone – are also full of genuine concern and practical advice, especially regarding the

[12] McClatchie, ed., *The Mahler Family Letters*, 48, 49, 30.

impractical and costly household that Justine established for them in Vienna, and the misadventures of his wayward brothers. Alois was finally allowed to go his own way in 1893 and disappears from their lives. Otto, tragically, committed suicide in 1895.

While Alma's characterization of the siblings can shade into caricature, elements are corroborated by a recently published letter of Bauer-Lechner. On the basis of Mahler's clear love and concern for his sister Justine, the recipient of most of the family letters, I was led in earlier works almost to dismiss Alma's portrayal of her as something of a drama queen, untrustworthy and manipulative. A recently discovered letter from Natalie indicates that I was mistaken: she recounts Justine's jealousy and manipulative nature, which revealed itself in lies and intrigues; her "ill-bred and unrestrained nature," which could also be happy and friendly, accommodating and sincere; and her great influence on Gustav. Natalie calls her the "most important source of happiness and also of misfortune in his existence" and draws attention to the quasi-incestuous aspects of its intensity: "had she not been his sister, she would certainly have been one of his greatest passions."[13] This dynamic, which I had regarded as latent at best, colors a comment that Justine made to her friend Ernestine Löhr in the wake of Mahler's affair with Anna von Mildenburg: "I have come to terms with the fact that I am no longer the nearest to Gustav's heart."[14]

When the young Gustav Mahler moved to Vienna in 1875 to study at the Conservatory, it was a severing with his past. Nevertheless, he continued to bear the imprint of the physical, social, emotional, and psychological circumstances of his upbringing in Iglau, both positive and negative. These experiences would surface in the themes of banishment, death, mourning, and brotherly love/hate that were to occupy Mahler's creative life and output. And yet Mahler emerged from the crucible of a difficult childhood and young adulthood capable of writing a remarkable letter to his sister that demonstrates a well-adjusted insight into human nature derived from the formative experiences of his family life:

> Always remember that every *human being* is a world to himself; one knows a large part of it – namely insofar as it is contained in oneself – but the rest of it remains a life-long secret to someone [else]. – If one establishes new rules, they are always suited for the piece of the world that one knows – (namely, because it is one's own) – . –

---

[13] Solvik and Hefling, "Bauer-Lechner on Mahler and Women," 38–40.
[14] Letter of November 5, 1896. McClatchie, ed., *The Mahler Family Letters*, 12.

But this leads too far afield! Just don't fight – don't be *suspicious* of each other – be content with what you have in common, don't criticize what you don't understand, and – *don't make any rules* for "the human race." – To the Lord *God* you are certainly all the same! – But seeing with human eyes, everyone is and remains an *unknown* world, yet with some small measure of sameness which makes *understanding* possible.

You are all bound together by this measure of sameness. Do not destroy the *connection* thoughtlessly.[15]

---

[15] Ibid., 137–38.

CHAPTER 2

A Childhood in Bohemia
Early Teachers and Friends

Reinhold Kubik

Translated by Juliane Schicker

Childhood in a city like Iglau around 1860 meant exposure to a degree of pluralism: Jews *and* Christians, Czechs *and* Germans, sentenced, as it were, to live together or alongside each other. But aversion and distrust notwithstanding, acceptance or at least tolerance were possible, and certainly better opportunities for mutual understanding than in a one-dimensional society. The Other was not exclusively villainized nor romanticized, but simply accepted, because it was inevitable. Every gradation of attitude existed, from hostility to toleration to an appreciation of potential gains. And a remarkable number of open-minded, unprejudiced, wise individuals emerged from this environment, enriching the palette of identities in the distinctive intellectual climate of Vienna around 1900: besides Mahler were Victor Adler, Sigmund Freud, Karl Kraus, Josef Hoffmann, Anton Hanak, Guido Adler, Heinz Friedjung, and Julius Tandler.

Aside from the familiar circumstances of Mahler's childhood, three factors formed his character: his musical upbringing, his formal education, and the influence of religion(s). This essay identifies in particular the people who embodied these factors in Mahler's childhood. I will only allude to other important stimuli and influences that critically affected Mahler's musical life, such as folk music, military music, and the sounds of nature; regarding these phenomena, we know general information about the people involved, apart from a few names associated with military music.[1]

The fact that Mahler's parents actively fostered his inclination toward music was a godsend not to be taken for granted in the house of a liquor manufacturer and distributor, even one eager for education. They allowed Gustav the installation of a piano from his grandparents' house and paid

[1] I wish to express my appreciation to my longtime colleague Helmut Brenner and also to Mr. Petr Dvořák, who graciously provided the information from Iglau (see note 6), and without whose tireless and friendly efforts this account would not have been possible.

for lessons in piano and elementary music theory from Iglau musicians, giving Mahler his first acquaintance with the fundamentals of harmony and form. The names of these teachers are known, but not the exact dates of instruction, and secondary literature concerning this issue is unhelpful.[2]

Franz Victorin (or Viktorin) was probably Mahler's first teacher. Born in 1832, this German Austrian was music director at the Iglau Municipal Theater between 1864 and 1868. Thereafter he performed at many theaters, lastly in Berlin, where he died in 1888. Victorin likely taught Mahler when he was between four and eight years old.

Victorin's successor was probably the pianist, composer, and music teacher Wenzel Pressburg (actual surname Pressburger). Born in Vienna in 1842, he probably lived in Bohemia/Moravia beginning in 1860; when he came to Iglau cannot be determined. In 1883, he successfully petitioned Mahler, his former student and then-music director at the Kassel State Theater, for a letter of recommendation.

Johann Brosch (Jan Brož) is another musician thought to have taught Mahler. He was born in Brtnice near Iglau in 1834 and became a professional violinist, making a name for himself in concerts of the Iglau Men's Choir Society and the Music Association. By the time he died in 1909, he was called "one of the most excellent violinists of our city." Brosch emerges as a piano teacher in the memoirs of Guido Adler, who had been taught by Brosch until Adler's departure from Iglau in 1864. Mahler's childhood friend Theodor Fischer related that Brosch also taught Mahler, but only after 1866.

Yet another string musician is mentioned in connection with Mahler's early music education: the Bohemian Jakub Sladky, who was born in 1816 in Beroun. Sladky was the double bass player in the orchestra of the Iglau Music Association, which included more than thirty musicians, about half of them professionals. The Music Association was disbanded in 1862, with a successor, the Municipal Orchestra, established in 1868.

Franz Sturm, another of Mahler's early teachers, served on the faculty of the Imperial and Royal *Hauptschule* (lower secondary school) in Iglau. While we do not know the substance of his instruction, he seems to have met the young Mahler through Sturm's participation as singer in choral events.

The most important musical figure for Mahler in this period was Heinrich Fischer. Born in Iglau in 1828, he was a founding member of the Iglau Men's Choral Society (1852) and became choirmaster in 1858.

---

[2] See the Appendix to this chapter for brief biographies based on current information.

In 1868 he was appointed as the Municipal Music Director, established the municipal orchestra, and by 1870 was the choir conductor of the two parish churches, St. Jacob and Maria Himmelfahrt (Church of the Assumption). Until 1872 he lived in Pirnitzergasse 264, adjacent to 265, the first home that Bernhard Mahler rented in Iglau. Mahler and Fischer's son Theodor (b. 1859) grew up together. Fischer likely taught Mahler harmony and compositional technique; he himself composed pieces for oboe and men's choir. The two exchanged letters sporadically throughout Mahler's entire life, the last being a postcard from Stamford, Connecticut, in April 1908. Fischer outlived his most famous student and died very old in 1917 from an accident.

Thanks to his teachers and his own hard work, Mahler excelled as a pianist, presenting his debut recital at ten years old at the Iglau Theater. Five years later, during a summer stay at Ronov by Čáslav (Czech Republic), his piano playing attracted the attention of the local estate owner Gustav Schwarz, who convinced Bernhard Mahler to send his son to the Vienna Conservatory.

Mahler's works contain special characteristics attributable to the music education he received during his childhood. His peculiar style of notation, for example, suggests a conservative education ignoring the norms of the Paris Conservatory, which had standardized advanced music education at the time. In a draft (mm. 203–15) of his early Piano Quartet movement in A minor, Mahler used the *Generalbassbezifferung* (figured bass notation), long obsolete at the time. Likewise, Mahler's old-fashioned notation of dotted notes (Symphony no. 3, no. 5, and no. 7) follows the Baroque tradition, largely unknown in Mahler's time, rather than mathematically precise modern notation; this seems to have been a peculiarity of Austrian composers. If we compare Schubert and what we might call his "Austrian provincialism" with Beethoven and his "progressive western education," as in the notation of triplets, we see a phenomenon duplicated in the tendencies of Mahler and Richard Strauss. Mahler also retained the traditional use of appoggiaturas in vocal music in his famous Mozart productions at the Vienna Court Opera.[3]

Regrettably, little evidence survives of Mahler's personal encounters with fellow students and teachers at the gymnasium. Considering his alert and inquisitive personality, numerous subjects and perhaps some

---

[3] Hartmut Krones, "'[...] doch behielt er jene Appoggiaturen bei [...]': Zu Gustav Mahlers Ausführung Mozartscher Rezitative," in *Musikinstrumente und Musizierpraxis zur Zeit Gustav Mahlers*, ed. Reinhold Kubik (Vienna: Böhlau, 2007), 261–96.

instructors were important to him; later in life Mahler remained proud of
his humanistic education, even though his grades confirm an aversion to
subservience and conformity. Alas, the people who shaped his development during this time are known only by name.

The same holds true for his schoolmates. We know their names from
documents in the Iglau Archives, but nothing is known about friendships
or personal aversions. Guido Adler, the only long-term friend from Iglau
besides Theodor Fischer, was five years older and left Iglau in 1864, before
the two became acquainted.

Mahler's attitude toward religion was also shaped by childhood experiences. He was a deeply spiritual and, indeed, religious person who strongly
believed in a divine order of the cosmos, in a bond shared by all humanity,
in his own destiny, and in his obligation to a god. He expressed this
attitude with great intensity in Symphony no. 2 and no. 8. Conversely,
Mahler did not recognize institutionalized denominations as legitimate
protectors of these principles, and he did not grant them the right to
determine his existence; as Alfred Roller shrewdly stated, "he required no
mediator between himself and God."[4]

Thanks to the right of mobility in the new constitution, an increasing
number of Jewish families moved to Iglau, among them Bernhard
Mahler's. The establishment of the Jewish community (see Chapter 1)
was overseen by the first rabbi in Iglau, Dr. Joachim Jacob Unger, who also
served as Mahler's religion teacher. Recalled at his death as a "good and
trusting gentleman," "one of the most noble persons, of a rare humility
and kindheartedness,"[5] Unger taught the Jewish religion at many schools
in Iglau. After Mahler's relocation to Vienna, when he was only remotely
connected with the Iglau gymnasium, the rabbi continued to serve as the
composer's private religion teacher. In 1877, Unger certified that Mahler
"had learned the substance of the Israeli religion through private study and
received a satisfactory grade on his exams."[6]

Bernhard Mahler's liberal view of religion was certainly an influential
example for his son. Mahler's family was quite connected to their Jewish

[4] Alfred Roller, *Die Bildnisse von Gustav Mahler. Ausgewählt von Alfred Roller* (Leipzig: E. P. Tal, 1922), 26.
[5] Moritz Antscherl, "Rabbiner Dr. Joachim Jacob Unger," *Ost und West: illustrierte Monatsschrift für das gesamte Judentum (1901–1932)* 13, no. 1 (1913): 79f.; Hugo Gold, ed., *Die Juden und Judengemeinden Mährens in Vergangenheit und Gegenwart. Ein Sammelwerk* (Brünn: Hickl, 1929), 245.
[6] Facsimile in *Státní okresní archiv v Jihlavě: Journey's Beginning. Gustav Mahler and Jihlava in Written Sources*, 2nd ed. (Jihlava: Okresní úřad, 2012), 125.

faith; for at least the important celebrations they visited the synagogue, and they had a good relationship with the cantor. However, the father's membership in the education committee of the Religious Society, which has been used to suggest the importance of the Jewish faith to Bernhard, is not relevant to Mahler's childhood; Bernhard Mahler became part of the committee only in 1878, when Mahler had long since departed for Vienna. Thus, Mahler's relationship with religion seems not to have been strict or rigorous, but rather tolerant and conciliatory. Apparently, his parents did not object to him going to Catholic high mass, and sometimes even to sing along, at least after 1870. Guido Adler recalled, believably if perhaps overenthusiastically, that "Catholic priests and the Rabbi Dr. J. J. Unger uniformly supported the religious raising of a child in family life, and tolerance was the guiding principle of the humanistic education taught in middle school by venerable teachers and had been prepared by excellent primary school teachers."[7] Mahler's oft-criticized conversion to Catholicism in 1897, though likely a result of career considerations, can also be seen through the lens of a childhood that unfolded as an intermingling of Jews and Christians.

Little is known about Mahler's life as a child among children. Most evidence can be attributed to Theodor Fischer, who, according to his own testimony, was a playmate and school friend and ultimately Mahler's companion through adolescence. Fischer has mentioned that Mahler, along with his brother Ernst (d. 1874) and other boys from Pirnitzergasse, played games in the Fischers' front yard, abandoned workshops, or "attics, accessible by means of a wooden staircase," in whose "mysterious darkness one could have adventures and amusing trepidation." Furthermore, "the municipal swim school was our playground, where we learned to swim very early, and passionately rowed our little boats." Mahler would retain his enthusiasm for water sports at least until his time in Maiernigg.

In Mahler's life before 1875, Emil Freund and Josef Steiner are the only friends known to have been present aside from Theodor Fischer. While the relationship with Emil Freund would be important only when he became Mahler's attorney much later, Mahler's contact with Josef Steiner was primarily relevant during his youth. In the summer of 1875, Mahler spent some time with Steiner in Ronov in the Meierhof Moravan close to Časlav; Steiner's uncle probably established the connection with the estate agent Gustav Schwarz, whose influence ultimately led to the interview with the

---

[7] Guido Adler, *Wollen und Wirken: aus dem Leben eines Musikhistorikers* (Vienna: Universal-Edition, 1935), 3.

Viennese piano pedagogue Julius Epstein, who spontaneously accepted Mahler into his piano class at the Vienna Conservatory. After the early death of Ernst Mahler, Steiner, a talented writer, produced the libretto to an opera, *Ernst, Duke of Swabia.* The text and whatever music may have existed are lost today. Steiner also wrote a second libretto, *The Argonauts* (after the play by Franz Grillparzer), which did not survive. In any case, there must have been a spiritual connection between Mahler and Steiner that went beyond a usual relationship. It probably originated before 1879, when Mahler sent the two famous letters from Puszta Batta to his former schoolfriend granting rare insights into his inner life. Later, Mahler might have regretted providing Steiner with such deep insight into his heart: though they both lived in Vienna, the former companions did not renew their acquaintance.

Brief Biographies of Relevant Figures

Johann Brosch (Ian Brož)

German-Austrian violinist, born on May 15, 1834, in Brtnice (south of Iglau). Lived in Iglau beginning in 1862, at 25 Spital Gasse (today: 23 Komenskeho), where he gave music lessons. Died April 29, 1909, in Iglau. Married to Pauline Brosch from Německý Brod (now Havlíčkův Brod) (1841–1910), with whom he had four children. Following his death "after long and hard suffering," the following note appeared in the *Mährischer Grenzbote* on May 2, 1909: "In the early years, Prosch [*sic*] belonged to the most distinguished artists of our city, and whenever the resounding notes of his violin rang out at High Mass in church or in the academies of the Music Association in the concert hall, everyone would listen, entranced, to his playing. Later as well, as the men's choir took the place of the Music Association, Prosch appeared publicly as a violin player. Only the struggle for his livelihood, the stress of his profession as a music teacher, and his increasing sickness compelled him to withdraw from the public eye entirely, so that likely only the older generation still knows that with Prosch gone, one of the most excellent violinists of our town has passed away."

Heinrich Fischer

Born on June 27, 1828, in Iglau. Until 1872 he lived at 264 Pirnitzergasse (today 6 Znojemská Ulice), next to the Mahler family's first residence (no. 265). Beginning in 1840 he studied oboe, harmony, and composition at the Prague Conservatory. Following his graduation in 1846, he became an oboist in Graz and at the Theater an der Wien. After 1850 he settled in Iglau and married Anna Benischko (1833–92), a native of that city, with whom he had a son (see below). In 1852, he was a founding member of the Iglau Men's Choir and was chosen as their choirmaster in 1858. He kept this position until 1909. In 1868, Fischer was appointed Municipal Music Director, founded the Municipal Orchestra, and by 1870 also was the choir conductor of the two parish churches St. Jacob and Maria Himmelfahrt (Church of the Assumption). In total, Fischer devoted fifty years to the development and maintenance of his hometown's musical life as Kapellmeister, choirmaster, organizer, and pedagogue who additionally taught at two middle and secondary schools and at the city's school for girls. Awarded the "Golden Cross of Merit with the Crown" by Franz Joseph I of Austria in 1912, Fischer died on January 31, 1917, after an accident.

Theodor Fischer

Son of Heinrich Fischer, born in 1859 in Iglau. Only a year older than Mahler, Theodor was the composer's playmate and then friend until their years at the University of Vienna. He studied law and worked hard to achieve a position as the president of the county court in Iglau, where he died in 1934.

Emil Freund

Born on December 13, 1859, in Želiv (district of Humpolec). After his school years in Prague, he attended the Iglau gymnasium starting in 1873, graduating in 1877. Subsequently, Freund studied law at the Karls-Universität in Prague and received his doctorate there in 1888. In 1893 he settled in Vienna as a lawyer; the last of his office addresses was Marc Aurel Street in the first district. He married the Viennese Josefine Barbara Jungwirth (1891–1980) in 1917. She was thirty-two years younger than her husband and survived him by fifty-two years. The marriage remained childless. After Mahler had become director of the Budapest Opera, Freund acted primarily as his lawyer, processing the inheritance after the death of Mahler's parents in 1889 and serving as a consultant on financial and legal issues. He managed Mahler's finances, preserved manuscripts, negotiated with publishers, and handled the sale of the villa in Maiernigg and the acquisition of the land in Breitenstein. He was also Mahler's executor and estate liquidator. Freund died on January 29, 1928, from "cardiac muscle degeneration." His urn was buried in the Jewish section of the Vienna Central Cemetery.

Wenzel Pressburg[er]

Pianist, composer, and music teacher. His name was actually "Pressbur-ger," as found on the documents of the Vienna Municipal and Provincial Archives and the Parish of St. Anton of Padua (Vienna – district of Favoriten). According to these sources, Pressburger was born June 17, 1842, in Wien Meidling and died at Ettenreichgasse no. 2 in Favoriten on August 23, 1906. He married Katharina Weinberg (1854–1929) in 1889. When and for how long he lived in Iglau is not conclusively known; the *Znaimer Wochenblatt* from January 1, 1860, has an announcement for a new "*Carneval*-Polka mazurka" by "Wenzl Preßburg." In 1883 he asked Mahler for support in his professional development, resulting in the following letter. Mahler had since been appointed as music director at the Royal Theater in Kassel and used his vacation to visit Iglau.

> Letter of Recommendation.
> With pleasure, I give confirmation to the music director Mr. W. M. Pressburg who is currently in Vienna, at his request, that I had the opportunity to get to know him as a conductor, teacher, and performing artist (pianist) – I myself was his student for many years – and that I can recommend him warmly as extremely appropriate for any artistic position, be it conductor or teacher.
>
> Yours respectfully,
Gustav Mahler
Prussian Royal Music Director
Court Theater of Cassel

(Present day) Iglau, August 10, 1883.
[Facsimile in: *Musikerziehung* 3, no. 1 (September 1949): 12.]

Jakub Sladky

Czech double bassist, born in 1816 in Beroun in Bohemia (west of Prague). Served in the orchestra of the Music Association until 1862, in the Municipal Orchestra from 1868. Taught in the home at 67 Pfarr Gasse (today: 9/85 Mincovny).

Josef Steiner

Born on August 31, 1857, in Bohemian Habry as the son of a Jewish salesman. Started school at the Iglau gymnasium in 1870, where he and Mahler attended different classes due to their age difference. In the winter semester of 1875–76 Steiner began studying law in Vienna and completed four semesters by the summer of 1877. He left the University without a diploma but returned for the winter semester of 1890–91 to audit classes, graduating on July 17, 1891, with a Juris Doctor. Settled in Prague, marrying Ida Salus (1879–1943) in 1899. The couple then moved to Vienna, where Steiner worked as "a lawyer and court interpreter for the Bohemian language." The couple had four children between 1901 and 1909. Professionally, Steiner was only moderately successful, and he died impoverished on April 28, 1913. He was interred in the Jewish section of the Vienna Central Cemetery.

Franz Sturm

Senior teacher at the *Hauptschule* in Iglau. He was born in 1817 in Štoky (district of Německý Brod, now Havlíčkův Brod) and married a woman from Iglau, with whom he had four sons. When he died on May 20, 1879, an obituary appeared in the *Mährischer Grenzbote* stating that Sturm had "worked in the school with tireless zeal to improve the well-being of those young people entrusted to him, and with an equally untiring devotion to the noble art of singing everywhere it was practiced."

Joachim Jakob Unger

Born on November 25, 1826, in the former Hungarian town of Homona (today, Humenné, Slovakia). He studied at a few Talmudic schools in Hungary, lastly in Lipník nad Bečvou near Olmütz, where he also received the rabbinate authorization. After passing the *Abitur* at the Royal Hungarian Gymnasium in Trenčín (now in Slovakia), he enrolled in the University of Berlin. In 1858 he received a PhD in the city of Halle (Saale) in Germany. On September 24, 1860, Dr. Unger took office in Iglau where he worked for fifty-two years. He married Johanna Fuchs (1841–1920), with whom he had two daughters. Unger, who also left behind an extensive body of literary work – Hebrew poems, patriotic speeches, and holiday and Sabbath sermons, among others – died October 16, 1912, in Iglau.

Franz Victorin (also František Viktorin)

Born around 1832 in Česká Kamenice. The place and duration of his studies have not yet been ascertained. The German-Austrian was Catholic and married. His earliest job was as music director for the spa town of Bad Ischl during the summers of 1860–62. Between 1864 and 1868 he was the music director of the Municipal Theater in Iglau, which was then led by the soprano Ottilie Moser (1837–1908). (Statements in the literature claiming that Viktorin was the leader of the theater are incorrect.) He then went to Krakow, Bílsko, and Budapest (1874–78). Beginning in the fall of 1880 he was music director at the Carl Schultze Theater in Hamburg, and then in 1881 assumed the post of music director at the Friedrich-Wilhelm Municipal Theater in Berlin, where he died on April 8, 1888. Both theaters specialized in operettas.

CHAPTER 3

Music in Iglau, 1860–1875

Timothy Freeze

> Just about the only impressions that become ultimately fruitful and pivotal for artistic creation are those that occur between the ages of four and eleven.
>
> —Gustav Mahler[1]

In October 1860, when Gustav Mahler was three months old, his family moved to Iglau, a provincial city of 20,000 that epitomized both the multiethnic character of the Austrian state and its liberal reforms of the 1860s. The third largest city in Moravia, but with its strongest cultural and economic ties to Germany and Bohemia in the west and Austria in the south, Iglau anchored a German-language enclave that included some eighty villages clustered along the Moravian-Bohemian border. Czech-speaking laborers and servants began settling in the city in the nineteenth century and made up 15 percent of the population by 1875, when Mahler moved to Vienna. Iglau served as a garrison town whose soldiers came from further reaches of the monarchy, especially Hungary and Croatia. Predominantly Catholic, it also had a Jewish community of about 1,000 that prospered from the educational and legal equality offered by the German liberal milieu of the 1860s and 1870s.

The primary contours of Mahler's youthful musical impressions were part and parcel of the city itself. The enclave's provincial location and ethnic diversity gave rise to a singular mixture of folk music traditions. The garrison's military bands made varied contributions to the city's everyday sounds and musical life. And as a bastion of German liberalism, Iglau sustained many social, sacred, and municipal organizations that promoted the cultivation and performance of music.

---

[1] Richard Specht, *Gustav Mahler*, 2nd ed. (Stuttgart: Deutsche Verlags-Anstalt, 1925), 170. All translations are the author's own.

Folk Music

Documentation of Iglau's folk music derives largely from late nineteenth- and twentieth-century ethnographic studies of nearby German villages and of Czech traditions as practiced in the broader region. Some portion of this music was certainly cultivated by city dwellers, who readily encountered local folk performers in the streets, restaurants, and courtyards. German and Czech peasants also organized dances to entertain the city's residents in nearby forest clearings.

Long-standing geographic separation from larger German communities to the west allowed for distinctive folk musical styles to develop among local Germans. Foremost among these was a type of fiddle quartet (*Fiedelmusik* or *Bauernfiedeln* [farmer fiddling]) that provided the dance music for peasant weddings, celebrations, and social gatherings. The ensembles resembled string quartets except that the simple, boxy instruments were akin to centuries-old ancestors of their modern equivalents. Most peculiar was the bass (*Ploschperment*), which was played flat on a table or lap, its pitch changed by pinching the thick metal strings. Vibrations between an adjustable screw and metal rivet in the tailpiece projected a loud, raspy buzz (*Schöbröjn*) suited to the instrument's rhythmic function. Sometimes its strings were even struck with the back of the bow to help propel vigorous dances.

The music of fiddle quartets consisted of march, dance, and song melodies spontaneously linked and varied in performance. The enclave's characteristic dance, the *hatschó*, was actually a series of such tunes. Beginning with a stately *Bairischen* (Bavarian) in triple time, it grew faster with the introduction of ländler and German dances (*Deutschen*). Eventually the dance switched to duple meter for a quick polka. When the lead dancer shouted "Hatscho!" a furious galop emptied the dance floor.

Among the best documented of Iglau's German folk songs are the four-liners that were often coupled with yodeling. Known in Alpine regions as *Gstanzl* (little stanzas) and *Schnaderhüpfel* (chattering hops), they went by *Tuschlieder* (fanfare songs) in this region for the brief instrumental flourishes that preceded each stanza. Such songs were common during the ritualized drinking that took place between episodes of dancing. Each epigrammatic stanza was sung by a different male dancer who tried to outdo the others with his humorous takes on love, drink, or everyday life.

Tuschlieder existed alongside many other types of folk songs that were practiced by the enclave's Germans. Some of the oldest were wedding and funeral songs unique to Iglau and similar eastern outposts of German culture. Others were known throughout the German-speaking world, including songs represented in *Des Knaben Wunderhorn*, which were sung in variants akin to those heard in northern Bavaria. The most recent folk styles came from Austria. In the second half of the nineteenth century, popular songs also made their way from the Empire's urban centers into the region's oral culture.

A similar mix of old and new traditions characterized the Czech folklore around Iglau. The hills and low population density of the region dampened cultural transfer with the neighboring crownlands. As a result, Czech villages preserved musical traditions that were disappearing elsewhere by the 1860s. Stylistically, these older traditions were oriented toward Bohemia. The folk songs were typically in the major mode and depicted scenes from peasant and soldier life. Common instrumental genres included the uhlan (*Hulán*), a moderately lively dance in compound duple meter, and laments (*žaloby*), which featured a plaintive solo accompanied by sparse interjections played "as if from a dream" by one or two other instrumentalists.[2] The polka did not emerge until the early nineteenth century, but its popularity persisted even as new styles of Czech folk music arose with the upheavals of industrialization. This newer style pushed further in the directions of satire and melancholy, its music blending aspects of classical Bohemian folk music with elements of urban popular song and the ballads of street singers (*Bänkelsänger*), who were an important conduit of its dissemination.

The documentary record of Iglau's folk music has several limitations. The clear-cut differentiation of traditions that the sources imply belies the mutual influence and overlap of the enclave's ethnic styles. German fiddle quartets became established in Czech villages, and Czech four-liners were sung at German dances. Some folk songs combined stanzas in both languages, and in both groups, funeral processions were followed by a turn to high-spirited music-making. Another limitation is the sparse documentation of traveling musicians. Given the geographic proximity, itinerant performers from Bohemia must have been regular visitors in the 1860s and 1870s. Such groups typically included three or four musicians playing a violin, clarinet (often in E-flat), and bass, with trumpet and flugelhorn becoming increasingly common after the introduction of valves. In contrast, groups performing Jewish klezmer music, of the kind that could be found further east in the empire, did not likely pass through the

---

[2] Vladimir Karbusicky, *Gustav Mahler und seine Umwelt* (Darmstadt: Wissenschaftliche Buchgesellschaft, 1978), 44.

enclave. In fact, there is scant direct evidence of any of the secular Jewish music practiced in Iglau. What can be said is that it was derived from Central (not Eastern) European styles and belonged to the same context of musical overlap and mutual exchange that characterized German and Czech repertoires.[3]

Military Music

Austrian battalions were stationed in Iglau throughout Mahler's entire youth. Their trumpet signals, drum rolls, and marches served practical functions for the troops and provided the populace with regular reminders of soldierly life. But the greatest contributions to Iglau's musical culture came from their bands. These ensembles consisted of a few dozen musicians, each proficient on a string instrument in addition to a primary wind instrument. The bands performed in a variety of configurations. Most iconic was the wind band formation (*Militärmusik*), but they also performed as full-fledged orchestras (misleadingly called *Streichorchester* [string orchestra] or *Streichmusik*). Chamber-sized derivatives of these ensembles were also common.

Military bands depended on public concerts for their financial well-being. As a result, they performed frequently and for a wide range of occasions. Iglau's military bands provided the entertainment for balls and dances and lent pageantry to civic and sacred processions. In the theater, military musicians reinforced the orchestra and provided stage music. The bands also held their own weekly concerts, most typically in restaurants or beer gardens but also in Iglau's remarkably expansive town square.

Stand-alone military band concerts offered a blend of the latest urban entertainment music with classical overtures and opera transcriptions. Their repertory included dances by the Strauss family, excerpts from the latest French and Viennese operettas, and pieces composed by military band conductors. Nearly every concert featured a lyrical solo for flugelhorn or cornet. Popular, too, were large potpourris that stitched together diverse tunes unified by a characteristic title. The following program for a beer-garden concert in 1875 typifies these performances:

---

[3] Jens Malte Fischer, *Gustav Mahler*, trans. Stewart Spencer (New Haven: Yale University Press, 2011), 31; *HLG4*, 474–76.

Franz von Suppé, Overture to *Flotte Bursche*
Johann Strauss, Jr., *Melodien-Quadrille*
Michael Balfe, aria from *The Bohemian Girl* (flugelhorn solo)
Dan Godfrey, *Les Gardes de la Reine* (waltz)
Giuseppe Verdi, Cavatine from *Nabucco*
[?] Heinrich, Concert-Polka
Giacomo Meyerbeer, *Fackeltanz* no. 1
Ludwig van Beethoven, *Fidelio* Overture
Josef Strauss, *Feuerfest* (polka française)
Franz Massak, *Musikalische Broschüre* (large potpourri containing fifty
    tunes from marches, dances, opera, and songs)
Johann Strauss, Jr., *Deutsche* (waltz)
Johann Strauss, Jr., *Unter Blitz und Donner* (polka schnell)[4]

In addition to such pieces, each military band had its own distinctive character. The 49th Infantry Regiment Band, for instance, stood out for the unprecedented attention it brought to symphonic music. Symphonies were among the most neglected genres in Iglau, where audiences favored styles rooted in song or dance. But on Christmas Day in 1874, the fifty-five-man ensemble performed the following works:

In wind band formation:
Meyerbeer, Overture to *Dinorah*
Mozart, Overture to *Le nozze di Figaro*

In orchestral formation:
Wagner, Overture to *Tannhäuser*
Mendelssohn, Scherzo [? from *Ein Sommernachtstraum*]
Haydn, Symphony no. 94, *Andante*
Beethoven, Symphony no. 5[5]

The concert was an exceptional event, for it provided one of only three complete performances of a symphony documented in the newspapers during Mahler's youth. Considering this ambitious repertoire, the significance of military bands for Iglau's musical life far exceeded the signals and marches that came to symbolize the ensembles in the popular imagination.

---

[4] *Mährischer Grenzbote* 4, no. 50 (June 24, 1875): 3.
[5] *Mährischer Grenzbote* 3, no. 102 (December 20, 1874): 2.

Music of Social, Sacred, and Municipal Organizations

The emphasis on *Bildung* and music by Iglau's middle classes found expression in diverse institutions. Among the most important of these for Mahler's development was the local library. Its collection of scores ran the stylistic gamut and contained much classical repertoire in piano transcription. As was the case for most of the nineteenth-century bourgeoisie, then, Mahler's primary experience of the classical canon, and especially of large-scale works, came from domestic performance at the piano. In addition, Iglau supported a thriving culture of special-interest groups (*Vereinskultur*). The frequent ceremonies and processions of the shooting club (*Schützenkorps*) and athletic society (*Turnverein*) required music, which was performed either by their own members or by those hired from military or municipal organizations. Other groups, however, found their primary purpose in music. The music society (*Musikverein*), founded in 1819, organized concerts and lessons that helped establish Iglau as a musical center of Moravia.

By the time the music society disbanded in 1862, it had been largely eclipsed by the men's choral society (*Männergesangverein*). Like many such groups throughout the German-speaking world, it was established in the ethos of heightened nationalist sentiment that followed the 1848 revolutions. Accordingly, its core repertory consisted of multipart folk songs and German romantic choral works. Nevertheless, it was among Iglau's most versatile musical organizations, hosting serenades and torchlit processions for distinguished visitors, including Emperor Franz Joseph I in August 1866. Each year, the choral society hosted a popular Carnival ball and organized two commemorative concerts, one for its founding and the other for Beethoven's birth. The society frequently provided light entertainment in local restaurants (*Liedertafel* or *Kränzchen*) and in the context of outings to the countryside (*Landpartien*). For these performances, it supplemented its core repertory with humorous and popular fare. Following the dissolution of the music society, however, the group channeled ever more of its energies into formal concerts. These programs included many chamber and orchestral works by Austrian and German composers, arranged as needed for the available instrumental forces. Such musical ambitions even led the society to mount a few isolated productions of opera, a genre rarely encountered in public performance in Iglau before 1870. And in 1872, the society established a women's chorus, which allowed them to expand their repertoire even further.

One of the choral society's founding members and directors was Heinrich Fischer, a distinguished musical figure in the city. An oboist and composer, he participated and held leadership positions in most of Iglau's major musical organizations. He was also an active teacher who counted Mahler among his pupils (see Chapter 2). It is through this connection that Mahler, who attended synagogue with his family at least occasionally, came to participate as rehearsal pianist and choirboy at St. Jacob's Church, where Fischer was also music director. For high days, Fischer drew on an impressive range of sacred music for chorus and orchestra, including compositions by Schubert, Donizetti, Cherubini, and Czech composers like Robert Führer and Albin Maschek. Some of the notable pieces he conducted were Rossini's *Stabat Mater*, Beethoven's *Christus am Ölberg*, and Haydn's *Die sieben Worte des Heilands*.

In 1868, Fischer was appointed Iglau's inaugural music director (*Stadt-kapellmeister*). Among his educational and civic responsibilities was direc-torship of the newly formed municipal band (*Stadtkapelle*), which consisted of twenty part-time musicians. The need for such an ensemble had grown steadily in the 1860s as the military band and men's choral society struggled to satisfy the city's growing musical needs. Accordingly, the municipal band's activities, like its repertoire, resembled those of the more established groups: civic ceremonies, balls, light entertainment in restaurants and the countryside, and formal concerts. One busy Sunday in 1872 can illustrate its multifaced activities. In the morning, it provided music for services at St. Jacob's Church and then a procession of textile workers. In the afternoon, it accompanied a parade celebrating the shoot-ing club's champion marksman. Then came a funeral procession. That evening, the ensemble held a benefit concert for the victims of a fire in a nearby village.

As indispensable as the municipal band was, it was the 1,020-seat theater that held pride of place in Iglau's cultural life. Its season lasted from late September to Easter. Performances were given six evenings per week and always in German. The repertoire spanned the spectrum from fully spoken plays to fully sung operas. Between these poles came a variety of genres, notably *Lustspiele* (comedies with some songs and couplets), *Posse mit Gesang* (farces with upward of a dozen musical numbers), and operettas. Although the theater had a stable of part-time orchestral musi-cians, it lacked a director, actors, and singers. To fill these positions each season, the city council hired an itinerant theater company. Its director managed the day-to-day operations, chose the repertoire, and oversaw the productions. Companies spent anywhere from one to three seasons in Iglau, usually nonconsecutively. Such frequent changes in leadership and performers resulted in variation in repertoire and quality, but one view remained constant throughout: the theater's highest artistic pursuit was to be found in opera and operetta.

In the 1860s and 1870s, musical stage works were produced ever more frequently, surpassing twenty performances in the 1866–67 season and fifty performances just seven years later. Within any given season, the relative blend of the genres was subject to change due in part to a fact of theater life: operettas were performed by singing actors, while operas more often required trained singers. During Mahler's youth, only one company, led by Gottfried Denemy, had a cast of opera singers. In the 1870–71 season, their first, the troupe presented nearly four dozen performances of canonical operas from the late eighteenth and nineteenth centuries together with a couple of more recent operettas:

Auber, *Fra Diavolo*
Bellini, *Norma*
Boïeldieu, *La Dame blanche*
Donizetti, *Belisario*
Donizetti, *Lucia di Lammermoor*
Donizetti, *Lucrezia Borgia*
Flotow, *Martha*
Hérold, *Zampa*
Lortzing, *Zar und Zimmermann*
Méhul, *Joseph*
Meyerbeer, *Robert le diable*
Mozart, *Don Giovanni*
Offenbach, *Le Mariage aux lanternes*
Rossini, *Il barbiere di Siviglia*
Rossini, *La cenerentola*
Verdi, *Il trovatore*
Weber, *Der Freischütz*
Zaytz, *Mannschaft an Bord*[6]

The season set the high-water mark for opera in Iglau. The next year, Demeny changed course, perhaps in response to the prevailing taste of the local theatergoers. This time he followed the strategy taken by other directors in Iglau, programming fewer operas and devoting a larger share of the musical stage productions to operettas by Offenbach and Suppé:

---

[6] Repertoire gleaned from the local newspaper *Der Vermittler*, nos. 1 and 2 (1870–71).

Balfe, *The Bohemian Girl*
Bellini, *I Capuleti e i Montecchi*
Conradi, *Beckers Geschichte*
Donizetti, *Belisario*
Donizetti, *La Fille du Régiment*
Donizetti, *Lucia di Lammermoor*
Donizetti, *Lucrezia Borgia*
Flotow, *Alessandro Stradella*
Flotow, *Martha*
Halévy, *La Juive*
Hopp, *Morilla*
Mozart, *Die Zauberflöte*
Offenbach, *Barbe-bleue*
Offenbach, *La Belle Hélène*
Offenbach, *La Chanson de Fortunio*
Offenbach, *Les Géorgiennes*
Offenbach, *La Grande-Duchesse de Gerolstein*
Offenbach, *Orphée aux enfers*
Offenbach, *La Princesse de Trébizonde*
Suppé, *Flotte Bursche*
Suppé, *Das Pensionat*
Suppé, *Die schöne Galathée*
Suppé, *Zehn Mädchen und kein Mann*
Verdi, *Ernani*
Weber, *Der Freischütz*
Zaytz, *Mannschaft an Bord*[7]

The greater frequency of opera and operetta productions was just one manifestation of a broader trend. By a stroke of good fortune, Mahler's youth coincided with a flowering of Iglau's musical life. Concerts became more frequent, and their repertoire more ambitious and oriented toward European metropoles. The Offenbach and Suppé operettas, for instance, typically appeared within a year or two of their premières in Paris and Vienna. Of course, these changes were among the wide-reaching effects of modernization, which ultimately left no corner of the monarchy untouched. During Mahler's youth, the venerable musical traditions cultivated in the nearby German and Czech villages were already registering

[7] Repertoire gleaned from the local newspaper *Der Vermittler*, no. 2 (1871) and *Mährischer Grenzbote* no. 1 (1872).

contemporary urban influences. And in 1871, when Iglau was connected to the railway network that would later convey Mahler across the continent, the post-horn signals that had long announced the arrival of postal carriages fell suddenly silent. In this way, Mahler's youthful musical impressions captured not only the ethnic character and cultural outlook of the Austrian monarchy but also its distinctive moment, perched between past and present, rural and urban.

CHAPTER 4

Student Culture in 1870s Vienna

Caroline A. Kita

Mahler arrived in Vienna in 1875 at the age of fifteen to begin his formal
training in piano at the Vienna Conservatory. He continued his basic
studies in his hometown of Iglau by correspondence and finally passed his
Matura, or secondary school exams, in 1877, allowing him to enroll at the
University of Vienna. Both the Conservatory and the University served as
bastions of intellectual and artistic life in the Habsburg capital, and they
provided Mahler with a foundational education in a wide array of subjects,
from music theory and music history to philosophy, art, history, and
literature. Yet perhaps even more important for his development at this
time were his informal intellectual engagements, fostered through the
friendships and acquaintances he made as a student, which would shape
the musician, conductor, and composer he was to become.

The Culture of the Vienna Conservatory

The Vienna Conservatory first opened its doors in 1817 under the auspices
of the Gesellschaft der Musikfreunde, an organization established in
1812 to cultivate musical life in the Habsburg capital. The Conservatory
began as a singing academy directed by Antonio Salieri, with its first class
including just twenty-four students.[1] Over the course of the next half-
century it grew steadily, eventually offering instrument instruction and
attracting a prestigious faculty. When Mahler arrived in 1875, in the heart
of the Conservatory's golden age, its students numbered 648.[2] The director during this period was Joseph Hellmesberger, a conductor, composer,
and violinist with a traditionalist mindset and sharp temper, known among

[1] Ernst Tittel, *Die Wiener Musikhochschule* (Vienna: Verlag Elisabeth Lafite, 1967), 14.
[2] Herta Blaukopf, "The Young Mahler, 1875–1880: Essay in Situational Analysis after Karl
R. Popper," trans. Stephen E. Hefling, in *Mahler Studies*, ed. Stephen E. Hefling (Cambridge:
Cambridge University Press, 1997), 6.

his students as "Old Hellmesberger." Having begun his tenure in 1851 (following the Conservatory's brief closure due to the political unrest of the 1848 revolutions), Hellmesberger remained in the position for forty-two years, transforming the school into one of the premiere institutions for music education in Europe. Prior to Mahler's enrollment, the increasing class sizes and a desire to expand performance space had led to the construction in 1869 of the Musikverein, located in the Bösendorferstrasse just blocks from Court Opera. The Conservatory occupied a prominent wing of the building, facing the imposing Baroque façade of the Karlskirche. Mahler remained at the Conservatory from 1875 to 1878, studying piano with Julius Epstein, composition with Franz Krenn (1816–97), and harmony with Robert Fuchs (1847–1927). His fellow students included Hans Rott, Anton Krisper, Rudolf Krzyzanowski, and Hugo Wolf.

Naturally, the culture fostered by Hellmesberger was conservative, with a curriculum designed to educate the next generation of performers and composers in the great Viennese classical music tradition. Contemporary composers also exerted their influence, above all Johannes Brahms, who served as artistic director of the Gesellschaft from 1875 to 1880 and judged many of the Conservatory competitions. Anton Bruckner taught organ, harmony, composition, and counterpoint at the Conservatory and the University. Mahler came to admire him as a mentor (despite his critical views of Bruckner's compositions), likely attending his lectures at the University though never formally enrolling in his class.

If Mahler's years at the Conservatory were rocky at times, due to a stormy temper and occasional stubbornness with his teachers, he was not alone. Wolf's famous expulsion, after claiming to Hellmesberger that he had "forgotten more than he had learned," illustrates the tensions between an aging faculty and rebellious pupils. A recurring point of contention was the longing for exposure to the newest trends in music, particularly the works of Richard Wagner. In the absence of formal opportunities within the Conservatory walls, an important counterpoint to Mahler's formal musical education took place at the Court Opera, where Wagner's works were becoming a regular part of the repertoire (*HLG1*, 42). Yet frustrations notwithstanding, Mahler received his diploma in 1878 with a degree in composition and several prizes in piano performance and composition. Typically for this era, his education included no coursework in conducting, the skill that would support him for the remainder of his career and eventually bring him back to the capital as director of the Vienna Court Opera from 1897 to 1907.

The Culture of the University of Vienna

Founded in 1365, the University of Vienna is the oldest institution of higher education in the German-speaking world. In the early decades of the nineteenth century, particularly during the neoconservative era of Franz Metternich following the Napoleonic wars, intellectual life in Vienna was highly regulated, reflecting the conservative social hierarchies of the ancien régime. Following the Revolution of 1848, which brought Emperor Franz Joseph (1830–1916) to the throne, educational reforms were initiated under the advisement of a Prague philosopher, Franz Exner (1802–53). These included the implementation of *Lehrfreiheit* (academic freedom), giving instructors more control over the subjects and modes of teaching;[3] the overhaul of the School of Medicine; and the establishment of institutes of history, philosophy, art history, and musicology.

Over the course of three semesters (winter 1877–78, summer 1878, and winter 1879–80), Mahler attended lectures at the University of Vienna given by some of the institution's most renowned faculty, notably Rudolf Heinzel (1877–1931), who taught German literary history (in particular Eschenbach's *Parzival*), and Rudolf Eitelberger (1817–85), the founder of the program of art history, who lectured on the art of the ancient Greeks. He also attended music history lectures by Eduard Hanslick (1825–1904), Vienna's famed and most feared music critic.[4] Although Mahler attended courses at the old campus in the city center, he witnessed the construction of the monumental Renaissance-style university building on the Ringstrasse, one of the centerpieces of Franz Joseph's massive urban renewal project that transformed Vienna in the late nineteenth century from a provincial capital into a *Großstadt* rivaling Paris and Berlin.

The liberal founders of the modern (post-1848) University of Vienna valued above all the principles of scientific materialism. They saw themselves as developing an "objective, realistic and rational" intellectual tradition, distinct from the "idealist, subjective attitudes of the Protestant north."[5] This blend of Enlightenment humanism and rational science, combined with the powerful influence of the Roman Catholic Church, produced a unique intellectual environment in Vienna, embodied, for

---

[3] Matthew Rampley, *The Vienna School of Art History: Empire and the Politics of Scholarship, 1847–1919* (University Park: Penn State University Press, 2013), 16.

[4] Blaukopf, "The Young Mahler," 17–19. For more on Hanslick's influence in Vienna, see Kevin Karnes, *Music, Criticism, and the Challenges of History* (Oxford: Oxford University Press, 2008).

[5] David S. Luft, "Schopenhauer, Austria, and the Generation of 1905," *Central European History* 16, no. 1 (1983): 60.

example, in Franz Brentano (1838–1917), a philosopher and ordained priest whose lectures Mahler attended. Brentano sought to reconcile Catholicism with modern science, seeking a scientific reason for the existence of God. Like his colleague in physics, Ernst Mach (1838–1916), Brentano championed the cause of empirio-criticism, claiming that the only phenomena that existed were those that could be perceived through the senses. Their views would achieve wide acceptance, influencing the young Sigmund Freud as well as the philosophers Edmund Husserl and Alexius Meinong and, later, the members of the Vienna Circle.

Student Organizations: The *Leseverein*, the *Rede Klub*, and the Pernerstofer Circle

This is not to say, however, that students in Vienna remained isolated from the influence of German Idealism. In student organizations and *Vereine*, another school of thought was cultivated: one focused on German nationalism rather than Habsburg patriotism, on mysticism and the occult rather than logic, and on the sublime and transcendent rather than the materialist and rational. Perhaps the most influential of these intellectual organizations in the 1870s was the Leseverein der deutschen Studenten Wiens (Reading Society of German Students in Vienna), founded on December 2, 1871. Until its dissolution on December 18, 1878, the Leseverein served as a center for student intellectual engagement and political resistance. The society's radical origins are evident from its name, which it took from the Legal-Political Reading Society that had played a critical role in the revolution of 1848.[6] Indeed, the Leseverein emerged in its own moment of political crisis, sparked by the decisive loss of the Austrian army to the Prussians at Königgratz (Sadová) in 1866, the consequent exclusion of Austria from the German Empire, and the *Ausgleich* of 1867, which formalized the Dual Monarchy of Austria-Hungary and catalyzed both pan-Slavic national sentiment and a responding German nationalist movement. The stock market crash of 1873, and the subsequent destabilization of liberal political hegemony in the capital, also left a lasting impact on this generation.

According to its annual report in 1877, the year Mahler enrolled at the university, the Leseverein membership included a remarkable 689 students

---

[6] William J. McGrath, *Dionysian Art and Populist Politics in Austria* (New Haven: Yale University Press, 1973), 34.

and 125 professors, and their events likely drew many more participants.[7] In support of their goals – to promote a German national solution to Austria-Hungary's political turmoil and to offer a powerful alternative ideology to liberalism – the Leseverein sponsored lectures, published pamphlets, and maintained their own library. Its early caretakers included the founder of the Austrian Social Democratic movement, Victor Adler (1852–1918).

A similarly disposed student organization whose membership overlapped with the Leseverein was the Pernerstorfer Circle, a group of young intellectuals who had first organized themselves as the Telyn Society at the Schottengymnasium in the late 1860s. Founded by Engelbert Pernerstorfer and Adler, along with classmates Max Gruber and Heinrich Braun, the organization's primary activities involved reading and discussing ancient Germanic myths along with the writings of Kant, Schopenhauer, and the early Nietzsche; under the influence of Adler the group increasingly engaged with socialist politics as well. The members of the Pernerstorfer Circle also formed the Rede Klub, a discussion society within the Leseverein focusing on history, philosophy, and the arts. Important speakers at the Rede Klub included Carl Rokitansky (1804–78), who sought to reconcile the evolutionary theories of Darwin with the philosophy of Schopenhauer, and the young philosophy professor Johannes Volkelt (1848–1930), one of the few outspoken champions of Kant's ethics and theory of knowledge at the university.

His engagement with the Pernerstorfer Circle acquainted Mahler with many of the ideas that would inform the musical world of his symphonies. The poet and philosopher Siegfried Lipiner (1856–1911), one of Mahler's primary interlocutors at this time, would have an especially profound impact. In 1876, Lipiner had published an epic poem, *Der entfesselte Prometheus* (*Prometheus Unbound*), a work deeply indebted to Friedrich Nietzsche's *Birth of Tragedy* (1872), which was widely read and discussed in the university's literary circles. Lipiner further promoted Nietzsche's writings in a lecture to the Rede Klub on April 28, 1877, entitled "On Nietzsche's Untimely Meditations: Schopenhauer as Educator." Shortly afterward, he authored a letter to Nietzsche, cosigned by fellow university students Max Gruber, Victor and Sigmund Adler, Heinrich Braun, and Engelbert Pernerstorfer, personally expressing their high regard for this work.

[7] *Jahresbericht des Lesevereins der deutschen Studenten Wiens*, VI. Vereinsjahr 1876–77 (Vienna, 1877), 8.

The success of *Prometheus* and the Nietzsche lecture earned Lipiner another coveted speaking engagement at the Rede Klub on January 19, 1878, in which he presented a groundbreaking lecture, "On the Elements of a Renewal of Religious Ideas in the Present Time." Here Lipiner offered a scathing critique of materialist philosophy, which he blamed for the degeneration of religion into "fetishism and dogmatism." Citing a diverse array of texts from Schopenhauer's *The World as Will and Representation* (1818; vol. 2, 1844) to the writings of psychophysicist Gustav Theodor Fechner (1801–87), and even the libretto of Richard Wagner's *Parsifal* (published already in 1877), "On the Elements" reveals the rhetorical prowess that earned Lipiner the admiration of Mahler and an enthusiastic following in Vienna and beyond. The lecture's conclusion, with its rousing call for a new embrace of myth and tragic art as the solution to the modern spiritual crisis, served as a rallying cry for students seeking an alternative to the ideas of materialist philosophy, logical positivism, and empirio-criticism dominating the lecture rooms of the University at this time.

Beyond the University: The Viennese Wagner Society, the Pythagoreans, and the Saga Society

In citing Wagner's libretto for *Parsifal*, Lipiner demonstrated his sensitivity to forward-thinking elements of Vienna's artistic and intellectual life, where Wagner was rapidly developing a cult following. In 1872, Guido Adler, Felix Mottl, and Kurt Wolf had founded the Wiener Akademisches Wagnerverein (the Viennese Academic Wagner Society) to promote Wagner's writings and musical works at a time when they were excluded from the Conservatory's repertoire. Wagner's early essays, such as *The Artwork of the Future* (1849) and *Art and Revolution* (1849), published on the heels of the 1848 Revolutions, proved especially popular, as they resonated both with the political disillusionment of Vienna's youth and their belief that art might pave the way for cultural rebirth and renewed spiritual unity. Adler organized a series of lectures on the first Bayreuth Festival production (1876) of Wagner's *The Ring of the Nibelungen* (1848–76) at the university in the winter semester of 1875–76, in which Lipiner and many other students and faculty members took part. Mahler joined the Wagner Society in 1877 with his friends from the Conservatory, Anton Krisper and Rudolf Krzyzanowski, and remained an enthusiastic member until 1879.

Around the same time, Mahler and Lipiner came into contact with the Pythagorean Group, led by Friedrich Eckstein, the personal secretary of

Anton Bruckner. This organization explored mysticism and occult spirituality through the philosophy of Pythagoras and the neo-Platonists, while also discussing the more contemporary work of psychophysicist Friedrich Zöllner (1834–82). Eckstein was a regular attendee at meetings of the Pernerstorfer Circle and shared with its members a fascination with Wagner's *Religion and Art* (1880). Under the influence of this essay, Mahler briefly adopted a vegetarian diet, which was believed to encourage the regeneration of the body and soul.

After spending the summer of 1880 conducting in Bad Hall, Mahler returned to Vienna and continued to develop his interest in mystical religion and Germanic myth by forming the Saga Society with Lipiner and a fellow university student, the writer Richard von Kralik (1852–1934) in 1881. According to Kralik, the goal of their organization was to live lives inspired by the great poets. Their meetings included listening to works by Wagner, reciting epic works such as the *Edda* and *Nibelungenlied*, and sharing their original compositions, among them Lipiner's opera libretto for composer Karl Goldmark, *Merlin* (1880, premiered at the Vienna Opera in 1886).

Jewish Students in Vienna

By the early 1880s, Jews made up one-third of all students at the University of Vienna.[8] A university education was seen as the path to assimilation; to receive a classical *Bildung* (spiritual and intellectual development and character formation) was to signal a commitment to a German cultural identity. Yet by the time Mahler arrived in Vienna, the tensions driven by increasing German nationalist sentiment had begun to create barriers for Jewish students. Vienna in the 1870s witnessed the rise of Georg von Schönerer, a young politician whose German nationalist program featured an openly anti-Semitic agenda that expressed itself in violence.[9] Another notable event that took place the year of Mahler's arrival in Vienna was the Billroth affair, sparked by a treatise published by the physician Theodor Billroth (a good friend of Johannes Brahms), who identified the increasing number of Jews in the University of Vienna's student body as detrimental and claimed that Jews could never belong to a modern German *Kulturnation*. The text's publication sparked student demonstrations and a response

---

[8] Steven Beller, *Vienna and the Jews 1867–1938: A Cultural History* (Cambridge: Cambridge University Press, 1989).
[9] Carl Schorske, *Fin-de-Siècle Vienna Politics and Culture* (New York: Vintage Books, 1981), 120–33.

by Victor Adler, delivered before the Leseverein in January 1876, that challenged Billroth's negative assessment of Jewish assimilation. The Billroth affair highlights a significant moment in the rise of German nationalist sentiment among Viennese students.[10] By the late 1870s, university fraternities began to bar Jewish membership, and increasing anti-Semitic sentiment came to dominate both the Viennese Wagner Society and the Pythagorean Group, leading to the alienation of many Jewish members, including Mahler.

After concluding his studies in Vienna, Mahler began his professional career with conducting positions in Laibach, Olmütz, Leipzig, Budapest, and Hamburg (see Chapter 6). He would not call the capital his home again for sixteen years. By the time he returned to take his position at the Court Opera, he was as an accomplished composer, with three completed symphonies, all of which bear traces of his musical and philosophical education in Vienna. The titles and programmatic descriptions of these works, marked by the worldviews of Schopenhauer, Wagner, and Nietzsche, as well as the mysticism of Fechner and the speeches and poetry of Lipiner, remain a testament to the formative influence of this period on Mahler's life and career.[11]

---

[10] For more on the Billroth affair and anti-Semitism in student culture in Vienna, see David Brodbeck, *Defining Deutschtum: Political Ideology, German Identity and Musical-Critical Discourse in Liberal Vienna* (Oxford: Oxford University Press, 2014), 106–34.

[11] For more on Mahler and Lipiner's relationship, see Chapter 21, along with Stephen E. Hefling, "Mahler's Totenfeier and the Problem of Program Music," in *19th-Century Music* 12, no. 1 (1988), 27–53; Carl Niekerk, *Reading Mahler* (Rochester, NY: Camden House, 2011); and Caroline A. Kita, *Jewish Difference and the Arts in Vienna: Composing Compassion in Music and Biblical Drama* (Bloomington: Indiana University Press, 2019).

CHAPTER 5

Viennese Musical Associates, 1875–1883

Charles Youmans

Mahler's arrival in Vienna as a fifteen-year-old student entering the Conservatory folded him into an artistic community of extraordinary stature. The composers, performers, teachers, and fellow pupils with whom he now rubbed elbows represented the upper echelon of European musical culture. Overnight, then, he traded the frustrations of a backwater existence in rural Moravia for daily contact with the most talented musicians anywhere. And he was poised to make the most of it; his musical ability, his capacity for work, and his fervent sense of ethical responsibility to the art encouraged him to draw all he could from this rich array of colleagues.

Who were they, and what did they reveal to him? A young musician as gifted and headstrong as Mahler – "tyrannical to the point of heartlessness, stepping on all obstacles in his path," remarked an associate from those years[1] – can hardly have been a passive object of influence. He did react, however, often intensely, and those experiences shaped his development. Friend or foe, the people surrounding him created the conditions out of which his identity emerged.

Foremost in the thoughts of an arriving student would have been the faculty, whose demands and efficacy would make the difference between completing the program or returning home defeated. Since 1851 the Conservatory had been run by the imperious Joseph Hellmesberger (see Chapter 4), who served for a time as concertmaster of the Court Opera orchestra and led a quartet that premiered works of Brahms, among other prominent contemporaries. Hellmesberger's mellifluous Viennese tone reflected a conservative outlook apparent also in his aesthetic principles and indeed in his dress, for example, the cane he brandished at overly independent students (*HLGI*, 31). "The sworn enemy of those who were talented but poor," Mahler would call him, having found himself on the

---

[1] Marie Lorenz, sister-in-law of his closest friend during the conservatory years, Rudolf Krzyzanowski. *HLGI*, 41.

wrong end of the grousing along with similarly disposed firebrands such as Hugo Wolf (*NBLE*, 23). Unlike Wolf, Mahler avoided dismissal, even though he embodied two of the director's three dislikes: "Jews, nearsighted people, and Jakob Grün" (who by 1875 had taken over as concertmaster).

What allowed Mahler to survive? Good relationships with the other faculty, perhaps, or at least grudging esteem. Julius Epstein, the pianist responsible for his admission, chastised Mahler for "arrogance" (*Übermut*) but sent his own son to him as a pupil. Epstein was fair-minded and honest, and more important, he had good musical judgment. A devout admirer of Mozart, editor of Schubert's piano sonatas, and close friend of Brahms, he shared his opinions freely and seems thereby to have tempered Mahler's fanatical admiration of Wagner; certainly, he drew his protégé's attention to repertoire by those composers who otherwise would have been ignored. Twenty-eight years older than Mahler, he outlived him by fifteen years, and their mutual respect never declined.

A similarly productive relationship formed between Mahler and Robert Fuchs, who took up his appointment as Professor of Music Theory in the fall of 1875, the semester of Mahler's arrival. Known as "Serenaden Fuchs" for his five string serenades – among the better-known works of a substantial oeuvre, and in a genre that marked him at the time as forward-thinking[2] – the young composer/pedagogue seconded Epstein's advocacy of classical repertoire, especially with respect to form. Fuchs also attracted the attention of Wolf, here again supplying a resolutely progressive student with a useful dose of the canon. But as if to complement the influence of this fresh-faced traditionalist, it was the sixty-nine-year-old Franz Krenn who most stimulated Mahler in his first year. Mahler did his best work at the Conservatory in Krenn's composition class, where a liberal attitude toward experimentation was grounded in comprehensive *Fachkenntnis* (expert knowledge; Krenn also taught harmony, counterpoint, and orchestration). Relative freedom from the stifling norm would make this environment an oasis for Mahler and his closest student colleagues.

Keeping one's sanity in a competitive, indeed, combative setting required friends with a similar disposition and gifts that measured up. Mahler managed to find several, and these relationships remained happy memories until the end of his life, though few continued meaningfully after he began his professional career. The most intimate would be Rudolf Krzyzanowski, a violinist two years younger but already in his third year of training when Mahler matriculated. They met in Krenn's composition

[2] Walter Niemann, *Die Musik der Gegenwart* (Berlin: Schuster & Loeffler, 1921), 8.

class, where Krzyzanowski showed promise rivaling that of Mahler and
their soon-to-be roommate, Wolf. Krzyzanowski distinguished himself
sufficiently that autumn to have a Quintet in C Minor performed at the
Conservatory's December concert of student works, and the following
September Mahler brought him to Iglau to play in a benefit concert at
the Czap Hotel, even opening the program with his Quartet for Piano,
Two Violins, and Viola. The critic for the *Mährischer Grenzbote* offered a
positive and detailed review, noting the "very carefully worked out development" (complete with double fugue), the striking return of the main
theme as a funeral march at the end of the first movement, and the high
quality of the thematic invention: "We can justifiably maintain that the
composer of this quintet [*sic*] has created a beautiful work, and that the
time will come when we can number him among the great."[3]

Krzyzanowski continued to distinguish himself as a composer through
Mahler's three years at the Conservatory. Wolf thought his own songs
inferior to Krzyzanowski's during this period, and in the spring of
1878 Mahler lost to him in the school's Lieder competition – an experience that Mahler remembered twenty years later when the two friends
encountered one another by chance at a café. (He even recalled the music's
opening and played it on a nearby upright piano.) But that student success
may reflect a less adventurous creative application of their shared Wagnerian enthusiasm. We cannot know who took the part of Brünnhilde when
the pair and Wolf were evicted on the spot for a raucous reading of the Act
II *Götterdämmerung* trio for Hagen, Gunther, and Brünnhilde, but Krzyzanowski was a keen participant there and in the score-readings sessions of
the Vienna Wagner Society, which the friends joined in 1877 (*ML*,
63–64). He was in any case a self-assured musician – "You must take
him as he is. He will always be a bulldog," Mahler observed – if also a
victim of his own success, as can happen with student composers who
please their elders (*HLG1*, 37).

If Krzyzanowski leaned in a more conservative direction than Mahler, or
at least prudently regulated his "modern" impulses, Wolf offered an
enthusiastic counterexample. His flagrant, fearless Wagnerism – conflicted
though it may have been in its compositional application[4] – put him in
open conflict with Hellmesberger, who, taken aback by an antagonist who

---

[3] *Mährischer Grenzbote*, 17 September 1876. The program names the work as a quartet and lists only
four performers; it may be that the quintet mentioned above, or another, was substituted.
[4] "He was both drawn to Wagner and repelled by him." Amanda Glauert, *Hugo Wolf and the
Wagnerian Inheritance* (Cambridge: Cambridge University Press, 1999), 3.

would not be cowed, oversaw the unfortunate expulsion in March 1877. Estrangements were to be the norm in Wolf's life; he held a genuine admiration for Brahms until the latter offered the well-meaning suggestion of counterpoint study with Gustav Nottebohm (for Brahms this tip indicated faith in Wolf's potential), and Mahler himself could not steer clear of his friend's legendary wrath. Having uncovered the fairy tale *Rübezahl* and pondering an opera on the subject, Wolf erupted when Mahler, eager to convince a skeptical Wolf that the work could be a comedy, wrote out the draft of a libretto (*ML*, 64). Stories such as these confirm a predisposition to overreact, but perhaps also an awareness, conscious or otherwise, of the capacity for such feelings to provide artistic inspiration. He was, in the compassionate image of Hermann Bahr, a handsome prince who had been changed into an animal.

Beneath the volatile exterior, as his friends knew, lay a massively talented musician, with a profound interest in the technical details of music and a moving conviction that music's importance touched on all spheres of life: emotional, philosophical, and social. Wolf's voracious appetite for repertoire drew his friends into a rigorous schedule of perfor- mance attendance: the months of December and January 1875–76, for example, included *Tannhäuser, Lohengrin* (conducted by Wagner), *Der fliegende Holländer, Don Giovanni, Lucia di Lammermoor, Les Huguenots,* Liszt's *Die heilige Elizabeth*, at least one concert of the Vienna Philhar- monic, and even a performance by the Hellmesberger Quartet. Temper- ament aside, the eagerness to learn is notable, and Mahler and Krzyzanowski shared it. As the years passed the three also ventured into the environs where turn-of-the-century socialism was forming – for exam- ple the Pernerstorfer Circle (see Chapters 4 and 22), where they met Victor Adler, soon to found the Social Democratic Workers' Party.

Wolf's sad end was anticipated by another friend, Hans Rott, whose considerable talent had only begun to reveal itself when he was committed to an asylum in October 1880. (He died only four years later, at twenty- five.) A born Viennese, his father a celebrated actor working mainly at the Theater an der Wien, Rott bore the weight of high expectations during his Conservatory years, singled out among Krenn's students as destined for greatness. As his student career unfolded, the lack of a Krzyzanowski-style success in student competitions weighed ever more heavily on him, and in 1878 he departed for abject obscurity as organist for the Piaresten Monastery. Whereas Mahler was unfazed by similar hiccups – he likewise did not win a prize for composition in his second year – the slights against

Rott enraged both of them; when Mahler won a head-to-head contest and related the story to his mother in dismay, she burst into tears.

Rott illuminates Mahler's natural empathy, often obscured by his troubles with anger management. A visit to Rott's quarters at the monastery, a single room furnished mainly with a string of sausages, would stick in Mahler's memory, as would Brahms's cruel advice that Rott abandon composition – though this was perhaps an overly rough attempt to steer him away from Wagnerian tendencies. Bruckner, Rott's principal mentor, held his rival responsible for the protégé's mental collapse, though he resisted making a scene at the funeral. In fact, Brahms did figure in the outburst that led to Rott's confinement; it began when Rott, startled on a train by a fellow passenger lighting a cigarette, attempted furiously to put out the fire while shouting that Brahms had planted dynamite on the vehicle.

Did such stories play on Mahler's mind when he suggested that Rott's Symphony in E Minor would become the "basis of a new genre"? "What music has lost with him cannot be measured," he claimed, and Paul Banks rightly notes the significance of Mahler's continuing interest in the work in 1900.[5] What Mahler had lost personally, a valued companion, may well have meant as much to him. His wistful recollection sounds like an elegy for a friendship: "We felt ourselves to be two fruits from the same tree, growing from the same earth and breathing the same air . . . We could have done great things together in our new musical epoch." Whether he exaggerated Rott's abilities we cannot know. The bond that was to develop with Richard Strauss, however, seems to have filled the void in a unique way. No other of Mahler's associates would receive the kind of humble praise that he reserved for these two.

Surveying the other members of Mahler's circle, many of whom went on to careers of true distinction, one senses that even at that early stage he had an eye for talent and did not suffer fools. Arnold Rosé, who would become Mahler's brother-in-law in 1902, entered the Conservatory in 1873 as a ten-year-old and took over as concertmaster of the Court Opera in 1881. Perhaps most impressive to Mahler when they met in 1875 was that Arnold played piano sufficiently well to be placed in a more advanced class than his new friend. (Arnold's brother Eduard, a cellist, entered the Conservatory in 1876 and would marry Emma Mahler in 1898.)

The most intellectually inclined of Mahler's musical peers was Guido Adler, also from Iglau and five years older. Adler had left the Conservatory

[5] Paul Banks, "Hans Rott and the New Symphony," *The Musical Times* 130 (1989): 142.

for the University by 1874, but he remained an important connection from Mahler's first day in Vienna until his last. No doubt his experiences studying with Bruckner and Hanslick were known to Mahler and figured in his decision to add University courses to his Conservatory work in 1877–78. Their relationship would bring important political advantages for Mahler, even when he served as director of the Opera; it was Adler, for example, who arranged (by means of a detailed, four-page report on Mahler's life and creative work) for the grant that funded the publication of the First and Third Symphonies by Waldheim Eberle in 1899.[6] But the foundation of the friendship was in the realm of ideas. Adler took part in the meetings of the Wagner Society from the beginning, and in spite of his academic bent he strongly supported what he pointedly called Mahler's "modern" inclinations.

Young Wagnerians in 1870s Vienna would naturally have been drawn to Bruckner, who championed their idol whatever the personal cost and had the special credibility of dedicating, with permission, a work to Wagner (the Third Symphony, in 1873). More important, Bruckner demonstrated more effectively than any other composer how Wagner's style might be adapted to the symphony and, by extension, to the classical genres on which composition students cut their teeth. If he thereby earned Hanslick's ire and Brahms's indifference, so much the better. To his young admirers he was a rare combination of high ability and benevolence, whose "happy, juvenile, almost childlike nature" intrigued Mahler sufficiently that he made it a mission "to comprehend his life and his ideals."

Why, then, did Mahler call himself a disciple of Bruckner but not a student? In his teaching, which included positions at both the Conservatory and the University, Bruckner hewed to a brand of conservatism that belied his tendencies in what must have seemed unimaginable ways. Ever faithful to the pedagogical methods of Simon Sechter, he believed it natural to remove the hat of teacher when expressing himself creatively.[7] "That is the rule," he confessed to his bemused students, "but when I'm at home, I disregard it!" Mahler took the composer to heart and accepted the teacher in small doses; in fact, he passed over Bruckner's courses at the Conservatory, and though he attended the lectures in harmony when he enrolled at the University in October 1877, he did not take the trouble to

[6] Edward R. Reilly, "Mahler and Guido Adler," *The Musical Quarterly* 58 (1972): 446–48.
[7] The complex relationship between the two, and relevance to Bruckner's influence on Mahler and Schoenberg, is discussed in Dika Newlin, *Bruckner – Mahler – Schoenberg* (New York: Norton, 1978), 9.

secure the required signature from his teacher indicating that he should receive credit.

None of this gave Bruckner any doubt about Mahler's musical ability, of course. The four-hand version of the Third, made by Mahler and Krzyzanowski (the latter unnamed on the title page), gave him such pleasure that for a time he believed he might dispense with the infamous "assistance" of the Schalk brothers. In off-hours he was known to spend time conversing with Mahler in cafés – a sure sign that he regarded him as a potential colleague, and this before the publication of the arrangement in January 1880. Bruckner would be grateful that Mahler maintained the relationship as his career ascended; one can imagine what it meant to have a report as caring and respectful as the following:

> At last I am fortunate to be able to write to you that I *have* performed one of your works [emphasis in original]. Yesterday (Good Friday) I conducted your magnificent and powerful "*Te Deum*." Both the performers and the entire public were gripped in the deepest way by the mighty structure and the truly sublime conception, and at the end of the performance I experienced what I consider the greatest triumph of a work: the public remained sitting in silence, without the slightest movement, and only when the conductor and musicians had left their places did the storm of applause break loose. The performance would have brought you joy. I have seldom seen a group of performers as enraptured as yesterday. (Mahler to Bruckner, April 16, 1892; *GMB2*, 121)

Here Mahler compensated, in the most meaningful way possible, for a late start in programming Bruckner's music, at a time when the older man could offer him nothing useful for professional advancement. But judging from the degree to which Mahler adopted Brucknerisms in his own pieces, the experience described here was more than mere flattery.

That Mahler managed to earn the respect of both Bruckner and Brahms is a testament to his underappreciated aptitude for politic behavior. A genuine friendship with the latter did not begin until December 1890, when Brahms was persuaded while in Budapest to attend a performance of *Don Giovanni* conducted by Mahler. "Quite excellent, tremendous – he's a devil of a fellow," he remarked after the overture, and soon would "pull strings" for Mahler in Hamburg and Vienna.[8] Little is known of any earlier contact, though the absence of an anecdote relating some vicious barb or insult during Mahler's apprenticeship, when the two inhabited the same spaces on a daily basis, counts as implicit praise, especially considering

---

[8] Jan Swafford, *Johannes Brahms: A Biography* (New York: Alfred A. Knopf, 1997), 570.

Mahler's ostentatious Wagnerism. In any case, Mahler's letter to Löhr after the Budapest experience (undated [January 1891]; *SLGM*, 130/*GMB2*, 112) conveys obvious pride, as though a goal of long standing had been accomplished. This after all was a composer who had known Robert Schumann, and thus who stood as a direct link to true musical Romanticism – he was a human embodiment of the Schillerian naive, confronting in Mahler a sentimentality second to none. And he was the composer who had done more than any other to revive the symphony, a project begun during Mahler's Conservatory years with the First (1876) and Second (1877) Symphonies.

A young musician sensitive to the political currents of 1870s Vienna, and hoping to build a career there in not so many years, would of course have recognized that he was living in the world of Eduard Hanslick. Mahler learned this lesson early and did not forget it. When he returned in 1897, he scrupulously followed the tradition of paying visits to the main critics in their homes; this was by no means a power play but a practical necessity, for the power was distributed equally at best. And in the world of music criticism in the last decades of the 1800s, Hanslick had no rival. For the Beethoven Prize that caused Rott such grief, Hanslick sat on the jury alongside Brahms, Karl Goldmark, and Hans Richter. The critic's appearance at the Leipzig world premiere of *Die drei Pintos* in January 1888 was as important to the work's widespread success as the presence of leading intendants and conductors. And his positive review of the Vienna premiere one year later meant that Mahler could legitimately call the work a critical success in spite of its brief run (three performances).

Hanslick could also promote composers by his opposition. As Peter Franklin suggests, Wagner became a hero to Mahler and his peers "precisely *because* the great critic Hanslick disapproved of him."[9] But that kind of productive scandal came less easily to Mahler than to Strauss, a reality vividly illustrated by the early history of *Salome*. Notoriety would strengthen that work and its composer through all of Europe, but it played no small role in driving Mahler across the Atlantic. And so he would learn, as had so many of his teachers, peers, idols, that living as a Viennese musician inevitably left scars.

---

[9] Peter Franklin, *The Life of Mahler* (Cambridge: Cambridge University Press, 1997), 33.

Becoming a Conductor
The Early Years in Mahler's Career

Peter Revers

Translated by Juliane Schicker

Within a few short years of professional life (1880–85), Mahler gained sufficient experience to become one of the leading young conductors in the German-speaking world. Despite the limited opportunities of undeniably provincial beginnings, in this brief period he absorbed the cherished repertoire that had long been his goal – above all, the operas of Mozart and Wagner. What interpretive abilities facilitated that rapid ascent? The central features of Mahler's character as a performer appeared early, and would remain consistent throughout his career. His meticulous rehearsals, and his attention to detail in all aspects of preparation, reflected the highest fidelity to the score and to the dramatic meaning of the underlying libretti. Moreover, already during his third engagement, at Olmütz in 1883, he began to exert influence on the production and staging – a tendency that, though tempered in Kassel and Prague, would define his mature work as a conductor.

First Steps: Bad Hall, 1880

In 1900, Gustav Mahler lamented to Natalie Bauer-Lechner that twenty years earlier his "damned employment as an opera conductor" had forced him to put aside his opera *Rübezahl* and other works from that time (*HLG1*, 73). In those days his precarious financial situation had motivated the decision to seek a conducting job, which succeeded in early 1880. Through the music publisher Theodor Rättig, Mahler met Gustav Lewy, an impresario who essentially managed the young conductor's career for the following ten years. When Lewy approached Julius Epstein, Mahler's piano teacher at the Vienna Conservatory, to find a theater conductor for the summer season at the Kurtheater in Bad Hall, Epstein recommended

Mahler, who in this first engagement would conduct "operettas and farces" as part of his duties.[1]

The wooden theater, comprising sixteen box seats, sixty-six lockable folding seats, and a standing section, lay "close to the spa garden, for which a demonstrably good crowd assembles at all times," and it enjoyed government subsidies "under the stipulation that the best and newest operettas, comedies, etc. must constantly be in the repertoire."[2] Performances served primarily to entertain the spa guests, with the spa hiring notable artists (e.g., the actor and operetta singer Alexander Girardi) as well as younger figures such as Mahler. Little evidence remains of Mahler's work in Bad Hall or of ancillary duties such as conducting the background music in the drinking hall where the spa-goers enjoyed "the lovely sounds of a Straussian Waltz."[3] "Considering the circumstances, I am well," Mahler remarked drolly in a June 21, 1880, letter to Albert Spiegler (*SLGM*, 63/*GMB2*, 38), and indeed he did gain his first conducting experience, working for three months with an ensemble of some fifteen to twenty musicians and mostly young, inexpensive singers.

From Kapellmeister to Dirigent: Laibach (1881–1882)

On May 6, 1881, the *Laibacher Zeitung* (*LZ*, p. 886) announced the theatrical hires for the "coming winter season 1881–82," among them "Kapellmeister Mahler from Vienna" at the Laibacher Landschaftliches Theater. Mahler was responsible for conducting opera and some operetta, which the newspaper reviewed often, albeit briefly. These reviews focused on the vocal performances; staging, the orchestra, and conducting were covered only partially and in general terms, with set design typically ignored. A detailed review of Nicolai's comic opera *The Merry Wives of Windsor* in the feuilleton (*LZ*, February 11, 1882, pp. 297f.) provides information about Mahler's working conditions. Noting that "the same Kapellmeister leads the operas and the operettas," the critic determined "to apply a less exacting standard to the opera performances," which suffered from an inadequate number of rehearsals. Already in Laibach, then, Mahler experienced the less enjoyable facets of repertoire theater, which would plague him throughout his career in the "opera business." Though reviews rarely acknowledged the Kapellmeister, the few mentions of Mahler were mostly positive.

---

[1] Helmut Grassner, "Kurorchester und Kurtheater Bad Hall – Wo Gustav Mahler seine ersten Sporen verdiente," *Oberösterreich. Kulturzeitschrift* 3 (1981): 60; Franz Willnauer, "Gustav Mahler und Oberösterreich," *Nachrichten zur Mahler-Forschung* 73 (June 2019): 56f.
[2] Franz Baar, *Fremdenführer von Bad Hall* (Linz: Vinzenz Fink, 1882), 23.   [3] Ibid., 83.

On September 24, 1881 a gala performance – Mahler's first public performance in Laibach – was given on the opening of the Carniola state parliament. The evening included Eduard von Bauernfeld's comedy *Bürgerlich und Romantisch* (Bourgeois and Romantic, 1835), introduced with Beethoven's *Egmont Overture*, which Mahler "led with precision" (*LZ*, September 26, 1881, p. 1852). On the premiere of Verdi's *Il trovatore* (March 19, 1881), the reviewer observed with similar efficiency that the orchestra had "given their all" under Mahler's direction. A milestone of Mahler's reception was unquestionably a production of Mozart's *Die Zauberflöte* that premiered on October 27, 1881. While on October 28 the *LZ* noted only that "the orchestra achieved excellence" (p. 2086), the following day a review of the second performance offered comprehensive praise, citing the "successful" ensemble work of the lead performers (both the female and male singers) and "no less the orchestra and choir" (*LZ*, October 29, 1881, p. 2094). The *Laibacher Wochenblatt* would commend this production even more emphatically: "Herr Mahler is indisputably a skilled Kapellmeister and earned substantial merit with the opera performance. Only rarely have we seen this orchestra execute its role with such precision, and the choirs offered, considering the circumstances, something truly amazing."[4] Mahler's last performance in Laibach earned similar tributes: "Kapellmeister Mahler conducts with precision and fire, observing the finest nuance; the solo and choir singers as well as the orchestra perform excellently" (*Laibacher Wochenblatt*, March 8, 1882; cited in Kuret, 65). Mahler's local obituary, published on May 23, 1911, under the title "Recollections of Gustav Mahler's Work in Laibach," specifically highlighted his conducting of *Zauberflöte*: "Critics described one performance of *Die Zauberflöte* during the 1881–82 season – which Mahler had to execute almost exclusively with operetta performers and which was repeated multiple times – as a model. Even then: Ex ungue leonem [from the point of the lion]!" (*LZ*, May 23, 1911, p. 1114).

The Merry Wives of Windsor likewise particularly taxed the ensemble, with Mahler first performing it on February 8 and 9, 1882. Although the number of singers was deemed inadequate, the production as a whole was described as "exact and satisfying" (*LZ*, February 11, 1882, p. 298). Three weeks after this premiere, Johann Strauss's operetta *Der lustige Krieg* stood on the program, and from early 1882 onward Mahler's approval in Laibach

[4] Primož Kuret, *Mahler in Laibach*, Wiener Schriften zur Stilkunde und Aufführungspraxis, Sonderband 3 (Vienna: Böhlau, 2001), 53.

grew. At a lucrative benefit performance on his behalf, conducting Friedrich von Flotow's *Alessandro Stradella* (March 24, 1882), he was "met with lively applause from the considerable crowd, with a fanfare from the orchestra, and he received a large laurel wreath. All of these gestures were well-deserved signs of recognition of this well-trained musician, who takes his difficult task quite seriously and who endured many trials and tribulations throughout the season" (*LZ*, March 24, 1882, p. 582).

Mahler's seven-plus months of wide-ranging activity in Laibach thus were unquestionably an important first step in his career, though in the end Alexander Mondheim-Schreiner, Laibach's theater director, did not extend his contract – partly because he customarily limited contracts to only one season but also because financial exigencies forced him to find another, cheaper Kapellmeister. Hence Mahler entered a new phase of uncertainty and financial insecurity, which he managed by giving piano lessons until Gustav Lewy once again found him employment, this time for three months as the Kapellmeister of the theater in Olmütz.

Frustrations and Success: Mahler in Olmütz (1883)

While few details survive of Mahler's work in Laibach, we know a great deal about his brief stay in Olmütz. Like his positions in Bad Hall and Laibach, this engagement happened on short notice. After the January 1883 dismissal of Emil Kaiser, the principal conductor in Olmütz, following a confrontation with theater director Emanuel Raul,[5] the urgent need for a successor was filled with the help of Lewy. Mahler arrived in Olmütz on January 12, 1883, and a few days later the daily newspaper the *Mährisches Tagblatt* (*MT*) shed light on the circumstances, while questioning Mahler's competence on dubious grounds:

> Our theater management informed us that today's scheduled opera – *Les Huguenots* by Giacomo Meyerbeer – is cancelled because the necessary orchestra personnel could not be secured from the local military bands. But we were also apprised that this performance was changed because the new Operakapellmeister Mahler did not yet seem adequately familiar with the local facilities. Opera performances are therefore set to resume only at the end of the coming week. Such a break in our opera performances would be rather objectionable, and thus we find it necessary to remind the

---

[5] Jiří Kopecký and Lenka Křupková, *Provincial Theater and Its Opera. German Opera Scene in Olmütz (1770–1920)* (Olmütz: Vydavatelství filozofické fakulty Univerzity Palackého v Olomouci, 2015), 145f.

management that, until such time as Kapellmeister Mahler has become
familiar with local conditions, the baton could be transferred to Kapellmeister Urban, whose diligence, competence, and discretion our audience
has in past years had sufficient opportunity to appreciate. (*MT*, January 13,
1883, p. 4)

These concerns, however, were clearly exaggerated. Only two days later,
Mahler conducted the second performance of *Les Huguenots*. The *Mährisches Tagblatt* critic withheld his judgment about Mahler's conducting,
because "the opera had already been rehearsed before Kapellmeister Mahler's arrival." But he effused that "we have here a youthful power, filled
with as much zeal as skill," and detected a "certain hastiness" before
quickly excusing it as "a result of his first [*sic*] and sudden debut, and all
the more understandable as the conductor had to read from a piano
reduction rather than a full score" (*MT*, January 16, 1883, p. 3).

As in Laibach, unqualified enthusiasm for Mahler's work emerged after
initial reservations. In the announcement of the dress rehearsals for Bizet's
Carmen (March 9 and 10, 1883), success was predicted in light of "the
extraordinary care with which it had been prepared by Kapellmeister
Mahler" (*MT*, March 9, 1883, p. 4). The extensive review of the premiere
carefully differentiated Mahler's prowess from the artistic shortcomings of
the organization (e.g., poor staging due to the approaching end of the
season, and unexcused absences from the choir members): "The fact that
the opera achieved success on our stage under all these circumstances is
thanks to Kapellmeister Mahler, who knew how to highlight the merits
and beauties of the opera in a way that at least partially covered the
deficiencies of the performance and especially the production and staging.
The orchestra achieved . . . excellence under his leadership and it deserves
the same praise" (*MT*, March 13, 1883, p. 6). By the end of Mahler's term
in Olmütz, discussion of his conducting commonly appeared at the
beginning of each review.

Mahler's departure would be felt as a distinct loss. The review of
Mahler's penultimate appearance on March 15, 1883, opens and closes
with unqualified praise: "Verdi's *Rigoletto* was performed yesterday to the
benefit of our splendid Kapellmeister Mahler"; "Kapellmeister Mahler [was
greeted] with applause and a magnificent floral wreath when he appeared
at the conductor's stand" (*MT*, March 16, 1833, p. 5). Yet Mahler felt his
departure for Vienna (after one last performance of *Carmen* on March 17)
to be a deliverance. Critics noted his exceptionally thorough rehearsals
almost universally; but for the young conductor, the experience of leading
inferior musicians was traumatic. "I'm in the worst mood," Mahler wrote

already on January 20, 1883, in a postcard to Fritz Löhr. Shortly thereafter, again to Löhr, he elaborated:

> I am paralyzed like someone who fell from heaven. From the moment I stepped into the Olmütz Theater, I felt like someone awaiting heaven's judgment. When one yokes the most noble horse together with oxen before a cart, it cannot do anything else but pull and sweat. I almost do not dare to see you in person – that is how dirty I feel. (*SLGM*, 68/*GMB2*, 43)

Evidently, Mahler had tried to avoid performances of Wagner and Mozart, "because I could not endure simply going through the motions of conducting *Lohengrin* or *Don Juan* here." Mahler writes further of the "unspeakable lack of feeling" of the ensemble members, who could not apprehend "that an artist can become completely immersed in the work of art. Often, when I am fired with enthusiasm and want to pull them with me toward a higher plane – and I see the astounded faces of these people as they smile knowingly at each other – my seething blood sinks down within me and I want to run away from them forever." Nonetheless, it was through this suffering under mediocre artistic conditions that Mahler developed his characteristic ideal of artistic perfectionism. In that respect, the months in Olmütz were formative in his development as a conductor.

"I would manage my position with conscientiousness and diligence": Kassel (1883–1885)

Only a few weeks after leaving Olmütz, Mahler encountered a new, appealing opportunity: "music and choir director" of the Königliche Schauspiele in Kassel. Mahler and theater director Adolph Freiherr von und zu Gilsa signed the contract in late May 1883. Lewy again provided a recommendation, calling Mahler "a zealous young man, musically educated through and through, and thus I believe you would not find anyone better for the vacant position." The director of the Royal Theater in Dresden, Karl Ueberhorst, had seen Mahler in Olmütz and called him "a young conductor of genuine distinction" and "a truly musical and energetic force."[6] Before the contract was signed, Mahler presented "trial services" between May 22 and 30: conducting Rossini's overture to *William Tell*, leading choir rehearsals, performing répétiteur work with female and male singers, and conducting Marschner's *Hans Heiling*.

---

[6] Hans Joachim Schaefer, "Kassel erinnert sich an Gustav Mahler" (lecture, November 20, 1990), supplement to Schaefer, *Gustav Mahler – Jahre der Entscheidung in Kassel 1883–1885* (Kassel: Weber & Weidemeyer, 1990), 17.

On August 21, 1883, Mahler took up the position, with his first production Meyerbeer's *Robert le diable*, premiering on September 19. The critic for the *Hessische Morgenpost* (*HM*, September 21, 1883) was immediately won over, describing "Maler" [*sic*] as "a conductor with as much energy as talent" and highlighting "his skill and calm, his perception, and his ability to communicate his ideas to performers." With regard to repertoire, however, Mahler had no choice; the majority of the operas (and especially those by Mozart and Wagner) were reserved for the principal Kapellmeister Wilhelm Treiber, whom Mahler disdainfully described to Löhr as the "most vacuous 4/4-beater I have ever encountered" (September 19, 1883; *SLGM*, 74/*GMB2*, 48). To Lewy, likewise, Mahler quipped darkly "that something unpleasant could suddenly befall Herr [Treiber] – but I should not say too much" (late October; *GMB2*, 50).

Mahler's conducting of Louis Aimé Maillart's opera *Les dragons de Villars* on October 23, 1883, was favorably reviewed. "Kapellmeister Mahler once again proved ... that he is a thorough, educated, conscientious, and very experienced conductor. May his ambition not tire and his zeal not grow weary in the future" (*HM*).[7] Conversely, reviews of Flotow's *Alessandro Stradella* (October 11, 1883) and Marschner's *Hans Heiling* were less euphoric. Mahler found his subordination increasingly depressing, and soon the situation felt unbearable. "I have allowed others to forge chain after chain on me, and now I have blundered into the old, shameful captivity," he told Löhr, and he confessed to Lewy at the end of October that he "would not withstand the position of second Kapellmeister too long" (*SLGM*, 74/*GMB2*, 48; *GMB2*, 50). In this state, he turned to Hans von Bülow at the end of January 1884, lamenting that his artistic ideals were "mishandled everywhere in the most unbearable way" (*GMB2*, 51). Bülow famously forwarded the letter to Treiber, inflaming the tensions and complicating a relationship that later would blossom in Hamburg.

Mahler handled a wide variety of tasks in Kassel, rehearsing the soloists, orchestra, choir, and actors, and conducting the works that Treiber had not claimed. He also prepared incidental music, including possible compositions. (His lost stage music for Joseph Viktor von Scheffel's *Der Trompeter von Säkkingen* probably resonated with critics and audiences the most, though it took him only two days to compose.) Additionally, this period saw Mahler's first opportunities as concert conductor; particularly noteworthy are the performances of Haydn's oratorio *The Seasons* on

---

[7] Also cited in Hans Joachim Schaefer, *Gustav Mahler – Jahre der Entscheidung in Kassel 1883–1885* (Kassel: Weber & Weidermeyer, 1990), 35.

February 13, 1885 (in Münden, praised as "model performance" in *HM*), and Mendelssohn's *St. Paul* on June 29, 1885.[8] The latter occurred at the opening concert of Kassel's Großes Musik-Fest on June 29–July 1, 1885, with a hastily assembled collection of musicians from the court orchestras in Meiningen, Weimar, and Braunschweig. Treiber, offended at being passed over for the honor, had agitated against Mahler with the Kassel players (not without anti-Semitic overtones), who refused to perform. Nonetheless, *St. Paul* was presented to a crowd of some 2,100 people, in a triumphant success for Mahler, under whose leadership the soloists, choir, and orchestra were "of one mind, one goal, one will."[9]

Despite the obvious burdens, Mahler's time in Kassel would constitute a breakthrough for him as conductor and as composer. Pressures entailed by hierarchy and regimentation fostered in him a longing for unfettered artistic self-expression, which would become a pillar of his mature artistic personality. It was no surprise, in any case, that in April 1885 Mahler requested an early release from his contract due to expire at the end of the season. Von Gilsa supported this request in a letter to the intendant, Botho von Hülsen, arguing that Mahler's contract with the Leipzig City Theater for the 1886–87 season – signed in early 1885 – had caused him to "completely lose his footing" and "receive frequent written warnings for misconduct, negligence, etc."[10] But in his next appointment, as first Kapellmeister of the Deutsches Theater in Prague under the directorship of Angelo Neumann, he was finally allowed to conduct the works kept from him by Treiber – *Fidelio, Die Meistersinger von Nürnberg, Tristan und Isolde*, a Mozart cycle, and so on – and his apprenticeship as a conductor had come to an end. Looking back in a letter to Löhr, Mahler confessed that "such tasks mold the musician . . ., especially if he mans the barricades and fights for what is holy as I do" (November 28, 1885, *SLGM*, 93/*GMB2*, 68). Mahler understood, then, the meaning of his time in Kassel, and in the end would express his appreciation to von Gilsa:

> Under your tutelage, I learned to obey in order to be able to command – which is the most difficult task – and to faithfully fulfill one's duty in order to be allowed to demand this of others. This unruly student often caused you hardship, and it may often have taken your broad-minded clemency not to lose patience with me. From now on, I hope to prove to you that I will not disgrace my master and that your well-meaning admonitions have fallen on fertile ground. (*GMB2*, 69)

[8] Ibid., 60.   [9] Ibid., 66.   [10] Ibid., 64.

CHAPTER 7

Between "Thrice Homeless" and "To the Germans in Austria"
Political Conditions in Mahler's Europe

Margaret Notley

Mahler's compositions are valued in part for their stylistic heterogeneity, a feature that calls to mind the linguistic and ethnic diversity of the regions in Central and Eastern Europe where he worked most of his life. For instance, he spent some of his most productive if also most stress-filled years (1897–1907) in Vienna, during a period of remarkable achievements in the arts and scholarly fields in the city. A correlation can again readily be seen between the efflorescence of creativity in Vienna and a populace that was diverse and becoming increasingly so.

Like Mahler himself, many newcomers were Jewish and came from the Czech regions of the Austro-Hungarian Empire. In the last two decades of the nineteenth century, about a quarter of Vienna's inhabitants had been born in Bohemia or Moravia, and the total number of immigrants increased until World War I.[1] Economic opportunities and, for certain groups, the appeal of an urban environment inspired an influx of new residents into a city that to at least some of the immigrants seemed more open to difference than the places they chose to leave. "Although in Vienna an anti-Semitic majority governed in the city council from 1895," write Michael John and Albert Lichtblau, "Vienna counted as a city with a liberal atmosphere to Jews, as the city of the Emperor who protected equal rights."[2] At the same time, pressure toward greater homogeneity was also apparent, there and elsewhere in Europe.

In a frequently quoted remark first by Alma Mahler, Gustav is said to have called himself "thrice homeless" because of his status as "a Bohemian among the Austrians, an Austrian among the Germans, and a Jew in the entire world" (*ML*, 109). His reported self-assessment invites

[1] Michael John and Albert Lichtblau, *Schmelztiegel Wien – einst und jetzt: Zur Geschichte und Gegenwart von Zuwanderung und Minderheiten; Aufsätze, Quellen, Kommentare*, 2nd ed. (Vienna: Böhlau, 1993), 14.
[2] Ibid., 114.

closer scrutiny of both the comment and the contexts in which he was active. Mahler was not, strictly speaking, a Bohemian. Rather, he was born in Kalischt and raised in Iglau, respectively, a Moravian village and small Moravian city on the Bohemian border. More importantly, Iglau was a German-speaking enclave within the largely Czech-speaking lands of the "Bohemian Crown," this last designation a relic of the Holy Roman Empire. In Mahler's day, the lands were part of Cisleithania, an unofficial name for the Austrian half of the Habsburg Empire; the Hungarian half was Transleithania, with the boundary marked by the Leitha River. Such were the complexities of the historical circumstances in which he worked.

The aspects of personal identity mentioned in Alma Mahler's account draw attention to political crises that, along with the notable creativity, marked this period in Vienna. Being considered Bohemian had certainly turned into a liability for many residents of Cisleithania in 1897, the year in which Mahler became a conductor of the Court Opera. On April 5, the Austrian prime minister, Count Kasimir Badeni, set off an extended crisis by abruptly declaring that the Czech and German languages would have equal status in official matters, a crisis that peaked in October and November 1897 and led to Badeni's dismissal.[3] Mahler's status as a Jew was, of course, the most consequential aspect of his own identity, and his appointment to the Court Opera on April 8, 1897 – three days after Badeni's decree – coincided with a regrettable watershed moment in the city's history: on that date, Vienna became the first European city to select an avowedly anti-Semitic mayor, Karl Lueger. This process had played out over two years and five city council elections, with behind-the-scenes manipulation of Emperor Franz Joseph by Badeni, who had his own political agenda.[4]

But what of the third basis of Mahler's sense of homelessness, his status as "an Austrian among the Germans"? This self-description is the hardest to grasp, in part because strong bonds between many Austrians and Germany obscure the source of the friction. Although Mahler did hold conducting positions in cities within the German Empire – Kassel, Leipzig, and Hamburg – the fraught relationship between the German and

---

[3] The April 5 ordinance applied to Bohemia; Badeni issued a second ordinance for Moravia on April 22. Bruce Garver, *The Young Czech Party, 1874–1901, and the Emergence of a Multi-Party System* (New Haven: Yale University Press, 1978), 243; and John Deak, *Forging a Multinational State: State-Making in Imperial Austria from the Enlightenment to the First World War* (Stanford: Stanford University Press, 2015), 223–26.

[4] John W. Boyer, *Political Radicalism in Late Imperial Vienna: Origins of the Christian Social Movement 1848–1897* (Chicago: University of Chicago Press, 1981), 316–410, especially 380–86 and 408–10.

Austro-Hungarian Empires would have conditioned his experiences in those cities. Under Otto von Bismarck, Prussia had defeated Austria in 1866 in one of the wars that preceded the founding of the German Empire. Well before Bismarck's death on July 30, 1898, however, Germany had adopted an official stance of nonintervention in Austria's domestic affairs. Amid this uneasy balance of power, many Austrian liberals felt an allegiance to Germany, and many German citizens took a keen interest in current events in Austria.

One such German citizen was Theodor Mommsen (1817–1903), a renowned scholar of Roman history, who, judging from the evidence in a number of anecdotes, viewed certain contemporary issues from an outlook colored by a pronounced sense of German nationalism. Mommsen had taught at the Friedrich Wilhelm University in Berlin until his retirement in 1887 and went on to win a Nobel Prize in 1902. His celebrity status around the turn of the century is made clear by the frequent appearance of his name in the *Neue Freie Presse*, as in an account of a memorial service in Berlin after Bismarck's death: "Now that Bismarck is dead, Theodor Mommsen is without doubt the most famous man in Germany."[5]

The newspaper's own bias toward a German nationalist perspective must explain why on October 31, 1897, there appeared on its front page an aggressive public letter by Mommsen addressed "To the Germans in Austria." This missive focused on the Czech presence in Austria and, in particular, Badeni's language ordinances and the unrest they had occasioned. In the opening sentences, Mommsen referred specifically to the 1866 Austro-Prussian War and the shared cultural heritage of the two realms:

> Believe only that as the Austrians look out toward Germany, so also do the Germans toward Austria, and that our hearts also bleed at these outrageous acts of dishonor and brutality. Yes, we separated ourselves from you, and the separation fight was harsh, but despite that we had hoped for the permanent standing together of two brothers peacefully coexisting after the difficult division of an inheritance. That the Alps of Salzburg and the Tyrol would also continue to belong to the nation as a whole, that the Danube would remain as German as the Rhine, the graves of Mozart and Grillparzer as German as those of Schiller and Goethe, even in the most heated struggle no one even among us cool north Germans doubted.

[5] "Ein Gespräch mit Mommsen," *Neue Freie Presse*, August 9, 1898: 1–2.

Mommsen then escalated his rhetoric, perhaps concerned about the street violence that Badeni's actions had set off, but choosing words that seem calculated to widen the divisions. He went so far as to assert that "we had believed the solidarity of Germany and Austria unshakably secured. And now the apostles of barbarism are at work burying the German labor of half a millennium in the abyss of their nonculture." Ultimately, he advocated the use of force if necessary: "The skull of the Czech is not open to reason, but it does respond to blows."[6]

Scholarship on Mahler has noted the significance of the language ordinances in the reception of his early work as a conductor in Vienna, but Mommsen's essay seems not to have elicited comment. Recent historical studies have noted the letter's impact,[7] however, and the powerful role it played in exacerbating the crisis was widely acknowledged at the time. To writers in Czech and other Slavic languages it seemed as inflammatory as Badeni's decrees had appeared to Germans and German Austrians; in the words of Berthold Sutter, "As the Germans had the Badeni language ordinances, the Czechs now designated Mommsen's letter an 'act of insurrection.'"[8]

Today the anti-Czech prejudice expressed in the letter seems not only repellent but baffling, for in 1880 Mommsen had taken a strong public stand against the anti-Semitism promulgated by another Berlin professor, Heinrich von Treitschke: Mommsen did not by any means share that particular prejudice. To be sure, anti-Semites with nationalist agendas at times enlisted Mommsen's fame for their own purposes – most notably (this continued into the Third Reich) by extracting from the third volume (1856) of his history of Rome a sentence in which he referred to Jews, stereotypically the quintessential international people, as "leavening of cosmopolitism and of national decomposition" in that ancient setting. But if the most incendiary lines from the 1897 letter were likewise often quoted out of context, the consternation felt by many of Mommsen's contemporaries at what seemed an uncalled-for virulence is nevertheless understandable, given the damning contents of the entire document. Surveying the damage, Sutter observed, "In Austria far more true dismay than joy about Mommsen's letter predominated – above all among

[6] "An die Deutschen in Österreich," *Neue Freie Presse*, October 31, 1897: 1.
[7] Garver, *The Young Czech Party*, 251–53; and Nancy M. Wingfield, *Flag Wars and Stone Saints: How the Bohemian Lands Became Czech* (Cambridge, MA: Harvard University Press, 2007), 64.
[8] Berthold Sutter, "Theodor Mommsens Brief 'An die Deutschen in Österreich,'" *Ostdeutsche Wissenschaft: Jahrbuch des Ostdeutschen Kulturrates* 10 (1965): 168.

moderate German politicians who sought an honorable compromise with the Slavic nationalities" (164).

Indeed, commentary in Austrian and German newspapers representing a wide spectrum of political views expressed outrage that a private German citizen had presumed to speak for his country, that he had inserted himself into Austrian affairs, and that he had done both so ineptly. *Das Vaterland*, a conservative, Catholic publication styling itself as the "Newspaper for the Austrian Monarchy," ran a front-page story sharply critical of Mommsen on November 3, 1897. Written by the newspaper's Berlin correspondent, the article questioned Mommsen's right to involve himself in the affairs of a neighboring state on the basis of the two states' shared national heritage and pointed out the dangers of irredentism practiced by any nation. The evening edition took up the issue again, quoting from a German daily, the *Hamburger Nachrichten*: "we must express our regret that a well-known German scholar is interfering in this offensive and unseemly fashion in the inner struggles of a state with which we stand in an alliance relationship."

On November 5, another Viennese newspaper, *Reichspost*, which called itself an "Independent Daily for Austria-Hungary's Christian People" and espoused anti-Semitic and pro-Lueger but not German nationalist politics, weighed in to complain that Mommsen had attacked anti-Semitism. The newspaper stated that it did not expect better of the *Neue Freie Presse*, the "organ of 'distinguished Jews,'" than to publish insults directed at Vienna by a foreigner. It then focused on the motivation: "In which interest, in whose favor was the public declaration drawn out?" *Reichspost* assayed an answer by considering at whom the essay's sharpest barb had been aimed, ruling out groups such as the Young Czechs and the Catholic People's Party before deciding that "anti-Semitic Vienna" was the target. Mommsen had in fact included in his letter a sentence that could be interpreted as a provocative challenge to the anti-Semites and their inclination to see Jews as the cause of all the problems in the multicultural empire: "How is it possible that when everything is at stake, such a relatively trivial matter as the position of the Semites in the state endangers unity?" To Mommsen, the Slavs represented a much greater threat, and he warned that "whoever gives in must realize that he is Czechizing either his children or at least his grandchildren."

Recent scholarship has noted the conjunction of intensified anti-Semitism and heightened anti-Czech feelings during the Badeni crisis.[9]

[9] Oliver Rathkolb, "Gewalt und Antisemitismus an der Universität Wien und die Badeni-Krise 1897. Davor und danach," in *Der lange Schatten des Antisemitismus: Kritische Auseinandersetzungen mit der*

Like Mommsen himself, however, some of his contemporaries did not share both prejudices – as noted earlier, a bifurcated position on these types of prejudice was also evident in *Reichspost*'s basic stance on imperial politics – or indeed either of them. For instance, Vatroslav Jagić, a scholar of Croatian extraction who had been Mommsen's colleague in Berlin and at the time of the crisis was a professor of Slavic studies at the University of Vienna, wrote a lengthy open response to the pessimism about Austria's future that Mommsen had expressed. Jagić did not mention Jews or anti-Semitism when he explained his optimistic vision, which depended on Austria remaining polyglot: "One should not think of Austria as a centralized, unified German state. Such a state next to Germany would be as much a source of difficulties as a Slavic state next to Russia." Adopting a conciliatory tone, he recognized German achievements and their positive effect on Slavic peoples in the empire but also asserted, "You know far too little about the intellectual and cultural life of Slavs."[10] On January 6, 1898, the *Neue Freie Presse* responded with less restraint than Jagić, accusing him of using a "quite unscientific" method because in his support of a bilingual Cisleithania he had not considered either "those extended regions of Bohemia where not a single Czech lives" or the size of the "coherent, purely German language area." In the end, neither the *Neue Freie Presse* nor Mommsen came off stronger as a result of this uproar; only Jagić emerged as reasonable.

That various ethnic groups asserted their particularity and the right to use their own languages undeniably resulted in occasional confusion. During the sixteen or so years that preceded his ascendancy to the Viennese position, Mahler had worked as a conductor not only in cities in Cisleithania and the German Empire but also, from October 1888 until March 1891, in Budapest, the capital of Transleithania. When he assumed the position at the Hungarian National Opera, Mahler indicated his intent to learn the Magyar language and to foster the composition and performance of operas in the language, but he does not appear to have succeeded in either endeavor. An anecdote from his tenure in Hungary demonstrates the complications that could arise from accommodating different languages. Toward the end of 1890, Lilli Lehmann went to Budapest to perform in several operas, and found herself in a bewildering multilingual

---

Geschichte der Universität im 19. und 20. Jahrhundert, ed. Oliver Rathkolb (Göttingen: V&R unipress, 2013), 69–92.

[10] "Mommsen und Jagić über den Kampf der Deutsch-Oesterreicher," *Deutsche Revue über das gesamte nationale Leben der Gegenwart* 23, no. 1 (January–March 1898): 43–47, here 45.

muddle: "I sang all the roles in Italian, only that of Rachel [in *La Juive*] in French since I had been given a choice and had no idea that Perotti [the male lead] would sing in Italian. All the others in addition sang in Hungarian, and one cannot imagine the cosmopolitan linguistic confusion of these performances, in which the foreigners, who sang without a prompter, had to remain true to their languages."[11] For his part, Mahler encountered Hungarian chauvinism during his time in Budapest – indeed, it ultimately led to his dismissal – as well as anti-Semitism; in this case, then, nationalism and anti-Semitism did converge.

Mommsen's stand against Treitschke's anti-Semitism made him a revered figure for many Jews, even though some of his comments in the 1880 essay exerted pressure toward the kind of homogeneity described at the outset of this essay. Remarking on the diverse peoples that had merged to create the German nation, he had suggested that Jews give up certain "special customs" and conform to German norms (these appear to have been Prussian), as a number of cities and states had to do when unification took place in 1871. Mommsen himself had been born in one of those states, Schleswig. His 1897 letter was far less diplomatic than the 1880 essay, of course, and its crude miscalculations were not isolated instances of his tactlessness; Mommsen was reported to have observed "in the presence of high Bavarian state officials at a formal dinner, as the talk came to Austria," that a Bavarian person formed "the transition from the Austrian to the human,"[12] though elsewhere this "witty remark" was attributed to Bismarck. In either case, the quip suggests the rude condescension that citizens of the German Empire felt free to express toward even German Austrians, a tendency that surely figured into Mahler's sense that he would remain "an Austrian among the Germans," that is, an intruder in this respect as well as the other two.

---

[11] Lilli Lehmann, *Mein Weg*, 2nd ed. (Leipzig: S. Hirzel, 1920), 367.
[12] Sutter, "Theodor Mommsens Brief," 167.

PART II
Performance

CHAPTER 8

Operatic and Orchestral Repertoire

Anna Stoll Knecht

Gustav Mahler's conducting career spanned three decades (1880–1911), bringing him to every corner of the Austro-Hungarian and German Empires before concluding in North America. He often complained about this activity – regarding it as a burden that kept him from composition – and his conducting repertoire did not always reflect his own taste, as he was at times subordinate to theater directors who made their own decisions. But by comparing his repertoire in the various positions he occupied, we can, at least partly, reconstruct his own vision. What are the characteristics of his preferred repertoire? Which composers did he favor, and whom did he neglect? What new music did he perform, besides his own? When did his choices match the norm, and when did they deviate from it? These and other salient features of Mahler's repertoire begin to emerge when his decisions are situated within the broader context of Austro-German operatic and concert traditions.

As the scope of this essay is limited to orchestral and concert repertoire in Austria and Germany (activity in the United States is treated in Chapter 12), I focus on two milestones in Mahler's international career: his tenures in Hamburg (1891–97) and Vienna (1897–1907). As director in Vienna, Mahler was in a position to make programming decisions. At the Hamburg City Theater, however, he took orders from the intendant, Bernhard Pollini. Comparing his repertoire in Hamburg and in Vienna thus allows us to determine which works he continued to perform when he was in charge. I will discuss operatic repertoire at greater length than the concert repertoire, since apart from concert tours and guest appearances, Mahler's career as symphonic conductor in Germany and Austria was limited to one season in Hamburg (1894–95) and three seasons in Vienna (1898–1901).

Operatic Repertoire in Hamburg

Mahler's engagement in Hamburg was crucial for his career as both conductor and composer. At the podium he expanded his operatic and concert repertoire considerably, earning recognition as a highly talented conductor. Creatively, it was during this period that Mahler set up the rhythm that he would retain until his death: composing during the summer when the theater was closed. Between 1891 and 1897 he managed to complete the First, Second, and Third Symphonies, working primarily from June through August.

Hired as First Kapellmeister in Hamburg, a step down from his directorship in Budapest, Mahler was obliged to accept repertoire choices motivated (in his view) by political or economic factors rather than artistic ones. He could propose works for performance, but his influence on Pollini was limited. Nonetheless, he did occasionally succeed, for example, during the initial negotiations in 1887, when he secured the rights to conduct Wagner, Mozart, and Beethoven, a helpful indication of his priorities as a conductor.

From the beginning of Pollini's tenure in 1874, performances of Wagner at the Stadttheater had increased annually, from nine in 1874 to an average of thirty-seven by Mahler's arrival in 1891. Moreover, in 1880 Pollini introduced an annual Wagner cycle that took place near the end of each season, so that when Mahler took up his position in March 1891, Hamburg was already a leading center for Wagner performances.[1] After a well-received debut with *Tannhäuser* on March 29, 1891, Mahler embarked on the annual Wagner cycle, performing ten operas in less than two months, including his first *Tristan*. In total Mahler offered 232 Wagner performances in Hamburg between 1891 and 1897 (out of 745 appearances), with his most frequently conducted works being *Tannhäuser*, *Die Walküre*, *Siegfried*, and *Die Meistersinger von Nürnberg*. Notably, after his arrival in 1891 the number of Wagner performances increased even further: from thirty-seven in 1890 and thirty-two in 1891 to sixty-four in 1892 and fifty-nine in 1893.

By comparison, Mahler conducted seventy-three Mozart performances during the period, most commonly *Die Zauberflöte* and *Don Giovanni* – the latter interpretation having made a lasting impression on Johannes Brahms in Budapest. Along with *Fidelio*, performed forty-three times during the Hamburg years, Wagner and Mozart would be the pillars of the operatic canon for Mahler throughout his career. "The perfect German opera composers," as he called them (*NBLE*, 180), grounded the repertoire

---

[1] In 1890–91, Hamburg totaled sixty-four Wagner performances, against fifty in Berlin, forty-nine in Dresden, and fewer than forty in Leipzig, Munich, Vienna, and Frankfurt.

in Hamburg: *Fidelio* was a "classic," and in 1881 Pollini introduced a Mozart cycle to complement the Wagner series.

Among works established in Hamburg and later retained in Mahler's repertoire were Weber's *Der Freischütz* (performed sixty-six times throughout his career), Verdi's operas (especially *Aïda* and *Falstaff*), and, to a lesser extent, music by Hermann Goetz and Anton Rubinstein. He tended to bypass large chunks of the then-standard repertoire: German Romantics such as Spohr and Kretschmer, Italian opera buffa (particularly Donizetti), or French composers including Auber, Boiledieu, and Halévy. Mahler never conducted *Samson et Dalila* by Camille Saint-Saëns, which had appeared in the repertoire in Hamburg during the 1881–82 season, and performed Gluck's *Iphigénie en Aulide* only a few times in Vienna, although it belonged to the core repertoire in Hamburg from 1877 on. Certain new works, however, found support from Mahler in Hamburg, particularly Engelbert Humperdinck's *Hänsel und Gretl* (performed fifty times) and Karl Goldmark's *Das Heimchen am Herd* (*The Cricket on the Hearth*; twenty-one). These operas disappeared from his repertoire after Hamburg, however, although he did perform two other Goldmark operas in Vienna.

More revealing of Mahler's own predilections are German premieres of two works by Tchaikovsky: *Eugene Onegin* in January 1892, in the composer's presence, and the first performance outside Russia of his last opera, *Iolanta*, a year later. Tchaikovsky remained in his repertoire in Vienna and in New York; indeed, *The Queen of Spades* would be the last opera Mahler ever conducted, on March 21, 1910 at the Metropolitan Opera. The Hamburg era also marks the beginning of Mahler's championship of the Czech composer Bedřich Smetana, with performances of *Dalibor*, *The Two Widows*, *The Kiss*, and *The Bartered Bride*, the latter a resounding success after its first Hamburg performance on January 17, 1894 (Mahler would conduct it there a total of thirty-seven times). Thus, while Mahler did not make definitive programming decisions, his six years left their mark on the Hamburg repertoire, through both tradition and innovation.

Operatic Repertoire in Vienna

As director of the Court Opera in Vienna, Mahler achieved a goal he could not manage in Hamburg, implementing a Wagnerian vision of opera as *Gesamtkunstwerk*. Effectively conductor, stage manager, and director, Mahler was finally in charge, both in the pit and on stage. He was a "total conductor," so to speak, training singers, musicians, and audiences. In most Wagnerian reforms he followed the Bayreuth model, though in one crucial aspect he would remain frustrated: "If only I could prepare a number of works flawlessly and present them as real festival performances, the way it's done in Bayreuth!... But the arrangement in our theatre is such that there must be a performance every day!... I have a repertoire in which the noblest works stand beside the most commonplace" (NBLE, 103–4). As in Hamburg, Mahler would be vexed by the repertory system, which entailed a reduced number of rehearsals for a large number of performances. But while the Festival model could not be transferred from Bayreuth to Vienna, Mahler's power to impose changes in the repertoire did allow him to institute reforms.

After his debut with *Lohengrin* on May 11, 1897, Mahler conducted 647 performances until his departure in June 1907. His progressive reshaping of the repertoire led, in the second half of his tenure, to the building of cycles and the conception of new productions. The historic nature of this achievement depended substantially on Mahler's encounter with Secession artist Alfred Roller in 1902. Beginning with the groundbreaking *Tristan* they codirected in February 1903, Mahler and Roller reinvented the canonic trinity together, revolutionizing set design, costumes, lighting, and acting to fulfill as nearly as possible the *Gesamtkunstwerk* ideal. After *Tristan* they designed a new production of Beethoven's *Fidelio*, premiered in October 1904 and performed nineteen times, including Mahler's last appearance as the director of the Vienna Hofoper on October 15, 1907. The pair then embarked on the *Ring* cycle, presenting *Das Rheingold* in 1905 and *Die Walküre* in 1907 before Mahler's resignation scuttled the project.

Along with their brilliant but incomplete vision for Wagner, Mahler and Roller revisited five operas for the Mozart Year of 1906: *Così fan Tutte* and *Don Giovanni* in 1905, and *Die Entführung aus dem Serail*, *Figaro*, and *Die Zauberflöte* in 1906. Thus as in Hamburg – and previously in Prague, Leipzig, and Budapest – Mozart and Wagner stood at the center of Mahler's repertoire in Vienna: the three most often performed operas between 1897 and 1907 were *Le nozze di Figaro* (fifty times), *Die Zauberflöte* (thirty-eight), and *Tristan* (thirty-seven). If Mahler increased the number of Mozart and Wagner performances during his tenure, both composers were already part of the traditional repertoire in Vienna (as in Hamburg), particularly from Hans Richter's appointment as a conductor in 1875. Comparing Mahler's repertoire in Vienna with that of Richter shows that, although they shared a common predilection for Wagner,

Mozart, and Beethoven, Mahler seldom conducted music by Meyerbeer, Gounod, Rossini, or Leoncavallo, who completed Richter's top ten and were firmly established in late nineteenth-century operatic repertoire in Germany and Austria. After Wagner, whose music Richter performed the most (899 performances), Meyerbeer occupies the second position (169), before Mozart and Beethoven. Mahler conducted some Meyerbeer operas throughout his career – most often *Les Huguenots* and *Robert le diable* – but only nine times in Vienna (*Les Huguenots* and *Le Prophète*). Gounod and Rossini, also highly placed in Richter's top ten (before Beethoven), were equally underrepresented in Mahler's repertoire: he never conducted *Roméo et Juliette*, *Faust* only four times in Vienna, and Rossini's *Il barbiere di Siviglia* only twice. Other favorites of Richter that Mahler tended to avoid include Leoncavallo's *Pagliacci*, Mascagni's *Cavalleria rusticana*, Cherubini's *Les deux journées* and Marschner's *Hans Heiling*. Massenet, who belonged to the traditional repertoire in Vienna, disappeared with Mahler's arrival in 1897.

As in Hamburg, Mahler battled to include new music as well as compositions that had not been heard in Vienna. He supervised the artistic direction of 101 premieres in ten years, challenging audiences with contemporary and marginal works, constantly striving to expand the repertoire to Slavonic, Russian, and French music. He was fighting on two fronts: against economic constraints, as productions that were not successful financially were threatened to be cut, and against censorship. Over time the battle took its toll, and the number of premieres progressively decreased: after twenty-four performances of new works between 1897 and 1900, Mahler conducted twenty-one between 1900 and 1904 and seventeen during the last three years.[2]

During his first season Mahler introduced three new operas, all successful financially and all presented earlier in Hamburg. Smetana's *Dalibor* was heard for the first time in Vienna on October 4, 1897, four days before Mahler's official nomination as director. The emperor's name day was usually celebrated with a premiere; that the soon-to-be director would pick, on that occasion, a Czech opera never performed in Vienna did not go unnoticed. Presenting a Czech work in German to mark the beginning of his directorship was interpreted as a politically charged step in a context of tension between Czech- and German-speaking populations. The Viennese newspapers deplored the presence of Czech members of the

---

[2] These numbers also reflect the decreasing number of performances that Mahler conducted: 320 (1897–1900), then 180 (1900–4), and finally 145 (1904–7).

parliament, as well as Czech students who had gathered en masse at the premiere. Nonetheless, Mahler kept *Dalibor* in the repertoire until 1904 (conducting it twenty-one times), though he declined to present another Czech opera during the remainder of his tenure.

He did, however, pick a Russian work as the second premiere of his first season in November 1897: Tchaikovsky's *Eugene Onegin*. Again, critics read political intentions behind this choice and ironically asked if the idea was to "celebrate the triumph of pan-Slavism in the Hofoper,"[3] which did not prevent Mahler from introducing *Iolanta* and *The Queen of Spades* a few years later. For the third new opera of his first season he chose Bizet's *Djamileh* (performed thirty-one times in Hamburg and Vienna), again a relatively exotic choice. Other notable Viennese premieres during the Mahler era in Vienna include *Der Corregidor* by Hugo Wolf, performed posthumously, and Verdi's *Falstaff* in German, in May 1904, with designs and costumes by Alfred Roller. The only Richard Strauss opera Mahler ever managed to program was *Feuersnot*, as Pollini had refused *Guntram* in Hamburg in 1894 and the Viennese censors would reject *Salome* despite Mahler's best efforts to broker a compromise. Finally, Mahler conducted world premieres of Goldmark's *Die Kriegsgefangene* (in 1899) and *Es war einmal* by Alexander von Zemlinsky in January 1900.

Orchestral Repertoire

After Hans von Bülow's death, Mahler became conductor of the eight annual Subscription Concerts in Hamburg, which in his single year of service took place between October 1894 and March 1895. Conducting concerts was not only a way to escape the madness of the opera house but also a lifelong ambition. Compared with Mahler's restricted decision-making power at the City Opera, the concert hall offered him a welcome degree of freedom, even though Pollini still had the last word on repertoire.

Bülow had established a solid Beethovenian tradition in Hamburg, performing all nine symphonies each season. Mahler followed this lead, picking a Beethoven work for every annual benefit concert. He also shared Bülow's taste for Berlioz, conducting the *Symphonie fantastique* for the first time at the Sixth Subscription Concert on February 4, 1895, and performing it twelve times in his career (making it his most-performed work in the realm of program music). Contrary to Bülow, Mahler did not particularly engage with Brahms's music, leaning rather toward Robert Schumann and

---

[3] *Neues Wiener Journal*, November 20, 1897.

Tchaikovsky. In the realm of new music, Hamburg heard Bruckner's Fourth Symphony for the second time under Mahler's baton, also in February 1895, as well as the Prelude to Act I of Strauss's *Guntram*.

Generally, Mahler's most favored works in the concert hall were by Wagner (235 performances) and Beethoven (166), after his own music (169). His first two symphonies were premiered during the Hamburg years, but in Berlin: the Second in December 1895 (after a performance of the first three movements in March 1895 under Richard Strauss) and the First (in its final form) in March 1896.[4] After Mahler's first season with the Subscription Concerts ended with a deficit, the series was discontinued. His mixed reception as a symphonic conductor seems partly due to his practice of altering scores (*Retuschen*). In fact, if his willingness to alter scores was admired at the opera, it alienated listeners in concert halls.

Mahler encountered similar difficulties in Vienna, where he served as director of the Philharmonic – chosen by the orchestra, following a long-standing tradition – between 1898 and 1901. An uneven reception came to a head when his performance of Beethoven's Ninth Symphony on February 18, 1900, was violently criticized. Mahler's reworking of Beethoven's orchestration was perceived as "barbarism,"[5] and some critics did not forgive him for having attempted to "improve" Beethoven.[6] In Vienna, as in Hamburg, Mahler's modern interpretations were welcomed in the realm of "new music," but rejected when he dared, as Bülow and many others had done before him, to reinterpret the "classics."

A third of the almost eighty works Mahler conducted during his three seasons with the Vienna Philharmonic were by Beethoven. Besides this traditional core, also including Wagner (although less often performed than in Hamburg), Mozart, Schubert, and Schumann, Mahler programmed Viennese premieres of works by three composers championed in his operatic repertoire: Tchaikovsky's *1812 Overture* and *Manfred Symphony* (performed only once, in January 1901, between its world premiere in Moscow in 1886 and 1971), Smetana's Overture to his "Festival opera" *Libuše*, and Bizet's concert suite *Roma*. As he had done in Hamburg, Mahler promoted the music of Richard Strauss, with two early works: excerpts from *Guntram* (February 1898) and the "Symphonic Fantasy" *Aus Italien* (November 1899). Other Viennese premieres of

---

[4] This was actually the fourth performance of the First, after November 20, 1889 (Budapest); October 27, 1893 (Hamburg); and June 3, 1894 (Weimar).
[5] Richard Heuberger, *Neue freie Presse*; see K. M. Knittel, "'Polemik im Concertsaal': Mahler, Beethoven, and the Viennese Critics," *19th-Century Music* 29 (2006): 295.
[6] Anonymous article in *Die Deutsche Zeitung*, November 1898.

symphonic poems include Franz Liszt's *Festklänge* (January 1899) and
Anton Dvořák's *Wild Dove* (December 1899). Apart from Bizet, French
music was represented by César Franck with the *Symphonic Variations* for
piano and orchestra, and by Berlioz: the *Symphonie fantastique*, which had
been in the repertoire since 1862, and two overtures, the *Carnaval Romain*
and the rarely performed *Rob Roy*, heard for the first time in Vienna under
Mahler in November 1900. Two world premieres took place during his
first season: another symphonic poem by Dvořák, *A Hero's Song* (in
December 1898), and Bruckner's Sixth Symphony (February 1899).
Mahler gave his last concert with the Vienna Philharmonic in February
1901, before resigning from his position in April. A few weeks later, the
arch-conservative Joseph Hellmesberger was elected to succeed him as
director of the Philharmonic. Mahler's career in the concert hall meanwhile took an upward tack: from 1901 his rising reputation as composer
led to frequent appearances as guest conductor throughout Europe, mostly
to promote his own music.

Comparing Mahler's operatic and orchestral repertoire in Hamburg and
Vienna shows clearly when his choices followed an established tradition,
and when they deviated from it. The "perfect German composers"
Beethoven, Mozart, and Wagner already belonged to the traditional repertoire in Hamburg and in Vienna before Mahler's arrival, but his radical
reinterpretations of the canonic trinity shook convention. As a rule, he
avoided conducting French grand opera or Italian opera buffa, genres that
were solidly in the traditional repertoire in late nineteenth-century
Austrian and German opera houses; but with regard to new music by
such composers as Smetana, Tchaikovsky, Strauss, and Bruckner, he
remained a tireless advocate.

CHAPTER 9

Collaborators

Anna Harwell Celenza

Descriptions of Mahler often emphasize his "outsider" status, his tyranni-cal bearing as an orchestral conductor, or his preference for composing in complete isolation. "Collaboration" is not a term regularly used to describe his artistic approach. But in the realm of opera, it was collaboration that eventually enabled him to realize, in living form, his artistic aspirations and to create what we commonly think of today as the role of the modern opera director.

Collaboration did not come easily to Mahler. His opera direction was informed by Wagner's *Gesamtkunstwerk* aesthetic, and, like Wagner, Mahler felt the need to control all disciplinary aspects of performance – the music, the acting, and the scenery. These dictatorial inclinations caused strife during his first appointments in Budapest and Hamburg, where he often clashed with colleagues, like Bernhard Pollini, who failed to embrace his ideas concerning reform. Once in Vienna, Mahler kept to this path, brooking little dissent. As a cellist at the Hofoper noted: "Mahler descended upon the opera house like an elemental catastrophe. An earth-quake of unprecedented intensity and duration shook the entire structure from its foundations to its gable. Whatever was not strong and vital was cast away and perished. In short order, the majority of the singers, conductors, and two thirds of the orchestra got sacked." Particularly during his first five years, Mahler comported himself as "quite the 'Master' type, endowed with the gift of commanding," and treated his colleagues "like a lion-tamer handles his animals."[1] But authoritarian manner not-withstanding, he also began to engage deeply with creative peers outside music, and through these encounters met his most influential collaborator, the innovative graphic artist Alfred Roller.

---

[1] Constantin Floros, *Gustav Mahler. Visionary and Despot: Portrait of a Personality*, trans. Ernest Bernhardt-Kabisch (Frankurt am Main: Peter Lang, 2012), 38–39.

The relationship formed in 1902, when Roller, then a professor of drawing at the School of Applied Arts and president of the Viennese Secession, oversaw the latter organization's fourteenth exhibition, famously designed around the unveiling of Max Klinger's *Beethoven Monument*. Mahler agreed to prepare an arrangement of Beethoven's Symphony no. 9 suitable for the opening and, though the performance would be a fiasco, experienced first-hand the Secession's efforts to push Viennese artistic taste in a new, avant-garde direction.[2]

Like Mahler, the Secessionists saw the future in the Wagnerian *Gesamtkunstwerk* – particularly Roller, an intellectual deeply interested in stagecraft. For the Beethoven exhibition, Roller created a large fresco, *Nightfall*, that served as a backdrop to Klinger's sculpture. Photos reveal that Roller's fresco gave depth to the sculpture, endowing it with a sense of mood and grandeur that would have otherwise been missing in a gallery setting. Mahler seems to have reacted positively, for a friendship developed quickly. Roller had been following Mahler's efforts to reinvigorate performances of Wagner at the Hofoper, and now he took the opportunity to share with Mahler his own ideas about the theater. Roller hoped especially to realize those aspects of Wagner's theories that he believed had never been actualized – namely, the visual elements of staged performance.

In *Art and Revolution* (1849) and *The Artwork of the Future* (1849), Wagner had called for the bringing-together, in equal measure, of the performing and visual arts: on one hand, music, dance, and spoken drama; on the other, architecture, sculpture, and painting. Although Roller believed that Wagner's productions had successfully integrated the performing arts, he maintained that neither Wagner nor his successors had taken full advantage of the visual arts. Arguing that Wagner's visual aesthetic was too rooted in naturalism, Roller advocated an approach to staging that would fuse realism and stylized symbolism.

Roller interpreted Wagner's vision through the lens of a contemporary theorist, the stage designer Adolphe Appia (1862–1928). For Appia, Wagner's handling of different branches of art as equal partners was impractical; he proposed that a hierarchy be instilled in the overall design of a stage production. Roller embraced this theory and applied it to his own conception of operatic design:

[2] Anna Harwell Celenza, "Darwinian Visions: Beethoven Reception in Mahler's Vienna," *The Musical Quarterly* 93 (2010): 514, 534.

The décor should never become an end in itself. Neither should it ever give the impression of a self-sufficient reality existing alongside or even above the work. It is there merely to set a mood at the rise of the curtain, the mood which the dramatist or the composer wishes to communicate to his audience. Everything concerned with the scenery plays a secondary role. The designer is only the servant of the work. He does not "decorate," does not illustrate the stage happenings, but instead creates with the utmost self-restraint the indispensable frame for the work of art.

The scenery and costumes should not fool the eye, Roller explained, but rather "create the atmosphere of the drama." And the primary tool used to create this atmosphere was light. "Like music, light is able to express all that belongs to the innermost essence of a phenomenon," explained Roller.[3] Light served as the catalyst of visual expression and enhanced the primary expressive element in opera: the music.

Mahler and Roller began to collaborate almost immediately. In January 1903 a production of Weber's *Euryanthe* featured Secession-inspired costumes by Roller. One month later, a new production of *Tristan und Isolde* premiered with all the visual elements (scenery, lighting, and costumes) designed by Roller. Thrilled by the production's artistic and critical success, Mahler singled out Roller's overall vision of the stage, "where everything is simply indicated, nothing [actually] exists."[4]

In his review, Max Graf focused similarly on abstraction, characterizing the production as a "symphony in three movements," each with its own color scheme – red, violet, and gray – and harmonic qualities. The ability of the lighting "to vary the color of a basic chord, spreading it out and changing it," was revolutionary. As Graf explained, Roller's set designs and costumes "brought something of the subtle *Tristan* chromaticisms to the world of the decorative arts." In short, Roller had created "musical impressions through the vibrations of air and color."[5]

Mahler, for his part, saw the collaboration with Roller as a turning point in his career as an opera director. Shortly after the premiere, he expressed his gratitude in a letter:

> My Dear Roller,
>   How you have put me to shame! For days I have been wondering how to thank you for all the great and wonderful things for which the Opera House and I owe you thanks. – And I have come to the conclusion that instead of

trying to put anything into words, I should simply remain silent. – I know
we are similar in one respect: in our completely unselfish devotion to art,
even if we approach it by different roads. And I was also fully aware that you
would not think me unappreciative or undiscerning if I did not try to put
anything into words about what you have come to mean to me.

And I should be very sad, as though it were some kind of farewell, over
our saying such things to each other now, were I not joyfully certain that
our collaboration hitherto is only a *beginning* and an indication of things to
come [emphasis in original].

The success of *Tristan* earned Roller a permanent appointment at the
Hofoper, where he served simultaneously as stage director, set designer,
and costume designer, responsibilities previously divided among various
individuals. Roller's indefatigable quest for perfection paralleled Mahler's
own. As one contemporary described it, Roller was "tireless in everything,
wandering from stage to stalls, from stalls to gallery, trying out filters,
colored lenses, light intensities, changing, improving, discovering nuances
imperceptible to the layman."[6] Together, Mahler and Roller mounted
twenty new opera productions, including, along with works of Wagner
and Mozart, Beethoven's *Fidelio* and Gluck's *Iphigénie en Aulide*.

Of course, to put on an opera requires more than music and scenery.
Singers, generally the focal points of opera productions, also played an
indispensable role in Mahler's collaborative process. At the Hofoper,
Mahler sought "a unified ensemble," not a "stable of stars," and had little
patience for performers opposed to his vision. "What you theater people
call a tradition," he once exclaimed in frustration to a singer, "is mere
convenience and slovenliness for you!"[7]

For Mahler, the ability to act was as important as the ability to sing, and
he was not averse to engaging singers with limited voices if their dramatic
capabilities were exceptional. "Unless every motion is stylized and translated into art, unless every step and expression is sublimated, the whole
performance becomes puerile," he claimed. But good acting did not come
naturally. Like good singing, it required study and hard work. "Considering that everything, even the cobbler's trade, has to be painstakingly
learned," Mahler argued, "why should an actor be expected to create a

---

[6] Ibid., 426; Stephen Carlton Thursby, "Gustav Mahler, Alfred Roller, and the Wagnerian
Gesamtkunstwerk: 'Tristan' and Affinities between the Arts at the Vienna Court Opera" (PhD
diss, Florida State University, 2009), 103; Emil Lucka, "Erinnerungen an Alfred Roller," *Deutsche
Zukunft* (December 17, 1933): 15.

[7] Stephen E. Hefling, "Liner Notes," in *Mahler's Decade in Vienna, Singers of the Court Opera
1897–1907* (Marston 53004-2, 2003); Fischer, *Gustav Mahler*, 416.

musical and dramatic role spontaneously and without guidance?" (*HLG2*, 295) In response to this rhetorical question, Mahler offered up as an example the success of his first prodigy, the soprano Anna von Mildenburg (1872–1947).

Mildenburg studied with Rosa Papier and made her debut in Hamburg as Brünnhilde in *Die Walküre* in 1895. Mahler conducted the performance and took credit for introducing her to the nuances of Wagnerian performance:

> Much the same way that I drilled her musically, I made her study every expression and gesture of her mime and acting in front of a mirror ... When she had memorized her part, I ... showed her every step, every pose, and every movement, and rehearsed her very precisely in relation to the music. Thus I studied the Wagner scores with her from A to Z.

Over the next two years, Mahler and Mildenburg worked closely together. Rumors of their romantic involvement dogged Mahler in Hamburg, and when he offered her a contract shortly after arriving in Vienna, it was with the understanding that their amorous relationship was over. Mildenburg became a guiding force among the Hofoper cast, having internalized Mahler's belief that everything a singer needed to interpret her role could be found in the score. Her performance in the 1903 *Tristan* blended exquisitely with the visual and aural settings devised by Roller and Mahler. As a contemporary noted: "[Mildenburg] had a very big voice" with a wide array of shadings, which "gave her an enormous range of expression ... Her appearance and movements had the same grandeur of style as her singing ... No other singer could as movingly convey Isolde's tragic figure and the wide range of her conflicting emotions" (*HLG2*, 575). Mildenburg's vocal score for the role shows notations in Mahler's hand, which track in detail her stage movements and gestures for each scene. The epitome of Mahler's singing actor, Mildenburg in later years published a detailed account of the collaboration and its practical results (see Further Reading).[8]

Mahler often relied on Mildenburg to coach the other singers, among them the soprano Marie Gutheil-Schoder (1874–1935), whom he recruited from Weimar in 1900 (*HLG2*, 296). Gutheil-Schoder debuted in Vienna with the title role of Bizet's *Carmen*, and as Mahler later noted,

---

[8] Stuart Feder, "Before Alma ... Gustav Mahler and 'Das Ewig-Weibliche,'" in *Mahler Studies*, ed. Stephen E. McClatchie (Cambridge University Press, 1997), 92; Paul Stefan, *Anna Bahr-Mildenburg* (Vienna: WILA, 1922), 37; Thursby, "Gustav Mahler," 39, 95–96.

the greatest strength of her performance was her acting: every expression and movement was "a revelation of the character she was trying to get inside." But she did not arrive at the Hofoper fully formed. "When I came to Vienna," she once explained, "I was strongly inclined towards portraying roles realistically." It was Mahler, in fact, who "showed me that every opera is a stylized work of art" and that every nuance must adhere to the score. "One thing I found interesting about Mahler . . . was his attention to detail, to the inner structure of a scene. He particularly liked pauses and silences. They were more important to him than anything. For it was through them that he created the inner life, the emotional content of the moment, the temperament, the humor." Gutheil-Schoder developed a broad repertoire under Mahler's guidance, in a true collaboration rather than simply following directions: "Mahler never came to rehearsal with a finished, worked-out directorial concept. Possibly he pictured in his mind's eye one important scene that was the focal point of an entire act, but he would also leave room for individuality to find expression . . . In this way he intensified everyone's . . . inspiration, developing it further with his own original ideas." Mahler in turn revered Gutheil-Schoder and Mildenburg as exemplars of what the singing actor should be. "They tower high above the rest . . . they reassure one that there is still natural talent on the stage, not just affectation, grease-paint and pretense."[9]

Several prominent male singers also came to Vienna during Mahler's tenure. One of the first was Erik Schmedes (1868–1931), a tall, blond tenor with chiseled features, who trained in Berlin and Paris before making his debut in Wiesbaden in 1891 as a baritone. After securing Schmedes a position at the Hofoper, Mahler convinced him to become a Heldentenor and cast him as Siegfried in 1898. Schmedes spent the rest of his career in Vienna specializing in Wagnerian roles. "He is the most musical singer that we now have!" Mahler would observe. Schmedes, in turn, claimed "absolute confidence" in Mahler "as a director and conductor": he "sustains the singer and protects him from all the pitfalls . . . [yet] is a strict critic," which Schmedes confessed made him "all the more pleased by his praise."[10]

---

[9] *NBLE*, 144; Marie Gutheil-Schoder, *Erlebtes und Erstebtes* (Vienna: R. Krey, 1937), 52 (cf. Kurt Blaukopf and Herta Blaukopf, *Mahler: His Life, Work & World* [London: Thames & Hudson, 2000], 156); Norman Lebrecht, *Mahler Remembered* (New York: Norton, 1988), 115–17.

[10] Christopher Norton-Welsh, "Singer Biographies," in Mahler's Decade in Vienna, Singers of the Court Opera 1897–1907; *Neues Wiener Journal* (June 26, 1904) (cf. Blaukopf and Blaukopf, *Mahler: His Life*, 136).

The bass/baritone Richard Mayr (1877–1935) likely shared this view, as he owed his career as a singer to Mahler. Mayr was studying medicine in Vienna when Mahler convinced him to enroll at the Conservatory. In 1902 he made his debut at the Bayreuth Festival and accepted a permanent position at the Hofoper, where he gained acclaim for his performances in the new Mozart and Wagner productions produced by Mahler and Roller. According to a contemporary, Mayr sustained the audience's interest with a "great variety of expressions" and his ability to build to an "impressive climax" during each performance. Although he was stout, and not particularly tall, his voice reportedly had the "depth and warmth of a trombone."

Friedrich Weidemann (1871–1919) studied in Hamburg and Berlin before making his debut in 1896. But only in January 1900, during a guest appearance in Vienna singing Kaspar in Zemlinsky's *Es war einmal*, did the baritone begin to realize his full potential. After conducting this performance, Mahler worked for several years to secure Weidemann a permanent position at the Hofoper, where he finally arrived in 1903 and spent the rest of his career. Like Mayr, Weidemann was regularly praised for his ability to "represent very movingly" every role he inhabited. He performed in an array of new productions mounted by Mahler and Roller, including *Das Rheingold* (1905), *Don Giovanni* (1905), and *Die Walküre* (1907). Weidemann also served as soloist in the world premieres of Mahler's *Kindertotenlieder* (1905) and *Das Lied von der Erde* (1912).

Without a doubt, the most famous of Mahler's collaborators was the tenor Leo Slezak (1873–1946), a towering, barrel-chested man with a voice to match. Although Mahler often chastised Slezak for his overindulgence of alcohol and cigars, he admired Slezak's extraordinary acting talent and infectious sense of humor. Slezak was hired by Mahler in 1901, five years after making his debut in Brno. Over the course of his career, he took on a wide range of roles (forty-four in Vienna alone), from *Guillaume Tell* to *Tannhäuser* and *Lohengrin*. Once during a performance of the latter work, Slezak revealed his ability to make light of the unexpected. Having failed to climb aboard the swan meant to transport him offstage, Slezak turned to the audience and asked wryly, "What time does the next swan leave?" Slezak's autobiographies – of which there are several – provide numerous amusing anecdotes and several fascinating accounts of his collaborations with Mahler. Although Slezak admitted to finding Mahler "the most gruesome of despots," he nonetheless valued the conductor's guidance when developing a role. "The rehearsals were a constant source of ideas," explained Slezak.

> [Mahler] was a martyr to the consuming flames of work, and he expected us
> to be the same ... Every remark was a gift for life. None of us would have
> ever dreamed of leaving the rehearsal room if Mahler was working on a
> scene in which we did not appear ... His way of working drew from the
> singer everything he had to give.[11]

Mahler's decade of collaboration at the Hofoper was exciting and fulfilling,
but too emotionally draining to be sustainable. Amid countless disputes,
especially between Roller and Mildenburg, Mahler regularly found himself
battling officials for additional funds. In the end, the parties went their
separate ways: Mahler to New York, Roller to the directorship of the
School of Applied Arts, and the singers to guest appearances across Europe
and the United States. But the legacy of their accomplishments lived on in
later innovative, interdisciplinary productions.

[11] Leo Slezak, *Meine sämtlichen Werke* (Berlin: Rowohlt, 1922), 247–48.

CHAPTER 10

A Perfect Storm
Mahler's New York

Joseph Horowitz

Though Gustav Mahler never realized it, the New York City he encountered in 1907 had for decades been one of the music capitals of the world. In the late nineteenth century, two towering personalities, Anton Seidl and Antonín Dvořák, had shaped the city's symphonic and operatic affairs – and memories of these men, and of their accomplishments, would cast deep shadows on Mahler's lesser New World achievements.

Seidl (1850–98) was arguably Richard Wagner's most important protégé. As a young man, he lived within the Wagner household at Bayreuth for seven years, an "uncle" to the children, a surrogate son to their father. He was assistant conductor for the first *Ring* in 1876. Wagner promoted Seidl as his conductor of choice – and it was Seidl who with the impresario Angelo Neumann toured the *Ring*. He arrived in Manhattan in 1885. Wagner had pushed him to go there, for both his own good and that of the cause.[1]

New York's Metropolitan Opera had been inaugurated in 1883 by wealthy socialites shut out from the Academy of Music, whose boxes were fully subscribed. When they discovered that Italian opera was more expensive than anticipated, they turned the vast house over to Leopold Damrosch, who could produce German opera at a much lower cost. But Damrosch died suddenly in 1885. Seidl was imported to take his place. The Metropolitan proceeded to host six historic German-language seasons under Seidl's baton. Seidl's Wagner ensemble was the equal of any abroad. He led American premieres of five Wagner operas. He acquired a zealous following – including cosmopolitan New York critics who knew Bayreuth and considered New York's Wagner performances better.

---

[1] On Seidl in America, see Joseph Horowitz, *Wagner Nights: An American History* (Berkeley: University of California Press, 1994), and Horowitz, *Moral Fire: Musical Portraits from America's Fin de Siecle* (Berkeley: University of California Press, 2012), in which the chapters on Henry Krehbiel, on Laura Langford and the Seidl Society, and on Henry Higginson are pertinent to the present essay.

The German seasons were abruptly terminated in 1891 – the box-holders, for whom the Wagner rites seemed alien and tedious, decided they'd had enough. Seidl was ousted. Though he would return in a lesser capacity in 1895, he mainly transitioned into a symphonic conductor. His most prominent podium was with the New York Philharmonic – in those years, an unstable musicians' cooperative with a long and erratic history. Seidl's Philharmonic tenure was both stabilizing and galvanizing. The same instrumentalists who stocked the ad hoc Philharmonic – a talent pool Seidl considered unique in the world – were regularly reconstituted, for Seidl, as the "Seidl Orchestra" or "Metropolitan Orchestra." Their most remarkable manifestation was alongside the elegant Brighton Beach Hotel on Coney Island, where Laura Langford's Seidl Society – a Brooklyn women's club unlike any other – presented Seidl in concert every summer. The 3,000-seat seaside Music Pavilion hosted fourteen such concerts per week. The repertoire was overwhelmingly Wagnerian, with Liszt in second place. Like so many facets of the Seidl story, Langford's Brighton Beach concerts had no equivalent abroad. Tickets cost 25 cents and less. Special railroad cars from Manhattan were provided for unescorted ladies. Brahms was shunned. The Music of the Future was wildly preponderant.

Seidl toured frequently in the northeastern and midwestern United States, with the Metropolitan troupe or with his own symphonic ensembles. Compared with Wagnerism abroad, the American variety was distinctively meliorist. As Wagner himself anticipated, there were no American Hanslicks or Nietzsches to cavil or rebuke. Wagnerism inflected American literature and visual art. It was a dominant topic in the better magazines and a major factor in general intellectual discourse. Americans identified with Siegfried the putative frontiersman, with Wagner the ostensible democrat. Concurrently, Dvořák (as we shall see) was musically inscribing basic ingredients of American identity. Never again would classical music so centrally impact on how Americans saw themselves.

As a purely musical phenomenon, Seidl introduced the United States to a new style of conducting. Previously, Theodore Thomas, a Kapellmeister type in its highest embodiment, had set standards for American orchestral performance. Seidl, by comparison, was a Wagnerite, invested in extremes of tempo and nuance as necessary aspects of interpretation. In Mozart and Beethoven, *Tristan* and *Die Meistersinger*, Wagner's pamphlet "On Conducting" (1869) was his bible.

Finally, Seidl the man was magnetic. Mysteriously taciturn yet not reclusive, he was recognized and greeted on streets and streetcars. Most Seidl acolytes were women for whom he was a raven-haired Romantic icon, and Wagner a liberating libidinal force. Crucially, Seidl embraced a democratic ethos. He took American citizenship. Estranged from Cosima's Bayreuth, he summered in the Catskills and rarely returned to Germany. An astonishing Seidl oration at Brighton Beach, preserved in a penciled manuscript, reads as a credo:

> We will play only good music; we know, the people *need* it, and this is the cause, that the noble ladies of the Seidl Society don't spare the large expenses and the terrible difficult and heavy work to give the *good* people, what he needs, and what he must have. It is not only right, to give the poor free music at the different parks, but the Bands must play *good* music. The people not understand it first, but later he will whistle it with more dash and vigor, as the rich, who sits in his box and – chatter, because – he does not understand it.[2]

The early death of this singular mythic artist was greeted as a national calamity. For his funeral, at the Metropolitan Opera House, women locked arms to force themselves into the overpacked auditorium. Downstairs, they outnumbered men twenty to one.

Seidl's closest friend in Manhattan, Antonín Dvořák, arrived in 1892 and left in 1895. Their relations were public: daily, they would convene at Fleischmann's Restaurant. What Laura Langford was for Seidl, Jeannette Thurber was for Dvořák. She enticed him to the New World to lead her visionary National Conservatory of Music. She cherished and challenged him. At Thurber's urging, Dvořák undertook to help found an "American school" of composition. Born a butcher's son, he was an instinctive democrat. A cultural nationalist, he fastened on African Americans and Native Americans, stirred by their plight, inspired by their songs. In Iowa in the summer of 1893, he nightly met with the members of the Kickapoo Medicine Show: Native American entertainers who sang, danced, and sold bottled remedies. At the Madison Square Garden Concert Hall in 1894, he led a black chorus and biracial orchestra in the premiere of his adaptation of Stephen Foster's "Old Folks at Home." The soloists were Sissieretta Jones, who as "the black Patti" was the most celebrated African American concert singer of her time, and Dvořák's assistant Harry Burleigh, who would become the composer most responsible for turning spirituals into concert songs.[3]

---

[2] Seidl's hand-written speech is reproduced in full in *Wagner Nights*, 211–12. I discovered it in the Seidl Society Archive at the Brooklyn Historical Society.

[3] On Dvořák's American style, see Michael Beckerman, New Worlds of *Dvořák* (New York: Norton, 2003). On Dvořák in New York, see ibid. and also Joseph Horowitz, *Classical Music in America: A History of Its Rise and Fall* (New York: Norton, 2005).

Dvořák's humanitarian stature was widely appreciated. His most famous, most influential, most controversial public utterance, in the *New York Herald,* prophesied that a "great and noble school of music" would be founded upon the "negro melodies" he adored. In New York, a city of immigrants, his prognosis was taken to heart. In Boston, he was denounced as a "negrophile." Meanwhile, he produced the instantly beloved *New World* Symphony (premiered by Seidl), an "American" String Quartet conceived in Iowa (whose landscapes it celebrates), and other exemplars of an American style that remain to be fully appreciated by Americans (let alone Europeans). Its keynotes included slave songs, Indian lore, and the vast and unpopulated American West. Its late embodiments – the *American* Suite, the Humoresque in G-flat – are as much the work of an assimilated American as Domenico Scarlatti's sonatas are Spanish; they no longer sound like "Dvořák."

Dvořák's National Conservatory students emulated his example. Concurrently, an American Composers' Concerts movement sponsored symphonic concerts exclusively presenting American works – a protectionist surge so powerful that it spilled into American Composers' Concerts in Germany, Austria, and France between 1889 and 1892, and in 1890 provoked one of its staunchest advocates, Henry Krehbiel (about whom more later), to write: "The American composer . . . after long suffering neglect, now seems to be in imminent danger of being coddled to death."[4] In the wake of Dvořák's *New World* Symphony, Krehbiel took the lead in espousing compositional strategies favoring homegrown vernacular elements. Of the participating conductors, Anton Seidl vigorously promoted Edward MacDowell (whom he considered "greater than Brahms") and Victor Herbert (whom he engaged as his frequent assistant); he also discovered, in George Templeton Strong's *Sintram* Symphony (1893), a Wagnerian American program-symphony of high caliber. This picture of electrifying growth and aspiration also importantly includes Boston, where Henry Higginson, a colossal cultural force, founded the Boston Symphony fully sprung in 1881.

All this momentous activity preceded the New World advent of Gustav Mahler, but so did a period of relative decline. Dvořák's 1895 departure and Seidl's death three years later were formidable blows. New York endured a leadership crisis. Because it lacked a sound administrative core, the Philharmonic was dependent on keeping a conductor with drawing

---

[4] Douglas Bomberger, *"A Tidal Wave of Encouragement": American Composers' Concerts in the Gilded Age* (Westport, CT: Praeger, 2001), 65.

power and panache. When post-Seidl it failed to do so, a "guarantors' committee" took over, intent on creating a permanent orchestra to rival Boston's or Chicago's. But the leading force, Mrs. Mary Sheldon, was no Henry Higginson, Jeannette Thurber, or Laura Langford; and she would incongruously become Mahler's boss.

Post-Seidl, the Metropolitan Opera created a species unknown in Central Europe: a world-class multilingual house with the resources to hire the most glamorous international vocal talent. Keeping this "golden age" on course was a strong manager, Maurice Grau. But after Grau's retirement in 1903, the Met was entrusted to the actor/impresario Heinrich Conried, who, as one wag put it, "knew no more about opera than the ordinary chauffeur knows about airplanes."[5] In Henry Krehbiel's assessment, "the fruits of wise endeavor and astute management" were being "frittered away by managerial incapacity and greed," Conried's signature move being to pack Enrico Caruso onstage as frequently as possible.[6] It was also Conried who in 1903 sensationally defied Cosima Wagner by staging *Parsifal*, which the Wagner family had intended to reserve for Bayreuth. Conried turned a handsome profit. But when in 1907 he presented the American premiere of Strauss's *Salome*, the anticipated sensation took the form of boxholder revulsion; Conried was forced to cancel the run after a "public rehearsal."

Concurrently, an operatic impresario of genius, Oscar Hammerstein, opened a rival Manhattan Opera in 1906 that surpassed the Metropolitan in every aspect save fashion. Like Higginson in Boston, Hammerstein knew music. The highlights of his second season included Offenbach's *Tales of Hoffmann*, then unknown in New York, and three important American premieres featuring the inimitable Mary Garden: Charpentier's *Louise*, Massenet's *Thaïs*, and Debussy's *Pelléas et Mélisande*. (Hammerstein would eventually present Garden as Salome, proving that it was the Met, not New York, that was unready to be shocked.) These complications, and Conried's failing health, impelled a final salvation strategy: bringing Gustav Mahler from Vienna. In short, both the New York orchestra Mahler would inherit and the opera company he would conduct were tarnished institutions attempting with inadequate administrative leadership to regain their luster.

[5] Stanley Jackson, *Caruso* (New York: Stein and Day, 1972), 106.
[6] Krehbiel, *More Chapters of Opera* (New York: H. Holt, 1919), v; Horowitz, *Classical Music in America*, 210.

Meanwhile, though the New World failed to entice a composer of international stature to take over from Dvořák, a substantial start on a native canon had begun. As this development remains largely unknown even to Americans, it is worth a moment's emphasis. Boston's musical community prominently included two formidable symphonists. John Knowles Paine composed a pair of big, sophisticated works of this description (1875, 1879) possessing a truly symphonic breadth of stride. Inspired by Paine, George Whitefield Chadwick composed two more American symphonies of note (Nos. 2 and 3, 1886 and 1894). Both contain whimsical scherzos that are gems of their kind. Chadwick's *Jubilee* (1897), in a similar vein, deserves to be an American symphonic staple.

Although Paine's music does not aspire to sound "American," some of Chadwick's does – and succeeds. Here, Dvořák's influence was crucial. With its vernacular panache – it quotes "Camptown Races"; its sunset coda clip-clops like Hollywood Westerns to come – *Jubilee* is practically a New World gloss on Dvořák's *Carnival* Overture. Chadwick's thirty-five-minute Fourth String Quartet (1896) is an explicit response to Dvořák's "American" Quartet (premiered in Boston). His Third Symphony was awarded a prize by Dvořák himself. The E-minor *Gaelic* Symphony (1894) of Chadwick's Boston colleague Amy Beach was Dvořák-inspired. Years after his departure home, Dvořák continued to matter.

In New York, the leading composer was Edward MacDowell, whose reputation has faded. But Victor Herbert, a Seidl protégé, produced a still delectable Second Cello Concerto (1894); Dvořák acclaimed the premiere (performed by Herbert and Seidl) and proceeded to compose an enduring cello concerto of his own. Finally, there are two important turn-of-the-century American composers whose "advanced" idioms foreclosed contemporary popularity. Arthur Farwell considered himself the first composer "to take up Dvořák's challenge." As founder of the Indianist movement in music, Farwell furnishes the closest American equivalent to Bartók. Such astringent Farwell piano miniatures as "Navajo War Dance no. 2" (1904) and "Pawnee Horses" (1905) transcend kitsch. And, of course, there is Charles Ives, who by the time Mahler left New York in 1911 had already completed his game-changing Second Symphony. Ives in 1911 remained wholly obscure – but not wholly unknown in New York musical circles.

How much of this music did Mahler know or care to know? According to rumor, he encountered Ives's Third Symphony in score and was tantalized. His sole "Anglo" program for the New York Philharmonic (February 14 and 17, 1911) comprised Elgar, Stanford, and four

Americans: Chadwick's *Melpomene* Overture, Charles Martin Loeffler's *La villanelle du diable*, MacDowell's *Die Sarazenen* and *Die schöne Aldâ*, and Henry Hadley's *The Culprit Fay*. Not one of these works attempts a consciously "American" voice.

No picture of New York's turn-of-the-century musical life would be complete without Mahler's nemesis-to-be, who brutally (but accurately) proclaimed Mahler's American career as a "failure" in a fifty-inch-long obituary.[7] This was Henry Edward Krehbiel, for decades the "dean" of New York's world-class musical critical community. We have already encountered him twice because he was ubiquitous. To observe that Mahler's biographers have misunderstood him would be an understatement; in the Mahler literature, Krehbiel remains an object of incomprehension and ignorance.

One reason is that he had no remote equivalent in the Old World. Born to immigrant German parents, he was a self-made American. He never attended any college. As a fledgling newspaperman, he covered murders and baseball games (for which he invented a new method of scoring) before turning himself into the music critic of the *New York Tribune*. The armchair critics of Mahler's Vienna were professorial and methodical; their reviews never ran the morning after. Krehbiel, by comparison, was a pragmatic activist of prodigious energy. He edited collections of songs and arias. He translated opera librettos from German and French (including Berlioz's *The Trojans*, whose first American performance he facilitated). He lectured and taught widely and prominently. He wrote a dozen books. The few surviving Krehbiel notebooks include inquiries in German and English into musical education in ancient Greece, the "Black Stone of the Mohammedans," the songs of Chief John Buck, and the hymn quoted by Dvořák in his *Hussite* Overture.

A genuine scholar-critic, Krehbiel could claim expertise in overlapping fields of inquiry, each of which Gustav Mahler would trample. To begin with, he was a considerable historian of German music. It was he who undertook to complete Alexander Wheelock Thayer's *Life of Beethoven*, a

---

[7] Every Mahler biography known to me recapitulates Mahler's ignorance of the New World. A partial exception is volume four (*A New Life Cut Short*) of Henry-Louis de La Grange's *Gustav Mahler* (*HLG4*), by far the most detailed treatment of Mahler in New York. I myself had occasion to apprise de La Grange of the significance of Anton Seidl, and he graciously amended his narrative accordingly. But de La Grange's admiration and love for Mahler the man and musician precluded any reconsideration of Henry Krehbiel. On Krehbiel's Mahler obituary, see Joseph Horowitz, *Moral Fire*, 117–18. On Mahler's "failure" in New York, see Horowitz, *Classical Music in America*, 185–95, and Horowitz, review of *HLG4*, in *Journal of the Society for American Music* 3, no. 1 (February 2009): 104–10.

monumental biography still consulted (albeit as revised by Elliott Forbes in 1964); with the addition of his own volume four, Krehbiel's 1925 third edition (for which he requested and received no compensation) numbered 1,137 pages. His *Studies in the Wagnerian Drama* (1891) ranged effortlessly among Greek, Roman, Norse, Egyptian, Hindu, and Persian sources while assaying the origins of the *Ring*. For *Die Meistersinger*, Krehbiel visited Nuremberg to scrutinize the historical record; he knew which Hans Sachs songs were authentic and which were not. His interpretive exegeses of these and other Wagner operas were wholly his own. And he acquired his own convictions about how the works of Beethoven and Wagner should be performed.

It was from Wagner, and from German art generally, that Krehbiel absorbed the notion that great music is nationally specific, that culture and race are bound as one. No other American of his time so diligently documented the folk music of Jews, Slavs, Magyars, Scandinavians, and Russians. A veritable ethnomusicologist, he transcended the biases of his era. At Chicago's World Columbian Exposition, he admired the rhythmic subtleties of African musicians others dismissed as savages. Also in Chicago, he used a phonograph – still a novelty – to record and transcribe the winter dances of the Kwakiutl Indians from Vancouver Island; in three substantial *New York Tribune* dispatches, he cited such features as duple rhythms atop triple meters. His 155-page *African-American Folk-Songs* (1914) is a landmark treatment that rebukes as "ungenerous and illiberal" Brahmin culture bearers who refused to equate "negro" with "American."

This research buttressed a further area of scrutiny: the quest for an "American" school of composition – grounded in turn in a historian's command of American musical history. Two Krehbiel books – *Chapters of Opera* (1908) and *More Chapters of Opera* (1919) – remain necessary resources. Finally, Krehbiel was arguably the most influential musical pedagogue of his generation. The many printings of his *How to Listen to Music* date from 1896 to 1924. And he was also the program annotator for the New York Philharmonic.

Because Krehbiel was himself a prominent and indispensable member of the musical community upon which he reported, he more than knew Anton Seidl and Antonín Dvořák. The former he counted a personal friend. When Albert Niemann studied the role of the *Götterdämmerung* Siegfried, his consultations at Seidl's East 62nd Street brownstone were witnessed by Henry Krehbiel, with Frau Seidl-Krauss sewing in a corner; afterward, the three men shared cigars and beer. When Dvořák arrived in Manhattan, Krehbiel fed him specimens of Indian and plantation song.

Previewing the *New World* Symphony for his readers, he produced 2,500 words and fourteen musical examples, an exegesis nationally reprinted. The composer had granted him an interview in his home. Weeks later, Krehbiel wrote to Dvořák: "I have had no greater happiness from 20 years of labor on behalf of good music than has come to me from the consciousness that I may have been to some degree instrumental in helping the public to appreciate your compositions, and especially this beautiful symphony."[8]

Krehbiel did have an ego. Though a man of warm feeling and affectionately regarded by many colleagues, he seemed insufferable to others. He would not brook ignorance – whether of Beethoven's intentions as he construed them or of the New World in the eyes of foreign observers. He insisted on the moral properties of art: either it uplifted the soul or – like Strauss's *Salome*, a prime object of his opprobrium – it didn't matter. Mahler's pollution of the sublime with the quotidian was bound to seem anathema to a listener with Henry Krehbiel's fixed aesthetic predilections.

And so it was that a perfect storm engulfed Gustav Mahler when all unknowing he sailed to America. A few examples will complete my story. Recalling Mahler's patronizing goal for the Philharmonic – "to educate the public," particularly "those who may not now have a taste for the best" – Krehbiel offered a wry postmortem: "He never discovered that there were Philharmonic subscribers who had inherited not only their seats from their parents and grandparents, but also their appreciation of good music." When in December 1909 Mahler performed his own First Symphony with the Philharmonic, Krehbiel, as program annotator, requested permission to reprint a letter in which Mahler described programmatic aspects of the work. Mahler in turn prohibited Krehbiel from writing anything at all. Krehbiel responded with hilarious impudence: "In deference to the wish of Mr. Mahler, the annotator of the Philharmonic Society's programmes refrains from even an outline analysis of the symphony which he is performing for the first time in New York on this occasion . . . All writings about music, even those of musicians themselves, he holds to be injurious to musical enjoyment."

Mahler arrived in America weakened and fatigued. His energy and idealism were aroused by the New World, but fitfully. He never discerned

---

[8] Michael Beckerman, "Henry Krehbiel, Antonín Dvořák, and the Symphony 'From the New World,'" *Notes: The Quarterly Journal of the Music Library Association* 49 (1992): 453.

the burden of expectation imposed upon him by the legacies of Seidl and Dvořák. With his colossal propensity for self-absorption, he could never have composed a New World symphony. Dvořák had Mrs. Thurber; Seidl, Mrs. Langford. Toscanini, instantly displacing Mahler at the Metropolitan Opera, would have his Gatti-Casazza. Mahler was handed Henrich Conried and Mrs. Sheldon. He remained a chronic outsider.

CHAPTER II

Celebrity

Eva Giloi

In 1907, the Metropolitan Opera in New York offered Gustav Mahler an astronomical engagement fee: 75,000 kronen for three months' work. As the highest fee ever offered to a musician, it was to crown Mahler's career as a star conductor and composer. He viewed the honor with ambivalence, however, unsure whether one could be both a celebrity and a genius. His successor to Viennese musical stardom, Arnold Schoenberg, famously insisted in 1946 that "If it is art, it is not for all, and if it is for all, it is not art" – no doubt echoing his mentor.[1] But while Mahler expressed a belief that the "celebrity genius" was an oxymoron, in practice he tacked between the poles of esoteric art and public acclaim, culminating in his move to New York, Vienna's New World counterpart, where he hoped to find an "unspoiled" audience that could be taught to understand his idiosyncratic music-making while heralding him as an artistic champion.

Mahler's ambivalence about celebrity genius reached back to his earliest days as a student and composer in Vienna in the 1870s. The imperial city had long been one of Europe's richest cultural centers, and the mechanisms for fame were well established. Vienna's musical renown rested on the lasting legacy of Haydn, Mozart, Beethoven, and Schubert, a tradition carried into the late century by Johannes Brahms. When Mahler arrived in 1875 the city boasted the internationally famous Burgtheater, with actors known throughout Europe, such as Charlotte Wolter, and a brilliant designer, Hans Makart, the "painter prince" who immortalized Wolter on canvas and whose "Makart style" and color palette were imitated widely in painting and home décor across the continent. This was the backdrop in which Mahler set out to make his mark. Already as a student (at the Conservatory in the fall of 1875, and two years later also the University) Mahler recognized the need to distinguish himself from Vienna's musical

---

[1] Alex Ross, *The Rest Is Noise: Listening to the Twentieth Century* (New York: Farrar, Straus and Giroux, 2007), 10.

91

orthodoxy as represented by Brahms and Eduard Hanslick. And he was
not alone in this endeavor: breaking with official taste was in vogue for a
host of young Viennese modernists inspired by Richard Wagner and
Friedrich Nietzsche (see Chapter 4). But Mahler also aspired to the
traditional markers of success, vying for the Beethoven Prize and other
established awards and competing successfully for a series of increasingly
prestigious conducting positions as he worked his way up in the profession, culminating in the directorship of the Vienna Court Opera in 1897.

In pursuing this dual agenda of integration into and distinction from
Vienna's culture industry, Mahler joined many other musicians, poets, and
visual artists, not just in Vienna but across Europe, who found audiences
responsive to the rituals of the *succès de scandale*. The fate of Oscar Wilde's
Salomé is a prime example. When Wilde first rehearsed his play in 1892, he
engaged Sarah Bernhardt, who was regarded as the greatest actress of her
time precisely because her roles embodied the contradiction between moral
rectitude and emotional abandon.[2] That she was described by contemporaries as a "perplexing dramatic outlaw" and "perverted Parisienne" did not
scare away throngs of adoring spectators, including respectable young
women not at all put off by her illicit affairs or the fact that she slept in
a coffin and kept pumas as pets. Wilde himself could not walk that line:
Salomé was banned from the English stage and the poet imprisoned for
homosexuality, even as Bernhardt found public success in the drama's
acclaimed Paris premiere in 1896. Richard Strauss's *Salome* (1905) recov-
ered Bernhardt's productive notoriety, with a musical setting hailed by
audiences as a great work of art despite its "satanic" storyline and experimental score. For Mahler, who regarded Strauss's opera as a masterpiece,
the audience's embrace of both music and subject matter would demonstrate more powerfully than any other single experience that genius and
popularity were not incompatible.

Salomé's example reflects contrasting developments among artists and
audiences. In terms of technique, the arts were radicalized at the fin-de-
siècle as younger artists rejected the traditional (or bourgeois) "cult of
beauty" and drove the arts toward expressionist, violent, and even intentionally ugly modes. Yet philistine audiences pursued these renegades into
ever more daring terrain as experimentation became a signal part of the
entertainment industry. The deliberate provocation of Serge Diaghilev's
staging of *L'après-midi d'un faune* in Paris in 1912 led to *Le Figaro*'s

[2] Susan A. Glenn, *The Female Spectacle: The Theatrical Roots of Modern Feminism* (Cambridge: Cambridge University Press, 2000), 9–39.

condemnation of the ballet as crude and inelegant, but also to highly inflated ticket prices the following year for Diaghilev's production of Igor Stravinsky's even more challenging *Le sacre du printemps*. Diaghilev tantalized the Parisian audience in the press teasers for *Le sacre* with promises of a thrill that would spark impassioned discussions. After a first night of catcalls and outrage, that same audience reveled in the ballet's intentionally alienating choreography in subsequent performances. Much the same was then underway in the visual arts, as the sensationalism of Secession movements in Paris, Vienna, and Berlin turned their exhibitions into must-see events.

Certainly, the popularity of provocation did not reflect a commitment to avant-garde experimentalism per se; audiences remained divided in their responses, cheering and jeering in equal measure. It was clear, though, that everyone wanted to be in on the fun and to have an opinion about the pieces. Even when some audiences and critics professed to be insulted by the works, as with *Le Figaro* following the premiere of *Le sacre*, they came back for more, testing the artworks against their aesthetic understanding and sense of taste. Such was the case, for instance, for Hermann Cohn, the renowned ophthalmologist and father of the author Emil Ludwig. As a scientist, the elder Cohn was a practical man, more comfortable among fellow researchers like Rudolf Virchow or Heinrich Schliemann than bohemian artists. The teenage Ludwig, in full generational revolt, lambasted him as a philistine who "cared not at all for culture" because he rarely read literature and preferred traditional plaster casts of Apollo and Diana over Max Klinger's modernist Prometheus drawings. And yet the elder Cohn was never missing from premieres at Breslau's Lobetheater, including the scandalous, avant-garde dramas of Henrik Ibsen, Gerhart Hauptmann, and Arthur Schnitzler. On each occasion, Cohn took pains to ensure that his acquaintances saw him present at these liminal events.[3]

Cohn's ritual participation in high art embodies the shifting definition of cultural capital that drove the educated middle classes into ever more daring artistic terrain. Securing cultural capital through art had a long history for the bourgeoisie, but being versed in high culture was now no longer enough: consuming abstruse art and aesthetic scandal in an urbane manner became the ultimate proof of cultural competence. The radicalization of audience reception rested on two tangential factors in particular that had a profound impact on who could participate in hero-worship and

[3] Emil Ludwig, *Gifts of Life: A Retrospect*, trans. M. I. Robertson (Boston: Little, Brown, 1931), 78–80.

how genius was defined: the development of a consumer economy, and the rising profile of the sciences as providing the metrics of success. As a result, and unlike the construction of celebrity today, the difficulty of an artwork became an integral and necessary component of its creator's fame. Far from being an oxymoron, then, the "celebrity genius" had become a fixture of audience expectations by ca. 1900.

The educated middle classes first turned to art as a source of cultural capital in the eighteenth century, when the enduring social divisions between aristocracy and bourgeoisie prompted the latter to seek an alliance with artists in the "aristocracy of the spirit." The glittering of nobility at the opera posed a distinct problem: the bourgeoisie's attempts to flaunt its wealth could not compete with their social superiors' prestige. And so middle-class audiences staked their claim to cultural capital on the earnest profession of a sublime love of art, including an openness to original works. This strategy played out during the first half of the century through a belief in the divine inspiration in Beethoven's compositions and Niccolò Paganini's performances, but also through a newly serious, thoughtful attention and an engaged intellect, in contrast to the noisier, more restless concertgoers of the past. By the time Franz Liszt toured Europe in the 1830s and '40s, still seeking social elevation by linking himself to Europe's elites and parading in the colors of the nobility, his concerts were most heavily attended by an educated bourgeoisie eager to flaunt its cultural finesse by appreciating his virtuosity.

The mid-century bourgeoisie also approached artists as kindred souls, in an emotional turn that rested in equal parts on hero-worship and personal identification. When the young poet August Heinrich Hoffmann von Fallersleben spent the bulk of his visit to Vienna in 1827 stalking Franz Schubert in various public parks, it was not just to see the great man but to find in the artist he called "my" Schubert a soul mate embodying Fallersleben's love of music. And this desire for personal validation through imitation remained strong at century's end, nowhere more so than at Monte Verità in Ascona, the famous spa founded by Wagner acolytes. Seeking to align modern man to his true creative and natural self, they self-consciously adopted Wagner's vegetarianism alongside alternative medicine, nudism, and modern dance, which they practiced on the "Parsifal Lawn" behind the spa's hotel. The desire for proximity to art also prompted an increasing number of bourgeois families to settle in artist neighborhoods: Ina Seidel's father, a physician, moved his family to Munich's Schwabing neighborhood specifically because he wanted to live among artists whose art he collected. For those who wanted mere passing contact, there was a growing "celebrity tourism" industry through which respectable citizens could conjure the fantasy of breaking taboos by visiting Europe's artist cafes and cabarets. Indeed, the desire for vicarious bohemianism became so popular that the *New York Times* ran regular features on the best bohemian bars to visit in Paris, Berlin, Vienna, or Budapest.[4]

Ostentatious attraction to innovative art and visionary bohemianism thus set the middle classes apart from the more traditional aristocracy, which relied on maintaining the status quo and an artistic canon that reflected hierarchy, legacy, and inherited value as the highest good. Nor could the aristocracy, as a class, identify with the Romantic ideal that raised artists' social standing because of their greater access to the sublime emotions of creativity. Most princes and high aristocrats regarded themselves as patrons of artists, not peers, and only occasionally did they tolerate artists – the most famous of them (e.g., Liszt) – in their midst. By 1900, meanwhile, the middle class's fascination with the artist's otherworldly nature would give way to a fixation on the scandal of the artwork itself. Feeling its cultural capital challenged by new rivals, from above and below, the educated middle class clung to its hard-won sense of cultural superiority by moving from a celebration of inspired works within the canon to new creations bursting its boundaries.

From above, the expansion of high finance banking and a second industrial revolution (especially in new technologies like electricity and chemicals) turned the new captains of industry into an admired and politically influential elite. As this financial haute bourgeoisie rivaled the aristocracy with its lavish lifestyle, the educated middle class redoubled its claim to cultural capital through erudition. At the same time, the financial upswing after the 1880s solidified Europe's consumerism and established a new class of consumer from below: lower middle-class, urban, white-collar workers, clerks, and service sector employees, who equally expected to participate in the cultural rituals of fame and the social prestige that art conveyed. Earlier in the century, a relatively small number of fans had the time and money to pursue their idols directly. By 1900, leisure time and disposable income had expanded down the social ladder, while changes in mass media, urbanization, and transportation made celebrity tourism

---

[4] See Eva Giloi, *Monarchy, Myth, and Material Culture in Germany, 1750–1950* (Cambridge: Cambridge University Press, 2011), 94, 102, and chapter 4 for celebrity tourism generally. Also: August Heinrich Hoffmann von Fallersleben, *Mein Leben: Aufzeichnungen und Erinnerungen*, vol. 2 (Hannover: Carl Rümpler, 1868), 52; Udo Bermbach, *Richard Wagners Weg zur Lebensreform* (Würzburg: Königshausen & Neumann, 2018), 10–11, 156–77; Ina Seidel, *Meine Kindheit und Jugend: Ursprung, Erbteil und Weg* (Stuttgart: Deutsche Verlags-Anstalt, 1935), 38–39.

accessible to a much wider social demographic. The theater, concert hall, and bohemian cafe still offered a spectacle for audiences eager to see celebrities, but a growing collectibles industry also made it possible to consume those celebrities in private and personalize them in the process. Schiller cakes, Wagner napkins, and Parsifal cheese were sold alongside Zeppelin cigarettes and Kaiser Wilhelm perfume, so that cultural heroes, social dignitaries, and political leaders became "glamorous accessories" that could be appropriated, metonymically, playfully, and temporarily, in the highly individualized pursuit of the self through consumer choice.[5] Fans also collected portraits of their idols, much as children today collect soccer or baseball trading cards. Celebrity portraits came first in the form of the *carte-de-visite*, invented in the mid-1850s by the French photographer Eugène Disdéri as the first mass-produced photograph. By the early 1860s, Disdéri offered 65,000 different celebrity portraits for sale, and photographers across Europe soon followed his lead. The portraits were collected in albums, where they could be taken out, examined, and put away again at will, so that consumers could fit celebrities into the time-space niches of their lives, at their own convenience.[6] Once sound came home with the phonograph, the barrier between home and theater, private and public, fan and celebrity was largely obsolete.

The intense personalization of the celebrity industry thus provided a rationale for the lower middle class to push up against the cultural capital of the educated bourgeoisie. Many white-collar workers and clerks responded to their surrounding culture by nurturing ambitions of their own. Schools taught them that poetry and art were a national treasure; their city streets were filled with monuments to "great men"; the popular entertainments of their free time immortalized creative genius; and changing school arts curricula reinforced the ideal of the cultural role model. Young aspiring poets and artists from lower middle-class backgrounds adopted these goals and, in tangibly increased numbers, sent their novice works to theater directors and museum curators, justifying their entry into the aristocracy of the spirit with the depth and authenticity of their creative desire. As a result, sincerity in art appreciation and intimate insight into

[5] On collectibles, material culture, and celebrity tourism, see Giloi, *Monarchy*, esp. 289–90. On celebrities as accessories, see Nigel Thrift, "The Material Practices of Glamour," *Journal of Cultural Economy* 1, no. 1 (2008): 9–23.
[6] Eva Giloi, "So Writes the Hand That Swings the Sword: Autograph Hunting and Royal Charisma in the German Empire, 1861–1888," in *Constructing Charisma: Celebrity, Fame, and Power in Nineteenth-Century Europe*, ed. Edward Berenson and Eva Giloi (New York: Berghahn Books, 2010), 41–51.

the canon of great works were no longer enough to secure the middle class's cultural dominance, since the classics were now accessible to their subalterns as well. Interaction with difficult, avant-garde art that required both taste and erudition restored separation of the educated bourgeoisie from the challengers below.

Along with their rising interest in the arts, white-collar workers developed a new passion for technical knowledge and popular science as a path to career training and social mobility. As the economist Werner Sombart noted sourly in 1909: "university professors carry education to the masses in popularized college courses; public libraries, public reading rooms shoot out of the ground in larger cities like mushrooms out of the earth; educational collections of all kinds open their doors to a mass public in order to disseminate natural science, ethnological and other knowledge."[7] The increased interest in popular science was symptomatic of the growing prestige of science and technology as the benchmarks for modern success, pushing the metrics of genius toward innovations that were not just groundbreaking but actively and intriguingly abstruse. In the sciences and technology, true genius was found in original discoveries that other people found difficult to comprehend, as exemplified by towering figures like Hermann von Helmholtz, Robert Koch, Max Planck, Fritz Haber, and Albert Einstein. And the metric of tradition-defying originality cast its shadow over the assessment of art and literature as well. Earlier in the century, artists were lauded for being innovative within a canon; later, only true novelty could stand as evidence of genius. Over the course of the century, Paganini and Liszt both went from geniuses to mere virtuosi in popular debates, while Wagner's status as a true genius surged thanks to the iconoclastic technical innovations of his compositions.

Thus, artworks too would now have to burst the bounds of traditional aesthetics to qualify as works of creative genius. But unlike the sciences, the arts did not have a practical gauge for value. New technologies either worked or did not, and scientific experiments could be replicated, proving their value. Arts and literature, on the other hand, could not be evaluated on the basis of objective utility, since their "efficacy" was rooted in their subjective "effect" on the audience. As the ideal of "art for art's sake" intersected with consumer culture, so that works of art had exchange value but only questionable "use value," it became increasingly difficult to establish a definition of artistic merit based on astounding originality.

---

[7] Werner Sombart, *Die deutsche Volkswirtschaft im neunzehnten Jahrhundert* (Berlin: G. Bondi, 1909), 445.

The long-term implications were troubling: if new artistic techniques were too far outside the traditional canon to be easily understood by the layman, how could a buyer, curator, or arts institution tell if a painting or score would hold its value in the future? This combination of factors, influenced by the sciences, inspired a pause in normalizing judgments. If one could recognize the artwork's legacy directly, it was banal; if one could not, it might reveal itself to be a work of genius later.

It was this ambiguity that prompted Cohn to hedge his bets by supplementing his annual pilgrimage to Bayreuth, where Wagner's originality had been tested by time, with unfailing attendance at avant-garde dramas, lest they turn out to be the classics of the future. Would Cohn have recognized that Mahler's symphonies satisfied both requirements? Working within the quintessential Viennese genre, reshaping formal and gestural traditions while leaving them sufficiently intact to be recognizable, and planting himself firmly in Wagnerian stylistic territory, Mahler introduced harmonic, orchestrational, and musico-rhetorical innovations every bit as "advanced" as what his scientific counterparts managed. For this reason, he eventually would earn the full commitment of the concert-going public, albeit after his death. And it was this desire to invest in future cultural capital, as the journalist Leo Lania later recalled, that turned Mahler and Schoenberg, alongside Freud and Klimt, into the vanguard of genius, establishing fin-de-siècle Vienna as the mesmerizing epicenter of modern thought, sound, and vision.

PART III

Creation

CHAPTER 12

The Composer "Goes to Press"
Mahler's Dealings with Engravers and Publishers in Vienna around 1900

Renate Stark-Voit

Translated by Juliane Schicker

> Among the many enemies of the living composer, one is the publisher.[1]
>
> —Alban Berg, from the beginning of his memorial address for Emil Hertzka, June 20, 1932

It is an open secret that a composer's path to the public – and therefore to posterity – leads, on one hand, through performances, and, on the other, through publication of the composer's works. The manner in which Mahler negotiated his way through the publication industry, particularly in fin-de-siècle Vienna, will be sketched here, along with the developments and personalities that fostered that process.

With the favorable response to his completion of Carl Maria von Weber's *Die drei Pintos* at the Leipzig Stadttheater in 1888, the young Mahler gained not only his first material success but also his first contract with a publisher. The work was accepted by C. F. Kahnt, and F. Bloch offered an exclusive distribution contract for all performances outside Leipzig.[2] In comparison to his more astute partner, Weber's grandson Captain Carl von Weber, Mahler received far less compensation than he deserved, but the agreement was nonetheless lucrative. Encouraged by this experience, Mahler then brought some of his own creations to a publisher (introduced by an intermediary), Dr. Ludwig Strecker, the director of the renowned publishing house Schott in Mainz: "For some years now I have collected a number of my own compositions in various genres – among other things: *a symphony* – a large-scale *fairy tale* for choir, orchestra, and soloists – a *symphonic* poem, and approximately *twenty* selected songs."[3]

---

[1] Robert R. Holzer, "Alban Berg Remembers Emil Hertzka: Composer and Publisher between Real and Ideal," in *Music and the Cultures of Print*, ed. Kate van Orden (New York: Garland, 2000), 96.

[2] Franz Willnauer, ed., *Gustav Mahler. Briefe an seine Verleger* (Vienna: Universal Edition, 2012), 67f.; the contract appears on pp. 70f.

[3] Ibid., 80 (emphasis in original).

Though his larger pieces were not accepted, he made a beginning with the
Lieder, which appeared in three books, for two vocal registers each, in late
1891 and early 1892. Mahler himself worked energetically to market them
and get the word out.

He followed up with more songs, this time in separate versions for piano
and for orchestra (the latter a relative novelty for this era). Originally, he
hoped to publish these five "Humoresques," written in the first three
months of 1892 to texts from *Des Knaben Wunderhorn*, with Schott as
well. But they were declined, along with the abovementioned works and
the *Lieder eines fahrenden Gesellen* (*Songs of a Wayfarer*), composed in
1884 in Kassel.

The preserved engraver's copy of both versions of "Das himmlische
Leben" ("The Heavenly Life") confirms that Mahler expected the works to
be published, including the songs for orchestra. His Hamburg copyist,
Ferdinand Weidig, had presumably finished this copy already in 1892, but
it was not used until a much later date (see the description below of J. V.
v. Wöss's work for Eberle and a link to this source).

Subsequently, Mahler offered his works for the first time to the
renowned Leipzig publishing house Peters, but he received a rejection.
Only for the "Gesellenlieder" was he able to sign a contract, which he did
on September 27, 1897, with Josef Weinberger, an influential publisher
who worked in Vienna and Leipzig.[4] One factor that smoothed Mahler's
path to public recognition was the introduction of copyright protection,
applicable also to musical works, in the *Reichsgesetzblatt* (Reich Law
Gazette) regarding the "Law of 26 December 1895 concerning copyright
in works of literature, art, and photography": "§1: Under the protection of
this law are the works of literature, art, and photography that have appeared
domestically; further, those that have originated with Austrian citizens,
whether the work has appeared domestically, abroad, or not at all." On
p. 671, section b, we find that the law applies specifically "to works of music."

From then, Mahler would have a bumpy ride through the publishing
business in Leipzig and Vienna; not until his successful move to Vienna
would it settle down. Of the first three completed symphonies, only the
Second was published during Mahler's time in Hamburg (engraved by
C. G. Röder). This occurred in 1896, thanks to financial support from two

---

[4] See ibid., 107, for the reproduced contract. In 1897 Weinberger would found the Gesellschaft der
Autoren, Komponisten und Musikverleger (Society of Authors, Composers, and Music Publishers),
which, however, Mahler did not join, as he already belonged to Richard Strauss's Berlin-based
Genossenschaft deutscher Tonsetzer (German Composers' Cooperative).

Hamburg sponsors: the wealthy Wilhelm Berkhan and, most importantly, the Hamburg musician and banker Hermann Behn, who also prepared the first piano reductions of the Second. Friedrich Hofmeister in Leipzig was commissioned to produce the score and the four- and two-hand piano reductions. Meanwhile, another sponsor took on the parts and eventually would assume financial responsibility for publishing the First and Third Symphonies: this was the Gesellschaft zur Förderung deutscher Wissenschaft, Kunst und Literatur in Böhmen (Society for the Promotion of German Science, Art, and Literature in Bohemia), an association that included Guido Adler, Mahler's compatriot and university friend. Adler convinced the other members to subsidize Mahler's works (see the resolution below), so that both symphonies could be prepared by the Viennese engraver Waldheim-Eberle. (In Vienna at this time a peculiar situation obtained in which the engraver determined what material they would offer, rather than the publishing house choosing the press, as is customary today.)

R. v. Waldheim and Jos. Eberle had merged in 1895. Both were lithographic printing establishments like Röder in Leipzig, and competitive and innovative presses with modern engraving methods that allowed large print runs. Mahler's original contract with this firm does not survive, but a draft contract with First Viennese Newspaper Company (*Zeitungsgesellschaft*) of February 1898, which formed the basis of business relationship with Eberle, has recently been published with commentary.[5]

Josef Stritzko (1861–1908), Josef Eberle's son-in-law, was named executive director of the Druckerei und Verlags-Aktiengesellschaft vorm. R. v. Waldheim – Jos. Eberle & Co. (Printing House and Publishing and Stock Company, formerly known as R. v. Waldheim – Jos. Eberle and Company), a name that had been in place since 1897–98. From the time he assumed his position, Stritzko was in contact with Mahler, but mostly verbally, one presumes, since no written correspondence has been preserved (with the exception of one letter in 1906 from Stritzko to Mahler about the mailing of the newly produced study score of the Fourth Symphony, including a formal answer-sketch in the hand of the stenographer).

A letter from the beginning of 1898 from Mahler to Behn, which concerns the material of the Second Symphony engraved in Leipzig, shows that Mahler recognized the advantages of the new Viennese constellation:

---

[5] Paul Banks, "Mahler and 'The Newspaper Company,'" *Nineteenth-Century Music Review* 1, no. 3 (December 2018): 329–52.

Vienna, 21 January 1898:
    I ask you to send the plates of the *score* and *of your piano reduction* to the
firm of
    Eberle and Company
    Vienna
    VII Seidengasse 3.
    Of course, Hofmeister's proprietary rights [*Commissionirung* (*sic*)] end
from that moment on.
    The firm [Eberle] is handling the matter on the *largest scale*: it has already
printed Bruckner's entire œuvre and will print mine completely as well,
including piano reductions and orchestral parts.
    Eberle and Company is exclusively an engraving company à la Röder,
but with tremendous operating capital (a stock company to *propagate
Austrian publishing houses*), and they promote publishers they deem worthy.
    ... It will ensure advertisement on a *large scale*.[6]

Shortly thereafter, on February 6, 1898, the *Prager Tagblatt* announced in
the section "Association News" (p. 10):

Society for the Promotion of German Science, Art, and Literature in
Bohemia. During the first general meeting of this year, which took place
on 28 January ...
    At the request of the Department of Composition, the German-
Bohemian composer Gustav Mahler, Director of the Court Opera in
Vienna (born in Kalischt), received a grant for the publication of his
orchestral works (three symphonies), which make use of the most modern
developments and have attracted the attention of the recognized experts.[7]

In this way Guido Adler had paved the way for his friend, and the first
three symphonies were published in Vienna. Josef Weinberger's presence
in Leipzig likely made it possible that the proprietary rights (*Kommissio-
nierung*) of the Second held by Hofmeister, mentioned by Mahler, would
end, that is, that thenceforth both score and reductions could be sold by
Weinberger's Viennese office (as described in Mahler's letter to Behn).
    Around 1900, the situation seemed to have changed once more: instead
of Weinberger, Bernhard Herzmansky of the publishing house Doblinger
now received the (proprietary) rights of the Fourth Symphony. Meanwhile, though Mahler's penultimate *Wunderhorn* song "Revelge" (1899)
was engraved in Vienna by Eberle (and corrected by Mahler, both versions

---

[6] Cited according to the original in the Bavarian State Library, Munich, Sign. Ana 600.A (emphasis in
    original).
[7] http://anno.onb.ac.at/cgi-content/anno?aid=ptb&datum=18980206&seite=10&zoom=33, accessed
    September 14, 2019.

being preserved), it was not printed there, but rather appeared together with other songs under the slightly misleading title *Sieben Lieder aus letzter Zeit* (*Seven Songs from Recent Times*) in 1905 by Kahnt in Leipzig. This development could point to an estrangement between Mahler and Weinberger, who had long since become a shareholder in the young Universal-Edition, if it were not for the fortunate circumstance that this new business soon (probably already in 1903) focused its attention on publishing Mahler's works as the first great flagship of contemporary music production, by taking on all of his music (besides the "Gesellenlieder").

The feat of bringing Mahler's compositions to publication was not accomplished definitively by this one-time "takeover." The special challenge of Mahler's works lay in the fact that they were never irrevocably finalized. No sooner was a first version of the print or proof sheet available than Mahler began multiple proofreadings to fill in his experiences from performances, to enter another critical revision, to correct mistakes, and to refine markings for articulation and tempo, and all these corrections had to be copied into the new plates. He would adhere to this process for the rest of his life. As a result, the proofreader or, more specifically, the editor increasingly became Mahler's most important contact person in the process of editing the music.

One individual in particular became a key figure for the editing and revising of Mahler's published works. He had worked as music editor at the printing house Waldheim-Eberle from its founding years, and then in 1907 was hired by Emil Hertzka (probably on the recommendation of Mahler) as chief editor for Universal-Edition. Mahler would express in unmistakable terms what this man meant for him in a 1909 letter from New York to director Hertzka concerning his Eighth Symphony: "Above all: the piano reduction by Mr. v. Woess is a *masterpiece*. I am genuinely delighted with this incomparably solid and finished piece of work." Mahler returned to this laudatory mode toward the end of the long letter, adding: "Now, I send my warm regards and, yet again, my thanks for this magnificent reduction, which is undoubtedly the *best* that I have ever encountered in this regard, and could only have been done by a musician as highly gifted and diligent as Woess."[8]

---

[8] Mahler to Hertzka, New York (Hotel Savoy, stationery, n.d.), postmarked November 26, 1909 (emphasis in original). Willnauer, *Gustav Mahler*, 204f. Here, quoted from the autograph: http://daten.digitale-sammlungen.de/0004/bsb00045323/images/index.html?id=00045323&groesser=&fip=eayayztssdaseayaeayaqrsxdsydxdsydwxdsydenyzts&no=6&seite=8, accessed September 14, 2019.

Figure 12.1   Josef Venantius von Wöss (1863–1943).
Used by permission of Universal Edition

But who was this musician whom Mahler respected so highly? Hans Heinsheimer would later depict him, from the perspective of the much younger publishing colleague, respectfully and impudently as a

> friendly, quiet, stout gentleman who, during my time, already had snow-white hair, wore dark, widely cut suits that befitted a church composer, and worked hermetically sealed off from the overheated bustle of our busy profession at the farthest end of the long, tunnel-like hallway in one of the few rooms of the establishment that did not allow one to hurry through to somewhere else, because it only had one door, a door that most often sent the terrified visitor into a bashful flight before he even dared to knock, with the help of the larger-than-life words PLEASE KNOCK.[9]

Josef Venantius von Wöss[10] came from the former Crown Land Dalmatia and was himself a composer (Figure 12.1). Because he was unable to

[9] Hans Heinsheimer, *UE – Die ersten 37 ½ Jahre*, UE 26333 (Vienna: Universal Edition, 2017), 25.
[10] Josef Venantius von Wöss (b. June 13, 1863, in Kotor, d. October 22, 1943, in Vienna) was the son of an Austrian captain and came to Vienna in 1866, where he studied at the Conservatory of the Gesellschaft der Musikfreunde from 1880 to 1882. Until 1907 he worked in the proofreading department of the engraving company Druck- und Verlags-Aktiengesellschaft R. v. Waldheim – J. Eberle in Vienna. Then, he continued to work as editor, but for Universal Edition, and prepared

generate sufficient interest in his own works (operas, overtures, chamber music, and, above all, church music), he worked as a skillful editor in the "background" of the music industry. Already in 1901 his handwriting can be found (probably for the first time) in a *Mehrfachmanuskript* (a manuscript in multiple hands) of Mahler: with meticulous editorial work, Wöss created from a draft of a piano reduction for the song "Das himmliche Leben," which had initially been prepared (unsuccessfully) for printing, an engraver's copy for the piano reduction for two hands of the sung finale of the Fourth Symphony for the company Eberle. Mahler himself had ordered the earlier piano reduction of the song at the beginning of the 1890s and corrected it himself from a transcription by his Hamburg copier Ferdinand Weidig. Wöss's version was published alongside the score of the Fourth Symphony (in addition to the reduction for four hands, also by Wöss).[11]

In exactly this momentous year of 1901, a publishing group (as one would call it today) formed in Vienna with the ambitious goal of confronting the large German traditional publishing houses with a new, Austrian model. The initiative originated with the Viennese banker Josef Edler von Simon, brother-in-law of Johann Strauß, the younger: together with other financiers and those publishers that were active in the monarchy at the time – Bernhard Herzmansky, Adolf Robitschek, and the Emperor's Council Josef Weinberger (once more he played an important role here, and soon turned "his entire [holdings]" of Mahler's music into capital, i.e., shares) – they founded a stock company in June 1901 (from twenty-five [!] shareholders, among them also Emil Hertzka, who later would become decisively important) for the purpose of "a joint creation of an Austrian musical collective edition, titled 'Universal-Edition.'" Their work was an attempt to put classical composers on the market in *Viennese* editions (and as teaching material as well). In the beginning, contemporaries were not yet among the published composers. This issue was approached in three steps: production, distribution, and protection of copyright, among which the "paper business" soon resulted in high debt. The year 1904, however, saw the successful acquisition of the publishing portfolio of the Munich

---

numerous piano reductions, i.e., for Mahler's Third, Fourth, Sixth, and Ninth Symphonies, as well as *Das Klagende Lied* and *Das Lied von der Erde*.

[11] Bavarian State Library, Munich, sign. Mus.ms. 22738; http://daten.digitale-sammlungen.de/0004/bsb00044005/images, accessed September 14, 2019. The *Mehrfachmanuskript* includes copied text by Ferdinand Weidig from 1892 (black ink), Mahler's corrections at the time (black ink), and Mahler's further instructions from 1902 to J. V. v. Wöss (blue pen) as well as the proofreading entries and changes by Wöss for the piano reduction that followed (red pen).

firm Josef Aibl, which included works by Richard Strauss (among them numerous tone poems) and Reger, the latter mostly still in arrangements.

It remains unknown when negotiations with Mahler took place, because, as mentioned above, no correspondence survives with Stritzko or any executive of the new corporation. In 1906, however, Eberle produced study scores (photomechanically miniaturized) of Symphonies 1–4, based on substantial corrections of the plates, which Mahler must have undertaken personally (though unfortunately no documentation survives, and even the corrected copies are only indirectly traceable); the unaltered conducting scores (and piano arrangements) that parallel these were available, all merely carrying the label "incorporated into the Universal-Edition."

Meanwhile, Mahler had resolved his contractual relations with Eberle and wrote in the middle of July 1903 to Bruno Walter, who had been asked to connect him with Henri Hinrichsen at Peters (where Mahler had been rebuffed six years earlier): "It fits perfectly that I just parted amicably with my previous publisher so that from now on, I *can freely dispose* of my works!"[12]

So began the phase of Mahler behaving like a good businessman, who dictated his worth instead of having to act as a petitioner, and who therefore again gravitated away from Austria and toward Germany with his new symphonies. Henri Hinrichsen at Peters now paid the impressive sum of 10,000 guilders for the Fifth, which was almost the equivalent of Mahler's salary as director.[13] For the Sixth, Kahnt outdid Hinrichsen by offering a sum that was again 50 percent higher. Only the Seventh posed problems, because the previous two were not well received by the audience and press, though it did finally land safely with Bote & Bock in Berlin.

At this same time, Mahler broke with Vienna, having resigned from the Court Opera, and Hertzka took over Universal-Edition (UE): "It was a stroke of genius. He [Weinberger] got rid of a person whom he could not order around. He got rid of UE, which had become a burden and a stone around his neck. And he left the annoying Hertzka a debt of 900,000 crowns, which presumably would soon finish him off."[14] Born and raised in Budapest in 1869, Hertzka first studied chemistry in Vienna, and only incidentally music and literature (Figure 12.2). His musical knowledge is described as rather modest, but he must have possessed other gifts and an

[12] Willnauer, *Gustav Mahler*, 117. "Frei" is underlined twice in the original.
[13] The richly insightful correspondence between Mahler and the publishing manager Henri Hinrichsen, which likely is complete, has been published multiple times and cannot be evaluated further here. See the items by Klemm and Willnauer in the Further Reading section.
[14] Hans Heinsheimer, *UE –Die ersten 37 ½ Jahre*, 16.

Figure 12.2   Emil Hertzka (1869–1932).
Used by permission of Universal Edition

extraordinary personality, because he seemed destined to "create" the musical modernity of Vienna, while giving his trust to countless composers of whom no one at that time expected a future.

He had first of all the skill to bind Mahler to Universal-Edition with his works up until the Fourth, and from the Eighth on, for the rest of his life. This formed the basis for Mahler's posthumous reputation, and at the same time marked Universal-Edition as "Mahler's Publishing House" for the foreseeable future. The surviving detailed and nuanced correspondence between Mahler and his "dear Herr Director" begins in June 1909 with the signing of the contract for the Eighth, and ends in February 1911 with Mahler's last letter from New York, in which he remains true to form: "Please, dear friend, be very careful to ensure that my symphonies are issued only with the revisions."[15]

> Among the few friends of the living composer, one was Emil Hertzka.
> —Alban Berg at the end of his memorial address for Hertzka

[15] Willnauer, *Gustav Mahler*, 236f.

CHAPTER 13

Mahler and Program Music

Constantin Floros

Translated by Juliane Schicker

Definitions of "program music" vary to a degree reminiscent of Babel. Broadly speaking, the term suggests heteronomous creations, that is, works inspired by extra-musical ideas: personal experiences, existential questions, philosophical and religious ideas, visual representations, literary works, and historical events.

To locate the sources of more recent program music, we look not to Clément Janequin or Greek antiquity (Pythian Nomos of Sakadas) but, rather, to purely instrumental works by Froberger, Frescobaldi, Kuhnau (*Biblische Historien*), Bach (*Capriccio sopra la lontananza del suo fratello dilettissimo*), and François Couperin (*Le Parnasse ou l'Apothéose de Lully*). During the final third of the eighteenth century, Paris saw the first performances of *symphonies à programmes*: symphonies for which programs were distributed containing information about the subject matter. Composers included François Lesueur, Berlioz's teacher, and, in the 1790s, Francesco Antonio Rosetti (= Franz Anton Rösler) and Carl Ditters von Dittersdorf.

The terms "program music" and "program symphony" seem to arise in German musical terminology first in the 1850s, having been restricted until then to the French-speaking world. In contrast, the related term "characteristic music" spread throughout most of Europe around the close of the eighteenth century. In countless printed and manuscript scores ca. 1800 the designation "characteristic" was applied to symphonies, overtures, sonatas, and other pieces.

A historiography of nineteenth-century European music could reasonably begin with the antagonism between so-called absolute music and program music. The Viennese music critic Eduard Hanslick would become the outstanding apologist of absolute music – coining in 1854 the now-famous phrase "sonically moving forms" (*tönend bewegte Formen*) – and, much later, composer Ferruccio Busoni would take up the cause in his *Entwurf einer neuen Äesthetik der Tonkunst* (1907). Program music, however, dominated the scene for a much of the century.

For many listeners, Hector Berlioz, Franz Liszt, and Richard Strauss are the most prominent representatives of program music. Yet their answers to similar basic questions differed greatly. Berlioz was inspired by the musical play, Liszt by the "philosophical epopee," and Strauss by literature, musical autobiography, and materials amenable to his personal brand of illustrative program music.

Berlioz referred to his *Symphonie fantastique* as an "instrumental play" (*drame instrumental*) in its first official program, published on May 21, 1830, in the Parisian newspaper *Le Figaro*. This term suggests a dramatic work – a play without words – with the program fulfilling the role of an opera's spoken text (i.e., the recitative). But the difference between providing an extensive program, as in this case, and only a title, as in Beethoven's *Pastorale*, is smaller than it appears, and by no means categorical. Both pieces belong to the genre of "soul painting" (*Seelenmalerei*), describing a series of images and mental states. Berlioz's program operates on a dreamlike, quasi-surrealist level, referring to the central figure of the beloved as an idée fixe, a term derived from the realm of psychiatry. Thus, while external events are represented, Berlioz, like Beethoven, was more interested in the expression of emotion – as we see in the name of the opening movement: *Reveries – Passions*. Berlioz's 1839 "dramatic symphony" *Roméo et Juliette*, by contrast, attempted for the first time to express a play (more precisely, the emotional content of several scenes) by symphonic means. Recognizing that a mere textual program explaining staged events would be insufficient, Berlioz included choirs and solos, to prepare the audience mentally, emotionally, and spiritually for the symphonically interpreted scenes of Shakespeare's tragedy.

Franz Liszt's self-declared artistic goal was the "inner amalgamation" of music with poetry (literature). But whereas Wagner saw a way forward in the music drama, Liszt turned to symphonic program music. In a letter to Agnes Street-Klindworth of November 16, 1860, he described the "principal idea" of his Weimar period (1848–60): "a renewal of music through its deepest connection with the art of poetry."[1] Specifically, in his groundbreaking work on Berlioz he would argue at length for the modern program symphony as a counterpart to the "philosophical epopee" of Goethe, Byron, and Mickiewicz. Instrumental music was an art of the

---

[1] Pauline Pocknell, ed. and trans., *Franz Liszt and Agnes Street-Klindworth: A Correspondence 1854–1886* (Hillsdale, NY: Pendragon Press, 2000), 187.

emotions, and the epopee a "telling of inner thoughts," encompassing mental states, affects, and passions.

The poetry and text adapted in most of Liszt's symphonic poems belong to the epic and lyrical genres. Liszt preferred philosophically reflective poetry: Victor Hugo's *Ce qu'on entend sur la montagne*, Lamartine's meditation *Les Préludes*, and Schiller's *Die Ideale*. Hugo's poem thematizes the dualism between nature and humankind, leading to a philosophical aporia: Why would God merge the harmonic sounds of nature with the clamor of humanity? Lamartine takes up the theme of life itself, construed as a series of preludes. And *Die Ideale* considers the relationship between art and existence, between artist and ideal. In all cases the programs are grounded in a fundamental idea, often pointing unmistakably to the epopee: sorrow, whose corpse's banner "extends through all times and places" (*Héroïde funèbre*); the dichotomy of suffering and triumph, understood as the artist's fate, culminating in the posthumous victory of great people and ideas (*Tasso*, after Goethe and Byron); the antithesis of misfortune and glorification, manifested in various changing forms such as boldness, suffering, perseverance, and salvation (*Prometheus*).

Richard Strauss's symphonic music is invariably programmatic (after the two early symphonies), imposing the expected demands on the audience: it presumes that listeners possess certain knowledge; it attempts to steer their imagination down a particular path; and it invites them to explore the correlation between subject and music. Strauss took inspiration from Berlioz and from Liszt, whom he greatly revered and consistently supported. Particularly during his younger years, Liszt's aesthetic would fascinate him; letters to Hans von Bülow and the Slovakian composer Johann Leopold Bella show that Strauss adopted Lisztian principles from the ground up. In program music, which Strauss considered the legacy of Beethoven, he located the only path to an "independent development of our instrumental music."[2] Like Liszt, Strauss believed in the superiority of content (the poetic idea) over form and in the ability of new ideas to create new forms. He understood music as the art of expression, and he flatly rejected Eduard Hanslick's autonomy aesthetics.

One difference between Liszt and Strauss, however, lies in their public commentary about absolute music. Liszt's essay on Berlioz, his classic defense of program music, did not include an attack on absolute music.

[2] Strauss to Johann Leopold Bella, December 2, 1888. Franz Zagiba, *Johann L. Bella (1843–1936) und das Wiener Musikleben* (Vienna: Verlag des Notringes der wissenschaftlichen Verbände Österreichs, 1955), 48.

In contrast, Strauss openly rejected absolute music as both anachronism and an inferior art form:

> Program music: real music!
>
> Absolute music: can be written with the aid of a certain routine and craftsmanship by any only moderately musical person.
>
> The first: art!
>
> The second: craft!
>
> Remarkably enough, present-day music took No. 2 as its starting-point and was made fully conscious of its true destiny only by Wagner and Liszt.[3]

What, then, was Strauss's role in the history of program music? Most agree that his symphonic achievements surpassed those of Berlioz and Liszt. Gustav Brecher praised his "recklessly realistic style," while Max Vancsa commended him on opposite grounds, as a leader of the "idealistic direction in program music."[4] This contrast fairly reflects the varied directions that Strauss gave to his work: illustrative program music, auto-biographical works, and tone poems as psychological dramas.

Strauss adopted the Lisztian brand of psychological drama in four of his tone poems: *Macbeth* (after Shakespeare), *Don Juan* (after Lenau), *Death and Transfiguration* (based on a scenario developed with Alexander Ritter), and *Thus Spake Zarathustra* (after Nietzsche). In literary terms, psycho-logical dramas are plays (mostly monodramas) involving a long psycho-logical development, and in particular a struggle toward catharsis. For Liszt, program music based on these subjects was intended to present not "true realities" – that is, plot details – but, rather, the "narration of inner truths."

In other tone poems Strauss distanced himself from Liszt, first through musical illustration and then by means of fictitious programs not based on literary models. *Till Eulenspiegel's Merry Pranks* (1895) and *Don Quixote* (1897) converted external incidents into music, shocking listeners with pictorial effects: broken pots and the death on the gallows in *Till Eulen-spiegel*, the bleating of sheep and the ride through the air in *Don Quixote*. While Mahler recoiled, telling Richard Specht that he preferred his music to be "misunderstood rather than perceived as purely rationalistic or,

---

[3] Strauss to Bella, March 13, 1890. Quoted in Willy Schuh, *Richard Strauss: A Chronicle of the Early Years, 1864–1898*, trans. Mary Whittall (Cambridge: Cambridge University Press, 1982), 148.

[4] Gustav Brecher, *Richard Strauss. Eine monographische Skizze* (Leipzig: H. Seeman, 1900), 36; Max Vancsa, "Zur Geschichte der Programmusik," *Die Musik*, 2, no. 23 (1903): 323–43, and 2, no. 24 (1903): 403–18.

indeed, as illustrative program music,"[5] he nonetheless eagerly conducted both works, in Europe and the United States. Illustration remained prominent in Strauss's three tone poems after *Don Quixote,* two of which, *Ein Heldenleben* (1898) and *Symphonia domestica* (1903), are momentous contributions to the genre of musical autobiography.

Mahler, who from his time in Leipzig considered himself primarily a symphonist, described the significance of modern program music in an important letter to Gisela Tolnay-Witt from February 7, 1893. "The new era of music" started with Beethoven: "From now on, the subjects of musical reproduction are no longer basic moods (like pure joy or sadness, etc.), but also the transitions from one to the other, conflicts, external nature and its effect on us, humor, and poetic concepts" (*SLGM*, 147/ *GMB2*, 130). Like many other composers (Liszt, Strauss, Tchaikovsky), Mahler was convinced that "inner" programs had inspired Beethoven's symphonies. Programmaticism thus amounted to a historical imperative, which explains why chamber music no longer satisfied him and why he needed a large "Wagner orchestra."

Mahler's symphonies too are based on inner programs, which he shared publicly up to the Fourth Symphony. Thereafter he did not officially disclose his programs, although he hinted at them in conversations with friends and confidants. A variety of reasons moved him (beginning in October 1900) to formally distance himself from program music. From the beginning, critics had ridiculed his hermeneutic expressions, and he realized that verbal programs were vulnerable to gross misunderstandings. He also felt it important to distance himself from Richard Strauss's illustrative program music. And finally, he was well aware that music criticism in Vienna was dictated by Hanslick, the archenemy of program music. But in spite of these adjustments to his works' public face, Mahler continued composing programmatically – thematizing existential questions by means of inner programs – even after the Fourth Symphony. With this choice he maintained faith with a set of core beliefs: in experience as the indispensable prerequisite of artistic creation, in a conception of art as the anticipation of destiny, in the priority of the intellectual (*geistlich*) over the material, and in the continuation of human existence after death.

In his review of the first two volumes of my Mahler trilogy, Carl Dahlhaus opined rather audaciously that "we must respect a composer's aesthetic decision that programmatic aspects do not belong to the subject

[5] Richard Specht, *Gustav Mahler* (Berlin: Schuster & Loeffler, 1913), 172.

matter itself, i.e., to the work as an aesthetic object." He claimed further-more that "how a musical work emerged and developed is a private affair of the composer"[6] – an astonishing statement given that analyzing the genesis of musical artworks is one of musicology's central tasks. It is now estab-lished fact that, as starting points for his symphonic works, Mahler used images, verses and poems, natural sounds, personal experiences, and literary, religious, and philosophical ideas – all of which he realized in music. Above all he valued music's capacity for plastic expression. Dal-haus's position suffers from his needless attempt to conceive of the finished work as an abstraction, without considering the process by which the music emerged.

Why then were the programs concealed? The answer is, for several reasons. Mahler withdrew the programs of his first four symphonies (in 1900) to distance himself from Straussian musical illustration, but also to avoid being misunderstood. Experience had taught him that his programs were too personal to publicize. Many of his colleagues held a similar view about programs, for example, Schoenberg, who began his compositional career as a program musician – with *Verklärte Nacht*, op. 4, after Richard Dehmel, and *Pelleas and Melisande*, op. 5, after Maurice Maeterlinck – but later suppressed the programs for the same reason as Mahler. Moreover, in an essay on Franz Liszt, Schoenberg reproached his colleague for using literary rather than inner programs; indeed, a large part of Schoenberg's music, and that of his student Alban Berg, would be decidedly autobio-graphical in a basically Lisztian sense.

Like many composers before him, Mahler used a range of techniques to provide extra-musical meaning to his creations. The most important of these include:

1. Borrowing from his songs. In his first three symphonies, Mahler adapted the instrumental substance of preexisting songs, surmising that these passages would retain the textual meaning of the work in which they originated.
2. Characteristic motifs and quotations. In portraying his inner world, Mahler employed a large number of "characteristic motifs" (a term coined by Liszt) borrowed from the symphonic and musico-dramatic traditions of the nineteenth century. These symbols include the inferno, the cross, the Grail, resurrection, and eternity, as found in

[6] Carl Dahlhaus, "Tönende Metaphysik," *Die Zeit* (October 1978); cf. Constantin Floros, "Carl Dahlhaus and Mahler's Programs," in *Gustav Mahler's Mental World: A Systematic Representation*, trans. Ernest Bernhardt-Kabisch (Frankfurt am Main: Peter Lang, 2016), 213f.

such works as the opening movement (*Inferno*) of Liszt's *Dante Symphony*, Wagner's *Die Walküre* and *Parsifal*, and others.

3. Leading harmonies (specific characteristic chord sequences, deployed in the manner of leitmotifs, i.e., "leading motives") and leading rhythms (which recur in semantically stable guises). The former include the major-minor seal; the latter, such famous rhythmic ideas as the death, battle, and fight motifs. A particularly important case here is the Sixth Symphony's combination of a prominent major-minor chord succession with the concise leading rhythm, which appears during the opening movement, the scherzo, and the finale.[7]

4. Idiophones and other sound symbols. The tam-tam, for example, symbolizes the realm of death; the hammer blows of the Sixth symbolize fate; the bells of the Third, eternity; and the string harmonics at the beginning of the First, nature. Likewise, the glockenspiel often serves as an aural prop suggesting the music of angels. And according to Mahler himself, cowbells indicate an "echoing earthly roar" one hears when standing "at the highest summit in the face of eternity."[8]

5. Musical conventions and genres. The term "conventions" encompasses musical movement types and genres with recognizable stylistic features and characteristic expressive qualities. Musical conventions of vocal provenance include instrumental recitative, arioso, chorale, hymn, and the song without words. Conventions drawn from instrumental traditions include the march, funeral march, pastoral, and a personal favorite of Mahler, "music from the farthest distance." The most common musical dance elements are the ländler, waltz, valse, and minuet. Each of these has its own distinct semantic field, by means of which Mahler's aspiration to a universal symphonic practice could reflect fundamental questions of humankind and the world.[9]

6. Inclusion of verbal texts. Significantly, to substantiate his poetic intentions, Mahler followed the example of Beethoven's Ninth and included "the word" in a few of his symphonies, using mixed choirs, a women's choir, a boys' choir, and vocal soloists.

While Mahler built upon Beethoven's principles, he also meant to unify those with the dramatic art of Richard Wagner, whom he revered deeply. Reconciling them proved challenging, however, as we see in a letter of March 26, 1896, to the critic Max Marschalk:

---

[7] Constantin Floros, *Gustav Mahler and the Symphony of the 19th Century*, trans. Neil K. Moran (Frankfurt am Main: Peter Lang, 2013), 207–37.
[8] Ibid., 249–50.   [9] Ibid., 77–146.

Right now we stand – of this I am sure – at an important crossroads that soon will separate the two divergent paths of symphonic and dramatic music forever. Those who understand the essence of music realize this. Even now, when you compare a Beethoven symphony with the sound structures of Wagner, you will recognize the essential contrast in their nature. – True, Wagner adopted the *expressive means* of symphonic music, just as the symphonist will justifiably and purposefully appropriate the expressive capacities gained for music by Wagner's life and work. In this sense, all arts are interrelated; indeed, art is even related to nature. But as yet there has not been enough deliberation on this topic, because we still have no *perspective* on it. (*SLGM*, 179/*GMB2*, 172)

Confessing that he was not the one to construct this system, Mahler remained wed to a view already formed while working on his first symphonies.

According to Alfredo Casella, Mahler himself categorized his oeuvre into three periods.[10] Across the three, however, he maintained faith in the necessity of an inner program grounded in personal experience. Even Mahler's three instrumental symphonies, Nos. 5–7, are in fact based on secret programs that he divulged to trusted confidantes: Alma, Bruno Walter, Willem Mengelberg, and others. Regarding the Sixth, Alma would claim that the three hammer blows in the finale seal the fate of the protagonist. Alfred Roller, arguably Mahler's closest colleague at the Vienna State opera, concurred: "His music speaks what his chaste mouth kept quiet." He continued:

On the evening after the dress rehearsal for the Sixth Symphony, Mahler asked a friend who was not a musician what his impression of the symphony was. That friend, still sobbing deeply from the shock evoked by the music, started stammering: "How can someone as gracious as you express so much cruelty and ruthlessness!" To that, Mahler replied solemnly and firmly, "Those are cruelties that have been inflicted on me, pain that I endured."[11]

Natalie Bauer-Lechner heard such confessions already in the summer of 1893, with Mahler claiming that "the work always is born from suffering and the severest inner experiences" (*NBLE*, 33). Likewise to Oskar Bie in April 1895: "My music is *lived* experience; how should those confront it, who do not *live*, who feel not a draft from the tempest of our great time?" (*SLGM*, 160/*GMB2*, 145). This statement suggests why many people today are touched by the authenticity of Mahler's music: the music and the human being remain inseparable.

---

[10] Alfredo Casella, "Gustav Mahler et sa deuxième symphonie," *SIM: Revue musicale mensuelle* 6, no. 4 (April 1910): 240f.

[11] Alfred Roller, *Die Bildnisse von Gustav Mahler* (Leipzig: E. P. Tal, 1922), 23f.

CHAPTER 14

Intertextuality in Mahler

Vera Micznik

Much has been written about Mahler's references, allusions, quotations, or borrowings from the widest varieties of music, from popular ("lowbrow") military marches or ländlers to cultivated ("highbrow") compositions such as Brahms's, Tchaikovsky's, or Wagner's. Mahler's early contemporaries in fact attacked and derided him precisely for this open referential quality of his music, which, to their minds, opposed the romantic notion of originality and authenticity. Not until the 1960s did it become clear that in the context of his time this feature constituted an extraordinarily daring modernist statement. Since then, many scholars have explored Mahler's music in light of his propensity to incorporate preexistent musical materials, often referring to it as "intertextuality." I propose here a reevaluation of this term and concept, as well as a clarification of its definition and, more specifically, the problems and benefits of its applicability to music in general and to Mahler's music in particular. As we shall see, the intertextual activity unveils in Mahler's texts further, unsuspected, hidden contextual meanings that can be uncovered through tracing the origins of the networks of codes embedded in them.

Julia Kristeva's original proposition of the term "*intertextualité*" in 1967 defines the opening of contemporary literary criticism, turning from the previously prevailing formalist methodology to a freer, semiotic, yet "translinguistic" practice, to an interpretation of the literary text as a "productivity" (*productivité*), as a "permutation of texts," an "intertextuality." Or, as she puts it elsewhere (attributed to Bakhtin), "any text constitutes itself as a mosaic of quotations, any text is an absorption and transformation of another text."[1] Following her, Roland Barthes explains that "the text is made of multiple writings, drawn from many cultures and

---

[1] Julia Kristeva, "Le texte clos," in Σημειωκη: *Recherches pour une sémanalyse (Extraits)* (Paris: Seuil, 1969), 52; Kristeva, "Le mot, le dialogue et le roman," in ibid., 85. All translations, unless otherwise specified, are mine.

entering into mutual relations."[2] The idea that texts (literary and other) cannot escape a common network of constellations which blend their origins, that they all belong to a sociolect that needs to be untangled by the reader in order to reach their broadest meanings, is not new. What is new, however, is a change in the philosophical hermeneutical position that goes hand in hand with (1) the contemporary liberation of the text's meanings from the assumed authorial seal and (2) the recognition that meaning emerges at the intersection of the intertextual networks projected by the text (regardless of what the creator intended) and those of the receiver (or the listener).

Subsequent scholars clarified further the conditions that best identify intertextuality as a heuristic tool. For Roland Barthes, for example, the intertextual production is not interested in recapturing the sources of a textual utterance, but involves more hidden, not readily recognizable links: "The intertextual . . . is not to be confused with some origin of the text: to try to find the 'sources,' the 'influences' of a work, is to fall in with the myth of filiation; the citations which go to make up a text are anonymous, untraceable, and yet *already read*."[3] There is no hierarchy that gives priority to older texts that might have inspired or influenced newer ones, there is no attempt to recapture the author's intentions – intertextuality's productivity goes in all directions, unsettling "notions of Authorship, of origin, of unity, and of identity." But, since the writing submitted to the intertextual activity is anterior to reading, the production of meaning is situated at the encounter of an already existent text with the reader who interprets it; and the focus of that production changes drastically from the author to the reader's competence. As Barthes states, the "multiplicity" of writings present in the text "is revealed in only one place, and that place is the reader, not, as was hitherto said, the author"; and for Michael Riffaterre, "[intertextuality] refers to an operation of the reader's mind, but it is an obligatory one, necessary to any textual decoding." This "reader-oriented hermeneutics" (as Linda Hutcheon calls it[4]) thus brings

---

[2] Roland Barthes, "The Death of the Author," in *Image, Music, Text*, trans. Stephen Heath (New York: Hill and Wang, 1977), 148.

[3] Barthes, "From Work to Text," in *Image, Music, Text*, 160.

[4] Jill Rosemary Schostak, "[Ad]dressing Methodologies. Tracing the Self in Significant Slips: Shadow Dancing" (PhD diss., University of East Anglia, 2005), vol. 2 (no page number available), Imaginativespaces.net, accessed September 9, 2019; Barthes, "The Death of the Author," 148; Michael Riffaterre, "Intertextual Representation: On Mimesis as Interpretive Discourse," *Critical Inquiry* 11, no. 1 (September 1984): 142–43; Linda Hutcheon, "Literary Borrowing . . . and Stealing: Plagiarism, Sources, Influences, and Intertexts," *English Studies in Canada* 12, no. 2 (June 1986): 237.

a radical change in the older perception of texts as carriers of authorially imprinted stable, unique, original meanings, and instead proposes flexible, fluid meanings emerging from the encounter between the reader's intertexts and those of the texts at hand.

In order to prompt an intertextual reading, the text has to suggest a "hidden, latent intertext" that provokes and challenges us, that "suggest[s] gaps that can be filled and references made to a yet unknown referent," by what Riffaterre calls an "ungrammaticality," a "signpost" that stands out as not fitting into the predominant style of the text. Riffaterre illustrates this process in his analysis of William Carlos Williams's modernist poem "The Red Wheelbarrow." This short poem seems blunt in its unadorned enumeration of objects in a barnyard, described succinctly, realistically, and inertly, as if making a statement of unwillingness to play by the rules of conventional poetic beauty. Yet beneath the modernist effect of aesthetic alienation, Riffaterre detects in the red wheelbarrow "glazed [with rain water]" a suggestion of an intertext. "Glazed [he writes] presupposes an artistic object with the finish of fragile, delicate China . . . [it] conjures up a vast intertext of artifacts made with aesthetic intent."[5] This reference contradicts the general mimetic dullness of the utilitarian objects enumerated, as this intertext of a more delicate painting invites the reader's imagination to re-project the colors and shapes of the poem onto a new artistic plane. This provocation, then, this word that belies the poem's dryness, opens up the text into the networks of all beautiful poetry ever written.

Can this theory be applied to music in a profitable way? Can it enable us to discern aspects of music that would be unreachable through available analytical and interpretive musical methodologies? And, especially, does it uncover facets of Mahler's music and context that would be difficult to reach otherwise?

In music, tracing correlations among artistic works is a common tool in analytical and critical interventions. It may identify the communality of codes, genres, topics, or of tonal or formal systems or strategies applied by composers to their works during the same or different time periods, which receivers usually recognize. Similarly, obvious connections among musical texts, such as allusions, quotations, references of one text to another as more or less consciously intended by the authors, have been productively

---

[5] Michael Riffaterre, "Compulsory Reader Response: The Intertextual Drive," in Michael Worton and Judith Still, eds., *Intertextuality: Theories and Practices* (Manchester: Manchester University Press, 1990), 57; Riffaterre, "Intertextual Representation," 144–48, 145.

explored.[6] Those concerns generally lie outside intertextuality in the strict sense described above, however, and therefore I shall discuss here only studies that invoke the term itself, to see the modes in which the concept is applied and what is gained from its implementation.

The relatively few explicit applications of intertextuality among musicologists vary in their acknowledgment of the word's more restrictive meaning for early literary critics. In particular, situating the intertextual process only in the listener's mind, thus ignoring the author's intentions or the historical and creative origins of works, poses a challenge to the most common historical and analytical methods. A survey of representative cases can be instructive. For example, Kevin Korsyn's deeply informative article, "Directional Tonality and Intertextuality: Brahms's Quintet op. 88 and Chopin's Ballade op. 38," argues for an intertextual connection between Chopin's Ballade no. 2 in F Major, op. 38, and the second movement of Brahms's String Quintet, op. 88.[7] Invoking the concept of intertextuality in conjunction with Harold Bloom's theory of "anxiety of influence," Korsyn ignores one of the precepts of intertextuality – that of disregarding notions such as authorship, origin, originality, and chronology – with a detailed assessment of Brahms's anterior knowledge of Chopin's work and ostensibly intertextual relationships in the practice of directional tonality. In addition to the purists' objection to the application of the term to just one work and its precursor as opposed to multiple textual sociolects, one might observe that Korsyn's arguments rely on deep (predominantly Schenkerian) analytical work, mostly ignoring the surface textual phenomena with which one might expect an intertextual reading to be concerned. If intertexts are triggered by "signposts," as Riffaterre calls them, commonalities of directional tonality buried well below the surface might not qualify as perceivable intertextual indices.

In other examples, intertextuality is seen as a sharing among various works of melodic "quotations" or "borrowings," which, presented each time in different contexts, enrich the meaning of the original music with new cultural and contextual connotations. Robert Hatten rightly

---

[6] See, for example, Christopher A. Reynolds, *Motives for Allusion: Context and Content in Nineteenth-Century Music* (Cambridge, MA: Harvard University Press, 2003); Peter Burkholder, *All Made of Tunes: Charles Ives and the Uses of Musical Borrowing* (New Haven: Yale University Press, 2004); David Metzer, *Quotation and Cultural Meaning in Twentieth-Century Music* (Cambridge: Cambridge University Press, 2003).

[7] Kevin Korsyn, "Directional Tonality and Intertextuality: Brahms's Quintet op. 88 and Chopin's Ballade op. 38," in *The Second Practice of Nineteenth-Century Tonality*, ed. William Kinderman and Harald Krebs (Lincoln: University of Nebraska Press, 1996), 45–86.

differentiates between the common building blocks that large numbers of works from the Western tradition share, which he calls "styles" (such as genres, conventional harmonic progressions, and topics, which are so prevalent as to be clear without intertextual analysis) and what he calls "strategies," which in his words are "the thematic ... elements and processes ... sufficiently characterized as to be 'marked' for the listener's attention."[8] Indeed, these latter cases are often the favorite object of putative intertextual musical analyses, in the form of a search for quotations, allusions, or other direct links – surface features, easily audible, that trigger a majority of intertextual readings of musical works.

Hatten offers as an example the often-cited intertextual chain of quotations starting with Mahler's *Des Knaben Wunderhorn* song "Des Antonius von Padua Fischpredigt," then used instrumentally in the third movement of his Second Symphony, and finally reworked in Berio's *Sinfonia* with other musical quotations and a discontinuous layer of verbal quotes from Beckett's novel *The Unnamable*. Referential resonances abound in this complex network: between the text and Mahler's original music capturing the irony and futility of the prayer; between the musical features – reproduced within the nonverbal symphonic context of the symphony – and the listener's (possible) knowledge of the verbal source of meaning; and then the plunge into Berio's "mosaic of quotations," including musical and literary ones, where the productivity of "absorption and transformation" of those previous texts results in the generation of new rich meanings, some reinforcing the irony of the original song, some proclaiming the end of meaning in a cacophony of spoken and musical enunciations gradually disintegrating. Whether this chain of quotations confines itself to a narrow definition of intertextuality is doubtful, as the existence of a precise quotation throughout the work contradicts Roland Barthes's finding that the intertext includes anonymous discursive practices, codes whose origins are lost.

A scholar hewing more closely to the narrow definition of intertextuality is Michael Klein, who takes exceptional care in reading intersections of musical codes, for example, by applying the concept of nonchronological and "ahistorical" connections. This approach leads him to argue in Bloomian fashion, for example, that in the intertext between Chopin and Bach, "Chopin is the precursor of Bach because he asks us to hear the earlier composer's prelude in a new way." Particularly relevant to

---

[8] See Robert Hatten, "The Place of Intertextuality in Music Studies," *American Journal of Semiotics* 3, no. 4 (1985): 70–71.

Mahler are also the studies of Raymond Monelle and Robert Samuels, which explore the intersections between semiotics and intertextuality in elucidating Mahler's works.[9]

In my own approach to intertextuality in Mahler, I am most interested in the ways in which intertexts penetrate the very essence of his musical language in the form of cells or gestures, present as subcutaneous veins, hidden traces, anonymous vestiges of other styles whose origins have become obscure. One of the hidden vestiges in Mahler's middle to late style is the presence of Bach's music. Mahler's interest in Bach is well known: there are abundant remarks in Mahler scholarship of his Bach performances, arrangements, and the generic allusions to Bach's chorales (e.g., Symphony no. 2/v, 3/vi, 9/iv), to fugues (e.g., 5/v, 9/iii), or, as Donald Mitchell notes, Bach's Passions in "Der Abschied" in the alternation of recitative and arias, or, as Julian Johnson mentions, to Motets and Cantatas in "Veni Creator Spiritus" of the Eighth Symphony.[10] Most of these examples make intentional references to older forms as topics. The chorales invoke reflective, recollected, heightened feelings, often serving as a musical device to produce respite to counteract agitated or tension-building states in musical processes; the fugues are used as endearing homage to Bach's baroque academic compositional practices (5/v), or, with blasphemous dissonances and contortions, they refer to the tradition, yet ironically mock it with the goal of suggesting alienation or decadence in modern times. These can be called intertextual, but in the broader sense of the term "styles" as described above by Hatten.

Yet the Mahlerian intertext is imbued, especially in the mature songs, with traces from Bach that are less often noticed. The instrumental introduction of "Nun will die Sonn' so hell aufgeh'n," the first song of the *Kindertotenlieder*, presents such a case (Example 14.1).

In the right-hand line one can hear the implied two-part upper contrapuntal voice C_5–D_5, B_4–C_5 as upbeat on the fourth to the first beats of the 4/4 measures, and the second voice $G\#_4$–A_4–B_4–C_5, sequenced one whole tone lower starting of $F\#_4$ in m. 2. In conjunction with the stepwise bass line of the left hand, implied in the voice leading are two parallel diminished seventh chords on G# and F# (#IV and #III of the tonic key

[9] Michael Klein, *Intertextuality in Western Art Music* (Bloomington: Indiana University Press, 2005), 8; Raymond Monelle, *The Sense of Music: Semiotic Essays* (Princeton: Princeton University Press, 2000); Robert Samuels, *Mahler's Sixth Symphony: A Study in Musical Semiotics* (Cambridge: Cambridge University Press, 1995).

[10] Julian Johnson, *Mahler's Voices: Expression and Irony in the Songs and Symphonies* (Oxford: Oxford University Press, 2009), 153ff.

Example 14.1   Mahler, *Kindertotenlieder*, "Nun will die Sonn' so hell aufgeh'n," mm. 1–4.

Example 14.2a   J. S. Bach, *The Well-Tempered Clavier*, Book I, Prelude in F Minor, mm.
12–13.

Example 14.2b   J. S. Bach, *The Well-Tempered Clavier*, Book I, Fugue in F Minor, mm. 1–4.

D minor). Defying a stable statement of the tonic, although these chromatic chords become diatonic in mm. 3 and 4, they lead, still awkwardly,
via a iv (G) minor chord, to D minor (i) in m. 4. Both the vocal texted
main melody beginning at m. 5 ("Nun will die Sonn' so hell aufgeh'n")
and the rest of the song rely on these sparse, evenly moving contrapuntal
lines, sometimes in inversion, conveying painful but subdued feelings of
despair mixed with heightened resignation.

   A sensitive reading of this passage leads one to "ungrammaticalities" in
the form of Bach-like formulas – interferences in what otherwise should be
a late nineteenth-century chromatic style. Segments from the Prelude and
Fugue in F Minor from the *Well-Tempered Clavier*, Book I, exemplify the
intertexts that I bring to the interpretation of Mahler's introduction
(Example 14.2).

   Linear motion in static durations of quarter- or eighth-notes, and the
sense of implied two-part polyphony (or compound melody) typical of
Bachian instrumental solo music, likewise have their effect. And dissonant

intervals such as diminished fourths and fifths resolved semitonally upward add the darkness of "pianto" baroque figures. A sense of rational construction is added by the steady stepwise and rhythmically repetitive, seemingly controlled motion at each level, and by short sequences in the inner voices, but this apparent emotional control and balance is counteracted by the registral separations, whose expressive leaps convey possible "sigh" topics, while the absent voices of the diminished chords heighten the expressive tension. The connotations of "high music," spirituality, and the resilience of the Passions fill in the intertextual gaps, much as for Riffaterre the red wheelbarrow glazed with rainwater provided the artistic validation in Williams's poem.

Similar intertexts of Bach's preludes and fugues accompany the dirge-like fourth song of the *Kindertotenlieder*, "Oh denk' ich, sie sind nur ausgegangen!" At mm. 65–68, near the end of the song, the contradiction between the father's words "im Sonnenschein, der Tag ist schön auf jenen Höh'n" (in the sunshine, the day is beautiful on yonder heights) and his inner pain at the death of the child is represented musically through the Bachian steady footing of the repeated quarter notes, connoting the imagined certainty of the untroubled world in which the father wants to believe, while the registral splits in the two-part chromatic counterpoint disguise the real sighing of the father.

The intertexts that these works invoke, however, are not necessarily particular pieces by Bach, but an indeterminate corpus of his music with these characteristics, which have become a recognizable sociolect of the musical literature. Thus, my musical segments do not claim origins in particular pieces, nor do they imply a direct – that is, witting – influence of Bach on Mahler. They are not quotations or allusions to Bach, but floating traces that have become part of Mahler's language absorbed from the generally available intertexts. I agree with Julian Johnson, then, when he writes that in Mahler, the significance of the "almost certainly accidental echoes of (mis)remembered fragments from other works … lies in the broader stylistic reference they imply rather than in any individual work to which they may allude."[11]

From the interpreter's recognition of various outside intertexts whose origins are lost or obscured, of which the composer might not even have been aware, result new signifying topics, part of a language shared among works (sometimes the composer's own works), thus problematizing the search for exact quotations from outside and inside sources with fixed

[11] Ibid., 154.

attached meanings. A few examples worth further exploration may be suggested here. Unsuspected connections between markedly different works like the Eighth Symphony and *Das Lied von der Erde* rely on common intertexts created by Mahler out of anonymous fragments, including newly created topics of discourse, for example, losing control; such passages can suggest erotic playfulness, subtly linking the youths' unleashed energy on horses in "Von der Schönheit" from *Das Lied*, and the angels' unholy frolicking in heaven in the Eighth's Goethe movement, erasing the differences of genre and national identity classification that distinguish these works. Other latent intertexts in Mahler's works, such as the ubiquitous traces of the "turn motive" or the "hurdy-gurdy" reso-nances, await further study as well. The openness that intertextuality proposes may challenge Mahler's interpreters to seek more traces whose participation in the construction of meaning they can elucidate.

Bringing new and relevant intertexts into the interpretation of Mahler's music enables us to discover strategies of meaning that are unique to his works. While Mahler's overt referentiality to other musics, especially his importing of recognizable quotations and allusions from surrounding popular and classical repertories, may tell us more about the context of his times, heuristic intertextual readings put the onus on the listener's competence to decipher the plurality of texts with reference not to an external reality but to other floating intertexts. As Schostak writes, para-phrasing Riffaterre, "Texts and signs refer to other texts and signs; they do not refer to the world, or even to concepts."[12] And since such readings do not compete with influences and sources,[13] we can consider both as equally relevant producers of meanings. The reader's (or listener's) respon-sibility for the intertextual productivity of a text does not consist of proving ultimate meanings, but rather of unsettling notions of authorship, origin, and decentering traditional boundaries. In Barthes's elegant for-mulation, intertexts are "what comes to me, not what I summon up; not an 'authority,' simply a circular memory. Which is what the inter-text is: the impossibility of living outside the infinite text."[14]

[12] Schostak, "[Ad]dressing Methodologies."
[13] Schostak cites Kristeva, who writes: "since this term [intertextuality] has often been understood in the banal sense of 'study of sources,' we prefer the term transposition because it specifies the passage from one signifying system to another." Julia Kristeva, *Revolution in Poetic Language*, trans. Margaret Waller (New York: Columbia University Press, 1984), 59–60.
[14] Schostak, "[Ad]dressing Methodologies," vol. 2, addendum; Barthes, *The Pleasure of the Text*, trans. Richard Miller (New York: Hill and Wang, 1976), 36.

CHAPTER 15

The Symphony, 1870–1911

David Larkin

"A gentle feeling of melancholy creeps over me, when, knowing completely and intimately the greatness of Beethoven and being penetrated by the profound meaning of his creations, I recall that there have been and still are many composers, who, after him, have undertaken to write symphonies."[1] Beethoven had been dead for over seventy years when Felix Weingartner penned these lines, and many distinguished composers had produced symphonies in the interim. Nonetheless, it was Beethoven's shadow that still loomed largest over the genre. Carl Dahlhaus has argued that the development of the symphony through the nineteenth century was "circumpolar," with each new composer primarily responding to Beethoven's exemplars rather than to the works of intervening symphonists.[2]

Although Weingartner thought Beethoven the unapproachable pinnacle of symphonic composition, he and many of his contemporaries continued to wrestle with the possibilities offered by the multimovement orchestral format. The sheer variety of works entitled "symphony" that were written in the decades leading up to the First World War is evidence of the diversity of ways in which this challenge could be met. In a much-reported 1907 conversation, Mahler and Sibelius, experienced symphonists both, put forward contrasting ideas as to what constituted the essence of the genre: the Finnish master "admired its style and severity of form, and the profound logic that created an inner connection between all the motives," whereas for Mahler "the symphony must be like the whole world. It must be all-embracing."[3] These two imperatives – formal stringency and an integrative breadth of vision – are not

---

[1] Felix Weingartner, *Die Symphonie nach Beethoven*, 2nd rev. ed. (Leipzig: Breitkopf u. Härtel, 1901; first published 1898), 1–2; alternative translation given in Felix Weingartner, *The Symphony Writers since Beethoven*, trans. Arthur Bles (Westport, CT: Greenwood Press, 1971), 2.

[2] Carl Dahlhaus, *Nineteenth-Century Music*, trans. J. Bradford Robinson (Berkeley: University of California Press, 1989), 152.

[3] Erik Tawaststjerna, *Sibelius, vol. 2: 1904–1914*, trans. Robert Layton (London: Faber and Faber, 1986), 77.

necessarily antithetical, of course; indeed, in different admixtures they can be found in many symphonies from this period.

The era of symphonic composition covered by this brief survey has famously been dubbed the "Second Age of the Symphony" by Dahlhaus. According to his interpretation, after Schumann's Third (1850) there was a "dead period" in which virtually no first-rate nonprogrammatic symphonies were written before the revival in the 1870s. During these intervening decades, the program symphony and especially the Lisztian symphonic poem, both of which could also claim an ancestry in Beethoven's symphonic output, offered progressive alternatives. David Brodbeck has recently challenged this notion of a dead period, noting that there were approximately 500 new orchestral compositions produced in the third quarter of the century, including a slew of symphonies dismissed by Dahlhaus as they deliberately avoided Beethovenian monumentality in favor of a post-Schubertian lyricism. These works satisfied market demands for new products, but aimed to be accessible rather than trying to match and surpass earlier masterpieces.[4] Symphonies of this sort continued to be written after 1870, but virtually none of this music is performed regularly today. Nonetheless, even if our aesthetic preferences have evolved or been shaped institutionally to prefer symphonies that are more epic and ambitious, it is worth being reminded that those works that have survived to become repertory staples are not fully representative of what was produced at the time under the title "symphony."

Building on Dahlhaus's work, James Hepokoski has usefully divided the Second Age into two "generational waves," the first consisting of works by those who were born between 1820 and 1845, including Bruckner, Brahms, Bruch, Borodin, Tchaikovsky, Dvořák, Franck, and Saint-Saëns. Succeeding these came the likes of Elgar, Mahler, Strauss, Sibelius, Nielsen, and Glazunov, all of whom were born around 1854–65 and who are regarded as late romantics or early modernists.[5] The first-wave composers wrote their symphonies against the backdrop of the increasing dominance of the canon of past works in concert programs. As a consequence, some composers, especially those based in Vienna, signaled their awareness of the history of the genre through stylistic allusions to works of the past, providing an orientation point for the cultivated listener. The

[4] David Brodbeck, "The Symphony after Beethoven after Dahlhaus," in *The Cambridge Companion to the Symphony*, ed. Julian Horton (Cambridge: Cambridge University Press, 2013), 73, 81.

[5] James Hepokoski, "Beethoven Reception: The Symphonic Tradition," in *The Cambridge History of Nineteenth-Century Music*, ed. Jim Samson (Cambridge: Cambridge University Press, 2002), 455–56.

modernists who followed had an even larger body of works to contend with; this, together with the increasing precariousness of the tonal language, led them to innovate and challenge some of the foundations of the genre.

1870–1889

Probably the most important and hotly awaited symphonic debut of the age came in 1876, when the First Symphony of the forty-three-year-old Brahms had its premiere. Brahms had made several abortive attempts at symphonic composition earlier in his career, and the fourteen-year gestation of the First bears out his contention that "one cannot 'fool around' these days with a symphony." That the First was launched in the same year as Wagner's *Ring* cycle is an irony of history. Wagner's much-publicized opinion was that Beethoven's Ninth marked the end of the symphony proper, with the incorporation of voices into the final movement proleptically pointing the way to music drama. By means of his overt engagement with the Beethovenian struggle-to-victory paradigm across the symphony as a whole and an unmissable nod to the "Ode to Joy" theme in the finale, Brahms offered a practical refutation of Wagner's thesis. To his supporters, the message was clear: the purely musical (i.e., nonprogrammatic and voiceless) symphony was still viable. While retaining the epic scale and dramatic character appropriate to this most public of genres, Brahms infused it with a sophisticated handling of motif hitherto more the province of chamber music. The disapproving Wagner described the result as "little chips of melody, like an infusion of hay and old tea-leaves."

Brahms was not the first to find in Beethoven's Ninth a font of symphonic inspiration. His antipode, Anton Bruckner, had by this point completed his first five numbered symphonies, although all of them were later revised. His obsession with Beethoven's final symphony can be seen in virtually all his symphonic openings, where fragmentary initial presentation of motifs backed by tremolo textures gradually coalesce and grow into thunderous tutti statements of the assembled themes. Another vital influence on Bruckner was Wagner, the dedicatee of the Third Symphony, whose advanced harmonic idiom and ways of sequencing motifs were adopted by Bruckner. This importation of Wagnerian resources into the hallowed genre of the symphony aroused the ire of Vienna's most prominent critic, Eduard Hanslick, a committed Brahms devotee. Thereafter, Bruckner's works became a political battleground, with supporters hailing

Example 15.1a   Brahms, Symphony no. 2, IV, mm. 234–41.

Example 15.1b   Mahler, Symphony no. 1, I, mm. 7–9.

his epic monumentality and aligning it with nationalist agendas, while detractors found his symphonies overblown and naive.

As a keen Wagnerian, one might imagine that Mahler would be drawn more to Bruckner than to Brahms, especially since he described the latter as a "die-hard member of the old school." Nonetheless, despite attending Bruckner's lectures and transcribing the Third Symphony for piano duet after attending its disastrous 1877 premiere, Mahler later confessed that he found Brahms's compactness and mastery of form "indisputably" greater than the "fragmentary character" of Bruckner's symphonies, despite the magnificence and inventiveness of the latter. It is surely no accident that the descending fourths idea that dominates the opening of Mahler's First is anticipated in a similarly mysterious passage in the finale of an earlier D major symphony, Brahms's Second (see Example 15.1). However, nods to Bruckner in Mahler's output are also plentiful: for instance, the tramping figure at the outset of Bruckner's First turns up in a more brutal guise at the start of Mahler's martial Sixth.

Despite their differences, both Brahms and Bruckner adhered to the normative four-movement structure that had been codified in the late eighteenth century. Furthermore, both publicly presented their works as absolute music, although the presence of the once-texted Alphorn melody in the finale of Brahms's First and the programmatic cues Bruckner privately communicated about his Fourth indicate a more complex reality. There is nothing in the oeuvre of either that provides a structural precedent for *Titan*, the five-movement symphonic poem in two parts that was the initial version of Mahler's First, although he later cut the central movement and withdrew the program. Purely in the matter of externals, a closer parallel can be found in the Vienna-based Karl Goldmark's 1876 Symphony no. 1, "Rustic Wedding," which has programmatic titles for each of its five movements, while Berlioz's *Symphonie fantastique* and Beethoven's *Pastoral* Symphony constitute influential earlier exemplars.

Another major symphonist working within the greater Austrian Empire was the Czech Antonín Dvořák. Compositionally as well as politically, he found himself between two cultures: his musical style is firmly grounded in mainstream Germanic precedents but flavored with elements of Czech music as, for instance, in the choice of a "Furiant" for the third movement of the Seventh. Richard Taruskin has noted that these "ethnic" elements contributed to Dvořák's initial fame and also his eventual marginalization in comparison with native Germanic symphonists such as Brahms: "Without the native costume, a 'peripheral' composer would never achieve even secondary canonical rank, but with it he could never achieve more."[6]

The fructifying effects of vernacular music traditions are also evident in Dvořák's best-known Symphony, the Ninth, "From the New World," where he claimed he drew on aspects of African American and Native American musical styles. The first movement of the Eighth exemplifies another important aspect of Dvořák's approach to symphonic writing: his lyricism. In this case, the sheer quantity of material challenges the structural control usually exerted by sonata form. Robert Layton has compared this movement to "a great novel, where the large cast of characters evolve and develop . . ., the author acting as a helpless observer of their personal dramas," an observation that echoes Adorno's remarks about Mahler's novel-symphonies overturning the classical "precedence of the whole over the parts."[7] Dvořák's turn in the 1890s to highly detailed narrative symphonic poems based on Czech poetic ballads was prefigured in the concert overtures he produced earlier in his career alongside his abstract symphonies.

---

[6] Richard Taruskin, "Nationalism §11: Colonialist Nationalism," in *Grove Music Online*, https://doi .org/10.1093/gmo/9781561592630.article.50846, accessed February 26, 2019.
[7] Robert Layton, *Dvořák's Symphonies and Concertos* (London: British Broadcasting Corporation, 1978), 44; Theodor W. Adorno, *Mahler: A Musical Physiognomy*, trans. Edmund Jephcott (Chicago: University of Chicago Press, 1992), 72.

Beyond the Austro-Germanic scene the symphony was taken up with particular relish by Russian and French composers. Where Germanic composers of this generation tended to cultivate either the absolute symphony or the symphonic poem, the likes of Tchaikovsky, Franck, and Saint-Saëns resemble Dvořák in composing freely in both genres without caring that they were straddling what was once a significant musico-political divide. The boundaries between absolute and programmatic symphonism are particularly permeable in the case of a work such as Tchaikovsky's Fourth. Unlike his *Manfred* Symphony, which was openly based on Byron's poem, Tchaikovsky published the Fourth as absolute music; however, the private explanatory program for the Fourth that he sent to his patroness, a detailed story of the workings of "fate" in the life of a protagonist, is surely too well tailored to the narrative course of the music to have been invented after the fact.

In two further ways Tchaikovsky's numbered symphonies are comparable to those of Dvořák: his use of native Russian material and his all-pervasive melodicism. The Second employs folk song in three of the four movements, with the tunes themselves subjected to variation procedures following the lead established by Glinka, Balakirev, and other Russian nationalist composers. In contrast to Brahms, whose music he detested, Tchaikovsky more typically adopts as his symphonic materials melodies that can be deconstructed, rather than building an assemblage of tiny cells into a theme as Brahms does (e.g., the latter's Fourth Symphony begins with a simple descending third, which is then catenated into a theme through inversion and sequence). As a result, lyricism in Tchaikovsky is not confined to what are traditionally the more tuneful parts of sonata form, such as secondary themes. Nonetheless, these remain moments of particular warmth and memorability, as in the case of the hyperromantic second theme in the opening movement of the *Pathétique* (Sixth) Symphony.

A common concern for many of those writing symphonies in this period was how best to create the sense of an organic whole across the separate movements. Saint-Saëns ostensibly divides his Third Symphony into just two parts, but within each of these is a linked pair of traditional movements (Allegro moderato – Poco Adagio; Scherzo – Allegro), the first and fourth movements preceded by slower introductions. Along with physically joining movements together with linking passages, Saint-Saëns also makes extensive use of thematic recycling, bringing back ideas from movement to movement and recasting them in new guises. These procedures are akin to Berlioz's handling of the idée fixe in the *Symphonie*

Example 15.2   Saint-Saëns, Symphony no. 3 (a) I, mm. 12–13; (b) II, mm. 384–85.

Example 15.3   Franck, Symphony in D Minor, II, mm. 201–4.

fantastique, or Liszt's thematic transformations. Example 15.2 shows the nervous minor-mode idea near the start of the first movement transformed into the triumphant major-mode tutti theme in the finale.

Cyclical thematic procedures are also employed in Franck's Symphony in D Minor, a work in three rather than the normal four movements. The Allegretto second movement here is a novel fusion of the slow movement and scherzo that typically occupy the center of the symphony. The opening Allegretto theme gives way in the middle to a more fleeting scherzo-like section; when the Allegretto music returns, the scherzo figuration is retained as a new backdrop (see Example 15.3). Within the Finale, the Allegretto passage returns again, as do a series of themes from the first movement. Although there are precedents for such summative intermovement thematic citation in Liszt's similarly three-movement *Faust* Symphony, Franck utilizes these cyclical devices without programmatic purposes.

1889–1914

The year 1889 has been a convenient dividing line in music histories and is particularly appropriate here in that Mahler's First had its premiere in this year. The emphasis so far has been on the ineluctably "historical" nature of symphonic composition: the notion that a creator was necessarily in a conscious dialogue with tradition by deciding to write a symphony. This imperative to establish a relationship with the past remained live for the "second wave" composers, but it was tempered by a newfound feeling of being in a transitional age, with all the exciting and potentially disorienting possibilities this opened up. Dahlhaus drew attention to the "breakaway spirit" of Mahler's First and Strauss's tone poem *Don Juan* (also launched in 1889), neither of which shows any signs of being trammeled by traditional symphonic practices, whether in the matter of structure, orchestration, harmonic language, or programmatic purpose.

Although Strauss had written two early symphonies in a conventional mold, his decision to focus on single-movement tone poems after 1886 represented a change of heart. Convinced by Wagner's theories, he had come to view the symphony proper as passé and also rejected inherited structural norms in favor of shaping his music to suit the poetic idea that inspired it. Like so many others, he claimed to have a Beethovenian imprimatur for his innovations, pointing to late works where one-off structures were devised to match equally novel ideas. Within the arena of orchestral composition he also acknowledged Liszt's programmatic symphonic poems as important precedents, summed up in the Lisztian slogan he adopted: "New ideas must search for new forms."

After seven tone poems, Strauss then returned to a nomenclature that more explicitly positioned his works as successors to the symphony with the *Symphonia domestica* (1904) and *Eine Alpensinfonie* (1915). Nominally single-movement works, they last ca. 45–50 minutes in performance, and thus are comparable in dimensions to many multimovement symphonies of the era. Of the two, *Domestica* is the more clearly in dialogue with symphonic norms: one can easily parse the ostensibly unbroken structure into four or five large sub-movements. Nonetheless, the explicit representational content of these works – respectively, a day in the life of Strauss's family and a day walking in Alpine scenery – align them firmly with Strauss's earlier tone poems. As a body, Strauss's programmatic orchestral works have been interpreted as a desacralizing challenge to the symphony thanks to their deliberately antimetaphysical focus.

Other composers of this generation who produced both programmatic works and symphonies – Elgar and Sibelius jump to mind – were less keen to fuse them together. Elgar, praised by the slightly younger Strauss as the first English progressive and who returned the admiration, produced a series of overtures and symphonic poems, but his First Symphony (1908), written when he was in his early fifties, is a work of absolute music. The opening A-flat major march exudes a nobility and assurance that is radically undercut by the chromatic D-minor theme that initiates the exposition proper. One could easily identify the former element with tradition and the latter with the music of modernity, and interpret the first movement and indeed the symphony as a whole as exploring the tension between these two forces, with the triumphant return of the march at the end of the Finale as a victory achieved in the teeth of nearly overwhelming opposition. The Second more openly invites metaphorical interpretation thanks to the lines from Shelley that preface the score, and it has been described as "nothing less than the *summa* of the modern institutional symphony."[8]

Perhaps the most significant counterpart to Mahler around the turn of century was Sibelius, who had produced four absolute symphonies by 1911 and another three after this. He had been composing programmatic orchestral works for almost a decade before his First had its premiere in 1899, and even after this date he continued to write works based on Finnish *Kalevala* legends. These nationalist leanings were also read into the apparently abstract Second Symphony, which was linked to Finland's aspirations for political autonomy. More important in the composer's eyes was the "wonderful logic (let us call it God) that governs a work of art," although the many thematic interconnections across each work were on his own testimony not always part of the conscious design and could only be recognized after the symphony's completion. This penchant for integration saw him join movements together, such as the swelling link from the Vivacissimo third movement into the Finale in the Second Symphony, or the more radical combination of Scherzo and Finale in the last part of the three-movement Third Symphony.

Most adventurous in terms of its musical language surely is the Fourth, written in the shadow of a cancer diagnosis in 1910–11. The opening four note idea C–D–F#–E can be seen as a subset of the whole-tone scale, with the F-sharp and E deployed as a tolling figure underneath the melancholy A-minor cello theme. Toward the end of the first movement, A major is established but never securely, and the whole-tone idea returns in distorted form as an acid coda. The Finale begins in A major with a folk-influenced raised fourth, but again it cannot hold, and the downbeat ending in A minor can be seen as a metaphor for the parlous state of the genre as a whole. Even though Sibelius would write three more symphonies, the heyday of the genre was past. In the second decade of the twentieth century, the symphony went into an eclipse along with the language of tonality that had sustained it.

---

[8] James Hepokoski, "Elgar," in *The Nineteenth-Century Symphony*, ed. D. Kern Holoman (New York: Schirmer, 1997), 340.

CHAPTER 16

Mahler and the Visual Arts of His Time

Martina Pippal

Translated by Juliane Schicker

.

A Difficult Relationship?

Gustav Mahler's indifference toward the visual arts and architecture is well documented. Friedrich Löhr reported that his friend purposefully avoided museums in Florence and Paris, and Alma Mahler-Werfel called the villa commissioned by Mahler in 1900–1 on the Wörthersee "hideous" (*scheußlich*), that is, awkwardly historicist (Figure 16.1).[1]

Alma, of course, had the benefit of an informed background. Daughter of renowned landscape artist Emil Jakob Schindler, she became in 1895 (at the age of sixteen) the stepdaughter of the affluent art dealer and artist Carl Moll, a founding member of the Vienna Secession and its president in 1901. At the Schindler–Molls' Jugendstil villa atop the Hohe Warte (Josef Hoffmann, 1901), she encountered other members of the Secession, including Gustav Klimt, Josef Hoffmann, Joseph Maria Olbrich, Kolo (Koloman) Moser, and Alfred Roller. It was in this milieu, in the fall of 1901 at the salon of the Jewish journalist Berta Zuckerkandl, that the twenty-two-year-old aspiring composer met the forty-one-year-old director of the Vienna Court Opera.

Mahler's cultural socialization, by contrast, began in earnest when at fifteen he arrived at the Conservatory in the still-liberal Vienna of Mayor Cajetan Felder. Immediately, he confronted examples of the historicism that dominated the city at that time: the late-Romantic Court Opera on the Ringstraße; the Hellenized Musikverein on Karlsplatz, housing the Conservatory where Mahler received musical instruction; and the so-called Kaiserforum (Imperial Forum), subject of a dispute that would teach the young musician the interdependence of culture and politics.

---

[1] *SLGM*, 405, n. 88/*GMB2*, 439, n. 61; Kurt Blaukopf, "Mahler und die Secession," in *Beiträge '79–81. Gustav Mahler Kolloquium 1979. Ein Bericht* (Kassel: Bärenreiter, 1981), 7–15; Alma Mahler, *Gustav Mahler: Erinnerungen und Briefe* (Amsterdam: Allert de Lange, 1940), 196.

Figure 16.1   Mahler's villa on the Wörthersee, Maiernigg, Austria. Friedrich Theuer, 1900–1901. Postcard, Alma Mahler to Arnold Schoenberg, with greeting from Gustav Mahler, August 23, 1902. Mahler's annotation, "two hands," may indicate that he is the rower pictured in the foreground.
Arnold Schoenberg Collection, Music Division, Library of Congress

Begun in 1871, the Forum would encompass a *cour d'honneur* (royal courtyard) reminiscent of the Palace of Versailles, spanning the length of the Imperial Palace from the royal stables to the ceremony hall. Gottfried Semper had sketched it in 1869, using a style of functional purism based on the Italian Renaissance. Carl Hasenauer, however, a colleague thirty years Semper's junior, gained the upper hand with plans that reflected the Imperial family's perspective: the Baroque as the glorious high point of their history, with the complex's two court museums as monuments to Habsburg taste and grandeur. Hasenauer championed architecture's narrative potential; in the sense of Wagner's Gesamtkunstwerk, painting and sculpture would subordinate themselves to architecture, with all media oriented toward Baroque style. The conflict peaked in 1871, with Semper leaving Vienna and Hasenauer helping to establish luxurious neo-Baroque late historicism across the city.[2]

[2] See Werner Telesko, Richard Kurdiovsky, Dagmar Sachsenhofer et al., eds., *Die Wiener Hofburg 1835–1918: Der Ausbau der Residenz vom Vormärz bis zum Ende des "Kaiserforums"* (Vienna: Österreichische Akademie der Wissenschaften, 2012).

Figure 16.2   Hans Makart, *Moderne Amoretten* (*Modern Cupids*, 1868).
Photograph by Johannes Stoll. Courtesy of Creative Commons Attribution-Share Alike 4.0
International license, https://creativecommons.org/licenses/by-sa/4.0/legalcode. Original image
is in color

With its top-down sociopolitical relations, the epoch of historicism involved an omnipresent desire for social advancement. Social success required not just establishing oneself financially but participating in symbolic capital and adopting the aesthetic standards of the next highest class, all the way up to the imperial family. By this means historicism spread throughout Vienna, across social strata (including tenements) and geographically to the outer regions of the monarchy. Mahler's rise would take account of such considerations, requiring, for Jews and Gentiles alike, conformity to the taste of the Christian majority population.

The Salzburg-born and Munich-trained painter Hans Makart embodies this mode of social advancement in the era of Mahler's Vienna apprenticeship. In *Moderne Amoretten* (*Modern Cupids* [1868], Figure 16.2), Makart liberated form from content by means of free composition. In large formats, he melded the Italian Renaissance with Rubens and Orientalist paintings.

Styling himself as the "prince of painters," Makart made his studio, acquired in 1869 with his professorship at the Viennese Academy, a "royal court" complete with curtains and Gobelin tapestries, carpets and bearskins, furniture, paintings, instruments, weapons, and exotic plants – a veritable Gesamtkunstwerk fit for staging legendary celebrations (Figure 16.3).

Figure 16.3   The studio of Hans Makart, ca. 1875.
Photograph by Josef Löwy

Prominent guests (Richard Wagner, Arnold Böcklin, Franz Liszt) were widely discussed, guests' costumes dictated fashion trends, and across the board Makart's studio influenced the style of living in the *Gründerzeit* (period of promoterism; literally, "founders' period"). The artist's influence culminated in the Makart-Zug, a festive procession he designed and choreographed for the celebration of the twenty-fifth wedding anniversary of Franz Joseph I and Elisabeth in 1879.

Having passed the *Abitur* in Iglau in 1877, Mahler took courses at the University of Vienna – in musicology, archeology, history, and art history – to complement his piano and composition studies. Though his Jewish ancestry and lack of financial means hindered his upward mobility, his musical talent and broad education would serve as tickets into elite society.

Wanderjahre (Journeyman's Travels)

Remarkably, the opera conductor Mahler, who held positions in eight different cities from 1880 until his return to Vienna in 1897, avoided the genre of opera as a composer. Makart too had longed for the precedence of form over content, and one senses a late historicist impulse in Mahler's attraction to the monumental: his First Symphony (*Titan*) included five movements in its early guise; the Second retained that scheme; and the Third Symphony grew to six movements (reduced from a projected seven!). Moreover, Mahler augmented the orchestra and integrated the human voice (soprano and alto soloists with mixed choir in the Second; alto soloist with women's and boys' choirs in the Third), finding a musical analogue for the monumentality of Viennese neo-Baroque architecture. Likewise, insofar as Mahler's music drew on a Gesamtkunstwerk aesthetic, it expressed a kinship with tendencies in architecture and the visual arts to encompass various media: painting, sculpture, and the applied arts. The repertoire of sounds – that is, materials – expanded, broadening the expressive spectrum as well as the narrative possibilities. For Mahler and for his artistic compatriots, the exuberance of Wagner's Gesamtkunstwerk meant unconstrained complexity.

In the grand themes of these early works, however – the meaning of life, the longing for death, the mystery of resurrection – Mahler already situated himself at the intersection of historicism and Symbolism. With titles and subjects overtly drawing on literary sources, and an awareness of the "false paths" (*falsche Wege*) that these might open for listeners, Mahler approached the Symbolist predilection for a suggestiveness that leaves room for subjectivity, including one's own memories and dreams.[3] "Landscapes" grounded in a mood of late Romantic mysticism become the site of creative individuation, manifesting itself aurally.

Mahler also shows flashes of the bizarre and grotesque, for example, in "St. Anthony of Padua's Sermon to the Fishes" (1893). Closely confronting the audience with an event held for centuries as holy, as requiring a respectful distance, Mahler echoed the Symbolist works of Swiss painter Arnold Böcklin. Böcklin's gods and their offspring, with their realistic human bodies and animalistic desires, breach that distance; naturalism becomes an unsuitable means of rendering the sublime. In fact, Böcklin painted Antonius's Sermon with the same irony in 1892 (Figure 16.4), and Mahler would cite him in 1900 as his model for capturing nature.[4]

Mahler anticipated the visual media of his time by using "lower" materials (Ländler [an easygoing Austria version of a waltz], klezmer) in his First Symphony. Only around 1900 were folk-art motifs integrated into nationalist Jugendstil architecture, for example, in Hungary and Scandinavia; the *Heimatstil* (regional style) in Alpine villa architecture –

---

[3] Mahler to Friedrich Löhr, n.d. [spring 1895]. *SLGM*, 161/*GMB2*, 147.

[4] Herbert Killian, *Gustav Mahler in den Erinnerungen von Natalie Bauer-Lechner*, rev. ed., annotated by Knud Martner (Hamburg: Karl Dieter Wagner, 1984), 182.

Figure 16.4   Arnold Boecklin, *Der heilige Antonius* (*St. Anthony*, 1892).

including the Mahler villa at Maiernigg – represents a similar phenomenon. But in Mahler's case, the tendency also has sources in decadence and socialism. Joris-Karl Huysmans's use of various dialects and technical terms from manual professions is at once naturalist and socialist, the latter an interest of Mahler's since his acquaintance with Victor Adler in 1879.[5]

Return to Vienna: Competing Currents

When Mahler returned to Vienna in 1897, the city still reveled in the neo-Baroque, Albert Ilg having declared it in 1880 the Austrian national

---

[5] Christian Glanz, "Gustav Mahlers politisches Umfeld," in *Mahler im Kontext/Contextualizing Mahler*, ed. Erich Wolfgang Partsch and Morten Solvik (Vienna: Böhlau, 2011), 13–31, esp. 20–31.

style.[6] The previously unfinished "Michael" wing of the Hofburg (Imperial Palace) was completed between 1889 and 1898, on Joseph Emanuel Fischer von Erlach's plans from the 1720s. In 1894–95, Rudolf Weyr created the hyper-Bernini-esque figures for the wall fountain "Die Macht zur See" (Power at Sea).

Other styles, however, began to make headway. Symbolism arrived in Vienna in 1895 with Karl Wilhelm Diefenbach, Rudolf Jettmar, and Adolf Hirémy-Hirschl. And although an appointment of the Leipzig Symbolist Max Klinger as professor at the Academy of Fine Arts fell through in 1896, the architect Otto Wagner published in the same year his theoretical treatise *Modern Architecture*, conceptualizing architecture derived from its function. Wagner associated himself with Semper but oriented himself toward Roman antiquity. As professor and leader of the architecture track at the Academy of Fine Arts (from 1894) and creator of a visionary general regulation plan for Vienna (1893) as well as complex infrastructure projects (suburban railway, 1898–99; city railway, 1892–1901), Wagner allowed function, form, and material to intertwine. Together these artists broke ground with a new aesthetics affirming modern life.

In 1897, the year of Mahler's return to Vienna, a group of mainly younger artists left the historicism-based Künstlerhaus (Society of Fine Arts; literally, house of artists) and founded the Vienna Secession. The city government of Vienna provided a building site for the group, and by 1898 the exhibition building designed by Joseph Maria Olbrich was completed, with financial support from the industrialist Karl Wittgenstein (father of Ludwig Wittgenstein). The nineteen members of the group, led by president Gustav Klimt, rejected the concept of historicism but did not replace it with a uniform style. Klimt was then drafting three Symbolist ceiling paintings for the new university building on the Ring; Josef Hoffmann, by contrast, initially adopted French-Belgian Art Nouveau before leaving his geometric-ornamental mark (adapted from the Glasgow School) on the Viennese Jugendstil. The group achieved public attention through its magazine *Ver Sacrum* and frequent exhibition activity.

At the Court Opera, Mahler proceeded just as radically as the Secessionists, setting upon the institution like a "natural disaster": "An earthquake of tremendous intensity and duration jolted the whole building from the gable to the foundation. Everything old, outdated, or not

---

[6] Friedrich Polleroß, ed., *Fischer von Erlach und die Wiener Barocktradition* (Vienna: Böhlau, 1995).

thoroughly viable had to give way."[7] In this same period, however, Mahler planned his Maiernigg villa with the taste of a moderate, indeed, conventional owner. Designed by his neighbor at Wörthersee, the Viennese architect Friedrich Theuer, the building was symmetrical and faced the sunless north, with a stonewalled veranda and wooden balcony. The prominent half-hip roof, a hybrid of a late Romantic small castle and a *Heimatstil* hunting house, matched the popular villa architecture of the time, assimilated with prevailing social taste.

In those years, Alma Schindler's heart also beat with a late Romantic pulse. Disregarding her surroundings, she composed songs in the spirit of Richard Wagner – consecration gifts for the departed father whom she had loved above all else. When she met Alexander Zemlinsky in 1900, she chose him as composition teacher – and lover, until leaving him in 1902 for Mahler, who promptly ended her creative work, though not for stylistic reasons.

Mahler and the Secession

On April 14, 1902, Mahler collaborated with the Secession artists for the first time, contributing the music for a private preview of the Beethoven Exhibition – the Fourteenth Secession Exhibition, dedicated to Max Klinger.[8] Klinger's monumental sculpture of Beethoven commanded the central room; for the left side room, Klimt had painted the Beethoven Frieze and Hoffmann had designed proto-abstract overdoors.[9] While Klimt had maintained the Symbolist style in content, he used all formal means to prevent the misreading of his images – the path of humankind (and especially the artist) from suffering to the fulfillment of the desire for happiness – as the reproduction of an event. He reduced the corporeality of the figures and emptied the space between them. But these open spaces are substantive, placing tension and serenity in equilibrium, while the beauty of the line and the decorative moment dominate. The forms are *figures*, not the fate-laden individuals depicted by naturalists; their gestures are not the expressive means of subjective feelings but referential signs,

---

[7] Franz Schmidt, composer, member of the Vienna Philharmonic (1896–1911), until 1914 solo cellist in the Court Opera Orchestra. www.wien.info/media/files/mahler-spaziergang.pdf, accessed September 10, 2018.

[8] The actual opening took place on the following day, April 15.

[9] See Marian Bisanz-Prakken, *Gustav Klimt. Der Beethovenfries. Geschichte, Funktion und Bedeutung* (Salzburg: Residenz, 1977); Dieter Bogner, "Musik und bildende Kunst in Wien. Konsonanz – Dissonanz – Nomos," in *Vom Klang der Bilder* (Munich: Prestel, 1985), 346–48.

synchronized like the movements of dancers. The piece expresses collective sensation, rather than the rigid synchronization of a movement as in classical ballet. Klimt's pigments are bright, rejecting the characteristic darkness of Symbolism for all the figures except a menacing beast.

For this pre-opening, Mahler had arranged excerpts from the Finale of Beethoven's Ninth Symphony for brass instruments – a rare case of small forces in his output. Instrumentalists placed away from the podium turned the entire hall into a sound *space*, serving the themes of separation, loneliness, and longing for death, and echoing the visual language of Klimt's frieze. Julius Korngold would compare the two artists in 1907, reviewing a performance of Mahler's Sixth Symphony and finding remarkably that Klimt lacked "the pathos," "the driving energy," and "that which excruciatingly churns the nerves."[10]

In fact, Klimt was opposed to precisely these expressive demands. In his Attersee paintings, a calm, square format supports works that are first and foremost paintings; the sun entangles itself in the mesh of brushstrokes – "frames full of seawater," for the art critic Ludwig Hevesi. Likewise, in Klimt's portraits of women, the face serves as an idealistic mask, the body a silhouette freed from corporeality, and both are absorbed by the painting's bright surface, abstract and thus ideal for interior design. The well-to-do emancipated Jewish individuals who commissioned this ambience (such as Fritz Waerndorfer) received a modern stage for a lifestyle freed from constraints, liberated from both late historicism and the assimilationist aesthetic of their parents and grandparents. In the period when the casual "reform dress" was offered to women to cast off the corset and Parisian fabrics, Berta Zuckerkandl trumpeted the Secession's contributions to securing Jewish patrons their place in the overall social structure.[11]

Why did Mahler spurn the Secessionists' style in his own personal living space? He may simply have been uninterested or perhaps aware of the accusation (from Karl Kraus and others) that a "*jüdischer Geschmack*" (Jewish taste) attached to the Secession style around Klimt.[12] German nationalism and anti-Semitism were on the rise as liberal politics lost

---

[10] *ML*, 36–37; *Die Musik* 6 (1907): 327; Ute Jung-Kaiser, "Gustav Klimts verschlüsseltes Mahler-Bildnis," *Archiv für Musikwissenschaft* 4, no. 3 (1998): 252–62, esp. 253.

[11] www.klimt-am-attersee.at/, accessed October 4, 2018; Elana Shapira, "Modernism and Jewish Identity in Early Twentieth-Century Vienna: Fritz Waerndorfer and His House for an Art Lover," *Decorative Arts* 13, no. 2 (2006): 52–92; Shapira, *Style and Seduction. Jewish Patrons, Architecture, and Design in Fin de Siècle Vienna* (Waltham, MA: Brandeis University Press, 2016), 58–60.

[12] Shapira, *Style and Seduction*, 58–60.

influence in Europe. But Mahler was bolder in his own profession. He stood by Arnold Schoenberg when riots broke out in 1902 at the premiere of *Verklärte Nacht*; Mahler supported the musical avant-garde publicly even when it was aesthetically foreign to him. And on the twentieth anniversary of Richard Wagner's death, Mahler invited the Secession's current president Alfred Roller to stage a new *Tristan* in the Royal Court Opera (see Chapter 9).

"Moneymental Style"

In 1909, Carl Moll commissioned Auguste Rodin to create a bust for Mahler's fiftieth birthday. That milestone would be marked as well by Mahler's greatest triumph as a composer: the Munich performance in September 1910 of his Eighth Symphony, under his direction and involving more than a thousand performers, including a huge orchestra, organ, eight female and male vocal soloists, two large mixed choirs, and a boys' choir. Though the colossal work might have seemed anachronistic when compared with the works of his contemporaries in visual arts – the newest generation of Viennese painters, including Richard Gerstl, Egon Schiele, and Oskar Kokoschka – impressions can be misleading. Late historicism in fact had a resurgence in architecture and the fine arts around the year 1910, most visibly at the Imperial and Royal Ministry of War on the Vienna Stubenring. At the 1907 design competition, forward-looking solutions like a skyscraper (Robert Orley and Franz Safonith), a functional building without inscriptions or emblems (Adolf Loos), and a design by Otto Wagner were rejected in favor of the gigantic neo-Baroque conglomerate of castle, military barrack, and administrative building designed by Ludwig Baumann, *Burgbauarchitekt* (leading architect in charge of the Vienna Imperial Palace) and the favorite of imperial heir Franz Ferdinand. It was not constructed until 1909–13.[13]

Monumentality was in the air, then, as Mahler underwent the "Pentecostal experience" of creating his Eighth Symphony, a hymn that burst all boundaries.[14] And this resonance with a resurgent historicism confirms the limitations of reading Mahler's music as part of contemporary artistic developments, such as Jugendstil. True, Mahler and the original

[13] Rudolf Kolowrath, *Ludwig Baumann. Architektur zwischen Barock und Jugendstil* (Vienna: Compress, 1985), 73–75.
[14] Jens Malte Fischer, *Gustav Mahler*, trans. Stewart Spencer (New Haven: Yale University Press, 2011), 526. "Moneymental style" is a neologism coined by the Viennese cultural philosopher Herbert Lachmayer.

Secessionists jointly pursued the ideal of Wagner's Gesamtkunstwerk, and along with it a certain radicality. And Mahler saw the value of Alfred Roller as a theatrical innovator. As a private owner, however, and in important creative respects, Mahler remained conservative. Predictably, he followed an independent and peculiarly Viennese avant-garde path, reaching out to modernist developments, to be sure, and appropriating "low" materials in a way that has no parallel in the contemporaneous fine arts of Vienna.

CHAPTER 17

Mahler and Modernism

Marilyn L. McCoy

Does one really need such a huge apparatus as the orchestra to express a great thought?[1]

When Gisela Tolnay-Witt, a plucky young girl from Budapest, posed this question to Gustav Mahler in a letter written around 1893, she must have hit a nerve. Gisela's original letter does not survive, but her query, quoted verbatim, was immortalized in the lengthy epistle the composer sent in reply. Assuming a pedantic tone at first, Mahler begins a long disquisition about the history of performance, performance indications, and musical expression. Bit by bit, as his chronological account approaches his own time, and his enthusiasm grows, one cannot help but note the importance of words like "new" and "modern" to his narrative of the music of his own present. Moreover, the composer consistently reaffirms that musical innovation is inextricably linked with inspiration from the past. With the adoption of "new elements of feeling" that could be portrayed in tones, the "new era of music" began with Beethoven; the "modern 'Wagnerian' orchestra" as well as that of "the 'New Ones' (die Neuer)" (i.e., present-day composers) grew from composers' search for one color per instrument. Then, at last, a declaration of membership: "We modernists (wir Modernen) need such a large [orchestral] apparatus in order to express our thoughts, be they grand or modest." Though Mahler usually balked at declaring himself a modernist composer, here he definitively aligns himself with the Austro-German early modernist cohort, who consciously sought out uncharted musical territory between 1890 and 1910.

Following the thread of the composer's own logic as demonstrated in the above letter, it is clear that as much as Mahler revered the musical past and tried to keep abreast of the trends of the musical present, he wanted to

---

[1] Quoted by Mahler in a reply to Gisela Tolnay-Witt, February 7, 1893. *SLGM*, 147–49/*GMB2*, 128–31.

write "new music for new ears," as Nietzsche put it. When he succeeds, these moments cannot help but attract our attention, because they are designed to do so. Nevertheless, the composer's "new music" often engages with the old, even as it makes the old sound new. Combining, recasting, extending past musical practice, and incorporating everyday sonic phenomena that fascinated him, Mahler continually managed to create music that sounded "unlike anything that has ever been heard before" – a description he applied to nearly every newly completed work. While he paid attention to early modernist trends – Wagnerism, Nietzschean thought, realism and naturalism, historicism, irony and humor – he felt no need to borrow from them. Richard Strauss, Mahler's close friend and rival, was the only composer whose music he assiduously followed and someone whom he would not dream of imitating. Sometimes, he found himself part of a movement he did not intend to join; and sometimes, he opened up as yet unexplored musical vistas that only he could envision and make manifest.

In this essay I will examine passages from four of Mahler's works whose novelty reveals how he navigated the multifarious contexts of musical modernism: the Second (1894), Fourth (1900), and Seventh (1905) Symphonies, and *Das Lied von der Erde* (1908). After investigating the kinds of compositional techniques the composer invented to achieve the "modernity" of each excerpt, I will show that Mahler's new ideas not only rested upon elaborations of similar ideas from the musical past but found a place in the aesthetic interests of his early modernist contemporaries.

The finale of Mahler's Second Symphony, completed in 1894, is a behemoth of sound, symbol, and drama. Lasting roughly forty minutes, its eschatological narrative falls into three large parts: a ten-minute introduction and exposition ruled by slow tempi, another ten minutes of explosive driving development meant to evoke the "march of the dead toward judgement," and the long-breathed crescendo of its cantata-like conclusion, where chorus and soloists usher us into the ecstasy of a humanistic resurrection. Mahler ultimately suppressed the program for the symphony, but the closing text reveals all the audience needs to know.

One of the most ingenious passages of the movement, and of Mahler's music in general, emerges from the silence that follows the climax and collapse of the march (m. 325). A sighing, metrically irregular melody, later defined by the alto as the voice of a fearful believer, creeps erratically upward, gradually taking on more substance and shape. Suddenly, its progress is interrupted by the more disciplined sounds of a distant offstage marching band. In the score (m. 343), Mahler's note to the conductor explains: "Here the author imagines something like a music scarcely apprehended, its isolated sounds carried by the wind." In an impressive technical feat, the two independent musical time streams interweave over a flurry of changing meters. Once they have been joined, the marching band grows louder as the passage unfolds, becoming the embodiment of apocryphal trumpets inexorably pulling the believer forward until both explode into the same musical space (m. 380), confronting the terrifying reality of the Last Judgment.

For all its compositional originality, Mahler's music-theatrical coup operates as a grand elaboration of the long-standing use of offstage sounds in opera to signal the approach of someone, or something, that precipitates the action in the following scene. The elaborate orchestral apparatus he applies could also be characterized as Siegfried's horn writ large. Mahler eschewed composing operas, but he conducted Wagner's works dozens of times annually, and he freely availed himself of Wagnerian orchestral color and complex textures. As he declared in a letter of March 26, 1896, to the composer-critic Max Marschalk: "Wagner indeed made the *expressive means* of symphonic music his own, just as now the symphonist, for his part, can grasp and bring over, fully justified and fully conscious, the expressive possibilities that music won through Wagner's work" (*SLGM*, 179/*GMB2*, 172). Finally, one must not overlook the intended realism of this passage, with its recreation of the real-life experience of hearing the intermingling of distant disparate musical strains – a phenomenon the composer loved and musically imitated all his life. Whether inspired by a whiff of Berlioz or a breeze from Richard Strauss, this too placed Mahler in the company of early modernists.

In more ways than one, the world of Mahler's Fourth Symphony (1899–1900) lies at a remove from the works that precede it. Its neoclassical Mozartian ease, transparent orchestration, and playful ironic tone baffled audiences. Somewhat obscured by the work's good humor and occasional seriousness, however, a pointed critique of the received formal conventions of Classical music lurks beneath its superficial traditional trappings. Mahler's unique mixture of evoking, satirizing, and treating the past with an attitude of detachment aligns with the early modernist trend of musical irony, an attitude he shared with Richard Strauss, who pursued similar goals with different musical priorities. Faced with a music-cultural context in which many composers perpetuated rather than questioned compositional norms, Mahler responded with peculiarly subtle daring.

Once past the shock of the opening sleigh bells – another feint at realism – the easygoing G-major theme of the first movement of the

Fourth, its balanced phrases passed among various instruments, seems to promise that the rest of the piece will be a smooth, untroubled ride. Subsequent themes unfurl effortlessly. After hearing two more repetitions of the first theme, listeners certainly anticipate a discernible recapitulation, but Mahler muddies the musical waters of that arrival. At the end of a zigzagging development, the full orchestra loudly exults in C major (mm. 209ff.), only to dissolve into a chaotic handful of fragments, none of them harmonically secure: a C-sharp-minor trumpet fanfare (later imported to the beginning of the Fifth), sleigh bells, and running melodic fragments that sound familiar. All at once, the wandering woodwinds stop, take a breath, and the strings play the closing gesture of the first theme exactly as they did at the beginning of the piece, as if nothing untoward has happened (mm. 239–40). If we listen more closely, the missing components of the first theme are all there, but scattered, played by different instruments, sometimes at the wrong pitch. Mahler delivers the spirit of a conventional recapitulation, but withholds its recognizable substance until the last minute.

The composer slips a similar stretch of unexpected music-formal anarchy and levity into the sublime Adagio double variations of the Fourth's third movement. After the first variation of the mournful second theme builds to an agonized climax and collapse, the strings return to G major for the second variation of the first theme, an Andante waltz (m. 222). Without warning, abbreviated variations of the first theme start to proliferate at an alarming rate, with tempi that accelerate until the structure degenerates into a disorganized, madcap race. Reaching into the tumult like a sonic deus ex machina, a majestic horn choir (m. 283) quells the pandemonium with a powerful sudden return to the Andante tempo that set off the entire sequence.

Mahler's ironic games with inherited musical conventions in this work show a different side of early modernist historicism. He proves that the more devotional evocations and reinterpretations of the music of Bach, pursued by early modernist colleagues such as Max Reger and Ferruccio Busoni, were not the only ways to revisit the musical past as part of a new aesthetic. As Walter Frisch notes, the ironies of Mahler's Fourth Symphony help audiences recognize "the unbridgeable distance between them and the musical past."[2] That past remains in human memory, not as a

---

[2] Walter Frisch, *German Modernism: Music and the Arts* (Berkeley: University of California Press, 2005), 213.

dead tradition to be reanimated but as a treasure trove for the modern artist to reinterpret in novel ways.

The music and writings of Richard Wagner and the philosophy of Friedrich Nietzsche were the most significant compositional and philosophical touchstones for early modernist composers. For nearly all of Mahler's contemporaries – Richard Strauss, Alexander Zemlinsky, Franz Schreker, Hans Pfitzner, and even Claude Debussy – following Wagner meant composing operas, a path Mahler decided not to follow. In addition, Mahler's oft-noted avoidance of the complex chromatic harmony of Wagner's operas is at odds with Strauss's accelerated, constantly evolving harmonic constructs, on the one hand, and the constricted contrapuntal twisting of Hugo Wolf's Lieder, on the other.[3] While Mahler would appear to be guilty as charged of this tonal predilection in nearly all of his pre-1907 symphonies, the Seventh Symphony (1904–5) resists this dictum. Furthermore, its first and last movements come close to fulfilling Nietzsche's demand, made in *The Case of Wagner*, that an essential prerequisite for modernity is the impossibility of large-scale coherence, of structural unity in works of art. Here, a very short excerpt from the long, complicated first movement of the Seventh must suffice as a demonstration of how tenuous conventional harmony and small-scale coherence can become when chord progressions and phrases yield to the unpredictable pull of several recurring motives.

The sound materials of the movement's introduction, which lasts two minutes, bespeak music a step away from unbridled violence, rent with dissonance and rhythmic sparks when they clash and collide. The passage could be heard in "B major-minor," but then one would have to leave out all the "wrong" notes, that is, those dissonant against the home chord. The opening B-minor chord, for instance, has been "sullied" with an extra note, G-sharp, that makes it sound disturbingly unstable. When the following tenor horn solo reconfigures these same notes into a melody that brings its stark tritone intervals into sharp focus (mm. 2–4), the discomfort intensifies. The slow forward march of the strings' thick funereal chords pounds its way upward, sideswiped by competing tunes in the woodwinds and trumpet, seemingly trembling with suppressed rage, building toward the moment when the violins add yet another dissonant note, A-sharp, to the same melody (mm. 12–13). The entire orchestra joins in, extending the opening melody into a more balanced entity while

[3] See Robert P. Morgan, "Ives and Mahler: Mutual Responses at the End of an Era," *19th-Century Music* 2 (1978): 73–74.

the tenor horn plays a countermelody against it. At last, they manage to tame this first section into closure, sinking into near silence before an unexpected turn to the next section.

Since the high level of dissonance and instability established at the beginning of the Seventh is not sustained for long stretches but, rather, flows into and out of stable episodes featuring more palatable Romantic tropes (e.g., sweeping love songs), one can be tempted to consider short-lived musical volatility as an insignificant anomaly within a traditional framework. But it is precisely this juxtaposition of discordant instability and soothing nostalgia that makes the Seventh modern. The "paradise" of the past cannot vanquish the burgeoning chaos of the present. Once Mahler had sonically actualized this realization, he had already crossed into the mystical world of his late works, written in 1907–10, before his untimely death on May 18, 1911.

Das Lied von der Erde (1907–8) came into being in the wake of overwhelming personal trauma. Though Mahler found the strength to continue composing, he realized that he no longer sought, nor cared about, the approval of audiences and colleagues. As he wrote to his close friend Bruno Walter on July 18, 1908: "Since the panicked shock I experienced back then [in 1907], I have sought nothing else but to turn away from seeing, away from hearing anything" (*SLGM*, 324/*GMB2*, 367). In *Das Lied*, the composer fully gave in to this impulse, bringing forth music that sounded unlike anything else written up to that time. Here the composer conceived his own sui generis contribution to early modernism: the emancipation of musical time.

The composer's loosening of conventional music-temporal structures in *Das Lied* was born of a paradox. The work's exotic musical world breathes the spirit of orientalism, an obsession of both French and German Romantic writers since the turn of the nineteenth century. The texts Mahler chose for his symphonic song cycle came from Hans Bethge's *Die chinesische Flöte* (*The Chinese Flute*, 1907), a collection of free German translations of eighth-century Chinese poems. As the composer pondered how to conjure the faraway landscapes of these texts in music, he fashioned a free-floating, flexible music-temporal language, one that would move in unforeseen ways that lay outside Western tradition. Thus, although the piece's mingling of standard harmony with stock oriental musical clichés such as pentatonic scales sounds comfortably familiar, the mutable quality of its fluid temporal underpinnings confirms its modernist credentials.

The opening of "Der Abschied" ("The Departure"), the extended final movement of *Das Lied*, is a stunning example of how Mahler manipulates the interplay of meter, rhythm, harmony, and counterpoint to pull the musical fabric along a temporal continuum that fluctuates among a hypnotic, trance-like immobility, tentative forward motion, and a settled, regular tempo. After two lingering gong-like "strikes" resound in the harps, low strings, tam-tam, contrabassoon, and French horn, the third "gong" coincides with a twofold exchange between the oboe's fluttering turn figures and sustained single articulations played by a pair of horns, spaced at regular intervals (m. 3). But just as the piece seems to be gaining momentum, its energy dissipates into an overlong silence. From here on, the irregular push and pull between long gong strokes in the low instruments, the seemingly random sighing figures in the horns, and the elastic undulations of the oboe figure continues sorting itself out until it gradually yields to a disciplined, even pace; at last, the music hits a regular stride (m. 10). Once attained, however, this newfound propulsion almost immediately disintegrates as oboe and flute soloists burst into impetuous roulades. The remaining notes of the harps and bassoons decelerate, then fall silent, clearing the way for the subsequent vocal recitative.

In this passage, the relative weight of the leading voices shifts, changing their interplay. While only the celli remain to sustain the C pedal, the flute has taken over the oboe's role and melodic material (m. 21). It now either plays a lithe countermelody against the free declamations of the vocalist or fills in the gaps once the vocalist has halted. The listener, hypnotized by the lavish, unrestrained melodic undulations of the flute, singing like a lonely songbird at dusk, realizes that the everyday world has disappeared when it falls silent. Mahler's musical spell of timelessness, skillfully cast, is now complete.

Mahler calls himself "modern" one last time in his letter to Gisela Tolnay-Witt, but the surprising twist he makes there unveils a fitting last word relevant to the composer's feelings about being a modernist. To stave off any further maddening questions, he exclaims: "That's just the way we are! We 'moderns'!" Mahler's scare quotes imply that he was just as proud to call himself a modernist as he would be to claim the opposite. In other words: if he were willing not to take the label seriously, he would be at worst an impostor, at best an artist who could be amused by his audacity to claim something for his music that just might be a joke or a passing fad. As we have seen, the composer's sense of humor, thirst for adventure, and ability to court risk and misunderstanding without fear make his music unique, idiosyncratic, and timeless. Whatever its inspiration, the new called to him, and he would give his all to achieve it. As he once remarked: "It's not just a question of scaling a summit previously unknown, but of plotting, step by step, a new pathway to it" (*HLG2*, 339).

CHAPTER 18

Reception in Vienna

Kevin C. Karnes

To honor Mahler's fiftieth birthday, the critic Paul Stefan solicited a book's worth of dedications (*Widmungen*) from the composer's colleagues and friends – composers, directors, performers, authors, designers, even a musicologist. Attesting to Mahler's extraordinary esteem in the world of the visual arts, the textual dedications are framed by photographic reproductions of a sculpture and a painting, each contributed by its famous creator. The sculpture is a lifelike bust of Mahler by Auguste Rodin. The painting, in contrast, is nowhere explicitly identified as an image of the composer: it is "The Knight" (*Der Ritter*) from the *Beethoven Frieze*, with which Gustav Klimt had adorned the walls of the Vienna Secession for its "Klinger–Beethoven" exhibition of 1902 (Figure 18.1).

From the time of the opening of the 1902 exhibition, contemporary observers had noted the likeness of Klimt's knight to Mahler's visage, and Mahler himself contributed to the event by conducting his own arrangement of the *Ode to Joy* in the Secession building's entrance hall. In the published exhibition catalogue, Klimt's frieze is described in allegorical terms. The panel in which the knight appears, it reads, depicts "the sorrows of feeble humanity," looking for aid in its "longing for happiness" from a "well-armored knight as an external force," and from "compassion and ambition as inner, striving forces."[1]

It is no surprise that Klimt would depict an admired composer as an allegorical, even mythical figure, for he had already built a considerable reputation for allegorical paintings on topics ranging from philosophy and jurisprudence to love. But a remarkable feature of Mahler's reception in Vienna in the years around 1910 is that so many others in the composer's

---

[1] Paul Stefan, *Gustav Mahler. Ein Bild seiner Persönlichkeit in Widmungen* (Munich: R. Piper, 1910), plate after p. 94; *XIV Kunstausstellung der Vereinigung bildender Künstler Österreichs Secession Wien. Klinger–Beethoven* (Vienna: Adolf Holzhausen, 1902), 25–26 (the authorship of the text is unclear).

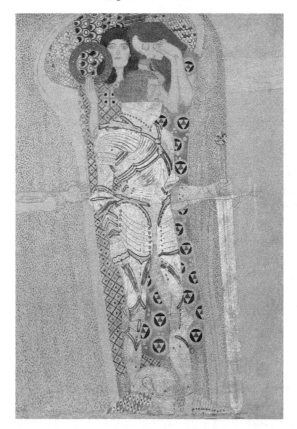

Figure 18.1   Gustav Klimt, *Der goldene Ritter* (*The Golden Knight*, 1902), in Paul Stefan, *Gustav Mahler* (1910).

orbit likewise framed his impact on music or society in allegorical terms. These included figures who had known the composer personally since youth, and others who barely knew him at all. And they included writers not otherwise prone to public displays of romantic imagining. Yet when confronted with the challenge of describing the impressions Mahler's work had made on them, all of them found themselves in a place like Klimt, conjuring images of strength and compassion, depicting embodiments of a powerful force that just might lead humanity, as a whole or in part, to happiness, wholeness, or transcendence.

"Gustav Mahler was a saint"

Arnold Schoenberg had been acquainted with Mahler since 1904 at the
latest, when he and Alexander Zemlinsky had recruited the elder composer
to participate in their founding of a "Vienna Society of Creative Musicians," their musical answer to the Vienna Secession. From that point
forward, the three composers socialized sporadically, with Mahler going
out of his way and risking considerable critical ire to show public support
for the music and organizing efforts of his younger colleagues. When
Mahler returned to Austria from New York in the summer of 1908, he
and Schoenberg reestablished contact. The following summer, which
Mahler again spent in the Austrian Alps, he worked to secure a salary for
Schoenberg from a pair of wealthy patrons, with the intention of freeing
his composer friend from distracting obligations to noncreative work. That
same year, Mahler lobbied the publishing firm Universal Edition to add
Schoenberg's works to its prestigious catalogue. Back in New York in
January 1910, Mahler wrote to confide to Schoenberg that he was
"homesick . . . for the handful of people by whom I wish to be understood
and whom I love." And "you," he added, "are among them, in the
front row." Perhaps most touching is Alma Mahler's recollection of her
husband's terminal decline in early 1911. "During his last days," she
wrote, "and while his mind was still unclouded, his thoughts often went
anxiously to Schoenberg." "If I go," Gustav reportedly uttered, "he will
have nobody left."[2]

Schoenberg had not always been an admirer of Mahler's music. That
changed in the autumn of 1904, when he first heard Maher's Third
Symphony in concert. Writing to Mahler in December to describe the
impression his symphony had made upon him, Schoenberg, whose analytical acumen was already becoming the stuff of legend, found himself
unable to convey the significance of the piece in musical terms. "I must not
speak as a musician to a musician if I am to give any idea of the incredible
impression your symphony made on me," he confided. "I can speak only
as one human being to another." Then, he unfolded a reading of Mahler's
work in allegorical terms, terms remarkably close to those used by the
Secession to describe Klimt's *Beethoven Frieze*. "I believe I felt your
symphony. I shared in the battling for illusion; I suffered the pangs of
disillusionment; I saw the forces of evil and good wrestling with each
other; I saw a man in torment struggling towards inward harmony;

[2] *HLG2*, 684–94; *HLG4*, 188, 449–50, 526; *ML*, 197–98.

I divined a personality, a drama, and *truthfulness*, the most uncompromising truthfulness."[3]

A well-known photograph of Schoenberg in his apartment from 1911 makes clear the centrality of Mahler's professional model to the younger composer's sense of creative selfhood. On the wall behind him is a photograph of Mahler; right next to that hang two of Schoenberg's portraits of the composer. In the days that followed Mahler's death, Schoenberg completed his famous oil painting, *Burial of Gustav Mahler*.[4] Later that year, Schoenberg's first book, his *Harmonielehre*, was published with a dedication to the elder composer. There, in a passage reflecting on Schoenberg's role as author in relation to his readers, he channeled the remembered words of his idol: "a *model* (as *Gustav Mahler characterized*, in a *single word*, the *essence* of the *teacher*)." Later in the book, though lacking concrete evidence, Schoenberg remarked that "it is possible, indeed it is probable" that Mahler's music had been a model for one of the key technical innovations that lent Schoenberg's work of the period its distinctive sound, the harmonic use of chords built of fourths. In response to Mahler's death (as he later remarked), Schoenberg composed the last of his *Sechs kleine Klavierstücke*, op. 19, in June 1911: a sparse, transparent meditation on fourth chords, a sounding tribute to his ideal teacher.[5]

Schoenberg did not contribute to Stefan's book of dedications to Mahler. But he published a memorial essay in a special Mahler issue of *Der Merker*, a Vienna music and theater journal, in 1912. "To Gustav Mahler's work!" he declared. "Into its pure air! Here is the faith that elevates us. Here is someone believing, in his immortal works, in an eternal soul. I do not know if our soul is immortal, but I believe it is. What I do know, however, is that men, the highest men such as Beethoven or Mahler, will believe in an immortal soul until the power of their belief has endowed humanity with one." Summing up: "Gustav Mahler was a saint."[6]

---

[3] Joseph Auner, *A Schoenberg Reader: Documents of a Life* (New Haven: Yale University Press, 2003), 46 (emphasis in original).

[4] Auner, *Schoenberg Reader*, 50; Schönberg, *Catalogue raisonné*, ed. Christian Meyer and Therese Muxeneder (Vienna: Arnold Schönberg Centre, 2005), plates 338, 339, 153.

[5] Schönberg, *Harmonielehre* (Leipzig: Universal Edition, 1911), 322, 451 (emphasis in original); Schoenberg, *Theory of Harmony*, trans. Roy E. Carter (Berkeley: University of California Press, 1978), 288, 404; Auner, *Schoenberg Reader*, 95.

[6] Schoenberg, "Gustav Mahler," *Der Merker*, March 1, 1912, 182–83; Schoenberg, *Style and Idea: Selected Writings*, ed. Leonard Stein, trans. Leo Black (Berkeley: University of California Press, 1975), 447–48.

"You lift us up to the godliness for which we long"

Guido Adler's relationship with Mahler went back to their student years,
when the future musicologist befriended the aspiring conductor at the
Vienna Conservatory in the 1870s. At that time, Adler was an avid
follower of Friedrich Nietzsche, who had recently challenged an imagined
community of German youth to "struggle on behalf of culture" by
fostering "the production of the genius." Adler took Nietzsche's challenge
to heart, and when Mahler, an artist of unquestionable genius, appeared in
the midst of his philosophically minded friends, Adler went to extraordinary lengths to ensure his material security and professional success. Adler
welcomed Mahler into the Viennese Academic Wagner Society in
1877 and immediately sought to secure work for him as conductor and
choirmaster. In the 1880s, when both of them found employment in
Prague, Adler consistently championed Mahler's accomplishments as conductor at the city's German Theater. A decade later, when both had settled
in Vienna, Adler spearheaded an effort to raise funds for the publication of
Mahler's early symphonies. In his substantial and persistent efforts on
behalf of advancing Mahler's work and professional life, Adler answered,
over the course of decades, Nietzsche's call to the young.[7]

Adler's friendship with Mahler, though never close personally, lasted
until the end of the composer's life, and his admiration for Mahler's gifts
and persona continued until the end of his own. A founding figure of
German musicology at the Universities of Prague and Vienna, Adler was a
crusading advocate for the application of what he regarded as scientific
methodologies to the project of music research – namely, empirical observation and inductive reasoning, all conducted within a systematic framework of methodological investigation. In a book on Mahler published in
1916, based on a memorial essay from two years earlier, Adler brought his
ideology of research to bear upon the task of summing up the life's work of
his departed friend. Invoking the mythological image of the "red thread"
that Theseus used to find his way out of the Minotaur's labyrinth, which
had long before been taken up as a metaphor for the audible function of
the leitmotif in Wagner's music dramas, Adler framed his musicological
project as an attempt to unlock the connection between Mahler's art and

[7] Nietzsche, "Schopenhauer as Educator," in *Untimely Meditations*, ed. Daniel Breazeale, trans. R. J.
Hollingdale (Cambridge: Cambridge University Press, 1997), 163; *HLG1*, 465–66, 475–76; Edward
R. Reilly, *Gustav Mahler and Guido Adler: Records of a Friendship* (Cambridge: Cambridge University
Press, 1982).

life. "Only someone who can trace the red thread through the life and works of an artist like Mahler can fathom his complex spiritual paths and reveal his human and artistic nature."[8]

Yet both Adler's obituary and his follow-up biography were elaborations upon a still-earlier essay on Mahler, which Adler wrote as his contribution to Stefan's dedication book of 1910. There, Adler made clear his sense of the impossibility of trying to frame Mahler's achievement historically while the composer still lived. So, he turned instead to a project akin to Schoenberg's of these same years: an attempt to convey the nature and depth of the impression that Mahler's music and presence had made upon him. "You are a child of our times," Adler wrote, "who has built upon the solid foundation of proven tradition. Your work is directed at everyone who can sense the pulse of what is to come. The sounds of your homeland and the ways of the nation to which we belong constitute the basis upon which you construct your houses of art." He continued in this allegorical mode, as if channeling the forces of Klimt's knight:

> You espy the child encircled by angels, the youth in the face of adversity, the man enfolded in strife and struggle, the warrior in acts of great courage, the wife in the throes of dearest love, humankind striving for immortality. You eavesdrop on the weavings of nature, the green meadow, the shadowy grove, the animals in the forest, the terrors of chaos and confusion. You lift us up to the godliness for which we long.[9]

"... to go in search of home"

Born in Prague just as Mahler and Adler were building their careers in the city, the composer and critic Max Brod probably never met the director of the city's German Theater. But in his first contribution to the inaugural volume of the periodical *Der Jude* (1916–17), Brod made Mahler the central figure in his discussion of Jewish music and an imagined Jewish cultural nation. Anti-Semitism had always shadowed the reception of Mahler's work as conductor and composer, and it was flagged by Adler as one of the causes of Mahler's break with the Vienna Court Opera in 1907. For Brod, as for many of Mahler's detractors, the composer's Jewishness permeated a great deal of what sounds in his music. But that,

---

[8] Adler, "Gustav Mahler," in *Biographisches Jahrbuch und deutscher Nekrolog, vol. 16: Vom 1. Januar bis 31. Dezember 1911*, ed. Anton Bettelheim (Berlin: Georg Reimer, 1914), 3–41; Adler, *Gustav Mahler* (Vienna: Universal Edition, 1916), 4; Reilly, *Gustav Mahler and Guido Adler*, 14.

[9] Adler, "Ein Fruendeswort," in Stefan, *Gustav Mahler*, 3–4.

in turn, made Mahler an exemplary member of the broadly European Jewish community of which Brod dreamt. In his contribution to Stefan's dedication volume, Adler had described Mahler's music as articulating and cementing the bonds of a collective extending limitlessly outward from wherever the composer might stand, embracing all of humankind and even nature itself. In contrast, for Brod, the collectivity inscribed by Mahler's music was limited and more specific. Alongside Heine, Mendelssohn, Meyerbeer, and numberless Hasidim from Poland and Russia, Brod's Mahler numbered among the "great sons of the Jewish folk, whose genius was compelled to wrestle with a specifically Jewish fate" (*Judennot*).[10]

The fact that Mahler's relationship to his Jewish heritage was fraught was irrelevant to Brod's thesis. "Judaism may have played no great role in Mahler's consciousness," he admitted. Rather, inspired by the periodical's founder, Martin Buber, Brod looked to images of Jewish communities in Europe's east, whose members he imagined as almost mystical peoples, uncorrupted by the assimilating pressures of Austro-German society. In launching *Der Jude*, Buber aspired to kindle a "communal feeling" among all European Jews, to awaken among them awareness of the "community of blood" to which each and every one of them belonged. That community, for Buber and Brod alike, transcended geography and self-identification, as well as the form that one's spiritual practice – or lack thereof – might assume. For the Jewish community of blood was rooted in a timeless, all-encompassing spirit, ensured by unbreakable genetic bonds.[11]

Like Schoenberg and Adler, Brod reflected on aspects of Mahler's musical vocabulary. Also like them, he read Mahler's musical texts allegorically, as indicators of things higher and deeper than notes or sounds. The symphonic marches for which Mahler was famous pointed to Hasidic songs the composer knew in his heart but likely never experienced directly, as did the distinct major/minor quality of his melodies and his tendency to elaborate a melodic line gradually from a single repeated pitch. To "western ears," these things might give rise to impressions of Mahler's music as "incoherent" or "bizarre," Brod wrote. But "one's perspective changes if they allow themselves to empathize with Mahler's Jewish soul." For Brod, that soul was expressed most fully in the final movement of Mahler's *Das*

[10] Adler, *Gustav Mahler*, 19–20; Reilly, *Gustav Mahler and Guido Adler*, 24; Brod, "Jüdische Volksmelodien," *Der Jude* 1 (1916–17): 345; Philip V. Bohlman, *Jüdische Volksmusik. Eine mitteleuropäische Geistesgeschichte* (Vienna: Böhlau, 2005), 222.
[11] Brod, "Jüdische Volksmelodien," 345; Bohlman, *Jüdische Volksmusik*, 221; Buber, "Die Losung," *Der Jude* 1 (1916–17): 2.

Lied von der Erde, and particularly in the closing utterance of its soprano ("ewig, ewig . . ."). With this thought, Brod concluded: "Upon hearing the sound of east-European Jewish folk song, I understood at last why it was necessary for his last song cycle, the Chinese *Song of the Earth*, to bewail his 'loneliness' and go in search of 'home': the Orient, 'eternally, eternally.'"[12]
In Brod's essay, as in the statements of Adler, Schoenberg, and Klimt, Mahler was a saint, a visionary, a cementer and proclaimer of community. He was a well-armored knight descended among us, leading us into a space of wholeness, maybe even happiness, for which we all long.

[12] Brod, "Jüdische Volksmelodien," 344–45; Bohlman, *Jüdische Volksmusik*, 221–22.

CHAPTER 19

Mahler's Press from London to Los Angeles

Karen Painter

Mahler liked to present himself, especially in letters, as an unrecognized genius whom future audiences would honor even if contemporaneous critics remained dismissive. If he had cause for disappointment with the German-language press, the foreign press often recognized his accomplishments. This essay focuses on Mahler coverage in the press in England, New York, and California, where positive reports and unflagging curiosity defy any presumptions of provincialism. Far-flung publications admired the conductor, awed if perplexed by his compositions, at a time when their Austro-German counterparts disparaged his music. Their attention did not result from a more profound understanding than in Central Europe; rather, staying abreast of foreign affairs, including musical, was a mark of cultivation. The stakes were simply not as high as in Vienna and in Germany, where protecting the integrity of classical music against the claws of modernism underlay so much reporting on Mahler.

Mahler's Reception in England (1892–1911)

Mahler won favorable notices in England already in mid-career, despite haphazard coverage. When Covent Garden engaged the Hamburg Opera to produce a brief season of German opera, *Siegfried* was an unequivocal success under "August Mahler," the audience in "rapt attention ... throughout the entire opera." *Tristan und Isolde* "was marked by rare intelligence and mastery of the score."[1] Later in that decade, the London *Musical Times* would rave about Mahler's work in Vienna. His *Fidelio* had "such excellent results that one can only wish that the master's work was in like manner given at all other theatres ... The performance of the music under Mahler was extremely fine." Ermanno Wolf-Ferrari's *The Inquisitive Women* "was brilliant in every way"; *Marriage of Figaro* "was truly

[1] "German Opera," *Musical Times* (July 1, 1892): 406–7.

magnificent." Finally, "Gustav Mahler has again distinguished himself as a conductor" in Hermann Goetz's *The Taming of the Shrew*.[2] (It is striking that the *Musical Times* did not track Mahler in America. A fleeting reference to his tenure at the New York Philharmonic came within an announcement that Samuel Coleridge-Taylor would travel abroad to conduct the Philharmonic in the premiere of his "Rhapsody on negro melodies."[3])

Recognition as a composer, not just a gifted conductor, came earlier in England than in Vienna (namely, with the premiere of *Kindertotenlieder* in January 1905). Announcing Mahler's move to the Vienna Court Opera in 1897, the *Musical Times* referred to "the well-known composer and conductor at the Stadt-Theater" in Hamburg. Even when there was no plan to cover Mahler, positive discussion of his music surfaced in 1899. *The Contemporary Review*, a London magazine that encouraged independent views in areas of debate within the church and politics, published a translation of Felix Weingartner's "The Symphony since Beethoven." The first installment was the second chapter, "The Romantic Symphony" (which covered more difficult aesthetic problems than the first chapter on the "classical symphony," published as the second installment). Weingartner heralded Mahler as an "important figure of our days, far too little esteemed as a composer" – a romantic genius, without concern for the vagaries of concert life or public success. Weingartner defended the first movement of the Second Symphony against detractors who "misunderstood" its thematic development; "[i]t is also a promising sign that the performances of his works have frequently met with undisguised opposition." Weingartner concluded, "Everything Mahler writes bears the stamp of a rich fancy and of a passionate and almost fanatic enthusiasm."[4]

Whereas earlier articles did not mention his music, the *Musical Times*'s report on the Allgemeine Deutsche Musikverein's 1902 festival highlighted Mahler over the ten other composers programmed. The Third Symphony generated "much interest," the Finale singled out for praise. A year later, the First Symphony was programmed in the Promenade

<hr>

[2] "In the World of Music," *New York Times*, April 9, 1899, translating from *Pester Lloyd*; Eusebius Mandyczewski, "Music in Vienna," *Musical Times* 45, no. 741 (November 1, 1904): 736; 46, no. 754 (December 1, 1905): 812; 47, no. 759 (May 1, 1906): 338; 47, no. 766 (December 1, 1906): 834.

[3] "Occasional Notes," *Musical Times* 50, no. 801 (November 1, 1909): 716. Although *The Bamboula: Rhapsodic Dance* was premiered under the composer at Norfolk that summer, in honor of the festival's tenth anniversary, the New York Philharmonic's performance came only later, honoring the fiftieth anniversary of the Proclamation of Emancipation (*New York Times*, January 3, 1913).

[4] "Foreign Notes," *Musical Times* 38, no. 648 (March 1, 1897): 196; Felix Weingartner, "The Romantic Symphony," *The Contemporary Review* (January 1, 1899): 436.

Concerts at Queen's Hall. The Vienna correspondent reported the positive reception first-hand ("The Konzertverein and the Tonkünstlerorchester performed two symphonies by Gustav Mahler with brilliant success") but blamed negative reception on the audience ("Mahler's First Symphony did not excite any special sympathy with the public").[5]

Recognition of Mahler's role in music history came indirectly in 1908. Under the headline "Is the Symphony Doomed?," the *Musical Times* professed that although no recent work continues the chain of great symphonic repertoire that ended with Brahms's Fourth, the genre was "not doomed to an early death." Mahler was listed first among composers who had recently or would soon premiere a symphony. The article concluded with the great English authority, Sir Hubert Parry, who argued that Brahms's bold applications of old symphonic principles showed the potential for individual development, even if "we can hardly hope that even the greatest composers of the future will surpass the symphonic triumphs of the past."[6]

The *Musical Times*'s obituary touted Mahler as "one of the foremost musicians of his day" but acknowledged that "he was little known to the public in England." The First and Fourth Symphonies, performed at the Promenade Concerts, had "failed to win popularity" – through no fault of the composer: "The English public were apathetic to his music probably because his naïveté of expression did not stir them and his high endeavour and scholarship, although doubtless admired, made no deep appeal; in the case of the symphonies a further obstacle to acceptance was their length." This alleged disinterest in Mahler's music was, however, at odds with the Musical League, founded in 1909 in Liverpool. While its programming focused on living British composers, foreigners such as Mahler, Debussy, Vincent d'Indy, and Max Schillings "promised to give their support and to endeavour to be present to conduct works of their own" at the society's first festival. It is possible that this endorsement spurred the Manchester Gentlemen's Concerts, which ran from 1799 to World War I, to program Mahler for the first time in 1909 – the Adagietto from the Fifth Symphony.[7]

---

[5] See *Musical Times* issues in May 1891, May and June 1897, June 1898, November 1901, and July 1902; "The Annual Festival of German Musicians," *Musical Times* 43, no. 713 (July 1, 1902): 481; "The Promenade Concerts at Queen's Hall," *Musical Times* 44, no. 727 (September 1, 1903): 610; "Music in Vienna," *Musical Times* 45, no. 742 (December 1, 1904): 810; "Music in Vienna," *Musical Times* 50, no. 794 (April 1, 1909): 260.

[6] "Is the Symphony Doomed?," *Musical Times* 49, no. 788 (October 1, 1908): 641.

[7] *Musical Times* 52, no. 820 (June 1, 1911): 383; "Occasional Notes," *Musical Times* 50, no. 795 (May 1, 1909): 311 (these plans fell through, and the festival was instead to feature seventeen British

London's *Monthly Musical Record* covered Mahler's conducting from 1886 to 1908, along with some compositions – not just his completion of Carl Maria von Weber's opera *Die drei Pintos* but also the Second Symphony (in Leipzig, 1897, and Berlin, 1898) and the piano arrangement of the Fifth Symphony. Whereas the reorientation of the *Monthly Musical Record* toward modern music is dated after 1912, the articles immediately after Mahler's death suggest otherwise: in addition to the obituary, Edgar Istel's lengthy article on Mahler came a month later.[8]

Coverage in California

Why would rural Californians, without access to Mahler's music or conducting, need to be kept up to date? The newspapers' physical layout of the reporting hints at the cultural status thereby attained. Colusa, north of Sacramento, reported that European and American music lovers gathered in Salzburg for a Mozart Festival that featured Mahler (among others) conducting. Colusans could feel superior by reading about unattainable luxury travel, then (immediately below) about a reunion of General Morgan's Confederate troops that summer, and (to the left) about the first basemen from local professional black baseball team who became "insanely drunk" and was arrested. (Colusa had gained national attention in 1887 when some 200 men kidnapped and hanged a Chinese immigrant the night after his murder conviction – a lynching both anticipated and widely praised, although the case would be reexamined in 1913.) Another town paper, in Truckee (near Lake Tahoe), reported not on the premiere of Mahler's Eighth Symphony in Munich but, two months later, on an incident during a break from its rehearsal – Mahler was mistaken for being a painter (Maler) and prevented from walking through a corridor that was being plastered and not ready to be painted. Struggling to fill its pages, the *Truckee Republican* devoted more space to advertising than to news; the Mahler anecdote was directly above reporting on the types of camels available for sale in Arabia, including their prices and functions.[9]

---

composers); "Occasional Notes," *Musical Times* 50, no. 798 (August 1, 1909): 516; "Music in Manchester," *Musical Times* 50, no. 801 (November 1, 1909): 740.

[8] The *Monthly Music Record* reports covered Mahler in Leipzig (1886), in Budapest (1889), in London (1892), in Hamburg (1894), several reports on Vienna (1897–99 and 1907), and in Munich (1908); Richard Kitson, introduction to the *Monthly Musical Record* on the Retrospective Index to Music Periodicals website (2011, rvd. 2013-14), www.ripm.org/?page=JournalInfo&ABB=MMR; *Monthly Musical Record* 41, no. 486 (June 1, 1911): 138, no. 487 (July 1, 1911): 169–70.

[9] *Colusa Daily Sun*, August 14, 1906; *Truckee Republican*, November 30, 1910. The articles appeared at the end of the newspaper, a mere four pages.

The *Los Angeles Herald*'s column "Stray Chords," which ran from 1896 through December 1904, featured Mahler eight times, from his engagement to Alma Schindler (February 1902) to Vienna's Gesellschaft der Musikfreunde inviting him to be director (May 1904). After Mahler's appointment to the Metropolitan Opera, discussed at length, readers were abreast kept of news. Mahler's fiftieth birthday was recognized – belatedly, in September 1910 – alongside the ninety-second birthday of the famous British clown James Doughty.[10]

In Sacramento there was no local newspaper from 1899 to 1906. Before then, the *Sacramento Daily Union* had reported on European musical life – for example, the completion of a symphony (Mahler's Second) "which will apparently beat the record" in the number of performers. A rumor that Mahler is "one of the great foreign conductors" being considered "to preside over the Boston Symphony Orchestra" prompted the new *Sacramento Union* to discuss Mahler's output. Speculation that Mahler "would prove an autocrat" advanced the bizarre claim that he had refused to produce an opera by a Count (Archduke Peter Ferdinand) unless the Emperor explicitly commanded him to do so.[11]

The *Los Angeles Times* had eclectic international reporting. Mahler's name first surfaced as a potential conductor of concerts in Warsaw that would be supported by a new company with leading Polish or Polish-born musicians as majority shareholders.[12] As Mahler coverage increased, limited resources led to peculiar decisions, such as reproducing a letter to the editor from Vienna that was likely prompted by Mahler's changed relationship to the Court Opera in the summer of 1904. (Married and with a second child, he became more interested in assuring his legacy – traveling to supervise performances of his music – than managing the minutiae of productions.) First appearing in the *New York Sun*, the letter was reprinted in the *San Francisco Chronicle* under the flattering headline, "Great Vienna Conductor: Something about Mahler and His Masterful Methods" and was centered in the spread of the week's arts news. The *Los Angeles Times*, however, opted for a bland title, "Mahler's Methods," and demoted the

[10] "Mainly Personal," *Los Angeles Herald*, September 4, 1910.
[11] "Music and Drama," *Sacramento Daily Union*, November 27, 1898; "Musical Items," *Sacramento Union*, June 3, 1906. HLG3, 61, note 102 gives the source of the anecdote as Max Graf.
[12] Arthur Nikisch was to be responsible for deciding which conductors to invite, including also Richard Strauss, Siegfried Wagner, Weingartner, Felix Mottl, and Édouard Colonne. The shareholders were pianists Ignacy Jan Paderewski and Josef Hofmann and tenor Jean de Reszke. The timing of this report (*Los Angeles Times*, November 12, 1899) is consistent with the establishment of the Warsaw National Philharmonic Orchestra in 1901.

letter to the last of nine segments in "Music and Musicians" that Sunday, the penultimate being an obituary for Eduard Hanslick (who had died four weeks earlier). The opening segment profiled at length Fanny Dillon (including a huge image), an aspiring composer of grand opera who had returned to California from composition study in Berlin.[13]

Local news again dominated when Mahler was appointed to the Metropolitan Opera. Casual praise of his music ("Mahler stands at the front of his rank") referenced the "great success" the Fifth Symphony with the Boston Symphony Orchestra. The author deferred to "competent critics" who regard the Fifth "very highly" and, on Mahler's conducting, quoted at length from his past colleague, the American singer Sara Cahier. More space was accorded to a gifted young singer from Los Angeles, Bessie Bulpin, who supported herself as a "telephone girl"; the Mahler bust pictured was one-tenth the size of Bulpin's full-length portrait.[14]

Negative Strategies in the New York Press (1910–1911)

Mahler continued to fascinate, if also provoking skepticism. Outright attacks, frequent in the German-language press, were more rare across the Atlantic. Yet the *New York Times* facilitated reporting that undermined Mahler as a musical leader in the United States. Readers learned within a report on Ferruccio Busoni's spectacular US tour that Mahler would conduct three concerts in Rome for the St. Cecilia Society. Interest peaked when, after the first concert did not go well, Mahler canceled the remaining two. The Rome correspondent pictured a rogue cowboy: "Gustav Mahler has shaken the dust of Rome off his feet in anger and a pretty legal fight is likely to result." The quotations, however, sounded authentic. After the first concert, Mahler was in a "terrific rage":

> They call themselves musicians he cried. "Why, they know nothing of music. They are bootblacks, and not very good ones at that." Friends tried in vain to calm him. "Me! Me! They want me to conduct those brigands! I have never come across such a set of undisciplined impertinent ignoramuses in my whole career, and I am off to-night."

The Rome correspondent chipped away at Mahler's side. The conductor took "grave exception" to the fact that "there was no one to receive him" – even though this was known to be customary in Italy. Moreover, the reviews

---

[13] *San Francisco Chronicle*, August 28, 1904; "Music and Musicians," *Los Angeles Times*, September 4, 1904.
[14] "Music and Musicians," *Los Angeles Times*, July 7, 1907.

"were not exceedingly complimentary ... [T]hey remarked that he had not offered the Roman public anything new in the way of interpretation." The correspondent (who did not attend the performance) concluded, "That the orchestra is as bad as Mahler declares seems impossible, as ... other great conductors have found little fault, and even praised the execution."[15]

The foreign desk more discreetly undermined the Eighth Symphony. Under the headline "Mahler Triumph Expected," the Berlin correspondent reported about the upcoming premiere, which American "friends and colleagues" would attend. Yet after briefly describing the symphony, the correspondent devoted more space to *another* composer and conductor: "Another event waited with interest by musical German is the première of the new dramatic grand opera *The Devil's Path*, by the brilliant young Polish composer Ignatz Waghalter." Waghalter was a fascinating figure in his own right – later the lead conductor at the new Deutsche Oper Berlin (1912–23) and briefly music director of the New York Philharmonic (1924–25), then, when he returned to America to flee persecution as a Jew, founding the American Negro Orchestra with Harlem Renaissance poet James Weldon Johnson. The Berlin correspondent showed overweening enthusiasm for the as-yet unperformed *The Devil's Path* ("The music is original, being very Slavic in character, and is brimful of rich modern orchestration and vitality") but remained at an arm's length from Mahler, blandly identified as "conductor of the New York Philharmonic Society," and the Eighth Symphony, only indirectly "said to represent the first serious attempt since Beethoven's 'immortal Ninth' to combine purely instrumental interpretation with realistic vocal effects." Blatantly promoting Waghalter as a replacement for Mahler, the correspondent told an apocryphal story of Waghalter's debut at the Komische Oper.[16] Whereas Mahler's discomfort with New York society and his distaste for the city were well known, the Berlin correspondent stressed that "Waghalter is married to an American girl and his parents live in New York" – the latter

---

[15] "News and Notes of the Musical World," *New York Times*, April 24, 1910; "Mahler Quits Rome after One Concert," *New York Times*, May 8, 1910. In the omitted phrase the author cites a Mühlberg as a conductor who praised the Roman orchestra. I have been unable to locate information about a conductor by this name.

[16] In his memoirs, Waghalter recounts the story differently. As second assistant conductor at the Komische Opera, Waghalter was notified earlier in the day by telegram that he would conduct the performance; he acknowledged that he had no prior access to the score but credits his teacher for teaching him to follow a difficult score while conducting. Ignaz Waghalter, *Aus dem Ghetto in die Freiheit* (Marienbad [Mariánské Lázně]: Adam Schnurer, 1936), 95. According to the garbled version in the *New York Times*, when no conductor was available that night, Waghalter volunteered, claiming "he knew the score of *Tiefland* by heart and could conduct it faultlessly."

an obvious error and the former difficult to verify. The article concluded, "Waghalter's skill as a conductor has come to the attention of American managers, and his [eventual] transfer to New York is already mooted."[17]

Given the erratic coverage of Mahler in the American press, one might wonder whether less attention might have served him better. The reports suggest, however, that American papers – perhaps provincial ones as urgently as those in the East Coast cities – needed to demonstrate that they followed new European trends. Mahler needed to be known about, even if only intermittently understood.

[17] *New York Times*, August 7, 1910.

PART IV

Mind, Body, Spirit

CHAPTER 20

Organized Religion

Stephen McClatchie

Richard Wagner's *Religion and Art* (1880) makes a distinction between inward faith, living and authentic, and outward religion, rigid and dogmatic. This distinction – which in our day is captured by the claim to be "spiritual but not religious" – has a long pedigree. It finds an important nexus in Austro-German lands in the latter half of the nineteenth century in three distinct areas: Jewish assimilation (including secularization and conversion); tendencies in Christianity, particularly Roman Catholicism; and the transference or sublimation of religious experience to the arts and particularly music (*Kunstreligion*). These areas are especially pertinent in the case of Gustav Mahler: a born Jew, convert Roman Catholic, and lifelong Wagnerian.

Judaism

Three aspects of nineteenth-century Jewish life in Austro-German lands are relevant to Mahler's Jewish ancestry: legal emancipation, the spread of Jewish Enlightenment culture (*Haskalah*) and Reform Judaism, and the increase of sociocultural assimilation.

After the Jews were expelled from Vienna in 1670, the largest number of Habsburg Jews, including Mahler's ancestors, was to be found in the Bohemian crown lands.[1] While new toleration laws allowing a number of Jews to marry and settle in certain centers were promulgated in the eighteenth century, the vast majority of Jews were bound to their birthplace and restricted to particular occupations (e.g., peddling). Mahler's relatives were certainly affected by anti-Jewish legislation; in many cases

---

[1] Here I draw on works by Steven Beller and Michael Haber (see Further Reading) as well as O. McCagg, *A History of the Habsburg Jews 1670–1918* (Bloomington: Indiana University Press, 1989); Robert S. Wistrich, *The Jews of Vienna in the Age of Franz Joseph* (Oxford: Oxford University Press for the Littman Library, 1990). See also Martin Goodman, *A History of Judaism* (Princeton: Princeton University Press, 2017).

they were unable legally to marry (neither of his parents was the product of a legal marriage), and the 1787 requirement that Jews adopt German surnames means that little can be discovered about his more distant ancestors.

Mahler was born into an era of legal emancipation for the Jews and before the advent of a new, racially based anti-Semitism that would have such a pernicious effect in German-speaking lands in the following century. In 1782, Emperor Joseph II introduced a Tolerance Patent for the Jews that allowed them to practice all trades; set up factories, businesses, and engage in commerce; and send their children to state schools and universities. Freedom of movement was still limited, however, and the restrictive marriage laws remained in effect. Such legal freedoms were a product of Enlightenment culture and a concomitant Christian secular rationalism that dismissed ancient anti-Jewish prejudices such as the blood-libel myth. They aimed to Christianize or at least secularize the Jewish people, by removing legal restrictions that bound them to their separateness and by insisting on their use of the German language, German education, and Christian dress. As a result, many Jews even in non-German-speaking parts of the empire developed strong social and cultural affinities with German language and culture.

Following the 1860 removal of restrictions on Jewish residence in industrial towns and ability to purchase real estate, increasing mobility fostered urbanization. In October 1860, Bernard and Marie Mahler moved with their three-month-old son Gustav to Iglau (pop. 17,000), just over the Moravian border from Bohemia. By the end of the decade, Jews comprised 5.4 percent of the population and had established a corporation, synagogue, school, and cemetery.

The Enlightenment culture that eventually led to legal emancipation also had significant impact within Judaism itself. Originating under Moses Mendelssohn and others in late eighteenth-century Berlin, the *Haskalah*, or Jewish Enlightenment, drew on long-standing rationalist strains within Judaism. Theologians and philosophers argued that Judaism was revealed Law, not revealed Truth, and had no dogma other than reason itself. Freedom of thought and inquiry are the bases of faith, which is achieved by study and by drawing conclusions from premises observed in nature. Given practical and liturgical expression several decades later under Abraham Geiger, these ideas led to what would be termed "Reform Judaism," which advocated the diminishment of traditional forms of ritual and piety in order better to accommodate Enlightenment society and culture. It favored the replacement of Hebrew with German in the liturgy, the excision of messianic and nationalistic passages about the return to and restoration of sovereignty in Israel from the rite, and the cessation of some Jewish rituals (even including circumcision). Like its Enlightenment progenitor, Reform Judaism stood against all that was superstitious and irrational.

In Habsburg lands the *Haskalah* first had an impact in Vienna, and its Jewish community served as a paradigm for the provinces. Legally constituted as the *Kultusgemeinde* in 1792, it offered support and assistance to members and, by 1826, opened the first synagogue in Vienna. Under Isaac Mannheimer, the Temple embraced some elements of Reform Judaism but maintained the Hebrew language and preserved much of the traditional service so as not to offend the provincial rabbis looking to Vienna for leadership. Musically, the leadership of its first cantor, Salomon Sulzer, was influential through the publication of his two-volume collection, *Songs of Zion* (1840–65). The new synagogue in Iglau that the Mahlers attended almost certainly followed this model under its first rabbi, Joachim Jacob Unger, who had been educated in Berlin.

The Habsburg Jews in the western provinces, most of whom were strongly influenced by the *Haskalah*, generally spoke German, settled in German-speaking enclaves, and essentially saw themselves as German (albeit loyal to the Habsburg dynasty). They valorized Western Christian culture for its ethical and moral values, embraced the rational individualism of the Enlightenment, and aspired to that "acquisition of middle-class respectability, good manners, and refined family life along with a patina of high culture" known as *Bildung*.[2] These affinities strongly undergird the rise of liberalism, with which most assimilated Jews strongly identified, seeing it as a form of spiritual asylum, whereby emancipation would be achieved through education with the goal of becoming fully human.

Given the influence of Enlightenment culture on Judaism, a seemingly inevitable consequence within the faith was increasing assimilation and even secularization. Steven Beller has shown that, at least among the cultural elite, religion became largely a matter of indifference, a "family heirloom." He argues that orthodox Jewish reverence for the Word, the prestige of sacred learning, and the life of the mind were transferred to the secular sphere and in fact became constitutive of Viennese fin-de-siècle culture. Alfred Roller noted that Mahler's lifelong interest in existential,

[2] Marsha L. Rozenblit, "The Jews of Austria-Hungary on the Eve of World War I," in *Reconstructing a National Identity: The Jews of Habsburg Austria during World War I* (Oxford: Oxford University Press, 2004), 24.

philosophical, and religious questions as well as his strongly developed ethic of compassion were the main things connecting him with Judaism.[3] Assimilation did not necessarily include formal conversion but "could entail the simple disuse of Jewish religious practice without any scornful rejection," implying instead "a more general interaction with gentiles, whether attendance at universities, practicing a profession, or taking part in political organizations" and often "included observing at least the secular side of Christian holidays, such as Christmas" – as was the case in Mahler's family.[4]

By the end of the nineteenth century, assimilated Jews were often seen as Other, accepted by neither orthodox Jews nor Christians. An "internalised socio-religious snobbery" (Maier) led to a schism with their orthodox, eastern co-religionists, and the emergence of German racialist anti-Semitism, which could not be assuaged by conversion, left them increasingly isolated. Ominously, the second generation of assimilated Jews in Vienna and elsewhere – including Mahler – were, like their Christian contemporaries, strongly influenced by antiliberal, antirationalist, and antimaterialist thought in the wake of the 1873 economic collapse. Following Nietzsche and other Wagner-influenced German irrationalists, they placed an emphasis on synthesis, wholeness, and feeling instead of rationality, individualism, and analysis. It was precisely out of this milieu that the new racially based anti-Semitism emerged and grew strong, with tragic consequences.

Christianity

While a majority of Jewish immigrants were assimilated to German society and culture, identified with the Habsburg dynasty, and retained membership in the *Kultusgemeinde* (as registration with a religious community was a legal requirement), some did convert to Christianity (often at marriage, given that intermarriage was illegal). Most chose Protestantism, although some, like Mahler, opted for the Roman Catholicism of the Habsburgs. As is the case with nineteenth-century Christianity in Europe in general, two contrasting tendencies prevailed in German-speaking lands, and ultimately in Mahler's conversion: first, Enlightenment rationality, furthered through

[3] Alfred Roller, introduction to *Die Bildnisse von Gustav Mahler* (Leipzig: Tal, 1922); translated by Norman Lebrecht as "A Portrait of Gustav Mahler," in *The Mahler Album*, ed. Gilbert Kaplan (New York: Kaplan Foundation, 1995), 15–28.

[4] Charles S. Maier, "Christianity and Conviction: Gustav Mahler and the Meanings of Jewish Conversion in Central Europe," *Simon Dubnow Institute Yearbook* 11 (2012): 135.

the growth of German scholarship and the political and social dominance of liberalism; second, the appeal of Romantic, mystical, and indeed irrationalist elements of Christianity, particularly Roman Catholicism.[5]

The first is part of the rise of the new German university on the model of the University of Berlin and the increasing prominence and influence of German theologian-philosophers like Schleiermacher and Hegel, which contributed to the burgeoning of German *Wissenschaft* throughout the century. The publication of David Friedrich Strauß's *Das Leben Jesu kritisch bearbeitet* (1834–35) and the increasing prominence of the Tübingen school under Ferdinand Christian Baur saw the application of new historical, philological, and critical methods to sacred scripture and the life of Jesus. Termed "higher criticism," this approach called into question the historicity of scripture and therefore also the idea of biblical inerrancy, which was particularly problematic for Protestants (the predominant faith of these scholars) owing to Protestant emphasis on the doctrine of salvation *sola Scriptura*.

There are parallels to be drawn between this rational and critical approach to scripture and the rise of liberalism, particularly in its influence on ecclesial life and communities:

> Liberalism in religion is the doctrine that there is no positive truth in religion, but that one creed is as good as another . . . It is inconsistent with any recognition of any religion, as *true*. It teaches that all are to be tolerated, for all are matters of opinion. Revealed religion is not a truth, but a sentiment and a taste; not an objective fact, not miraculous; and it is the right of each individual to make it say just what strikes his fancy.[6]

Constantin Floros plausibly connects Mahler's religiosity with such theological liberalism, which finds political and cultural expression in the general anticlericalism (particularly Roman) in the late nineteenth-century Germany of the *Kulturkampf* (culture struggle).[7] While this was more muted in the Catholic Habsburg empire, it did find sympathy among

---

[5] Useful surveys include Nicholas Atkin and Frank Tallett, *Priests, Prelates, and People: A History of European Catholicism since 1750* (Oxford: Oxford University Press, 2003); Michael B. Gross, *The War against Catholicism: Liberalism and the Anti-Catholic Imagination in Nineteenth-Century Germany* (Ann Arbor: University of Michigan Press, 2004); and Christopher Clark and Wolfram Kaiser, eds., *Culture Wars: Secular-Catholic Conflict in Nineteenth-Century Europe* (Cambridge: Cambridge University Press, 2003).

[6] John Henry Cardinal Newman, "Biglietto Speech," May 12, 1879, available at www.newmanreader .org/works/addresses/file2.html#biglietto, accessed September 14, 2019.

[7] Constantin Floros, "'Eine musikalische Physiognomik': Über Theodor W. Adornos Mahler-Interpretation," *Simon Dubnow Institute Yearbook* 11 (2012): 240.

liberals (and assimilated Jews in particular) and an eventual outlet in Georg von Schönerer's *Los-von-Rom* movement.

Reactions to these developments came in both official (from Rome) and sociocultural forms. The influence of higher criticism, historicism, and liberal theology provoked a reaction from the Roman Church in the form of papal encyclicals (e.g., *Quanta cura* and its appended Syllabus of Errors, 1864) and in the convocation of the First Vatican Council (1869–70). Most famous for its definition of papal infallibility in *Pastor aeternus*, its other constitution, *Dei filius*, focused on God, revelation, and faith, and explicitly condemned rationalism. Post-1848 Catholicism is also notable for a strong turn away from political liberalism (understandable, given that the pope was also the temporal sovereign over the Papal States until the unification of Italy) and an increasing tendency toward the centralization of authority known as ultramontanism.

Socioculturally, the reaction found expression in a revival of forms and expressions of Christianity that may be linked with the wider Romantic movement and writers like Schleiermacher, Schelling, and Novalis. Roman Catholicism, in particular, with its emphasis on transcendence, mysticism, and sacramentality – all essentially irrational – attracted increasing numbers, particularly in its nondogmatic forms of popular piety that were both manifested and reflected in the significant increase in the number of Marian apparitions in nineteenth-century Europe, with Lourdes (1858) and Marpingen (1876) being particularly notable.

It is within this milieu that we may situate Mahler's conversion to Catholicism. The reasons behind it were multiple and probably contradictory: career advancement, a Romantic and Wagnerian infatuation with idealist and irrationalist thought, and a personal inclination toward Catholic mysticism noted by Alma and others.[8] His baptism into the Roman Catholic Church on February 23, 1897, would have been preceded by a period of catechesis into the doctrines and dogmas of the faith, which we

---

[8] Mahler told Ludwig Karpath, for example, that he had long been inclined to Catholicism. The rationale for and extent of Mahler's conversion is contested in the literature, although most commentators doubt that it was on the basis of authentic religious conviction. See, in addition to standard Mahler biographies, Maier, "Christianity and Conviction"; Daniel Jütte, "His Majesty's Mahler: Jews, Courts, and Culture in the Nineteenth Century," *Simon Dubnow Institute Yearbook* 11 (2012): 149–62; and Gerald Stourzh, "An Apogee of Conversions: Gustav Mahler, Karl Kraus, and *Fin de Siècle* Vienna," in *From Vienna to Chicago and Back: Essays on Intellectual History and Political Thought in Europe and America* (Chicago: University of Chicago Press, 2007), 224–47. Given his position in society, it is almost certain that he was buried according to the full rites of the Roman Church, that is, laid to rest in consecrated ground following a Requiem Mass and Absolution.

know from a letter from Mahler's sister to a friend began no later than December 1896,[9] as well a formal, legal exit from the Jewish *Gemeinschaft*. It required a formal, public profession of faith, likely the so-called Creed of Pius IV, recently reaffirmed by the First Vatican Council, which incorporated the Nicene-Constantinopolitan creed and specifically Catholic doctrines.

Some tensions within Austro-German Christianity were particularly fraught for Jewish converts, especially those to Roman Catholicism. The attractions of irrationalist thought often shaded into anti-Judaism, with Judaism being attacked as a religion overly focused on rationality. Increasing nationalism throughout the century meant that the German social and cultural values toward which many Jews aspired were seen as rooted, indigenous, and largely Protestant – an identification often at odds with Habsburg Catholicism. Within this context, Catholicism itself was seen as feudal and irrational, with Roman conviction and dogmatism regarded as cosmopolitan, international, and external (and hence "Jesuitical" or even "Jewish"). For Mahler and many of his contemporaries, the German, nationalist, irrationalist, and anti-Semitic Wagner was the central figure and source of some of these tensions. He was also a decisive influence on the early Nietzsche, who provided a philosophical basis for the admiration of German culture among the Jewish members of the Pernerstorfer circle in Mahler's student days (see Chapters 4 and 22).

Kunstreligion

An essay entitled *On the Elements of a Renewal of Religious Ideas in the Present* (1878), by Mahler's friend Siegfried Lipiner (1856–1911), was a key mediator of these tensions.[10] Lipiner makes a distinction between true religious feeling – beyond reason and nature, positive, and revelatory – and the aridity of dogmatic, organized religion. For Lipiner, religious renewal will occur through a deterioration of religious forms, ceremonies, and dogmas into a religious expression that embodies revelation beyond the rational, that is intuitive, and that is based on feelings, expression, and experience. He favors the application of the tools of "dogma-murdering"

[9] Stephen McClatchie, ed., *The Mahler Family Letters* (New York: Oxford University Press, 2006), 5–6.
[10] Stephen E. Hefling, "Siegfried Lipiner's *On the Elements of a Renewal of Religious Ideas in the Present*: Introduction and Translation (with Original German Text)," in *Mahler im Kontext/ Contextualizing Mahler*, ed. Erich Wolfgang Partsch and Morten Solvik (Vienna: Böhlau, 2011), 91–151.

historicism and higher criticism to religion so that the "tasteless and insipid physical wonder[s]" of its external forms will wither and religion itself will then "become myth, and as myth, that is, as the artistic representation of something beyond reality, never cease to seize beings" (131). The world itself can then be seen *"as a work of art.* In such moments our sensibility is filled by the most sacred religious shudder, and the world as artwork, which is assuredly not the world of reality, this world of religious intuition it [our sensibility] will faithfully and reverently call *God.* This is the general relationship of art to religion" (133). Wagner picks up on these themes in *Religion and Art*, writing that "when religion becomes artificial it falls to art to salvage the kernel of religion." Mythic symbols have figurative value that, by revealing deep and hidden truth, delivers the divine message of Christianity ideally. The artist, then, becomes something of a Poet-Priest.

Such thought is part of a broader Romantic move, with roots in late eighteenth-century aesthetics and philosophy (Schelling and Kant), toward seeing art as religion and religion as art. The term "Kunstreligion," coined by Friedrich Schleiermacher in 1799, has particular resonance with Schopenhauerian thought and thereby to Wagner and the Wagnerian expressive aesthetic position that was central to Mahler throughout his life. Schopenhauer's valorization of art in general and music in particular in revealing the Truth beyond and behind the appearance of things is well known, as his idea that the aesthetic contemplation of art is one means of stilling the relentless restlessness of the Will.[11]

Both Wagner and Mahler were fascinated by themes of transcendence and transfiguration or resurrection as well as by the idea of redemption through suffering and love. These ideas and others underlying Kunstreligion have a profoundly Christian basis, rooted in aspects of nineteenth-century German theology. Wilhelm De Wette, for example, argues that art "bring[s] down to us from heaven the divine in earthly form" and that aesthetic perception serves as a "living image of divinity." He draws on Jakob Friedrich Fries's concept of aesthetic sense (*Ahnung*) as the mediating force between knowledge and faith or belief; it reveals a sense of a truth or reality that remains inexpressible.[12]

In terms of religious feeling, then, we may safely call Mahler an adherent of Kunstreligion, with its aesthetic notions of genius, inspiration, and

---

[11] It is less frequently recognized that Schopenhauer also sees the effect of grace in Christianity as providing similar relief; see *World as Will and Representation*, vol. 1/iv, §67–71; §34, 36, 38.

[12] Thomas Albert Howard, *Religion and the Rise of Historicism: W. M. L. de Wette, Jacob Burckhardt, and the Theological Origins of Nineteenth-Century Historical Consciousness* (Cambridge: Cambridge University Press, 2000), 38, 48.

transcendence. Like many contemporaries, Mahler uses language with a strongly religious bent to describe artistic inspiration – once even referring to it as the "immaculate conception" (*SLGM*, 212/*GMB2*, 223). Indeed, there is a compelling parallel between such *Einfälle* (inspirations) and the Christian doctrine of grace as the free, unmerited gift of God. Alma mentions Mahler's sense of himself as chosen by the Holy Spirit (*Gnadenwahl des Geistes*) and perhaps even, blasphemously, of the creator occupying the place of the Creator; Alfred Roller commented that Mahler needed no intermediary to God, but that, like a prophet, he spoke with him face to face.[13]

Conclusion

While the importance of his conversion to Roman Catholicism and the ongoing influence and impact of his Jewish upbringing is open to conflicting interpretations, like many of his contemporaries it is clear that Mahler's commitment to organized religion – if by this is meant dogmatic religion – pales next to its sublimation into the religious sensibility that is captured by the Wagnerian ideal of Kunstreligion. He was drawn to those aspects of mysticism and striving for transcendence that were characteristic not only of second-generation assimilated Judaism but also of certain streams of theology and popular piety typical of ultramontane Catholicism – a thought that would have horrified Wagner. Indeed, Mahler himself once wondered whether his "manner and [his] musical content ... might perhaps be merely Catholic mystical humbug."[14] It is in such expressions of religiosity that one may discern the origins of contemporary professions of areligious spirituality – an orientation that, as the years pass, is itself starting to look increasingly organized as a belief system.

---

[13] Roller, "A Portrait of Gustav Mahler," 27.
[14] Natalie Bauer-Lechner, November 14, 1900; first published by Stephen E. Hefling and Morten Solvik, "Natalie Bauer-Lechner's 'Mahleriana': A Review of the Sources and the Passages on Brahms," in *Naturlauf: Scholarly Journeys toward Gustav Mahler. Essays in Honour of Henry-Louis de La Grange for his 90th Birthday*, ed. Paul André Bempéchat (New York: Peter Lang, 2016), 270–71.

CHAPTER 21

German Idealism

Morten Solvik

Throughout his life, Gustav Mahler cultivated an unusually keen interest in philosophy, not only as a committed intellectual but also as an artist. Indeed, for him, life and art were inextricably intertwined. It would be entirely apt to interpret many of Mahler's works as forms of musical expression deeply invested in plumbing the fundamental questions of existence. As he wrote of his Second Symphony:

> *What did you live for?* Why did you suffer? Is it all only a vast, terrifying joke? – We *have* to answer these questions somehow if we are to go on living – indeed, even if we are only to go on dying! The person in whose life this call has resounded, even if it was only once, must give an answer. And it is this answer I give in the last movement. (Mahler to Max Marschalk, March 26, 1896; *SLGM*, 180/*GMB2*, 172–73)

It may seem odd that a composer would feel called upon to address the question of mortality in a musical composition, but the philosophical ambitions evident in this passage are far less the result of hubris than a symptom of the thinking at the foundation of Mahler's worldview.

Mahler came of age as a thinker in the late nineteenth century, a time of great intellectual upheaval and contesting philosophies regarding the world and humanity's place within it. The epistemological and ontological debates of this era saw idealism and materialism, empiricism and rationalism, as well as many other strands of thinking propagated in the search for a fundamental understanding of life. The intensity of the debate and the diversity of answers proposed would continue to grow during the early twentieth century as developments in science and politics came to challenge age-old tenets of identity and belief. In the wake of Darwin's exploration of the origins of humanity, Nietzsche's declaration of the death of God, and Freud's exposure of the irrational workings of the mind, there emerged a profound questioning of supposed truths that no longer seemed self-evident. The impact of this turmoil was both thrilling and terrifying.

Had religion been demolished? Were we but creatures that had flattered ourselves into thinking we were exceptional in the scope of being? Had our morality and purpose been unmoored? At the same time, with the advent of X-rays, photography, and other technologies were we not celebrating seminal achievements resulting in the comforts and miracles of modern life? Had human ingenuity and understanding of the material world not rendered old beliefs unnecessary?

It is daunting to reduce this tangled web of perspectives to a handful of terms, but a more general view of the intellectual landscape sharpens the focus on key issues that preoccupied Mahler and his contemporaries. Central to the debate in Vienna and the German-speaking world was its indebtedness to German Idealism, a philosophical movement often identified with the writings of Kant, Fichte, Schelling, and Hegel in a roughly fifty-year period from 1770 to 1830. Idealism comes in many variants, but at its roots it argues for the primacy of the mind as the fundament of all reality (ontological idealism) or as an unavoidable agent in knowing reality (epistemological idealism).[1] At its foundation, idealism contends that reality consists only of ideas, since all we can truly know to exist are our thoughts; physical things may induce perception, but they are not directly knowable because sensory input is not equivalent to the thing itself. This position was presented much earlier than the German Idealists by the likes of George Berkeley (who theorized a "subjective idealism") and, indeed, Plato.

The leading figure in German Idealism was Immanuel Kant (1724–1804), whose Transcendental Idealism attempted to construct a connection between realism and idealism by separating the ontological and epistemological elements of the debate. In the *Critique of Pure Reason* (1781), Kant explores the limits of what we can know. Perception itself, he argues, imposes subjective but necessary ways of representing objects to the mind through the categories of space, time, and causality. He does not, however, deny the real, independent existence of the objects we perceive. This synthesis of epistemological idealism and ontological realism also merged rationalist and empiricist tendencies, acknowledging the unavoidable presence and limits of mind in a demonstrable engagement with matter. It is important to point out that, while this treatise seemed to narrow the scope of human knowledge, as such, and certainly shut the door on meaningful speculation regarding anything immaterial, it did not

[1] See "Idealism" in the *Stanford Encyclopedia of Philosophy*, https://plato.stanford.edu/entries/idealism/, accessed September 14, 2019.

insist on the impossibility of immaterial existence (e.g., Kant needed to acknowledge the concept of God). This back door to ontological speculation left his acolytes with numerous interpretive possibilities.

The impact of this philosophy on German-speaking culture was profound, as it pervaded the Romantic movement of the early nineteenth century in the works of such influential figures as Jacobi, Jean Paul, Schleiermacher, Novalis, Hölderlin, E. T. A. Hoffmann, Wackenroder, and Tieck. Explorations of nature, love, and the profound insisted on the primacy of feeling and the ephemeral forces of life in what could be seen as a rejection of the rational sensibilities of the Enlightenment that preceded it. Knowledge in the broader sense, that which mattered to human existence, resided far beyond our faulty reason.

Of course, not everyone saw the world from this perspective, and as the nineteenth century continued, science emerged as an increasingly powerful tool in the understanding and harnessing of nature. Chemistry, physics, and biology were bounding ahead with ever new discoveries. Innovations such as X-rays, photography, motion pictures, telegraphy, telephones, and faster modes of travel astounded the public and made daily life ever more convenient. It seemed that understanding the world in its mechanical essence might finally solve the philosophical problem regarding the makeup of existence. After all, the success of technology was predicated on a material model of the world in which the interaction of its constituent parts consistently mirrored and anticipated reality. For many it was not much of a leap to suspect that everything consisted of matter, not only physical objects but also feelings and the mind.

The philosophical shift to materialism and positivism in certain quarters of German-speaking culture can be found, for instance, in the critique of religion espoused by Ludwig Feuerbach (1804–72), in the numerous extrapolations of Darwin's evolutionary thinking by Ernst Haeckel (1834–1919), and in the philosophical reflections inspired by scientific thinking in the work of Ernst Mach (1838–1916) and Ludwig Boltzmann (1844–1906). With Moritz Schlick (1882–1936) and the Vienna Circle of the 1920s, Vienna would become a hotbed of logical positivism in which aesthetics, ethics, religion, and any other philosophical perspective that did not rely on empirical evidence was roundly rejected. Their purpose was to construct a logical methodology to validate knowledge far from the speculations of metaphysics.

By Mahler's time, these challenges to idealism were well established, but some thinkers remained adamant about their opposition to materialism. The resulting syncretic theories often sought to overcome the apparently incommensurable gap between physics and spirit. One approach involved the concept of monads, originally introduced by Gottfried Leibniz (1646–1716). In its simplest outline, this theory proposed that the world consisted of basic particles, each of which possessed an inner identity. The main proponent of this mystical scientism was Rudolf Hermann Lotze (1817–1881), whose *Mikrokosmus* (1856–64) was one of Mahler's favorite books. Lotze's theory of sentient particles called for a two-fold perspective on the behavior of atoms. From the outside, monads moved according to patterns that could be explained by laws of mechanics. Internally, however, each monad acted in realization of a willing consciousness. All of these individual expressions of will in turn were joined together into a harmonious whole that fulfilled the divine intent of God. Thus, Lotze formulated a philosophy that could satisfy both the spiritual and rational tendencies of the time, a quasi-scientific formulation of animistic philosophy.

Another leading antimaterialist was Friedrich Albert Lange (1828–75), whose *Geschichte des Materialismus* (*History of Materialism*, 1866) also drew Mahler's sustained attention. Lange, like Lotze, presented a massive amount of scientific information on the world amended by a thoroughgoing treatment of the philosophical implications of knowledge. The manner in which we view scientific findings is not merely an epistemological issue, argued Lange, but also an ontological one. While a description of existence that confines itself to material substances may succeed in defining the reality accessible to our cognitive faculties, it cannot reach to the thing-in-itself. According to Lange, even a mechanical explanation of the world that proved consistent with the laws of nature as we perceive them failed to provide a true measure of reality. The critical shortcoming stemmed from the ephemeral nature of perception itself: "Therefore, one can surely no longer espouse any form of materialism, for even if our researches based on sensory perception must unavoidably assume that for every mental function there must exist a material cause, then this material and all that comes from it is only an abstraction of our images of representation."[2] Mahler openly expressed his enthusiasm for the works of Lotze, Lange, and others. He was, after all, deeply invested in a world in which the immaterial mattered. Art, devoid of practical purpose yet so crucial to the human spirit, formed the centerpiece of his existence. And as an individual driven by philosophical inquiry into life's essential questions, these issues mattered crucially to him.

---

[2] Friedrich Albert Lange, *Geschichte des Materialismus und Kritik seiner Bedeutung in der Gegenwart*, 2nd ed., vol. 2 (Iserlohn: J. Baedeker, 1873–75), 430 (author's translation).

Mahler's philosophy of art lay deeply embedded in the Idealist tradition. Here the towering figure in the composer's thinking was Arthur Schopenhauer (1788–1860) and his magnum opus, *Die Welt als Wille und Vorstellung* (*The World as Will and Representation*, 1818, 1844). Borrowing freely from Plato and Kant, Schopenhauer posited material reality as the physical rendering of ideal forms, themselves emanating from a single force at the basis of being he termed the Will. This scheme, of course, also encompasses humans, and most people are incapable of attaining insight into the true workings of being because they are trapped in individual subjectivity. As Kant insists, we are beholden only to sensory impressions from without and thus do not perceive the things themselves. Schopenhauer ekes out some exceptions here, most notably for artists, who, in moments of inspiration, escape the principle of individuation to become one with the universe. Returning to their conscious selves, these individuals then render their profound experience in works of art, abstractions of their inspiration manifested in the material means available to them, using paint, objects, symbols. The audience that then engages with the resulting painting, poem, or composition can catch glimpses of the truths that sparked the artwork's creation. Schopenhauer thus merges aesthetics with ontology and elevates the artist to a divinator of the profound.

Schopenhauer repeatedly makes the point that, of all art forms, music ranks highest by virtue of its abstract essence – as a direct representation of the Will, bypassing the Ideas – and its having suffered the least loss from its original source of inspiration in being manifested so ephemerally in a material setting.

> Therefore music is by no means like the other arts, namely a copy of the Ideas, but a copy of the Will itself, the objectivity of which are the Ideas. For this reason the effect of music is so very much more powerful and penetrating than is that of the other arts, for these others speak only of the shadow, but music of the essence.[3]

Mahler expressed precisely this view of creativity in general, and music specifically, on numerous occasions. "The need to express myself musically – in symphonic terms – begins only on the plane of *obscure* feelings, at the gate that opens into the 'other world,' the world in which things no

---

[3] Schopenhauer, *The World as Will and Representation*, trans. E. F. J. Payne (New York: Dover, 1966), 257.

longer fall apart in time and space" (Mahler to Max Marschalk, March 26, 1896; *SLGM*, 179/*GMB2*, 171). It is not difficult to see the mystical core of Mahler's worldview and the seriousness, indeed, the burden he felt, in creating his works. The mission went beyond the individual artist or even the specific artwork, for lurking in this brand of idealism was a type of responsibility to humanity. It was a view that Mahler owed in part to one of his best friends, Siegfried Lipiner (1856–1911). The two met in the late 1870s at the University of Vienna, where young intellectuals frequently gathered to discuss the pressing philosophical problems of the day. At one of these meetings, Lipiner gave a rousing speech, "Über die Elemente einer Erneuerung religiöser Ideen in der Gegenwart" ["On the Elements of a Renewal of Religious Ideas in the Present"], in which he argued that "the fundamental premise of materialism has been repudiated; ... this manner of explanation is not even adequate for making intelligible the outermost endpoints of the phenomenal world: the ultimate components of matter and consciousness."[4] To address this adequately it would be necessary to elevate life into a privileged realm through art, a mystical, religious awareness: "at instants of the greatest longing for art, it may well divine the greatest thought, *the world as a work of art*."[5]

Lipiner's speech was shot through with references to Lange and Schopenhauer and bristled with a call for fundamental changes in attitudes that would subsume art, faith, and society in a grand vision for the future of humanity. This attempt to revitalize religion in the name of an artistic overcoming of material reality represents perhaps an extreme aspiration, but the sincerity and urgency of the call must have inspired Mahler.

For Mahler, creative thinking itself constituted a mystical act, one that brought the artist into the realm of prematerial existence, privy to truths beyond the ken of daily perception. In the composer's view of the world, matter was but a portal to something more. As he wrote eloquently to a friend:

> Actually I cannot understand how it comes that you – with a musician-poet's soul – do not believe = know. What is it then that delights you when you hear music? What makes you light-hearted and free? Is the world less puzzling if you build it out of matter? Is there any explanation to be got

---

[4] Siegfried Lipiner, "Über die Elemente einer Erneuerung religiöser Ideen in der Gegenwart/On the Elements of a Renewal of Religious Ideas in the Present," in Erich Partsch and Morten Solvik, eds., *Mahler im Kontext/Contextualizing Mahler* (Vienna: Böhlau, 2011), 143.

[5] Lipiner, "Über die Elemente," 133.

from you seeing it as an interplay of mechanical forces? What is force, energy? *Who* does the playing? You believe in the "conservation of energy," in the indestructibility of matter. Is that not immortality too?

Shift the problem to any plane you choose – in the end you will always reach the point where "your philosophy" begins to "dream." (Mahler to Max Kalbeck, June 22, 1901; *SLGM*, 251–52/*GMB2*, 283–84)[6]

---

[6] Note Mahler's rendering of the first law of thermodynamics: heat is a form of energy, and thermodynamic processes are therefore subject to the principle of conservation of energy.

CHAPTER 22

Nietzsche

Lesley Chamberlain

When he was still little-known and widely ridiculed, Nietzsche found his earliest followers in Vienna. Learning of their existence in the 1870s, he admired their acumen. It was a group of artists and intellectuals known as the Pernerstorfer Circle who found his rare favor. They organized readings and lectured each other on the early works even as they appeared. In 1877 they made Nietzsche aware of their "heavy responsibility" in deciding "to follow you as our shining and captivating example ... and to strive like you ... to realize that ideal which you have outlined in your works."[1] This vision, as we shall see, was not so much of the *Übermensch*, the individual striving to master reality by turning it into a supreme artistic game. Nor did it owe a debt to the philosophically more complex Nietzsche of perspectives and masks, strategies not developed until the next decade, to assert the antimorality of "beyond good and evil." It was, rather, an infectious excitement at how the young Nietzsche had reinterpreted the world of the ancient Greeks.

The principal Viennese Nietzschean was a young poet and journalist by the name of Siegfried Lipiner (1856–1911). Having at aged twenty translated – in the widest sense – Nietzsche's barnstorming 1872 essay *The Birth of Tragedy Out of the Spirit of Music* into verse, Lipiner sent it to Nietzsche in 1877 and received an enthusiastic response. As the German philosopher declared:

> Now I know that there exists a poet. So tell me now without inhibition whether with regard to your origins you stand in some relation to the Jews. The thing is I have recently had many experiences which have aroused in me very great hope of young men of this origin. When my book is published I would like urgently to meet you in person.[2]

---

[1] Translation (slightly amended) from Martin Liebscher, "'Lauter ausgesuchte Intelligenzen': Admiration for Nietzsche in 1870s Vienna," *Austrian Studies* 16 (2008): 32–50.

[2] Nietzsche to Siegfried Lipiner, August 24, 1877. The occasion was Nietzsche's thirtieth birthday. Friedrich Nietzsche, *Briefwechsel: Kritische Gesamtausgabe* II/6 (hereafter *KG*), ed. Mazzino Montinari and Giorgio Colli (Berlin: DeGruyter, 1967–), 663, and Lipiner's reply, p. 693.

Today we would prefer Nietzsche not to make any racial or religious distinction, but we can be sure that Lipiner passed on the encouragement to his Jewish friends in the Pernerstorfer Circle, and in the Leseverein der deutschen Studenten Wiens (Reading Society of German Students in Vienna) that many of them also attended. Since a stock market crash in 1873, Viennese Jewish intellectuals had found their lives all the more constrained.[3] Jewish Pernerstorfer Circle members included the Social Democrat Victor Adler, the future founder of the Austrian Republic. Gustav Mahler, no stranger to anti-Semitism, joined the Circle in 1878.

Remarkable for the character of the Austrian Nietzsche in these days was his profile as a left-wing liberator keen to undermine sclerotic social and political conventions. Nietzsche instructed the Pernerstorfer Circle that only "the empire of youth" could stop the onslaught on "true culture" at the hands of the money-makers, the state, and the scientists.[4] And yet Nietzsche's philo-Semitic outburst and the political pendant attached to it misleads us in the case of the real connection between the philosopher and the composer. What would unfold from Mahler's reading would be a deep but hardly political affinity,[5] mediated in the first instance by Lipiner.

Lipiner's *Der entfesselte Prometheus* (*Prometheus Unbound*, 1876) had impressed Wagner as well as Nietzsche. Very soon Lipiner and Mahler formed a friendship that would last a lifetime, and it has been suggested that the very power of Lipiner's hold on the composer prompted his wife Alma's virulent objections. Nietzsche wrote, with his own early bond to Wagner in mind, of a "star friendship."[6] The closeness between Lipiner and Mahler was based on their love of Nietzsche and desire to learn from him. Though little came of Lipiner's own early artistic promise, it created a situation in which Mahler's creative personality from time to time resembled Nietzsche's, in its tumultuousness, its search for a new musicality, and its post-metaphysical hollow laughter.

Rohde in startlingly anti-Semitic terms had reminded Nietzsche to answer Lipiner (June 18, 1877), pp. 559–60.

[3] Lipiner himself converted to Protestantism and became mildly anti-Semitic. See Liebscher, "Lauter ausgesuchte Intelligenzen," 40.

[4] Quoted in Melvyn Ingleby, "Nietzsche's Vienna: The Reception of Nietzsche's Philosophy in 19th Century Vienna, 1870–1900" (PhD diss., University College London, 2014), 7. See Nietzsche, "On the Uses and Disadvantages of History for Life" (1874), in *Untimely Meditations, KG* III/1, 241–330.

[5] Henri-Louis La Grange, *Mahler*, vol. 1 (London: Gollancz, 1974), 69, leaves the question of Mahler's passing socialism open but suggests that the Pernerstorfer Circle had itself become anti-Semitic by the time he left it in 1883. This chimes with Lipiner's conversion. See above, note 3.

[6] Cf. Lesley Chamberlain, *Nietzsche in Turin* (London: Quartet, 1996), 49–50.

Lipiner's themes were all either directly or obliquely Nietzschean (e.g., the *Buch der Freude* [*Book of Joy*, 1880] and *Bruder Rausch (Fragment eines Epos)* [*Brother Intoxication (Fragments of an Epic)*, 1883]). One project, which he shared with Mahler in a four-hour presentation in 1896, and which lasted his entire life, was prompted by a desire for the renewal of Christianity. Lipiner had in 1878 lectured at the Leseverein on just that topic.[7] Where Nietzsche as the author of *Thus Spake Zarathustra* (1884) and *The Antichrist* (1887) had expressed a lyrical pessimism in response to the death of God, Lipiner planned "a trilogy on the life of Christ, intended for the musical theatre." Its three parts were "Mary Magdalen," "Judas Iskariot," and "Paul in Rome." Surely, the hope was that Mahler would write the score. Mahler's friend the violinist Natalie Bauer-Lechner described the scene in which Mahler listened intently to the proposal while she and Lipiner's wife looked on:

> While Klementine [Lipiner] and I took shelter under the roof of the café terrace, Lipiner and Mahler, in the middle of their conversation about Christ, stayed below in the hefty downpour, each holding only an umbrella. We saw how Lipiner was bent forward towards Mahler and spoke without interruption and gesticulated wildly with his free arm, his head and his body, while Mahler, in the posture of one who was listening intently, stood there as if he was rooted to the ground and only now and again, as was his way, when something especially deep seized and excited him, lifted his feet and stamped like a wild boar. All this happened to the great puzzlement and delight of the numerous audience gathered on the terrace, as they followed with ever-increasing curiosity the movements of the silhouettes of our two dear men standing in the pouring rain, until at last they all stood up, surged forwards and stared down at the two figures who might have been taken for the escaped inmates of a lunatic asylum, so that Klementine and I thought it wiser to abandon our shelter and to assemble the two men and start out on the way back with them, despite the unremitting downpour.[8]

The two friends were in their middle years by the time this encounter took place, but still they shared their youthful excitement over the style and the message of Nietzsche's first book, *The Birth of Tragedy*. That was a story, in fact, of the rebirth of ancient dramatic culture in the contemporary

---

[7] Siegfried Lipiner, "Ueber die Elemente einer Erneuerung religiöser Ideen der Gegenwart. Vortrag gehalten im Leseverein der deutschen Studenten Wien" ("On Aspects of a Renewal of Religious Ideas in Our Time. A Lecture Given at the Reading Society of German Students in Vienna") (Vienna: Leseverein der deutschen Studenten, 1878). For a commentary, see Liebscher, "Lauter ausgesuchte Intelligenzen," 39.

[8] *NBLE*, 54–55.

German-speaking world, and it was to happen through, and inspired by, a new kind of music.

The Pernserstorfer Circle and the Leseverein members who interpreted its Promethean spirit politically had strong artistic reasons for doing so. The playwright Arthur Schnitzler, the writer and critic Herman Bahr, the great poet Hugo von Hofmannsthal, and the fiction-writer and chronicler Stefan Zweig were all outraged by the stagnant culture of the educated Viennese. This middle class had so instrumentalized patronage of the arts, had so trivially turned it into a symbol of wealth and status, that the result was the death of art. Not the murdered God whom Nietzsche would lament in *Zarathustra*, but Art in Vienna had lost its life. The new generation set about resuscitating Art, and with that came the capacious and vague hope for a rebirth of spirituality. The Pernerstorfers argued that liberalism's individualist greed could be overcome only through reawakening the emotional elements of a culture, which would bring "the Dionysian liberation from the fetters of the individual." Moreover, by attaining Dionysian "one-ness," the political collective would be able to achieve greatness far beyond the reach of isolated individuals.

"Dionysian" was, of course, the key term of *The Birth of Tragedy*, counterposed against the Apollonian. But it is important to understand that, just as Nietzsche had not intended his essay politically, so these terms were also not opposing political forces but instinctive moments in the creative process. They related as dream to intoxication. Their inventor used them to set the very creation of artistic forms against the dissolution that our experience of their beauty might inspire. As in each of us our love of formal beauty is transformed into a feeling of cosmic oneness, so we leave our individuality and our cherishing of Apollonian art behind. Nietzsche contemplated the work of the individual creator in relation to the self-sublimation he believed all humanity was capable of. Both utopianism and self-destruction inhered in human nature. Through these twin impulses humanity related to nature as such.

For the student of Mahler to reread Nietzsche's original 1872 essay, with the rebirth of music still in its title,[9] it seems that this unique and unclassifiable work sets out a program that Mahler would follow, in some places to the letter. For those who believed, with Nietzsche, that "art is the highest task," the model was to be found in Greek tragic drama. Tragedy

---

[9] Nietzsche changed the title and wrote a later preface. See Michael Tanner, "Introduction," in *Friedrich Nietzsche: The Birth of Tragedy*, trans. Shaun Whiteside (hereafter *BT*) (London: Penguin, 1993), vii.

was what it was *because* it was set to music. Tragedy, introduced by a satyr chorus and played out on panpipes, made life "both possible and worth living." The music Nietzsche had in mind was an intricate blend of those Apollonian and Dionysian elements I sketched just now. The Apollonian impulse conjured images and sounds to delight eye and ear. Its business was the happy illusion that sustained the individual will to live. Freud would soon want to investigate the quirky dreamwork of neurosis, but for the time being Nietzsche's Apollonian interest was in the sunlit uplands of the daydream. As he went on: "Indeed, it might be said of Apollo that the unshaken faith in that *principium* [*individuationis*] and the peaceful still-ness of the man caught up in it have found their most sublime expression in him, and we might even describe Apollo as the glorious divine image of the *principium individuationis*, from whose gestures and looks all the delight, wisdom and beauty of 'illusion' speak to us."

Both complementary and distinct from this happiness was the sudden apprehension of the formless, unindividuated, and unending nature of existence, or "the dread that grips man when he suddenly loses his way amidst the cognitive forms of appearance." The Dionysian was the intense experience of disorientation and spiritual pain, not a delight in the beauti-fully formed image, but an ecstatic terpsichorean moment of abandon. "Under the influence of the narcotic potion hymned by all primitive men and peoples, or in the powerful approach of spring, joyfully penetrating the whole of nature, those Dionysian urges are awakened, and, as they grow more intense, subjectivity becomes a complete forgetting of the self." To this basic distinction Nietzsche added the most luxuriant imagery:

> In [Greece and] medieval Germany too, the same Dionysian power sent singing and dancing throngs, constantly increasing, wandering from place to place; in these dances of Saint John and Saint Vitus we can recognize the Bacchic choruses of the Greeks, with their prehistory in Asia Minor, as far back as Babylon and the orgiastic Sacaea ... The chariot of Dionysus is piled high with flowers and garlands; under its yoke stride tigers and panthers. If we were to turn Beethoven's Hymn to Joy into a painting, and not to restrain the imagination even as the multitudes bowed awestruck to the dust; this would bring us close to the Dionysian.[10]

If at this point – and we are only a few pages into the first chapter of *The Birth of Tragedy* – we feel a premonition of the fantastic gilded processions approaching castles in the air evoked by Mahler's symphonies, and of that phantasmagoria of dream-like states that is no one person's experience but

[10] *BT* [1], 16–17.

more like collective exaltation – then we must also be ready to have our visions abruptly undermined by everyday stolidity. "Some people, either through a lack of experience or through obtuseness, turn away with pity or contempt from phenomena such as these as from 'folk diseases,' bolstered by a sense of their own sanity; these poor creatures have no idea how blighted and ghostly this 'sanity' of theirs sounds when the glowing life of Dionysian revellers thunders past them."[11] These moments too seem all too familiar to us from the symphonies, with their caricatures of public pomposity and their abrupt slides from the sublime into the ridiculous. Talking of "truth as phantasmagoria" and "panic epiphany," the last German Nietzschean, Theodor Adorno, wrote that "Mahler was the first to draw the musical conclusion from a state of consciousness that commands nothing but the hastily bundled profusion of its own impulses and experience and the hope that something might arise from them which as yet they are not, but without falsification." He went on:

> Since Kant and Beethoven, German philosophy and music had been a single system ... The originality of Mahler's music takes up Nietzsche's insight that the system and its seamless unity, its appearance of reconcilia-tion, is dishonest. His music takes issue with extensive life, plunges with closed eyes into time, yet without installing life as a substitute metaphysics ... His potential to do so derived from the partly prebourgeois feudal, partly Josephinistically sceptical Austrian air, untouched by German Idealism, while symphonic integrity was still present enough to protect him from an attitude to form that made concessions to a weakly atomistic mode of listening.[12]

It is against the Nietzschean influence on both Mahler and Adorno that this penetrating analysis needs to be read. Mahler seemed to view Vienna's heavy and ornate historicism, and the political unreality of the last years of the Habsburg Empire, to be conjured up a last time with humor and nostalgia, before it was dissolved in the spirit of Dionysus.

Nietzsche's dialectical interweaving of the Apollonian and the Diony-sian meanwhile offered an account of suffering that showed how art might redeem the present age. Nietzsche had hoped to supplant the Christian myth of delivery through the Redeemer by his return to ancient Greece. The word "redemption," *Erlösung*, recurs in *The Birth of Tragedy*, and throughout his career it remained connected to how he originally saw

[11] *BT* [1], 17.
[12] Theodor Adorno, *Mahler: A Musical Physiognomy*, trans. Edmund Jephcott (Chicago: University of Chicago Press, 1992), 62, 64.

Wagner's role in the rebirth of German musical culture. In the 1872 text a sometimes Schopenhauerian/Wagnerian vision, as when Tristan and Isolde embarked on their ecstatic love-is-death journey into a final oneness with the universe, served to illustrate it. But the text also contained Nietzsche's own version of how to deal with metaphysical pain. Nietzsche said, in essence, that we create the illusions of art because we are ourselves illusions. With regard to "the mysterious foundation of our being, whose phenomena we are,"

> the more I become aware of ... omnipotent art impulses in [our] nature, and find in them an ardent longing for illusion and for redemption by illusion, the more I feel compelled to make the metaphysical assumption that the truly existent, the primal Oneness, eternally suffering and contradictory, also needs the delightful vision, the pleasurable illusion for its constant redemption.

Apollo is our Redeemer: "Only through him does the perpetually attained goal of primal Oneness, redemption through illusion, reach consummation. With sublime gestures he reveals to us how the whole world of torment is necessary so that the individual can create the redeeming vision, and then, immersed in contemplation of it, sit peacefully in his tossing boat amid the waves." The Apollonian artist "psalmodizes ... with his phantom harp-notes." Prometheus, by contrast, went beyond Apollonian bounds. "For his Titanic love of man Prometheus had to be torn apart by vultures."[13] For Nietzsche, art delivers us from having to dwell on the suffering of Christ on the Dionysian cross. We do not need to render ourselves artistically helpless by accepting the old Christian story. The "Resurrection" of the Second Symphony carries this message.[14]

What humanity was, the nature of "that being, whose phenomena we are," both troubled and liberated the age of Nietzsche. He made himself the spokesman for "the animal whose nature is not yet finally established" (*Beyond Good and Evil*, section 62). Writing about Mahler, Adorno picked up that theme and attached it to that symphony we think of as the most Nietzschean, the Third. Mahler's setting of the verses from *Zarathustra*, "Um Mitternacht ... ," has long since established the connection. But Adorno was ahead of critics of his time in understanding that the Mahler/Nietzsche connection was more fundamental than the borrowing of certain lines or images. Adorno wrote, "The Scherzo of the Third Symphony,

[13] *BT* [4], 25, 26.
[14] Cf. Stephen E. Hefling, "Zweite Symphonie," in *Gustav Mahler: Interpretationen seiner Werke*, ed. Peter Revers and Oliver Korte, vol. 1 (Laaber: Laaber, 2011), 272–73.

like that of the Second, is prompted by animal symbolism ... Through animals humanity becomes aware of itself as impeded nature and of its activity as deluded natural history ... for [Mahler], as in Kafka's fables, the animal realm is the human world as it would appear from the standpoint of redemption, which natural history itself precludes."[15]

That "natural history" was, of course, Darwin's. Moreover, the philosophical impact of the theory of evolution is traduced if we only think of it in terms of natural selection.[16] What mattered to so many artists and to the occasional philosopher in the Germanophone world was the death of the myth of creation. Where for so long it had been the task of art and the artist to imitate God's work, art and artist were now cut free whether they wished it or not. Mahler was no exception in confronting this measure of the age.

A great banality and a deflating literalness had entered the culture with, concomitant with Darwinism, the collapse of the Christian myth. In a strange way, Nietzsche qua philosopher was part of the problem as well as offering a potential solution. "Though it is hard to define, there is a real affinity between on the one hand, Nietzschean biologism and the 'philosophy of life' or 'vitalism' to which it gave rise ... what they have in common is their attempt to discover the ultimate legitimation for all values in the natural or primitive situation of man, uninfluenced by scientific prejudices or other habits peculiar to civilization."[17]

But let us remain with the Nietzsche who, in the light of what natural history had recently revealed, directly inspired Mahler to pose the question of the future of human spirituality. Like Nietzsche, Mahler could not answer the question, but he could keep conjuring fresh images and taking up new narrative threads. It seems to be that in the texture of the symphonies there is a glorious perpetuation of illusion, death, and rebirth. New stories arise, new paths keep opening up. The human voice grows out of this welter of possibilities – like an answer to the mystery of evolution.

Again, in *The Birth of Tragedy*, Nietzsche had shown the way. In deference to Schopenhauer's universe, in which artistic representation held off the brute force of the will of nature for a few blissful moments, he quoted: "The genuine song is the copy or impression of the whole of this mingled and divided state of mind." But it was Nietzsche's own schema

---

[15] Adorno, *Mahler*, 8–9.

[16] I take up this theme in Lesley Chamberlain, *A Shoe Story: Van Gogh, the Artists and the West* (London: Harbour, 2014).

[17] Leszek Kolakowski, *Positivist Philosophy from Hume to the Vienna Circle* (Harmondsworth: Penguin, 1972), 126.

that was surely destined to inspire Mahler. "The Dionysian musical enchantment of the sleeping man now sends out sparks of images, lyric poems which, at the peak of their evolution, will bear the name of tragedies and dramatic dithyrambs." In the Second, Third, and Fourth Symphonies, where extraordinary orchestral passages culminate in sung movements, everything seems to prepare for this moment of emergence. For Nietzsche, folk song linked the ancient world with the present; he repeatedly mentioned Clemens Brentano's collection *Des Knaben Wunderhorn* as an example.[18] Mahler incorporated *Wunderhorn* settings in all three of his Nietzschean symphonies.

In short, Mahler, adapting Nietzsche to his own purposes, announced the provocative rebirth of symphonic music, and supremely of the song, out of the tragedy of human banality. Nor did he ever forget the impact that Nietzsche had on him at the start of his career: he dedicated the third movement of his valedictory Ninth Symphony to "my brothers in Apollo."

[18] *BT* [5], 31; [5], 29; [6] 33.

CHAPTER 23

Fechner

Michael Heidelberger

Translated by Juliane Schicker

The physicist, psychophysicist, physician, and philosopher Gustav Theodor Fechner – an intellectual force occupying Mahler from his student years in Vienna through the composition of *Das Lied von der Erde* – is often described as a "mystic" or a "speculative thinker" whose fantastical philosophical system attempts to reconcile mechanistic science with an "animistic non-rational world-view."[1] Accordingly, his theories are usually dismissed today as curiosities. But though Fechner's views may appear strange, on closer examination they are not mere arbitrary convictions; rather, they have a rational foundation. Furthermore, it can be demonstrated that Fechner, unorthodox thoughts notwithstanding, made important contributions to the natural sciences. If his "speculations" went awry, he erred not by incorrect substantiation but by overestimating the power of his evidence – betrayed by his own "somewhat oracularly uttered sentences," as William James once phrased it.[2]

In this chapter I will introduce Fechner's life and work, before discussing "psychophysical parallelism," his highly original and influential conception of the relationship between the body and the soul. This crucial idea lies at the heart of his thought and touches on virtually all his other subjects, including panpsychism and pantheist religion. The third section examines Fechner's "day view" (*Tagesansicht*), his answer to the materialist and mechanistic "night view" (*Nachtansicht*) espoused by many of his contemporaries. Finally, the fourth section considers the reception of his philosophy through World War I.

---

[1] Morten Solvik, "Mahler and Germany," in *The Mahler Companion*, ed. Donald Mitchell and Andrew Nicholson (Oxford: Oxford University Press, 1989), 137.
[2] William James, "Introduction," in *Gustav Theodor Fechner: The Little Book of Life after Death*, trans. Mary C. Wadsworth (Boston: Little, Brown, 1904), vii.

Fechner's Life and Work

Fechner was born in 1801 to a Lutheran pastor's family in Groß-Särchen (today Żarki Wielkie in Poland). At sixteen he began studying medicine at the University of Leipzig, where he slaked his thirst for knowledge in other departments, for example, with Herbart's philosophical psychology, and so-called Late Idealism, an incipient critique of German Idealism. Having embraced atheism during his medical studies, he experienced inner struggles and a conversion of sorts after encountering the *Naturphilosophie* of Oken and Schelling, which inspired a new spiritual attitude. In future years Fechner would oscillate between atheism and a kind of natural religion.

As a student he earned his living with copious translations of French scientific works, then in 1823 began lecturing in medicine and physics at the university. Distanced once more from *Naturphilosophie*, he wrote scientific articles and literary satires, pursuing a vast array of projects. In 1834 he was offered the chair of physics at the University of Leipzig, after publishing a series of experiments on Ohm's theory of the electrical circuit. The next year would see an entirely new type of work for him: *Das Büchlein vom Leben nach dem Tode* (*The Little Book of Life after Death*, 1836), the prelude to his philosophy, written under the pseudonym Dr. Mises. Whereas late idealists preached a personal God – rejecting Hegel's "absolute spirit," which granted no space for human autonomy in historical development – Fechner's book reads like a proof that life after death can be reconciled with the sciences.

According to Fechner, in the transition from the worldly life to the beyond, a person's previous body is indeed destroyed, but the causal effects of a person's life continue to exist. "Every cause retains its effects as eternal property."[3] The "beyond" is thus no extraterrestrial realm but another form of earthly existence. Just as an old man shares no atoms with the child he once was, life's material aftermath continues to bear the person's consciousness and personality, though it retains nothing from the body. A single physical system can carry different consciousnesses simultaneously, just as different memories can inhabit one brain.

Exhausted by overcommitment, arduous optical experiments, and struggles for a clear worldview, Fechner suffered a profound mental crisis at the end of 1839. Emaciated and confined by a phobia of light to a completely darkened room, he lost his academic post and seemed beyond recovery.

---

[3] Fechner, *Das Büchlein vom Leben nach dem Tode* (*The Little Book of Life after Death*) (Dresden: Ch. F. Grimmer'sche Buchhandlung, 1836), 131.

But after five years, a short manic phase and megalomania led to rapid improvement, and in 1846 the university provided a modest salary with the requirement to resume lecturing. Once again Fechner could write, and he produced satires, philosophical essays, and other pieces, with little subsequent change in the external circumstances of his life.

In his first publication after the crisis, *Über das höchste Gut* (*On the Highest Good* [Leipzig: Breitkopf & Härtel, 1846]), he outlined a eudemonistic theory of ethics based on the "pleasure principle": to maximize worldly pleasure and minimize displeasure. *Nanna oder über das Seelenleben der Pflanzen* (*Nanna, or, On the Inner Life of Plants*) followed in 1848, further developing the claim, already suggested in the *Büchlein*, that plants and other nonhuman beings have a mental side (see below, section on "Fechner's Solution to the Mind–Body Problem").

In the three-volume *Zend-Avesta* (1851), which he regarded as his main work, Fechner attempted to deepen and generalize the ideas of his earlier philosophical writings. The first two volumes, the "Things of Heaven," compile the similarities between earth and humans. From this evidence he infers that the earth has a soul, just as we can infer from evidence that our fellow humans have minds. Conversely, the differences between people and earth make "the earth appear as a more living, autonomous, and unique being than we are ourselves" (vol. II, p. 388). After death, our bodies and spirits will belong to the higher body and spirit of the earth, just as the bodies and spirits of the earth and the stars will belong to the body and spirit of God. The third volume, the "Things of the Beyond," considers the relationship between our lives in the now and the hereafter, which mirrors "the life of memory that arises from the life of perception" (vol. III, p. 388). Fechner was convinced that "nothing unnatural or supernatural happens [in this] world order" (vol. III, p. 396).

After *Atomenlehre* (*Atom Theory*, 1855), a defense of the existence of atoms on a physical and philosophical basis, the two-volume *Elemente der Psychophysik* (*Elements of Psychophysics*, 1860) quickly made him famous. This work marked a turning point in the history of experimental and quantitative psychology. Fechner coined the term "psychophysics" to describe "an exact theory of the relations between body and soul." Its highlight is the proof of the "fundamental law of psychophysics": the intensity of a sensation (S) is proportional to the logarithm of the physical stimulus (R): $S = \log R$. Fechner considered his new theory to be an ideologically neutral foundation, from whose empirical and theoretical progress the exact nature of the relationship between the body and the soul would one day be determined. Aside from the preface and the introduction, the term "soul" is used only three times in the entire work, and a connection between psychophysics and Fechner's other theories is only indicated in chapters 45 and 46.

From about 1865 Fechner worked intensively on an empirical aesthetic that culminated in the *Vorschule der Aesthetik* (*Elementary Aesthetics*, 1876). In addition to other books, particularly on psychophysics, he published *Die Tagesansicht gegenüber der Nachtansicht* (*The Day View versus the Night View*) in 1879 – a book in which for the first time he took a detailed position on the various philosophical movements of his time. After his death in 1887, an extensive manuscript of *Kollektivmaßlehre* (*Theory of Measuring Collectives*, 1897) was discovered unexpectedly, in which he had developed a new theory of mathematical statistics based on methods he had established in his empirical aesthetics and elsewhere.

Fechner's Solution to the Mind–Body Problem

Fechner's fundamental philosophical concern is the so-called mind–body problem, that is, the relationship between the soul and the body, the mental and the physical. The traditional theory, deriving from Descartes and Christian-Platonic ideas, defines humans as comprised of two substances: the corporeal substance of their bodies and the spiritual substance of their souls. Fechner believes, however, that to assume the existence of substances in the world is not warranted. We are not given substances but only "[sensory] phenomena." Phenomena (*Erscheinungen*) are mental if they are only available to those who have them; when I feel pain, it is available exclusively to me (though others can infer it). In contrast, physical phenomena, like material objects, are directly available to others, and in principle to everyone. Persons thus have a double perspective of themselves. When I appear to myself as I do to no one else, I perceive inner phenomena, that is, mental states and processes; conversely, when I appear to myself as I appear or could appear to others as well, then physical phenomena are available to me (e.g., when I see my hand or look at myself in the mirror). For Fechner, the physical and the mental are aspects of one and the same being, a position that was called "dual-aspect monism."

In developing an alternative to Descartes, Fechner proposed a "psychophysical parallelism" in three levels of strength. The first version is an empirical postulate every scientist has to follow. The second is the scientifically most probable interpretation of the empirical data, as, for example, atoms are for the physicist. The third is the most probable metaphysical worldview associated with the former levels. In the first, weak form of psychophysical parallelism, a being cannot have mental processes without correlated physical processes – in any case, no one has experienced the converse thus far. Fechner calls such a correlation a "functional dependency," acknowledging that the connection between body and soul is understood scientifically as the relation between variables in a mathematical function. Fechner here neither asserts nor denies a causal role of the body or the soul, deferring that question to future empirical and theoretical insights.

In its second, stronger form, psychophysical parallelism introduces a causal interpretation of the mind–body problem and asserts a metaphysically based "identity view." Traditionally, when two types of events are correlated, it means either that one causally influences the other, that the events have a common cause, or that they are different aspects of the same event. Fechner argues for the third possibility, thereby advocating a kind of Spinozism. For example, the heads and tails of a coin are correlated, but neither the heads cause the tails nor vice-versa. They are aspects of an identical object, and if, for instance, the coin were bent, the changes of heads and tails would react in parallel without any relationship of causal influence of the one on the other. The identity view is thus no longer neutral, because it rejects a causal interpretation of the mind–body relationship, a view Fechner saw as consistent with contemporaneous scientific expertise.

In the two forms of psychophysical parallelism discussed so far, an asymmetry exists between the physical and mental phenomena in the world: there is no mental change without a physical change, but not necessarily vice-versa. In its third form, however, psychophysical parallelism asserts the inverse as well: there is no physical change in the world without a mental change. This clearly holds true for certain regions of our brain, but Fechner extended it to other physical changes, in a cosmological hypothesis applicable to the entire universe. At bottom – or so he claimed – there is no physical reality without a spirit that is aware of it.

How could Fechner seriously make such an assertion? Here he offered two arguments. First, mental properties are not necessarily always realized as they are in humans. A being, or more broadly, a material system, does not necessarily require nerves to have a mental side. Nature and technology offer countless examples where an ability is realized in different ways: a healthy person can see with their eyes, but so can a crab with a completely different visual system; we can play the same melody on a violin but also on a flute, even though both instruments are built differently.[4]

---

[4] Fechner, *Nanna oder über das Seelenleben der Pflanzen* (*Nanna, or, On the Inner Life of Plants*) (Leipzig: Leopold Voß, 1848), 38f.

Second, from external circumstances we can conclude that our fellow humans have "souls," that is, minds. From the behavior of the crab we deduce that it also sees, although we cannot verify that directly. Why should we not also deduce the inner mental side of other beings from structural and systemic properties? If the physical systems and behaviors of plants are analogous to those found in humans, then we can presume that plants have a mental side, too, although they lack nerves. And the same logic holds for the earth, the planets, and the universe as a whole.

For Fechner, a "soul" is thus not a substrate but, rather, a function, which in principle can be realized differently than in humans. Of course, the question of whether Fechner's panpsychism is logically possible remains separate from whether such a theory is empirically probable. The former has no bearing on whether the conclusions Fechner draws from the analogy between one material system and another (e.g., comparing humans with the plants or the earth) are sufficiently probable to require acceptance of panpsychism.

Fechner combined his psychophysical parallelism with Herbart's ideas about the intensity of sensations and the "threshold of consciousness." A physical stimulus is consciously perceived as a sensation only when it has a certain intensity; below this threshold the sensation remains unconscious. Likewise, the difference between two sensations can be noticed only when it exceeds a certain inner threshold. This fundamental law arose from Fechner's close experimental analysis of barely noticeable differences involving the various senses.

The concept of the unconscious provided Fechner the opportunity to explain how a being can be part of a higher consciousness, for example, how the human body and soul can be part of God's body and soul. The divine consciousness, which also includes the consciousnesses of all people, has a very low threshold, if any at all. A human's threshold of consciousness, however, is significantly higher than God's. The individual thus cannot become aware of the sensory life of God or other people, although the individual is still part of the divine consciousness in their unconscious. Fechner tries to find analogies for these circumstances in the human brain. An example is hearing a sound that is masked by our attention to a different sound source. The inner threshold of hearing the sound becomes higher than it would be without the other stimulus. Through the shift in our attention, we become aware that we "heard" the sound when in fact we were unaware of it.

The Day View over the Night View

With his view of "sensory phenomena" as the only empirical evidence of scientific hypotheses about the world, Fechner advocates a radical empiricism, grounded in his anti-Cartesianism regarding body and soul. His critique also pertains to the idea of the "*Ding an sich*" (thing-in-itself).

Fechner developed what one might call a "bundle theory" of matter: physical and mental objects are nothing more than bundles of phenomena connected by natural law, with no substantial underlying object of any form. In his *Tagesansicht*, Fechner combined these views with a theory of perception known today as "direct realism." It teaches that the properties of objects, such as color, smell, taste, and acoustic properties, actually belong to the things themselves and do not emerge solely in the awareness of a perceiver.

This theory opposes a powerful philosophical tradition, in place since John Locke, that views all these so-called secondary qualities as belonging to consciousness or perceptual states. Without a perceiving being, they would have no reality; they would be only "a feigned inner state, an illusion."[5] Fechner calls this latter theory the "night view," in contrast to the "day view" of "natural people," who believe in "a glow and sound through the world beyond them and from outside into them."[6] For Fechner the night view includes German idealism, materialism, Kant, the Neo-Kantians, and the views of philosophers in vogue at the time: Schopenhauer, Hartmann, Strauß, and others. Only the day view, Fechner says, gives people confidence in their direct experiences: that, as he puts it, flowers and butterflies do not "lie" with their colors, nor violins and flutes with their sounds.[7] Only in the day view are humans actually a part of the world and, with their consciousness, not strangers to it.

Whereas the night view offers a mechanistic conception of nature, with living beings "strange exceptions therein,"[8] the day view appraises the mental alongside the physical, as an equally real aspect of nature. One must, as like-minded American philosopher Charles Sanders Peirce wrote, make space "to insert the mind into our scheme [of the universe], and to put it into the place where it is needed, into the position which, as the sole self-intelligible thing, it is entitled to occupy, that of the fountain of

---

[5] Fechner, *Die Tagesansicht gegenüber der Nachtansicht* (*The Day View versus the Night View*) (Leipzig: Breitkopf & Härtel, 1879), 4.
[6] Ibid.   [7] Ibid., 3.   [8] Fechner, *Zend-Avesta* (Leipzig: Leopold Voß, 1851), vol. I, 8.

existence."[9] For Fechner, as for Peirce, this place lies in the identity of the physical and the mental. Only then does the true unity of nature emerge, with the mental and organic aspects of the universe no longer understood as negligible exceptions.

The Reception of Fechner's Work

The reception of Fechner's writings has been inherently split; those who accepted Fechner the scientist typically rejected his *Beseelungslehre* (theory of ensoulment) and panpsychism, and vice-versa. Likewise, Fechner's influence on scientific developments has often been ignored, for fear of association with the notion that plants and other parts of the world had souls. In any case, Fechner's greatest influence lay in his psychophysical parallelism, which for the overwhelming majority of psychologists, physiologists, and many other scientists became the unquestioned foundation of the natural sciences into the twentieth century.

One such figure, Albert Einstein, responded to a Swiss journal's query on the mind–body problem by citing Fechner explicitly: "To avoid a collision of the different kinds of 'realities' that physics and psychology deal with, Spinoza, or rather Fechner, invented the doctrine of psychophysical parallelism, which honestly completely satisfies me."[10] Evidence suggests that even modern neurophysiology, without making it explicit, is based on psychophysical parallelism – at least in its first and second version, insofar as it avoids causal assertions about the mind–body relationship and contents itself with the notion of a "neural correlate" of mental functions. Psychophysical parallelism's chief merit is that it respects the subject of psychology without reducing it to physiology or, indeed, physics, as do other mind–body theories. Thus it was significant that Fechner proved the compatibility of his view with the law of conservation of energy – proof still lacking today for substance dualism.

In 1896, the philosopher Kurd Laßwitz published a scientific biography of Fechner (*Gustav Theodor Fechner*, 3rd ed., 1910) still worth reading today. Laßwitz led a notable Fechner revival around the end of the nineteenth century, which saw the republication of works long out of print: *Zend-Avesta* in 1896 (3rd ed., 1919), *Nanna* in 1899 (4th ed., 1921), *Vorschule der Aesthetik* in 1897–98, and *Über die Seelenfrage* in 1907 (2nd ed., 1928). In Austria, the prominence of Herbartianism in the teaching

---

[9] Charles S. Peirce, "The Doctrine of Necessity Examined," *The Monist* 2, no. 3 (1892): 335.
[10] E. Bovet, "Die Physiker Einstein und Weyl," *Wissen und Leben* 15 (1922): 902.

reform of 1848 particularly favored Fechner's reception. Despite its own metaphysical premises, Herbart's philosophy was critical of metaphysics, open to empiricism, and set against German idealism (especially Hegel). Moreover, Herbart's views focused on psychology, which he understood as an empirical and quantitative science even before Fechner. The concept of a threshold of consciousness, which Fechner took up, originated with Herbart. Though panpsychism emerged from other sources, Fechner's philosophy seems, through Herbartianism, to have been more favorably received in Austria than in Germany – a factor perhaps not incidental to Mahler's enthusiasm.

CHAPTER 24

Literary Enthusiasms

Jeremy Barham

In memoirs of his association with Mahler during the 1891–97 Hamburg years, the music critic Ferdinand Pfohl highlighted the composer's bookish pursuits (with the help of a quotation from the Prelude to Part I of *Faust*): "Mahler was a literary musician, not only in his works but also in his need for intellectual stimulation and education. He was one of those people who, as Goethe puts it, are 'formidably well read.' He really did read an endless amount, and only things of great worth."[1] That this was no isolated view is corroborated by other friends, colleagues, and early biographers, including Ernst Decsey, Paul Stefan, Guido Adler, and Bruno Walter, as well as by Mahler himself, who frequently discussed his literary interests in letters, describing his books as "the only friends I keep by me! And what friends!. . . They become ever more intimate and consoling to me, my true brothers and fathers and lovers."[2]

From 1902 onward, he also had access to the vast library his wife Alma had continued to accumulate since her privileged formative years, and he often debated the finer points of literary works with her in correspondence and in their lives together. Given Mahler's (albeit comparatively humble) Bohemian-Moravian upbringing in a German *Sprachinsel* (linguistic enclave) by a nevertheless culturally aspirational bibliophile father, a gymnasium education in Iglau that was almost certainly orientated toward classical literature, and early friendships with a number of cultured figures, many of whom would go on to play distinguished professional roles within the Austrian (often specifically Viennese) intelligentsia (for example, Adler, Friedrich Löhr, Emil Freund, Josef Steiner, Anton Krisper, Albert Spiegler, and Siegfried Lipiner), it is perhaps not surprising that Mahler's life would develop strongly intellectual dimensions, both creatively and

[1] Ferdinand Pfohl, *Eindrücke und Erinnerungen aus den Hamburger Jahren*, ed. Knud Martner (Hamburg: Karl Dieter Wagner, 1973), 20.
[2] Mahler to Friedrich Löhr (undated; late 1894/early 1895); *SLGM*, 153/*GMB2*, 141–42.

207

personally, and that in his early years he even toyed with the idea of pursuing a literary career.

That said, it is not necessarily easy, or desirable, to attempt a precise diagnosis of Mahler's mindset on the basis of his reading habits. Though there are many clues, there are also ambiguities, gaps, and enigmas, as is to be expected from the mind of an artist as sensitive and questioning as Mahler's that was engaging deeply with a bewildering array of written cultural artifacts, past and present. More difficult still is to determine the full extent of how his intellectual and creative activities intertwined, since even on the subject of musical text settings he was conflicted. On the one hand, he admitted that there were often times in his large-scale works when he had to resort to the word to carry his musical idea (Second, Third, and Fourth Symphonies), but, on the other hand, he believed that music expressed infinitely more than those words could.

While Mahler developed no systematic theoretical approach to music aesthetics, such apparent contradiction nonetheless showed a keen aware-ness of nineteenth-century traditions of thinking about the meaning of music and its relation to *logos* as idea/word, and revealed the artistic challenge he faced in navigating a compositional path through the heavily symbolic, text-laden, and multimedial post-Wagnerian world in which he lived and worked. Plurality was Mahler's cognitive stock-in-trade, how-ever, and it is in this spirit that discussion of his creative and literary interests is best undertaken. For one thing, his reading covered a huge range of repertoire stretching from the ancient Greeks to contemporary philosophy and science, and there were certain writers about whom he remained ambivalent, such as Nietzsche (1844–1900), whose poetic lan-guage he admired but some of whose ideas he rejected.

Literary Settings

Nietzsche was, of course, one of the writers Mahler felt moved to set to music (the "Midnight Song" from *Also sprach Zarathustra* [1883–85] forms the initial pivot to a realm of sung texts as the Third Symphony's fourth movement), an act that inevitably plunged him into contemporary debates about the place of Nietzsche at the intersection of religious, philosophical, and artistic thought. He was struck most of all, however, by the musicality of Nietzsche's language. This intriguing cross-medial perspective was one that Nietzsche himself adopted not only in the title and content of his early monument to ancient Greek tragedy and the music dramas of Mahler's compositional hero Wagner, *The Birth of Tragedy out of the Spirit of Music*

(1872) – which Mahler almost certainly studied as a member of student reading groups in Vienna – but also in his perception of the inherent music in the verse of one of the greatest of German Romantic poets and kindred spirit of Mahler, Heinrich Heine (1797–1856).

The Nietzsche-influenced commentator Theodor Adorno would later both liken Mahler's musical forms to literary narration and the novel and credit by proxy Mahler's folkish and paroxysmal music with the ability finally to release the poetic music in Heine, so close were the deep veins of irony, lyricism, melancholic loss, and sudden *Stimmungsbrechungen* (disruptions of mood) from the exalted to the absurd shared by writer and composer. Mahler's only definitive Heine setting was an incomplete youthful attempt, probably from 1875–76, to work with "Im wunderschönen Monat Mai" from the well-known collection *Buch der Lieder* (1827). This ostensibly went against the grain of his subsequent reluctance to set verse of the highest quality (since there was little left for music to add to it) and, together with the difficulty of managing the legacies of Schumann's *Dichterliebe* (1840) and Wagnerian chromatic harmony that the setting rather diffusely dabbles in, may account for its unfinished state and Mahler's future subtle shift of direction in choice of texts.

Thereafter for his early vocal works Mahler would turn either to the work of less celebrated writers (Richard Leander – pseudonym of surgeon-turned-poet Richard von Volkmann [1830–99] – for "Frühlingsmorgen" ["Spring Morning"] and "Erinnerung" ["Memory"] and Tirso di Molina – pseudonym of the Spanish monk Gabriel Téllez [c. 1571–1648] – for "Serenade" and "Phantasie" from *Don Juan*), or to his own literary skills ("Im Lenz" ["In Spring"], "Winterlied" ["Winter Song"], "Maitanz im Grünen" ["May-Dance in the Countryside"] /"Hans und Grete"), leading to his first major works *Das klagende Lied* (*The Song of Lamentation*) and *Lieder eines fahrenden Gesellen* (*Songs of a Wayfarer*).

This body of repertoire demonstrates three significant facets of his literary disposition. First, the substantial text for *Das klagende Lied* illustrates a shorter-lived fascination with fairy tale, myth, and old German legends (especially Romantic revivals of these), harking back in tone to unrealized operatic projects *Herzog Ernst von Schwaben* (text by Josef Steiner) and his own *Rübezahl*. Completed in 1880, *Das klagende Lied* was most likely inspired by works of the same name by the little-known Munich-based poet Martin Greif (Friedrich Hermann Frey, 1839–1911) and the fairy tale collector Ludwig Bechstein (1801–60), as well as by the same eerie narrative device used by the Brothers Grimm in *Der singende Knochen* (*The Singing Bone*).

Second, a continuing sensitive ear for the refined lyrical side of Heine led Mahler eventually to two orientalist poets. For the *Kindertotenlieder* and five *Rückert-Lieder*, he turned to the hugely prolific and then-resurgent – though viewed by some contemporaries as somewhat Biedermeierish and mawkish – Friedrich Rückert (1788–1866), whom he claimed as a close spiritual relative alongside psychophysicist Gustav Fechner (1801–87), the latter having reviewed the poet's complete works in 1835 and cited extensively from his *Die Weisheit des Brahmanen* (*The Wisdom of the Brahman*, 1836–39) in one of his own more generalist religio-philosophical tracts, with which the composer expressed close affinity: *Zend-Avesta oder über die Dinge des Himmels und des Jenseits* [*Zend-Avesta or On the Things of Heaven and the Beyond*], 1851; see Chapter 23). Later, for *Das Lied von der Erde* (1908), Mahler would take up the delicate antique chinoiserie of Hans Bethge's (1876–1946) adaptations of eighth-century Chinese verse in *Die chinesische Flöte*.

The third, and perhaps most important, strand of Mahler's developing literary preoccupation spoke to the earthy and earthly realities of his youthful environment as a Jewish assimilationist, lower-bourgeois budding artist immersed in the life of rural and small-town Moravia-Bohemia. In all likelihood it was in his early school years that Mahler came to know the *Des Knaben Wunderhorn* collection of "alte deutsche Lieder" edited and assembled by two aspiring young (and notably wealthy) literati, Ludwig Achim von Arnim (1781–1831) and Clemens Brentano (1788–1842), and published in the German cultural stronghold of Heidelberg in 1805–8. Undoubtedly inspired by the *Volkslieder* anthology compiled in 1779 by Johann Gottfried Herder (1744–1803), one of the most influential promulgators of a broad German national sentiment, this part archive repository (of 700 folk poems) and part nationalistic anti-Napoleonic political statement provided Mahler with a rich smorgasbord of bucolic, romantic, religious, and military texts with which he strongly identified, on which he had modeled his own *Lieder eines fahrenden Gesellen,* and to which, like the book's culturally elite editors, he frequently made additions and changes for his own artistic ends. This creative literary engagement was like no other composer's relationship with this material, lasting from 1888 to 1901, the time of more than twenty song settings and the deep entwinement of many of them with four symphonies in which variously idealized and hauntingly realistic sentiments of loss, death, suffering, sacrifice, and poverty rub shoulders with joy, romance, absurdity, parable, and pastoral evocation, all communicated through innovative reworkings of art-song, folk-song, ballade, and dance genres.

Des Knaben Wunderhorn was dedicated by its editors to Goethe (1749–1832), whose exhortation in an 1806 review of the first volume that its contents would ideally lend themselves to musical setting whether with traditional or newly composed melodies in order to do full justice to the verses seems to have been taken completely to heart by Mahler. Indeed, if there was one star in the composer's literary firmament, then it was Goethe. Mahler owned more than one edition of the complete works, and had detailed knowledge of Eckermann's *Gespräche mit Goethe in den letzten Jahren seines Lebens* (*Conversations with Goethe in the Last Years of his Life*; first published in 1837 and 1848), which added further nuances to many aspects of the writer's life and ideas. Goethe was of course an intellectual giant of German cultural history. His thought traversed the realms of art and science in works of astonishing diversity that shifted through Rococo, *Sturm und Drang*, Classical, and early Romantic phases and embraced an eclectic range of forms and genres from essays, novels, poems (lyric, epic, ballad), plays, memoirs, letters, and diaries.

The *Faust* drama, in particular, which occupied Goethe intermittently for most of his mature working life, and from Part II of which Mahler drew the text for the second movement of his Eighth Symphony, was both a historical literary monument in and beyond Germany and a complex multifaceted expression of the human condition of suffering, striving, moral challenge, and redemption. Its reception peaked in the mid-nineteenth century at the time of the centenary of Goethe's birth, but it was not actually staged complete until 1875 (in Weimar), in the early days of the newly unified German Empire, for which it came to serve as a potent political symbol. Epitomizing Goethe's fragmentary working practice, the drama combines the timelessly archaic, mythic, and spiritually allegorical with the timeliness of peculiarly modern, and German, elements – the universal with the particular – in a way that for certain representatives of an emergent fin-de-siècle Viennese modernism, such as Hermann Bahr (1863–1934), held double-edged significance: as anchor and source of succor in an 1890s period of febrile artistic instability, but at the same time as outdated glorification of a Gothic-styled ancient history presented with Goethe's typical susceptibility to stylistic vagary.

Even one of the earliest and most popular Goethe biographies (that by George Henry Lewes, published in 1855 and mentioned in a letter by Mahler) considered *Faust* Part II to be a poetic failure because it sacrifices linguistic beauty to philosophical concepts. When Mahler turned to it relatively late in its reception history in 1906 for his Eighth, alongside the mediaeval Christian hymn "Veni Creator Spiritus" (by Hrabanus Maurus,

c. 780–856) – a Pentecostal invoking of the Holy (and for Mahler, the creative) Spirit that was much admired by Goethe and which he translated and wished to have set to music – it was partly in the sense of one magnum opus created in honor of another, for the Eighth with its huge array of musical forces was Mahler's self-declared gift to the nation and his most resounding public success. It was also a clear descendant and development of his setting of Friedrich Klopstock's (1724–1803) "Resurrection" ode in the finale of the Second Symphony – a movement of similar metaphysical exploration and grand scale whose universalizing message was enhanced by Mahler's omission of those obviously denominational verses of the ode which referred to Jesus, and by the addition of his own material reinforcing the general idea of ultimate salvation after struggle (the Eighth's *Faust* setting remains little altered by comparison). Though using *Faust* exposed Mahler to the risks associated with treating such a hallowed text, it may also be that he appreciated the untimely progressiveness of its structural and symbolic diversity in ways that some of his modernist compatriots could not, for he responded to it with one of the most generically and thematically heterogeneous symphonic movements of his output, one that goes some way toward actualizing the transitory and indescribable of Goethe's final lines in, as Mahler put it, the entire resounding universe and the circling planets and suns of his music-making.

Literary References and Absences

For his understanding of Goethe's *Faust*, Mahler was very probably indebted to his lifelong friend Siegfried Lipiner (1856–1911), who wrote various commentaries on the work, including a doctoral dissertation in 1894 entitled "Homunculus: A Study of Faust and Goethe's Philosophy" (now presumed lost). It is likely that Mahler paraphrased Lipiner's thoughts in a deeply philosophical letter of 1909 in which he discussed the conclusion of the drama with Alma – a letter that is as interesting for the patriarchal tone of literary educator that he adopted toward his much younger, radically modernist wife as it is for his highly sophisticated reading of the key Faustian idea of the "Ewig-Weibliche" ("eternal femi-nine"), especially in light of his subsequent dedication of the Symphony to Alma at the time of its first performance in 1910, made in an attempt to salvage his failing marriage.

Mahler famously urged his bride-to-be at one of their first meetings in 1901 to cast her complete Nietzsche edition into the fire, seemingly distancing himself from earlier interest in the philosopher at least up to the time of the Third Symphony. He would later berate Nietzsche together with Schopenhauer (1788–1860), Maeterlinck (1862–1949), and Otto Bierbaum (1865–1910) for their respective misogyny and muddled, fanciful thinking. This complex attitude suggests (1) that Mahler saw his quashing of Alma's compositional activity (a condition of their marriage) as, if anything, more a sign of respect for her "duty" as a full-time early twentieth-century spouse than as an act of male suppression; (2) that he readily made distinctions in his evaluation of different ideas from the pen of the same writer (holding Schopenhauer's music aesthetics in high regard, for instance); and (3) that he held very specific views about what constituted valid forms of mysticism, namely, those that were embedded in the kind of ancient religious practice exemplified by Jakob Böhme (1575–1624), Meister Eckhart (1260–c. 1328), Angelus Silesius (c. 1624–77), and Giordano Bruno (1548–1600) – all of whom have been linked to Mahler in the secondary literature of biographers and acquaintances – and not those steeped in contemporary decadent occultism.

Lipiner and other figures associated with the student groups to which Mahler belonged (Engelbert Pernerstorfer [1850–1918], Victor Adler [1852–1918], Heinrich Friedjung [1851–1920], and Richard von Kralik [1852–1934]) were instrumental in fostering German-nationalist sentiments and ideas of the artistic renewal of society from readings of Nietzsche, Wagner, and German mythical sagas. In considering this alongside the University courses Mahler evidently took in the history of old German literature, and the middle-high German epics *Parzival* by Wolfram von Eschenbach (c. 1170–c. 1220) and *Iwein* by Hartmann von Aue (c. 1160–c. 1210), the heroic flavor of Mahler's late-teenage cultural context and its link with aspects of his early musical interests become clear. Although later, in the early years of the new century, Mahler may have moved away from the writings of Nietzsche and Wagner (though never from the latter's music), he was still to be found reading works of antiquity (*Parzival* and Gottfried von Strassburg's *Tristan*) with Alma in 1907.

Despite a period of silence driven by Alma's antipathy toward Lipiner, the poet remained a crucial intellectual conduit for Mahler. Lipiner was a remarkable "networker" who made contact, either personally or by correspondence, with Fechner, Nietzsche, Wagner, and even Freud. His early writings *Der entfesselte Prometheus* (*Prometheus Unbound*, 1876) and *Ueber die Elemente einer Erneuerung religiöser Ideen der Gegenwart* (*On the Elements of a Renewal of Religious Idea in the Present*, a lecture to the Reading Society of German Students in Vienna, published in 1878) reinforced his circle's (and surely Mahler's) quasi-religious belief that metaphysical and spiritual dimensions were needed as a 'completion' of material reality. Couched in a Goethean struggle of the human spirit, this thinking, which undoubtedly led Mahler to the late-idealists Fechner, Rudolf Hermann Lotze (1817–81), and Friedrich Albert Lange (1828–75, especially his *Geschichte des Materialismus* [1866)]), was continued in *Adam*, the prelude to an unrealized dramatic trilogy *Christus*, which Lipiner and Mahler discussed in great depth at the time of the Third Symphony's completion (1896), and whose Dionysian qualities were lauded by the composer.

Mahler's skepticism toward certain "modernist" or "realist" writers who were favored by Alma or his younger friends and associates – for example, Richard Dehmel (1863–1920), Frank Wedekind (1864–1918), Gerhart Hauptmann (1862–1946), Henrik Ibsen (1828–1906), August Strindberg (1849–1912), and Oscar Wilde (1854–1900) – should perhaps not be overexaggerated, though it is evident that he had little or nothing to say about his fellow Viennese artists Hugo von Hofmannsthal (1874–1929) and Arthur Schnitzler (1862–1931). It is clear that Mahler felt a great deal more kinship with various forms of older literature: Shakespeare (for him, the greatest poet), the Weimar Classicism of Goethe and Friedrich Schiller (1759–1805), and the early Romantics Heine, Friedrich Hölderlin (1770–1843), Franz Grillparzer (1791–1872, on whose Euripides-inspired *Das goldene Vlies* [1818–21] he most likely based the libretto for his early unrealized opera project *Die Argonauten*), E. T. A. Hoffmann (1776–1822, particularly for his view of music as embodiment of the all-important noumenal realm, and the archetypal operatic trope of doomed female singer in *Rat Krespel* [1816]), and Jean Paul (1763–1825, whose eccentric *Bildungsromane* with their startling imagery, diffuse narrative style, and meditations on religious [non-]belief (for example, "Rede des toten Christus" in *Siebenkäs* [1796–97]) had profound effects on Mahler's creative outlook and programmatic conceptions).

Nevertheless, it is a typically Mahlerian paradox that, alongside these and the equally weighty and morally challenging *Gedankenliteratur* of his reputed favorite novel, Dostoyevsky's (1821–81) *The Brothers Karamazov* (1879–80, with its provocative atheistic deliberations), and Tolstoy's (1828–1910) *Resurrection* (1899), the composer found inspiration of very different kinds for the structure and characterization of his own works in, from one end of the spectrum, the humor and bold narrative innovations of Laurence Sterne's (1713–68) *Tristram Shandy* (1759–67), and

Cervantes's (1547–1616) even earlier *Don Quixote* (1605–15), which he had known since childhood, and, at the other end, the homespun sincerity of Peter Rosegger's (1843–1918) simple *Heimatkunst* (regional art) novels of rural and *volkstümlich* (folkloric) Austria – a writer whom in 1911, perhaps with a note of gentle irony, Mahler described as the most important contemporary poet.

CHAPTER 25

Romantic Relationships

Charles Youmans

Mingling with the DC elite at a 1981 French embassy affair, Leonard Bernstein, Mahler's leading twentieth-century advocate and closest American equivalent, fielded an innocent query from Maryan Stevens, wife of Supreme Court Justice John Paul Stevens: What emotions took hold while conducting a great work of music? "It's like fucking in a cathedral," came the forthright response – a deft piece of self-characterization both embracing and spurning his idol.[1] Mahler would have smiled at an unexpected intrusion of the coarse and catchy in an haute bourgeois setting. But in his world, cathedrals, of stone or of notes, were sex-free zones – "too sacred almost," Alma would write of the Mahlerian theater (*ML*, 15) – and what happened in the bedroom (or occasionally the office) stayed there.

Why bother, then, to survey Mahler's romantic relationships as a context for his music? True, there is plenty of material to contemplate: he participated in at least a dozen sexual liaisons, from his teen years through his marriage at age forty-one. Yet virtually none of that erotic energy found its way into his compositions. Certainly, he avoided the *Tristan*-esque chromatic/contrapuntal *Steigerungen* that were the bread and butter of Richard Strauss; if a knack for exhibitionist libidinal intensification led Strauss to overindulge in graphic musico-sexual fantasies, Mahler was equally inclined to fantasize about chastity. But how do we reconcile this aesthetics of abstinence with the composer's persistent claims that his art originated in his experience of life?[2] Does his music offer us censored autobiography? A higher degree of sublimation than Bernstein advocated? Something different altogether?

---

[1] John Paul Stevens, *The Making of a Justice: Reflections on My First 94 Years* (Boston: Little, Brown, 2019), 190.

[2] He made this assertion both early in his career ("My first two symphonies contain the inner aspect of my whole life; I have written into them everything that I have experienced and endured" [*NBLE*, 30]) and late (*Das Lied von der Erde* was "probably the most personal [work] I have made so far" [Mahler to Bruno Walter, September 1908; *SLGM*, 326/*GMB2*, 371]).

The relationships themselves suggest an answer. From the beginning, Mahler had no less trouble building a healthy connection with a romantic partner than he did putting to rest the existential doubts that drove him to compose. The categorized nature of the symphonies, that is, the repetitions of attitude and approach – religiose grandeur in the Second and the Eighth, manic "joy" in the Fifth and the Seventh, otherworldy resignation in *Das Lied von der Erde* and the Ninth – mirror a tendency in his choices of female companions, who likewise embody types: the tormentor, the masochistic pupil, the replacement mother. His attraction to these established itself early in his life – earlier, in fact, than his defining traits as conductor or composer. There are reasons to conclude that the latter depended on the former, and thus that Mahler's experience overlapped with Bernstein's more than we might expect.

Josephine Poisl, the Iglau postmaster's daughter generally acknowledged as Mahler's first love, morphed in less than a year from forgettable to unattainable. Naturally, she was a musician; their acquaintance began in the summer of 1879 when she and her sister studied piano with this already fierce taskmaster. Soon he nursed her vocal ambitions as well, and none too tenderly, marching her through the role of Senta. When the couple found their way out of the studio and into the woods, instruction continued, with stories of Wagner's *Ring* that evidently bored her; whereas Mahler's autumn letters from Vienna wistfully recall afternoons spent huddling under trees waiting out rain showers, hers from Iglau report current amusements: sleigh rides, outings to gather crayfish, and, in supplementary accounts from her mother, a fondness for waltzes and young professors with beards.

Thus the student became the teacher, inflicting wounds all the deeper for her lack of malicious intent. Now the dedicated admirer of *Winterreise* and *Dichterliebe* would be compelled to live them out. In correspondence that Mahler considered sufficiently important to stow away in a secret file discovered by Alma at the late date of 1930, we learn unexpectedly and from Josephine's own pen that Mahler was once an "enthusiastic dancer." Not for long! As summer turned to fall and face-to-face encounters became epistolary, humiliation ensued, Mahler pleading for a reconciliation: "I have never humbled myself before anyone. Look, I kneel before you!" Annoyed by his persistence, and short on time thanks to one Herr Wallner (later to become director of Iglau College), she turned matters over to her father's ruthlessly bourgeois negotiations: "Whatever position you took, you would only lose our respect, if you tried, against our will and without or approval, to persuade our child to leave the path which has been indicated to her as being beneficial to her and her interests." Matters soon closed, by means of a final "Have mercy on me!" anticipating the sketches for the Tenth (not altogether farcically) (*HLG1*, 62, 65–67).

Another curious anticipation of Alma in the Poisl episode was the presence of a mother who felt more kindly toward Mahler than did the daughter. Fanni Poisl took pains to console him, especially after he returned to Vienna and found himself jilted. Learning that he had managed to get lost for most of a day by walking the wrong way on the Danube, she observed flatly that he was too "gloomy and sad[:] one might think that you have been abandoned in some gloomy corner of the earth, instead of the gay Imperial city." He should be indulging the carefree pastimes of that stage of life: "have fun with other young people," she urged, obliviously citing the poisonous example of the beloved herself. And so he sank deeper into despair, and she retired from the relationship as not the last older woman to offer Mahler good advice that his personality would not allow him to heed.

The young lover did find a silver lining, however: he composed poetry, which he shared with his friend Anton Krisper. The content, maudlin in the extreme, matters less than the new habit. Suffering inspired him, he found, and the exceptional cases in which a creative work came from some other source would haunt his more sensitive followers (e.g., the finale of the Seventh, which prompted Adorno to complain that "Mahler was a poor yea-sayer").[3] Indeed, the outburst in which he summed up his misery for her could serve as an artistic creed, or at least of a summary of his principal works' content: "I saw myself so close to my goal ... and now, just before the gates of heaven, my fate should lure me back into the deepest abyss." If all three types of female companion introduced themselves in Poisl, then, it was the inducer of productive anxiety that left the deepest imprint.

The next significant affair, with the soprano Johanna Richter, followed a similar course, and here we have more details, about the person, the relationship, and the catastrophe. Once again love blossomed in pedagogical circumstances, that is, coaching sessions (now at Kassel), which would become Mahler's preferred hunting ground. The opportunities for tense exchanges would have been multiplied by the extraordinary demands

---

[3] Theodor W. Adorno, *Mahler: A Musical Physiognomy*, trans. Edmund Jephcott (Chicago: University of Chicago Press, 1992), 137.

on young singers at smaller theaters. Richter sang dramatic roles, lyric roles, and everything in between, occasionally dipping into the coloratura repertoire. If she did none of it especially well – critics regularly complained of poor high notes, problematic rhythm, and bland interpretation – she was undeniably beautiful. As with Poisl, the attraction did not depend on artistry but on ordinary human concerns.

Matters escalated in late summer 1884, and Mahler seemed aware that he was asking for more heartache. "All I can say is: God help me!" he wrote to Fritz Löhr (August 1884; *SLGM*, 80/*GMB2*, 56). The Poisl disaster had precipitated steps to avoid this kind of trouble, including vegetarianism, the "moral effect" of which allowed him, at least for the month of October 1880, to manage the "voluntary subjugation of my body" (*SLGM*, 64–65/ *GMB2*, 40). But now the body would have free rein, until New Year's Eve, when this fleeting obsession – "everything that is lovable in this world" – waited for the midnight songs to begin and then dismissed him from her apartment.

What he found in the street, however, as he wept among the revelers, was inspiration. And this time he better understood what to do with it: the *Songs of a Wayfarer* would be a direct result. He had already written the poems, having seen the writing on the wall, and the music emerged over the next months as the lovers played out a series of reunions and breakups. The cyclical nature of suffering was crucial; in the previous spring he had lamented, "I see no end to it. It makes me live through each day, each hour anew." Likewise, her cold formality, much like Poisl's, proved stimulating, so much so that he credited "the great stage-manager of the universe [*Weltenregisseur*]" who "arranged it all according to the requirements of art." The songs were "light in that darkness," a jolt of energy called into existence by romance-induced gloom.[4]

It pays, then, to examine the *Wayfarer* poems as an artistic manifesto, inspired by a partner who filled Mahler's need for creatively productive romantic distress. There is nothing reductive or simple-minded about accepting at face value, particularly in this case, Mahler's own repeated claims about the autobiographical nature of his work. It simply opens up a layer of meaning – only one among many, obviously, but an urgent one since perceptive artistic colleagues such as Max Steinitzer believed during these years that Mahler's true creative talent lay in poetry, not music. If being a poet means divining fundamental, genuinely applicable truths

---

[4] The details of the Richter affair are found mainly in correspondence with Löhr, from spring 1884 through summer 1885 (*SLGM*, 76–90/*GMB2*, 51–67); see also *HLGM1*, 113–14, 117–27.

about human experience – what Wagner would call "eternal moments" when interpreting Liszt's symphonic poems – then Steinitzer was on to something. The themes of these songs would be the themes of Mahler's oeuvre: loss, loneliness, and grief, amid an indifferent world; adoration of nature, complicated by pathological skepticism of genuine communion; pain, exacerbated by memory and positing death as a way out; blissful dissolution in an all-encompassing oblivion.

It was hardly coincidence, then, that Mahler's first great achievements as a composer emerged during his relationship with Marion von Weber (1856–1931), "the greatest of [his] loves," according to confidante and would-be spouse Natalie Bauer-Lechner (landing a jealous but respectable blow on Alma).[5] Wife of Carl Maria von Weber's grandson – whose inherited sketches of *Die drei Pintos* Mahler would arrange, thereby earning his first public success – Marion offered a set of qualities for which the considerably younger Mahler would leap straight off the cliff. Most significantly, she was the first good musician he ever loved, a pianist who could play his works with him four-handed from the full score, including his first attempt at a symphony, the genre that was his goal. Reading *Tristan* brought them to an admission of love, though for Mahler that passion grew as well from adoration of her gifts as a mother. With the Webers, Mahler experienced for the first time a happy home, a trauma-free existence, in which three children and a dog played without care and folded the young man into their cheerful clique. (Photographs of him with his own children convey that glow, missed in his youth but seized all too fleetingly in adulthood.)

Also significant for both partners was the simple fact of interesting conversation, which they craved. The husband, neither interested in nor inclined to share meaningful thoughts, facilitated the relationship by lengthy absences, to the point that both sweethearts believed they had unspoken approval to transform their "endless" conversations into a full-fledged love affair. Marion resisted Mahler's ill-advised inclination to seek explicit approval; his obsessive morality won out, and he quickly found himself writing letters again (and facing the prospect of a duel). This was all to the good, however, for in Marion's words, "only now did our real love begin." Like Mahler, she gained fulfillment by depriving herself of personal happiness on moral grounds, refusing to leave her children and

[5] Morten Solvik and Stephen E. Hefling, "Natalie Bauer-Lechner on Mahler and Women: A Newly Discovered Document," *The Musical Quarterly* 97 (2014): 30.

husband. The unattainable brought greater satisfaction, poured into letters that would leave Mahler's sister Justine in awe: "Frau Weber must have written from morning till night, otherwise the length of them would be inexplicable."[6]

For a third time, then – and this the most painful – Mahler found himself in an impossible situation, and once again hopelessness became his muse. "I was carried to the highest heavens through ardor and spiritual fulfillment, let my creative powers expand into the infinite." Even as he built a symphony from the Richter songs, a new and richer source of inspiration revealed itself: *Des Knaben Wunderhorn*, which he read with Marion's children. Peter Franklin observes that Mahler cannot have discovered them at this time, as he claimed.[7] But why would his memory fail him? Perhaps because he now grasped how to make creative use of a familiar text? If so, then this curious episode, with Mahler cast as the fun babysitter attracting the attention of a bored housewife, turns out to have launched three crucial pieces of his career as composer: the "arrangement" (*Die drei Pintos*) that spread his name through Europe; his first major work, a symphony that, despite a checkered early history, would eventually establish itself in the standard repertoire; and his meaningful connection with the programmatic source of the remaining three symphonies of his first creative phase. By now romantic disappointment had provided so many stimulants to composition that Mahler would need the better part of the 1890s to work through them all.

For the better part of the next fifteen years, from the Weber affair until the arrival of Alma, Mahler's emotional relationships with women settled into a pattern of compartmentalization forecast by these early experiences. On one hand were the caretakers, Justine and Natalie, who managed his household and his moods, shooed away noisy neighbors, and acted as sounding boards as best they could. Natalie was certainly right to raise an eyebrow at the odd closeness with Justine; she had good reason to conclude that only the blood tie kept them from living as spouses. And while Natalie did convince him twice to suspend his "entirely senseless celibacy," believing it a detriment to him "both physically and psychologically," the melancholy consummation brought her not a step closer to her goal of settling in as his wife.[8] Why not, when she seemed to unite all

---

[6] Ibid., 28.
[7] Peter Franklin, *The Life of Mahler* (Cambridge: Cambridge University Press, 1997), 66.
[8] Solvik and Hefling, "Natalie Bauer-Lechner on Mahler and Women," 40.

those qualities he most valued: intelligence, musicality, solicitousness, and sexual availability? Mahler's two brutally honest answers do not quite tell the story. If he could announce, "I detest the constant mothering," he nonetheless needed it, indeed, demanded it, though the predictable effect was to make the provider detestable.[9] And of course he did need physical beauty, as he explained to Natalie with cruel candor, though one wonders if with a less accommodating personality she might have met this standard.

The other side, which we see in a series of flings with singers, seems ordinary enough for a world in which abuse of power was the norm. What emotional needs were fulfilled for Mahler by Jenny Feld, Anna von Mildenburg, Sophie Sedlmair, Rita Michalek, Selma Kurz, and all the others, known and unknown? One was the need to dominate. A year after his death, Mildenburg marked the occasion by sharing in the *Neue freie Presse* a few anecdotes about her first private coaching with him in Hamburg. What she revealed was a grooming process, deployed by a routine application of fear and praise. Still a "half-child" as a newly hired twenty-two-year-old dramatic soprano, Mildenburg awaited "the Feared One" in a rehearsal hall with a répétiteur soon rudely dismissed by a "little man," "cross," "curse-inclined," and "face burnt negro-brown by the sun," who flew through the door and set to work on Act II of *Die Walküre* without any hint of an introduction. Though she was prepared for the worst – "my colleagues outdid each other in their fantastical descriptions of his tyranny and pedantry" – Mildenburg made it through only one "Hojotoho" before she "laid her head on the piano and began to cry." And at that moment, following the standard playbook for this kind of manipulation, the bully became a pussycat. He laughed, stood up, cleaned his glasses, told her that she had sung superbly, and she melted as "a feeling of infinite security came over me, even then, in our very first moment together."[10] To sing female lead roles under Mahler was to play out this familiar scene, if rarely the kind of long-term dependency that evolved in Mildenburg's case.

Also familiar were reading assignments, at least for the women he took seriously. Mildenburg recalled prolonged lectures about Wagner, in which "he advised me urgently to deepen my knowledge of his writings above all." To clinch the point, he bought her a complete edition of Wagner's

---

[9] Mahler to Justine Mahler, May 6, 1894; Stephen McClatchie, ed., *The Mahler Family Letters* (New York: Oxford University Press, 2006), 279.
[10] Anna Bahr-Mildenburg, "Meine ersten Proben mit Gustav Mahler," *Neue Freie Presse*, May 26, 1912.

writings, and likewise provided suggestions about what she should not be reading, as he would seven years later with Alma (Nietzsche being the principal concern in that case). Artistic and intellectual accomplishment thus served him as a weapon of sorts, grounding his authority and boosting his confidence as he attempted to build relationships with accomplished women.

It seems to have been Alma's willingness to speak to him on his level – to talk like a man, as it were, in spite of her youth, feminine beauty, and seeming naiveté – that intrigued him at the fateful Zuckerkandl dinner party. And she could back it up, with quasi-professional musical chops (how many modern-day undergraduate music students can comfortably play and sing Wagner's piano-vocal scores?) and a knowledge of the visual and literary arts (including personal connections to important figures) that here and there surpassed his own. In her case we have harsh evidence of his methods of domination, most vividly in the letter explicitly requiring her to give up composition. "If, at a time when you should be attending to household duties or fetching me something I urgently needed ... – if at such a moment you were befallen by 'inspiration': what then?" Here Mahler planted the seeds of his own doom, notwithstanding his claim to reject "that philistine view of marital relationships that sees a woman as some sort of a diversion." What stuck with her was that "he considered Robert and Clara Schumann's marriage, for instance, to have been 'ridiculous'" and that he required what she characterized as "self-imposed asceticism." That ultimately she strayed is no surprise; what seems odd is that she agreed to this arrangement in the first place (*GMLW*, 82–84).

Among the sources of depression in Mahler's last days was surely the knowledge that his final romantic relationship situated him firmly on the receiving end of the punishment. Alma's ostensibly terminated affair with the architect Walter Gropius continued, the sad pleadings of the previous summer yielded only the appearance of a reconciliation, and his emotional existence was entirely given over to the tender mercies of a woman who in the end would not be controlled. If Alma began the relationship by taking orders, and continued it by managing his needs, she finished as his most brutal muse, her influence painfully inscribed in the sketches for the Tenth Symphony ("Have mercy!" [*HLG4*, 1489]). But the grim reality of her continued infidelity introduced a dreadful ordinariness, which we find as well in her diary's detailed account of their first sex act.[11] The scene unfolded not in a cathedral but in the Director's *Büro*, the physical space symbolizing the authority that he used to coax women into trysts. There Alma experienced not a glimpse of the infinite but a mundane calamity of masculine middle age. Thus we confront the importance of Bernstein's "like"; the simile protects us from unpleasant reality, albeit a reality that for Mahler seems to have been necessary. His music imagined places that do not exist, by means of painful emotions and memories that he may well have wished did not exist, at least when one considers them in the harsh light of day.

[11] Alma Mahler-Werfel, *Diaries 1898–1902*, selelected and trans. Antony Beaumont (Ithaca, NY: Cornell University Press, 1999), 467.

CHAPTER 26

Mahler and Death

Carl Niekerk

Spinoza writes in his *Ethica* (1677): "A free man thinks of death least of all things, and his wisdom is a meditation of life, not of death."[1] We know that one of Mahler's favorite authors, Goethe, admired Spinoza, something that is highlighted throughout the former's nineteenth-century reception. We also know that Mahler's friend Siegfried Lipiner read Spinoza and made use of his ideas in his dissertation on Goethe's *Faust*. Whether or not Mahler himself was familiar with Spinoza's texts, then, we do not know, but he must have been aware of Goethe's interest in Spinoza, and particularly of their shared attitudes about death. Goethe is known for having avoided the topic whenever possible, an aversion that is illustrated in an exemplary way by the events surrounding the death of his best friend, Friedrich Schiller, in 1805: none of Goethe's friends or relatives dared to inform him about Schiller's death, and they went to great lengths to hide the fact from him until Goethe himself guessed what had happened.[2] Yet there is also a strong impetus in Goethe's work to translate death as an experience into a philosophy of life. Humans find a reason to live precisely because of an awareness of their mortality. Spinoza and Goethe were modern thinkers and sought to make sense of life in the here and now, not in some hereafter in which they did not believe. Mahler adopted this modern, postmetaphysical perspective, and it is in fact central to his philosophy of life (and death), in spite of the predilection for eschatology and (at times obsessive) fascination with death that he and Goethe shared (and that is nowadays often associated with Mahler's work).

What was death like as an everyday reality in Mahler's day? Around 1900, of the average number of 188,153 children born in Austria per year,

---

[1] Spinoza, *Ethics*, in *Complete Works*, ed. Michael L. Morgan, trans. Samuel Shirley (Indianapolis: Hackett, 2002), 355 (vol. 4, proposition 67).

[2] See Hans Gerhard Gräf, ed., *Goethe und Schiller in Briefen von Heinrich Voß dem jüngeren* (Leipzig: Philipp Reclam jun., [1895]), 83–84.

39,787 did not live to see their first birthday – a figure that equals slightly over 21 percent and that was high for Europe at the time.[3] Mahler saw many of his siblings die. Of his thirteen brothers and sisters, seven died in infancy. But that was not all: his brother Ernst (1862–75), to whom Mahler was close and at whose prolonged deathbed he was present, died at age thirteen; his sister Leopoldine (1863–89) died at age twenty-six; and his brother Otto (1873–95) committed suicide at age twenty-two. Death and its often gruesome details were an everyday reality for Mahler and his contemporaries. At the same time, a veritable "death cult" existed in Vienna around 1900, an aestheticization of death that may strike us today as disproportionate. A visible example of this, still today, is the city's interconfessional Central Cemetery (*Zentralfriedhof*) – one of a series of ostentatious infrastructure projects undertaken in the final decades of the nineteenth century – with its major church, graves of honor for prominent Austrians, and lavish funerals.[4] Mahler's own funeral in 1911 is illustrative of the public spectacle the death of a famous person entailed. (Mozart's funeral in 1791 was, in contrast, a rather anonymous affair – something that in an exemplary way illustrates that cultural perceptions of death had changed.)

Death is ubiquitous in Mahler's music. His first major work, *Das klagende Lied*, concerns fratricide and its consequences; the First and Fifth Symphonies contain funeral marches; the first movement of the Second Symphony was originally called "Todtenfeier"; the final movement Sixth Symphony is famous for its three (or two) hammer blows, which are often read as announcing death; the second movement of the Eighth sets Faust's death to music; the Ninth is often considered a product of Mahler's own struggle with death; the final movement of the Tenth reproduces the sound of funeral drums; and many of the *Wunderhorn* songs thematize death, as does the *Lied von der Erde*, of which the lengthy final movement is called "Der Abschied" (The Farewell). And then there are of course the *Kindertotenlieder* – songs about the deaths of children, composed in

---

[3] See H. Czermak and H. Hansluwka, "Infant Mortality in Austria," in *British Journal of Preventive and Social Medicine* 16 (1962): 197.

[4] See "The Death Cult in Vienna: Of Joyful Mourning and Macabre Pleasures," in Nicholas Parsons, *Vienna: A Cultural History* (Oxford: Oxford University Press, 2008), 73–74, 76. One could argue that through his Second and Eighth Symphonies Mahler participated in this death cult and thereby in what Pieter Judson has termed the "cultural war" of the Habsburg empire: Mahler too belongs to "Austria's German liberals" who "creatively deployed a variety of cultural symbols," and through references to its cultural heroes – in the cases of the Second and Eighth, Klopstock and Goethe – sought to create a cultural space for their ideas and aesthetic agenda. See Pieter M. Judson, *The Habsburg Empire: A New History* (Cambridge, MA: Belknap/Harvard University Press, 2016), 280.

1901 and 1904 when there was little reason for Mahler to think of the topic.

According to the psychoanalyst Stuart Feder, Mahler suffered from a "morbid fear of death," like Freud[5] (and, one could add, Goethe). This anxiety is noted by other biographers; Jens Malte Fischer writes that Mahler "[t]hroughout his entire life ... was manifestly preoccupied by the idea of death." Mahler did not like to speak about death, even if it concerned people in his immediate vicinity like his brother Otto or his daughter Maria (Putzi), although he was greatly affected by both. According to Alma, her husband did not want to witness his daughter's death and "fled the house, unable to bear the sight and sound of his dying daughter."[6] And yet, is this what really happened, is it Alma's perception of what happened, or is it Alma's attempt to stylize Mahler as a Goethe-like genius struggling with death?[7]

Feder, though, goes a step further than diagnosing a simple fear of death when he writes of "Mahler's lifelong romance with death" (274) – death is not something only to be abhorred; it is also something to be desired. This romance has a philosophical dimension, a question underlying Mahler's symphonies in particular: How can we face death as an inevitable part of the human condition and yet embrace life? How can we heed Spinoza's proposition to invest in life and not death? Mahler's music, in many different ways, offers answers to this question. The lines "Sterben werd' ich, um zu leben" (I will die, in order to live), the first line of the final strophe of Mahler's Second Symphony, formulate one of his answers – they are lines that Mahler added himself to Klopstock's poem and that constitute the core of the Second's finale, and the answer they supply points to the centrality of emotions in order to make sense of life. It is an answer that Mahler would work out in more detail in the second part of the Eighth Symphony, based on the final scenes of the second and final part of Goethe's *Faust*.

But Mahler's response to death is not merely philosophical. Mahler's "romance with death" has a clear aesthetic dimension as well – it not only takes us to the core of his creativity but explains what in Mahler's mind is valuable about his art. In order to explore this dimension of Mahler's

---

[5] Stuart Feder, *Gustav Mahler: A Life in Crisis* (New Haven: Yale University Press, 2004), 222.

[6] Jens Malte Fischer, *Gustav Mahler*, trans. Stewart Spencer (New Haven: Yale University Press, 2011), 330, 551.

[7] In other words, in Alma's view, Gustav's fear of death may have been another example of the "anxiety of genius" often associated with Jews; see Sander Gilman, *Smart Jews: The Construction of the Image of Jewish Superior Intelligence* (Lincoln: University of Nebraska Press, 1996), 47–71.

music, it is productive to look at Mahler's compositions based on Rückert's poetry. Rückert, at first sight, may seem an odd choice for musical setting in the 1890s. Although his work went through a brief revival in 1897, when several editions of his poetry were published simultaneously, Rückert's poetry in general was perceived (with good reason) as archaic and – in spite of his experiments with oriental verse forms – too naive to be interesting. The focus on Rückert also diverted Mahler from his taste for creating enormous public works of art, a tendency evident before and after his Rückert experiment.

What Rückert's poetry, in particular, his collection *Kindertodtenlieder*, did offer Mahler, however, was a form of emotional authenticity: Rückert wrote his poems briefly after the deaths of two of his children from scarlet fever at the ages of three and five in late December 1833 and early January 1834. The text of the song "Oft denk' ich, sie sind nur ausgegangen" ("Often I Think They Have Merely Gone Out"), the fourth of Mahler's *Kindertotenlieder*, depicts a father for a moment believing his children have not died but just have gone outside as they used to do. The poem can be read as a report on an everyday occurrence and shies away from poetic language (symbols, metaphors, comparisons). The assumption is that the reader/listener will recognize such an everyday scene and, through this recognition, will be able to participate in the emotions the narrating subject experiences. There is no philosophy here, just an evocation of emotions associated with the recent loss of a child – emotions that, in spite of their seeming simplicity, are also complex.

Mahler composed the *Kindertotenlieder* in the summers of 1901, 1902, and 1904 in tandem with songs based on four other poems by Rückert, among them two from the collection *Liebesfrühling* (*Love's Spring*), "Ich bin der Welt abhanden gekommen" ("I Am Lost to the World") and "Um Mitternacht" ("At Midnight"), that thematize death in the manner of the cycle. Together these poems draw a complex picture of Rückert's mindset, a feature of Mahler's choices that has long been overlooked. Two of the poems are from 1833, immediately before the deaths of Rückert's children; the *Kindertodtenlieder*, dating from early 1834, work through the tragic loss; and the *Liebesfrühling* poems, though prepared for publication shortly thereafter, come from the time of courtship with his future wife. Taken together these poems express a traumatized swerving among normalcy, loss, desperation, and reminiscences of earlier happiness – a complex psychogram of Rückert's state of mind around 1834.[8] It illustrates a

---

[8] See my study *Reading Mahler: German Culture and Jewish Identity in Fin-de-siècle Vienna* (Rochester: Camden House, 2010), 192.

pattern we find more often in Mahler's work: through death, we return to life – and, one could add, to what is valuable in life.

The timing in particular of the initiation of Mahler's Rückert's project is significant. Mahler himself had survived a major health crisis during the night from February 24 to 25, 1901, a severe hemorrhaging that doctors had trouble bringing under control. Mahler himself believed this crisis to have been a "genuine threat to his life."[9] This necessitated a surgical procedure that took place in the early summer, and he started work on his Rückert songs while still recuperating. The last of the *Wunderhorn* songs, "Der Tambourg'sell" ("The Drummer Boy") – the lament of a drummer boy awaiting the gallows, presumably for desertion – was composed during the summer of 1901 as well. Here, too, it is hard not to think of Mahler's own brush with death a few months earlier, though he uses German cultural history to step away from his personal concerns and selects images depicting death not as a dramatic event but as part of everyday life.

Songs at the occasion of the deaths of children have a long, now mostly forgotten tradition in German literature. The genre was more or less initiated by the poem "Auf den Tod eines Kindes" ("On the Death of a Child," 1666) by the Baroque poet Paul Fleming (1609–40); Friedrich Hölderlin (1770–1843) and Ludwig Uhland (1787–1862) published poems with the same title; Joseph von Eichendorff (1788–1857) published "Auf meines Kindes Tod" ("On My Child's Death," 1832), part of a cycle of three poems occasioned by the death of his two-year-old daughter; Gottfried Keller (1819–90) published the poem "Bei einer Kindesleiche" ("At the Corpse of a Child," 1845); Hermann Hesse (1877–1962) wrote "Auf den Tod eines kleinen Kindes" ("On the Death of a Small Child," 1930); and the poem "Du lächelst, um nicht zu weinen" ("You Smile, So as Not to Cry," 1956) by the Dadaist Hans Arp (1886–1966) works through the death of a child. Beyond these literary examples, the genre was often practiced by women mourning the loss of children. The poems are part of a genealogy that resists literary trends but also ideological use or abuse. In a sense they express the limits of the aesthetic: they deal with emotions so personal that aesthetic form no longer matters, and that quality certainly leaves them far removed from Vienna's ostentatious "death cult."

Mahler's Rückert settings pointed to a specific musical tradition as well: Robert and Clara Schumann, whose interest in the poet began with a collaborative effort to set poems from *Liebesfrühling* to music in 1841,

---

[9] Feder, *Gustav Mahler*, 66.

shortly after their own marriage.[10] "Liebst du um Schönheit" ("If You Love
for Beauty") in fact was set to music by Clara Schumann before Mahler, and
it is the only song from the *Rückert-Lieder* that Mahler composed after he
got to know Alma (it dates from summer 1902). This information sheds
interesting light on Mahler's interest in Rückert: along with the poems'
imagery of death, there is also a desire for intimacy and companionship in
Mahler's Rückert compositions (although Gustav certainly did not invite
Alma to embark on a compositional project with him). Robert Schumann
based more than fifty compositions on texts by Rückert, none of them
drawing on the *Kindertodtenlieder*.[11] Like Mahler, he did set the final scenes
of the second part of Goethe's *Faust* to music. It is instructive to think of
Robert Schumann – with his literary interests, emotional extremes, and
obsession with death – as an artistic model for Mahler in these matters.

Conventional wisdom has it that Mahler was too superstitious to name
one of his symphonies the Ninth because he thought he might not survive
it.[12] Similarly, it is sometimes assumed that Mahler, late in life, embraced
theories of reincarnation or transmigration of the soul, as articulated in
works by Fechner (with his ideas of an independent life of the psyche after
death until it finds a new body; see Chapter 23) and Hartmann (arguing
that there is a spiritual life underlying all of nature[13]) that Mahler had read.
Both cases are based on factual information about Mahler, and yet they
also suggest an irrationality at odds with our broader picture of Mahler's
personality. It strikes me as likely that Mahler's hesitation regarding his
Ninth Symphony simply reflects the enormous symbolic value of the
number nine in the symphonic tradition, harking back to pinnacle of
Beethoven's oeuvre as an accumulation of all his musical and worldly
wisdom. Did Mahler truly believe Fechner's and Hartmann's theories, or

[10] See Rufus Hallmark, "The Rückert Lieder of Robert and Clara Schumann," *19th-Century Music* 14,
no. 1 (1990): 3–30.
[11] See Rufus Hallmark, "Schumann und Rückert," in *Schumann in Düsseldorf. Werk – Texte –
Interpretationen*, ed. Bernhard R. Appel (Mainz: Schott, 1993), 91–118.
[12] The source of this story is William Ritter, who reported that at the premiere of the Seventh
Symphony in September 1908, Alma told him, under the condition that he will keep this secret,
that the broad outlines of Mahler's Ninth Symphony, based on ancient Chinese poetry, had been
completed but that he would give the piece a title rather than a number, because he was horrified by
the number nine; the next symphony, also already outlined, would be number ten. See William
Ritter, "Le Chant de la terre de Gustave Mahler," *Gazette de Lausanne* (November 26, 1911): 1–2.
However, Ritter wrote that this decision was motivated rather more by "respect" than by
"apprehension and superstition" ("bien plus de respect que d'appréhension et de superstition";
ibid., 1). After Ritter, Arnold Schoenberg discussed the idea of the finality of Ninth symphonies
(referring to Beethoven and Bruckner in addition to Mahler) in his 1912 essay "Gustav Mahler," in
Style and Idea (New York: Philosophical Library, 1950), 34.
[13] See Fischer, *Gustav Mahler*, 686–87.

was he merely seeking a perspective on death beyond the Judeo-Christian tradition? Tensions among a theoretical perspective, the imagery it provides, and those images' symbolic functions are likewise evident at the end of Goethe's *Faust II*, when in the scenes depicting Faust's death there is a sudden abundance of Catholic imagery. But that did not mean that Goethe, at the end of his life, had converted to Catholicism. What may have intrigued Mahler about Fechner and Hartmann was their ability to produce a vision of continued existence – life after death – built on a non-Western and complex belief that the essence of what a human being produces lives on after its physical demise. Like Goethe at the end of *Faust II*, Mahler was looking for specific imagery that would illustrate how what was essential in a person's life might live on; he was not endorsing a vision of life after death.

Spinoza believed that the mind could transcend the death of the body – that the mind could continue to exist after death through the knowledge it had acquired, a knowledge that "expresses the essence of the body" and has a "representational" but also "an affective aspect."[14] Human beings may not endure as individuals in their mortal bodies, but they do survive in the ideas they articulate and in the emotions accompanying these. Gretchen, Faust's main love interest, dies at the end of the first part of Goethe's *Faust*, but it is his memory of her, his love for her, that keeps Faust from giving in to Mephistopheles and moves him to keep striving for a better world, a decision that eventually saves him. It may be that Mahler's music still intrigues us today because of the texts and ideas it promotes, but it does also because of its highly complex emotional subtext that concerns death and life, and how we navigate both.

---

[14] See Don Garrett, "Spinoza's Ethical Theory," in *The Cambridge Companion to Spinoza*, ed. Don Garrett (New York: Cambridge University Press, 1996), 282–83; see also Garrett's "Introduction," 1.

PART V

Influence

CHAPTER 27

Posthumous Reputation, 1911 to World War II

Stephen Downes

In the years from his death to the outbreak of the Second World War, Mahler's music was in various degrees admired, misunderstood, celebrated, condemned, and ignored. The challenges were clear from the start. Mahler's death was marked in *The Musical Times* (June 1911) by a single paragraph that did not sound a promising forecast of Mahler's posthumous status as a composer. It reported an "apathetic" attitude toward his music from English audiences, who found that the naive aspects of Mahler's symphonic expression and his proclivity for great length "made no deep appeal." Even prominent apologists acknowledged the difficulties that Mahler's music raised. In 1914 Guido Adler noted that a "strange mix of the naïve and sentimental creates enigmas that are not easy to unravel."[1] In "crass contrasts," to use Adler's strident phrase, between the simple and complex, lay dangers of misunderstanding. But this music always had its public and private advocates.

Arnold Schoenberg dedicated his *Harmonielehre* (1911) to Mahler the "martyr," but his compositional relationship to Mahler's music was ambivalent. His 1912 essay "Gustav Mahler" professed great admiration while admitting little direct influence. Mahler's sometimes adventurous use of fourth chords (which Schoenberg quoted in *Harmonielehre*) may be reflected in the last of *Six Little Piano Pieces*, op. 19 (1911); these, according to Egon Wellesz, were composed as a response to Mahler's funeral. Schoenberg's music is closer to Mahler, however, when irony and parody are prominent, for example in *Pierrot lunaire* (1914) and the *Serenade*, op. 24 (1920–23). Alban Berg was a more straightforward devotee. Drooling admiration for the first movement of Mahler's Ninth was expressed in an unpublished fragment from 1912, and there is a palpable Mahlerian tone in the *Three Orchestral Pieces*, op. 6 (1914–15).

---

[1] Guido Adler, "Gustav Mahler" [1914], in *Gustav Mahler and Guido Adler: Records of a Friendship*, ed. Edward R. Reilly (Cambridge: Cambridge University Press, 1982), 40, 72.

In Berg's first opera, *Wozzeck* (1925), both the grotesque realism of the tavern scene (Act 2, Scene iv) and the emotive post-romanticism of the Symphonic Epilogue directly recall Mahler. The latter, which evokes the "Viennese voluptuousness" and "rapture" that Theodor Adorno heard as Berg's great connection with Mahler, is again prominent in passages of the incomplete *Lulu*. Berg's Violin Concerto (1935) ends with clear echoes of *Das Lied von der Erde*, and its inclusion of diverse musical allusions – folk song, Bach chorale, dance forms – compares closely with Mahler's often provocative stylistic juxtapositions. By contrast with Berg's occasionally effusive lyricism, in the music of his fellow Schoenberg student, Anton Webern, echoes of a Mahlerian *Naturklang* (nature-sound) are often heard in maximal expressive compressions.

The work of the conductors Oskar Fried, Willem Mengelberg, and Bruno Walter was especially crucial in sustaining a persuasive concert presence for Mahler's music. The activity of these and other prominent conductors belies the myth that during the period immediately after Mahler's death his music fell into rapid and widespread neglect. Walter conducted posthumous premieres of *Das Lied* (Munich, November 20, 1911, when, incredibly, it was coupled with a performance of the Second Symphony) and the Ninth (Vienna, June 26, 1912). His interpretations were, however, often considered rather conservatively couched, downplaying the catastrophically tragic and more modernistic aspects of the symphonies (he never conducted the Sixth). Otto Klemperer (though also selective in his appreciation of the symphonies), Hermann Scherchen, and Wilhelm Furtwängler all conducted Mahler, the latter, between 1912 and 1932, often with the Berlin Philharmonic, for whom Mahler's works were a prominent part of the repertory before Nazi prohibition.[2] Fried made important early recordings of the Second (1924) and *Kindertotenlieder* (1928), but perhaps the most influential recordings were Walter's of *Das Lied* (1937) and the Ninth (1938).

While important early cycles of Mahler's symphonies were performed during the Viennese season of 1918, at the first German Mahler festival in Wiesbaden (1921) and, in the same year, by Scherchen in Leipzig,[3] these have been overshadowed by Mengelberg's celebrated Amsterdam festival of May 1920. The critic Oskar Bie hailed the event as a postwar "celebration

[2] See Lewis Smoley, "Mahler Conducted and Recorded: From the Concert Hall to DVD," in *The Cambridge Companion to Mahler*, ed. Jeremy Barham (Cambridge: Cambridge University Press, 2007), 243–61.

[3] Christopher Metzger, "Issues in Mahler Reception: Historicism and Misreadings after 1960," in Barham, ed., *The Cambridge Companion to Mahler*, 203–16.

of peace" in which Mahler's music would promise reconnection, consolation, and reconciliation to a wounded continent. There were nine concerts and lectures given by leading Mahlerian advocates, including Adler and Richard Specht. Mengelberg's interpretations were lauded by keepers of the faith such as Adler and Paul Stefan, sustaining the acclaim that had greeted his many performances of Mahler with the Concertgebouw between 1911 and 1920.[4]

In a 1926 review for *Der deutsche Rundfunk*, Kurt Weill ascribed a prophetic significance to Mahler's Ninth, claiming it as exemplifying the principles of contemporary music, through emancipation from the obligations of both traditional harmony and form. As a student, Weill declared Mahler to be a "thoroughly modern person" and Mahler's music to be a manifestation of the "ultimate in modernism."[5] The influence of Mahler's music was evident throughout Weill's compositional career but is especially prominent in the 1920s and '30s. For example, from early performances, Mahler's Seventh Symphony was identified as probable formal model for Weill's Violin Concerto (1924). Adorno also heard Mahlerian aspects of the Concerto in its expressive idiom and what he described as its "surreal" effects. Adorno was an important critical voice in proclaiming Mahler as a precursor of interwar artistic trends such as surrealism, but he cautioned that Mahler should not be "summarily severed" from Romanticism; rather, he "remains dialectically linked to it" and its "archaically corroded material."[6]

In "apathetic" England, T. E. Clark hoped that his translation of Paul Stefan's groundbreaking 1911 monograph would "pave the way for Mahler in England."[7] But it was to be a slow path across stony ground. The incomprehension that had greeted Henry Wood's English premiere of the First Symphony during the 1903 Proms season resurfaced when the symphony returned to the Proms in 1930. The critic of *The Musical Mirror* described it as "a great disappointment. The work as a whole is devoid of all sense of style"; Mahler composes "commonplace" melodies and uninteresting developments within a "weak" structure. Elsewhere, however, Mahler met with more a positive response. On Hamilton Harty's

[4] See Eveline Nikkels, "Mahler and Holland," in *The Mahler Companion*, rev. ed., ed. Donald Mitchell and Andrew Nicholson (Oxford: Oxford University Press, 2002), 326–37.
[5] For sources and further discussion, see Stephen Downes, *After Mahler: Britten, Weill, Henze and Romantic Redemption* (Cambridge: Cambridge University Press, 2013).
[6] Theodor Adorno, "Mahler Today" (1930), trans. Susan H. Gillespie, in *Essays on Music*, ed. Richard Leppert (Berkeley: University of California Press, 2003), 603–10.
[7] Paul Stefan, *Gustav Mahler*, trans. T. E. Clark (New York: Schirmer, 1913), v.

first English performance of the Ninth with the Hallé Orchestra earlier that year, the critic of *The Musical Mirror* praised a "controlled and sympathetic reading," and Donald Tovey sustained an advocacy for Mahler's music in program notes throughout the 1920s and '30s.[8]

Benjamin Britten's Mahlerian awakening is often identified with his hearing the Fourth Symphony while a student at the Royal College of Music in 1930. In many diary entries from the 1930s he expresses admiration for Mahler's music in response to concert performances, BBC radio broadcasts, and listening to records. Britten described the repetitions of "*ewig*" (forever) in Mahler's "Der Abschied" ("The Farewell"), which he heard in Walter's pioneering recording: "It has the beauty of loneliness & of pain: of strength & freedom. The beauty of disappointment & never-satisfied love. The cruel beauty of nature, and everlasting beauty of monotony."[9] Several of Britten's compositions from this period (e.g., *Our Hunting Fathers* [1936], *Variations on a Theme of Frank Bridge* [1937], and the *Sinfonia da Requiem* [1940]) strongly echo Mahler, especially in passages of ambiguous negotiation between gestures of negation and collapse and aspirational moves toward fulfillment and redemption.

Concertgoers in France, meanwhile, were offered little Mahler. Henry-Louis de La Grange has identified just ten performances between 1927 and 1945, and between 1912 and 1927, "Paris heard not a single note of Mahler."[10] But the private realm tells a different story. Aaron Copland reported that Mahler scores were often discussed during his studies with Nadia Boulanger between 1921 and 1924. Boulanger annotated her Mahler scores with analyses of motivic and contrapuntal content, a reflection of her well-known appeal to her students to listen "horizontally." She had held a prominent role in promoting Mengelberg's 1920 festival, but in her review of the event she declared that "the architecture, the aesthetics of Mahler, by its dimension, its size, go against the French mind, made of moderation, of harmony." In a spirit of international reconciliation, however, she declared that an understanding of the importance of this music

---

[8] For more details on Mahler performances in Britain between the wars, see Donald Mitchell, "The Mahler Renaissance in England: Its Origins and Chronology," in Mitchell and Nicholson, eds., *The Mahler Companion*, 547–64.

[9] Donald Mitchell, ed., *Letters from a Life: The Selected Letters and Diaries of Benjamin Britten*, vol. 1 (London: Faber, 1991), 493.

[10] Henry-Louis de La Grange, "Mahler and France," in Mitchell and Nicholson, eds., *The Mahler Companion*, 138–52.

must be grounded in recognizing and valuing the differences between Mahler and "Frenchness."[11]

Copland's own public declarations of Mahler's importance date from the mid-1920s. In April 1925, after hearing Mengelberg conduct the Second Symphony, he wrote to the *New York Times* acknowledging Mahler's tendency to the "bombastic" and the "banal," but highlighting (in an echo of Boulanger) that the sustained relevance of Mahler is founded in his mastery of counterpoint and orchestration. Copland had encouraged Serge Koussevitzky to program Mahler, leading to a performance of *Das Lied* in Boston in 1928. (Koussevitzky gave the US premiere of the Ninth in October 1931; Leopold Stokowski's pioneering performances of the Eighth in Philadelphia on March 2, 1916, and his US premiere of *Das Lied* on December 15, 1916, should here be noted.) In several essays of the 1930s and '40s Copland discussed the influence of Mahler on the music of Honegger, Hindemith, Shostakovich, and Britten. *Das Lied*, which Copland described in especially glowing terms in a review of Walter's iconic recording, was a particular favorite for both Copland and his protégé, Leonard Bernstein. Mahler was a crucial aspect of the dialogues between Bernstein and Copland in the late 1930s, before Bernstein's big career breakthrough when he famously deputized at the last minute for Walter in 1943.[12]

Copland's public advocacy of Mahler was proclaimed in conscious counter to the skepticism often expressed in American criticism. Only *Das Lied* escaped the scathing pen of Olin Downes. Deems Taylor, reviewing the first New York performances of the Ninth (November 1931 and January 1932), thought that "the great Mahler war" would be over if someone would cut this symphony down to twenty minutes. Allan Lincoln Langley, a member of the New York Philharmonic, wrote a plea, "Justice for Gustav Mahler,"[13] which begins with an array of citations from New York critics, whose hostility ("abusive rather than critical") he deems out of step with broader opinion, a reaction he dates back to a performance by Mahler's "greatest interpreter," Mengelberg, in 1921. Langley condemns the anti-Mahler New York critics, by contrast with the more positive reception he saw in Chicago, Philadelphia, and Boston, for not raising Mahler to a rank equivalent with Bach, Beethoven, and the great

---

[11] Matthew Mugmon, "An Imperfect Mahlerite: Nadia Boulanger and the Reception of Gustav Mahler," *The Journal of Musicology* 35 (2018): 76–103.

[12] Matthew Mugmon, "Beyond the Composer–Conductor Dichotomy: Bernstein's Copland-Inspired Mahler Advocacy," *Music & Letters* 94 (2014): 606–27.

[13] *The Musical Quarterly* 12, no. 2 (April 1926): 153–65.

German tradition. Mahler's status with regard to this tradition also informed articles in the early 1930s in the journal *Chord and Discord* (published by the Bruckner Society of America), in which Mahler was positioned as "progressive" by contrast with Brahms, a discourse initiated by Gabriel Engel's "Mahler's Musical Language," which appeared in the first issue (February 1932). That year Engel published the monograph *Gustav Mahler – Song Symphonist* (1932); it was slim, but the first of its kind in America.

Chord and Discord recorded the Mahlerian activity of Walter and Klemperer in the 1930s. Some years earlier these conductors were celebrated guests in Russia, their performances feeding a growing interest in Mahler during the 1920s, especially in Petrograd/Leningrad. There was keen discussion of Mahler's music among students and composers. The leading figure was Ivan Sollertinsky, who wrote the first book on Mahler in Russian (1932), which aligned Mahler's music with the social and psychological turmoil of the time. For Sollertinsky, the third movement of the Ninth evoked "city clangor," and more broadly he heard Mahler's music as "compulsive, paradoxical, nervous," and containing passages in which lyricism is darkened by the grotesque, and a "profoundly humane feeling disguised by the self-protective mask of buffoonery." Such descriptions resonate especially closely with the edgy subjectivity, ironic humor, destructive forces, and mechanical energetics that inform passages of Shostakovich's Fourth Symphony (1934). The Mahlerian aspect of this symphony is also reflected in the finale's combination of monumentalism with multiple generic allusion – funeral march, scherzo, dance medley. The symphony's long fading coda, with celeste adding the sixth and ninth, is a clear, if despondent, descendant of the end of *Das Lied*.[14]

Mahler's national and ethnic identity was a sustained and often deeply problematic issue in his reception between the wars. (A further common thread between the music of Shostakovich and Mahler lies in a shared prominence in several works of material with Judaic qualities.) The Jewish question was a prominent driver in the American reception of Mahler through the cultural influence of exiles driven from Europe by the rise of Nazism.[15] Many of Mahler's earliest advocates, Paul Stefan and Paul Bekker, for example, had sought to assure Mahler's place in the Germanic

---

[14] Inna Barsova, "Mahler and Russia," in Mitchell and Nicholson, eds., *The Mahler Companion*, 517–30.
[15] Marc A. Weiner, "Mahler and America: A Paradigm of Cultural Reception," *Modern Austrian Literature* 20 (1987): 155–69.

line, and Specht's 1913 biography had downplayed the Jewish question. Adolf Weissman (*Die Musik und der Weltkrise*, 1922) was one of the first to describe Mahler's music as a symbiosis of German and Jewish elements, but for critics of the 1930s who declared (implicitly or overtly) National Socialist sympathies, Mahler became a target for condemnation. His use of German folk song (a tradition sacralized by Nazism) was especially problematic: for Richard Litterscheid, Mahler had failed to understand the depth and value of German folk song because of his Jewishness, and as a result composed music of "excess" and "sentimentality."[16]

Such views lie at an extreme end of a tendency to hear Mahler's music as an overtly autobiographical testament. This was a trope given immediate critical impetus on Mahler's death, and the premieres of the Ninth and *Das Lied* that quickly followed. Specht described the latter as "agonizing," a "renunciation," as both Mahler's "greatest work" and a "great farewell."[17] Clearly, however, Specht hoped that this performance was not really a farewell but, rather, a new beginning for the posthumous reputation of Mahler's music.

[16] Karen Painter, "Jewish Identity and Anti-Semitic Critique in the Austro-German Reception of Mahler, 1900–45," in *Perspectives on Gustav Mahler*, ed. Jeremy Barham (Aldershot: Ashgate, 2005), 175–94. On the supposed dangers of Mahler's music identified by Nazi critics such as Otto Schumann and Karl Blessinger, see Leon Botstein, "Whose Gustav Mahler? Reception, Interpretation, and History," in *Mahler and His World*, ed. Karen Painter (Princeton: Princeton University Press, 2002), 21–28.

[17] "Feuilleton: *Das Lied von der Erde*," *Neue Freie Presse* (December 4, 1911); translation in Painter, ed., *Mahler and His World*, 334–37.

CHAPTER 28

Mahler and the Second Viennese School

Wolfgang Rathert

Translated by Juliane Schicker

Gustav Mahler's dictum that his time would come has become a topos of the composer's image. Behind it lies a myth, of a saint and martyr of music history, established by Arnold Schoenberg in his Prague lecture on Mahler of March 25, 1912, and carried deep into the twentieth century by his oldest and most loyal students, Anton Webern and Alban Berg.[1] It survived in 1973, for example, in Leonard Bernstein's Harvard lecture *The Unanswered Question*, albeit in a sharp differentiation of Mahler from Schoenberg, whose embrace of dodecaphony Bernstein read as the downfall of modernism. Yet when examined from historical distance, the myth dissolves into historical, cultural, and music-historical facets whose problematic nature can illuminate Mahler and also the composers of the Second Viennese School: their self-image, reception history, and works. The triumvirate championed their idol with determination and perseverance, to make a place for him in the centuries-long progression of Western compositional history, and to establish as the culmination of this history (at least provisionally) their own works, with Schoenberg's twelve-tone method as its most advanced expression.

But another, backward-looking Second Viennese interpretation of Mahler's music existed from the beginning: as the last manifestation of a musical paradise eternally closed to subsequent composers, who, unlike Mahler, rejected the commandment to leave tonality intact. (In Prague, Schoenberg casually identified Mahler's "quite tonal" idiom as the basis for his unique melodic constructions; the astonishing claim, however, that "Mahler did not yet have many resources of harmonic contrast at his disposal" is comprehensible only by means of a teleological model of progress.) After a performance of Mahler's Third Symphony, Berg wrote to his future wife of a "removal from the world [*Weltentrücktheit*], as if in

---

[1] Arnold Schönberg, "Gustav Mahler," in *Style and Idea*, ed. Leonard Stein, trans. Leo Black (New York: St. Martins Press, 1975), 449–72.

the whole world there were nothing more than this music and I who enjoyed it." Before the premiere of *Das Lied von der Erde*, Anton Webern told Berg that he expected the "most wonderful sound there is," something "of such beauty as never has existed."[2] As self-styled heirs, then, the Second Viennese School faced an irresolvable dilemma: their succession through an initially "atonal" and then dodecaphonic language required the destruction of this paradise, which existed on a tonal foundation. As Walter Benjamin remarked in his *Theses on the Philosophy of History*, what we call progress is the storm "blowing from paradise" by the wings of the Angel of History.[3]

To prevent Mahler's aesthetic destruction by a dogma of progress, his work must be reinterpreted as the product of his own Janus-faced modernism. Even at the cost of Mahler's status as a transcendent classic, the resulting paradox is extraordinarily productive, considering how Schoenberg, Webern, and Berg reacted to it. For Schoenberg, the debate over compositional methods mattered less, perhaps, than the aesthetic reverberation of Mahler's music-historical achievements and their consequences; one recalls that the dedication to Mahler of the *Theory of Harmony* (1911) was later removed. In his 1955 Kranichstein lecture on the young Schoenberg, Theodor W. Adorno described what, in his mind, inextricably tied Schoenberg to Mahler: the idea of clarity, that is, Mahler's abandonment of the "colorful intoxication" in favor of defining "every musical event ... by the disposition of its colors." "What Schoenberg actually adopted" was "this circumstance, the fact that color serves to make the structure perfectly clear ...," and thus the actual subordination of color to the principle of composition." Looking past the tonal excesses of the *Gurre-Lieder* and the Straussian qualities of the *Chamber Symphony*, op. 9, Adorno here followed Egon Wellesz, Mahler's friend and the author of the first biography of Schoenberg (1920). Wellesz had interpreted Mahler's instrumentation (including his *Retuschen* [orchestrational revisions] of Beethoven and Schumann's symphonies) as an overcoming of the coloristic usage of the orchestra in favor of elucidating the linear and motivic structure. In this way, his orchestral pieces attained the compositional and

---

[2] Arnold Schönberg, "Mahler," in *Style and Idea*, 459; Alban Berg, *Briefe an seine Frau*, ed. Helene Berg (Munich: Langen, 1965), 21; letter from November 30, 1911, cited in Friedrich Wildgans, *Anton Webern*, trans. Edith Temple Roberts and Humphrey Searle (London: Calder & Boyars, 1966), 59.

[3] Walter Benjamin, "Über den Begriff der Geschichte," in *Illuminationen. Ausgewählte Schriften* (Frankfurt: Suhrkamp, 1977), 255. The intellectual-historical and religious background shared by Mahler and Schoenberg given their Judaism still awaits thorough study.

tonal ideal of a clear, expressive, and functionally legitimate (in every detail) music such as the Second Viennese School now hoped to achieve.[4]

For his part, Adorno noted that Schoenberg's counterpoint, in comparison with Mahler's, was grounded not in an organic unfolding of heterophonic lines accompanying the melody but, rather, in a simultaneously antithetical and complementary construction of a multidimensional musical space.[5] This difference resulted from a music-historical constellation around 1900 that led to a new understanding of linearity; Mahler had experienced and helped shape its origins in musical historicism, but not its radicalization after World War I. This was the founding phase of "New Music," when Paul Bekker and others demanded the end of prioritizing the vertical dimension over a purely melic or, rather, melodic polyphony. In the last of the *Six Short Piano Pieces*, op. 19, which Schoenberg wrote as an homage to Mahler one month after his death, the primacy of sound (*Klang*) was still present. And even the third of the *Five Orchestral Pieces*, op. 16, "Colors" ("Farben"), can be interpreted as realizing this ideal of clarity. In the main works of the 1920s (*Suite*, op. 25; *Variations for Orchestra*, op. 31), a contrapuntal-linear style dominates, whose rigor Schoenberg emphasized through dodecaphonic construction, that is, by abandoning the "old" tonality. Here Schoenberg distanced himself furthest from his predecessor, even as he strictly implemented Mahler's idea of a comprehensive polyphonizing of musical texture (*Satz*).

For Anton Webern, re-creative efforts as conductor of Mahler's works took pride of place; the direct traces of Mahler's influence, still discernible in Webern's early work, receded more and more after 1909 as his nontonal and dodecaphonic musical language radically broke with the old tonality. Mahler's reduced influence was also related to a changed view toward large musical forms, which the Second Viennese School avoided. The only symphony produced by a Second Viennese composer – Webern's Symphony, op. 21 (1923) – demonstrably rejects any approximation to traditional symphonic form and likewise to a movement-character such as the scherzo, in which the grotesque or burlesque would have found a place. This may also have to do with Webern's resigned observation, expressed in a letter to Berg in 1912, that Mahler's symphonies represented the ne plus ultra of that hybrid endeavor to raise the work of art beyond a mere symbol

---

[4] Theodor W. Adorno, *Kranichsteiner Vorlesungen*, ed. Klaus Reichert and Michael Schwarz (Berlin: Suhrkamp, 2014), 114–15; Egon Wellesz, *Die neue Instrumentation. II. Teil: Das Orchester* (Berlin: Max Hesses Verlag, 1929), 18–34 and 48–59.

[5] Adorno, *Kranichsteiner Vorlesungen*, 167–69, n. 5.

to an actual reality. Clearly, an organizational mode of thought remained in effect; it is found already in one of Webern's diary entries, in which he recorded discussions with Mahler and Schoenberg from 1905. Mahler had recommended "nature" as a model of modern counterpoint: "Just as the whole universe evolved in it [nature] from the primordial cell, from plants, animals, and people up to God – the supreme being – so a larger sound structure should develop [in] music from a single motive, which contains the seed of everything to come."[6] Webern's own form of twelve-tone technique, featuring the greatest possible unification and economization of the material on the basis of a never-ending variation principle (distinct from the Brahmsian "developing variation" adopted by Schoenberg) may be thus interpreted as an abstract, obsessive fidelity to this one idea. It likewise dominates Webern's well-known lectures from the early 1930s on the New Music and twelve-tone technique, in which Mahler is situated as an intermediary.

Conversely, Alban Berg reacted with unrelenting intensity to the Janus-faced, heterogeneous quality of Mahler's expressive means, which in the realm of harmony vacillate between the simplest and most advanced tonal materials. This inner connection of apparent opposites runs through Berg's entire oeuvre, in particular the *Three Orchestral Pieces*, op. 6, and the Violin Concerto, which maintain the duality of Mahler's worldview: on one hand, the sense of foreignness and premonition of death; on the other, transfiguration and apotheosis. Whether Berg's use of tonality in the Violin Concerto is a new stage of a "meta"-tonality (with major/minor tonality almost artificially generated through the tone row) or an artistic but sentimental return to a historically outdated language remains an open question. Post-1945 music history gave various answers to this question, which at least in postmodernism – as in Wolfgang Rihm's early symphonies, following in Mahler's footsteps – allow "regression" to appear as true "progress." In the end, the currency that Mahler gained after 1980 was motivated by compositional history and not merely a moral rectification.

This variety of reactions to Mahler's work persists in Schoenberg's later students, ranging from complete identification (Karl Horwitz) to a subtle development of certain tonal proclivities (Viktor Ullmann) up until an ideologically unambiguous but musically ambivalent dissociation (Hanns Eisler). In the next generation, with Schoenberg's posthumous son-in-law

---

[6] Letter from July 12, 1912, cited in *Opus Anton Webern*, ed. Dieter Rexroth (Berlin: Quadriga, 1983), 86; cited in Hans Moldenhauer, *Anton von Webern. Chronik seines Lebens* (Zürich: Atlantis, 1980), 65.

Luigi Nono, myth returns, but now abstract and universal, critiquing the
devastations of modernism by exposing enlightenment itself as myth.
Nono named Mahler's First Symphony as a taking-off point for the
space–time fragility of his *Prometeo*; the *Naturlaut* (natural sound) of the
violins at the opening of the First – empty octaves and harmonics on A –
served as the premonition of an acoustically open musical multiverse.[7] But
whether this universe contains the promise of a utopia or the seed of
dystopia or catastrophe, one cannot say.

Given the financial success and high reputation as a conductor enjoyed
by Mahler after the turn of the century, and given the controversy that
continued to surround his compositions through the mid-twentieth (compared, for example, with Richard Strauss), the Mahler Renaissance of the
1960s (see Chapter 29) was less the fulfillment of that prophecy from
1902 and more an ambivalent and even hypocritical act inexplicable
without the historical upheavals of the twentieth century. But it did mark
the moment when his work permanently caught on, and it was accompanied by a complete reversal of the aesthetic judgment of Mahler's music,
bringing the general critical assessment in line with the Second Viennese
perspective. The oeuvre's greatest critical vulnerability to that point, its
musical and cultural syncretism (also disparaged as *Kapellmeistermusik*),
now appeared as its true strength. Precisely this turn made Mahler's music
historically "incommensurable" and equipped it to mock all previous "style
categories of program and absolute music,"[8] Adorno would claim in a
book emblematic of this 180-degree reversal and appearing in the anniversary year of 1960. Yet this reversal also implicitly offset the anti-Semitic
and racially motivated ostracism that met Mahler's music after 1933,
initially in Germany and, with the outbreak of World War II, in the
European countries occupied by Nazi Germany as well.

It is difficult to gauge how Mahler's music would have been received
under "normal" historical circumstances. Would it have gained the retrospective nimbus that turned it into a blank canvas for contemporary
catastrophes, serving the initially negative and later positive stigma of social
exclusion? After his death, Mahler's former assistants Bruno Walter and
Otto Klemperer, Mahler's friend Oscar Fried, and Leopold Stokowski
cultivated his work and made it known internationally (see Chapter 27).

---

[7] See Luigi Nono, "Verso Prometeo. Conversazione tra Luigi Nono e Massimo Cacciari raccolta da
Michele Bertaggia," in *Scritti e Colloqui*, ed. Angela Ida de Benedictus and Veniero Rizzardi, vol. 2
(Milan: Ricordi, 2001), 349.
[8] Theodor W. Adorno, *Mahler. Eine musikalische Physiognomik* (1960), in *Gesammelte Schriften*,
vol. 13 (Darmstadt: Wissenschaftliche Buchgesellschaft, 1998), 152.

And yet public reactions in Europe after 1918 remained mixed, as the first age of modernism came to an end and made room for other ideals like neoclassicism and the *Neue Sachlichkeit* (New Objectivity). According to Hanns Eisler, Mahler, together with Schumann, Wagner, and Strauss, represented traditional (bourgeois) musical Romanticism. In his article "On Modern Music," published in the communist party newspaper *Die Rote Fahne*, Eisler wrote that these composers – in contrast to the revolutionary Beethoven – created meaning only to express a "personal, private experience" or a "personal, extremely private '*Weltanschauung*' [world-view]." Even twenty-seven years later, in a lecture ("Arnold Schoenberg and His Work") designed to help rehabilitate his teacher in the German Democratic Republic, Eisler mentioned Mahler only incidentally, in a single place. He spoke of Mahler's and Bruckner's "bombastic symphonies," from which Schoenberg broke away in 1908 with a music that was "uncomfortable" and marked by the "fundamental tone of despair": "[Schoenberg] had expressed the feelings of people in air-raid shelters long before the invention of the bomber plane; he expressed musically that the world was not beautiful. Thus he did not make things easy for his listeners or for himself. For who wants to hear that the world is not beautiful?" (Notably, however, Eisler would rely heavily on Mahler's style, and not Schoenberg's, in his score to Alain Resnais's Auschwitz film *Nuit et Broulliard* [1954]!) And it is more than paradoxical that Adorno attributed almost exactly these same traits to Mahler's music, suggesting that Mahler "incites anger in those who find the world agreeable, because he reminds them of what they must expel from themselves. Inspired by the inadequacy of the world, his art did not satisfy its standards, and for this the world celebrates its triumph."[9]

The shift by which Mahler became Schoenberg's antipode according to Eisler, but his precursor according to Adorno, is in all its contradictions a defining element of Mahler's reception by the Second Viennese School. It already characterized Schoenberg's examination of Mahler and has been discussed in the secondary literature for decades. Initially, Schoenberg positioned himself as a determined opponent of Mahler's music. In the following years, however, through the intercession of Guido Adler and others, Schoenberg and Mahler encountered each other in ever closer personal and professional situations, culminating in Mahler's

---

[9] Hanns Eisler, "Über moderne Musik," in *Materialien zu einer Dialektik der Musik*, ed. Manfred Grabs (Leipzig: Reclam, 1973), 41; Eisler, "Arnold Schönberg," in ibid., 235; Adorno, *Mahler*, 153–54.

1904 appointment as honorary president of the *Vereinigung schaffender Tonkünstler* (Society of Creative Musicians), cofounded by Schoenberg. The Vienna premiere of Mahler's Third Symphony in December 1904 then became an awakening for Schoenberg, converting him from "Saul" to "Paul," as he later wrote in his Prague speech. The letter that Schoenberg addressed to Mahler shortly thereafter can hardly be surpassed for pathos and common feeling; he states that he saw Mahler's soul in his work, and it was "naked, bare naked."[10] The change from an aesthetic to an emotional and existential level also marks the tone of the Prague speech: for Schoenberg, Mahler's essence and oeuvre were the epitome of an absolute that transcended the realm of art, wiping out the usual categories.

These exaggerations may also have signified humility and gratitude; Mahler had quickly recognized Schoenberg's talent and soon became one of his most important supporters and defenders in Vienna's music scene. But at its core it was a solemn declaration that Mahler's music signified a turning point in the history of composition, achieved by the power of his ingenious personality. The compulsion and necessity to express himself elevated the alleged banality and sentimentality of Mahler's themes and the fragmentation of his stylistic idiom – often misunderstood as "potpourri" – to a component of a secret overarching master plan that merged all contradictions within itself. By this means, Schoenberg could read Mahler's instrumentation too as "objective," that is, depersonalized, and say that, in the Ninth Symphony, the author almost disappears, rendering the work "no longer in the first-person."[11] Here, Schoenberg already prefigured central aspects of his own aesthetics (or, rather, ethics) of composition: Mahler's music is already the manifestation of an "idea" (*Gedanke*, and not a "style"), and its compositional radical nature the "necessary" consequence of the highest expressive need. The compositional act follows an unconscious, intuitive strategy of producing the greatest possible inner integration, so that in the end the highest subjectivity turns into the highest objectivity.

Werner Hofmann holds that at bottom Schoenberg's Mahler cult is grounded not on musical considerations but on a projection: Mahler became a saint because Schoenberg projected his own mission onto his teacher, thereby deriving his own sense of purpose from a general attitude

---

[10] Therese Muxeneder, "Gustav Mahler war ein Heiliger. Arnold Schönberg und Gustav Mahler," in *Gustav Mahler und Wien: "leider bleibe ich ein eingefleischter Wiener,"* ed. Reinhold Kubik and Thomas Trabitsch (Vienna: Brandstätter, 2010), 220.

[11] Arnold Schoenberg, "Prager Gedenkrede," in *Gesammelte Schriften*, vol. 1 (Frankfurt a. M.: S. Fischer, 1976), 23.

of protest "that was the fundamental ethos of Viennese modernism." Schoenberg had internalized this protest attitude early on as a member of the so-called Fourth Gallery[12] of the Court Opera, the most important site for his spiritual and musical socialization in turn-of-the-century Vienna. And it is still present in a text written in the United States on August 8, 1936, now part of the composer's *Nachlass*. It carries the title "Twenty-Fifth Anniversary of Mahler's Death" and begins as follows:

> It was the twenty-fifth anniversary of Mahler's death and a few months later Karl Kraus died. Recently, Adolf Loos and Alban Berg passed away (not to mention Franz Schreker) – I am only left with a few from the old guard, with Kandinsky, Kokoschka, Webern. I am really the only one from the old generation, because my peers, besides Loos, were rather reserved, hesitant, always stayed a few steps back. They only followed when it was high time. The younger ones from Stravinsky and Hindemith's time were always insecure cantonists. They fancied everything that was contrary to the idea: folklore, *Volkstümlichkeit* (popularity), objectivity, usability. While they were flirting with these concepts, we were fervently occupied with fortifying the boundaries of artistic-moral permissibility to make them impenetrable ... We led or aspired to lead our lives like national heroes, with purity of motive, incorruptibility of ethos, steadfastness of character, serenity in attack, knightly valor in defense. We attested to more respect for the past than its traditional guardians, whose behavior was always disrespectfully in the present, and who always couched this past in terms that, had they been realized, would not have been worth their hat. We made the teachings of the past our own, possessing them in a cultural form that considered the past not as an end but as a step, which we honored even as we stepped over it. Culture enabled us to think ahead. We had a legacy to preserve and knew instinctively that what does not grow, dies. Conservatism of any other kind means doom, because it led here. But at no time had conservatism caused more decay than in our time ... Remarkably, however, none of these men were connected with radical politics. We were all rather conservative – conservative, however, in the sense of recognized or anticipated needs.[13]

These recognized or anticipated imperatives of Schoenberg and the Second Viennese School would determine twentieth-century music history, even if Schoenberg's hopes to ensure the aesthetic hegemony of German music for

[12] Werner Hofmann, "Mahler: Halbgott oder Vollmensch," epilogue to Arnold Schoenberg, *Rede auf Gustav Mahler am 25. März 1912 in Prag* (Hamburg: Europäische Verlagsanstalt, 1993), 69; Christopher Hailey, "Die Vierte Galerie. Voraussetzungen für die Wiener Avantgarde um 1910," in *Bericht über den 2. Kongress der Internationalen Schönberg-Gesellschaft*, ed. Rudolf Stephan and Sigrid Wiesmann (Vienna: Lafite, 1986), 242–47.
[13] Arnold Schönberg Center Wien, Nachlass Schönberg Mus 376 (Call Number T36.16), pp. 1–5.

the next hundred years were not fulfilled. That they did not come to fruition rests also on the dialectic of the relationship between the Second Viennese School and Mahler's oeuvre. His works' heterogeneity, openness, and, at the same time, hopelessly nineteenth-century inner world counteracted a linear and perhaps also dictatorial conception of progress. Leonard Bernstein referred to this dialectic in 1973 when he characterized Mahler's Ninth Symphony as a "reluctant and protracted farewell to tonality," while noting that Schoenberg's twelve-tone technique no longer followed the "intuition of tonal relationships" but, rather, the "rules of an artificial language."[14] Today, we no longer dare to assert as resolutely as Bernstein what is "natural" and "artificial" in music. At best it is safe to say that this conflict, hidden in the myth of the "saintly" Mahler, brought about unforeseeable, fascinating artistic implications for twentieth-century music.

[14] Leonard Bernstein, *The Unanswered Question: Six Talks at Harvard* (Cambridge, MA: Harvard University Press, 1976), 265, 283.

CHAPTER 29

The Mahler Revival

James L. Zychowicz

The Mahler Revival of the early 1960s, a movement galvanized by the centenary of the composer's birth, bears scrutiny for the ways in which the renewed interest manifested itself and shaped the reception of his music. The term "revival" perhaps overstates the case, by connoting a resuscitation along the lines of Mendelssohn's 1829 performance of the *St. Matthew Passion*. As Stephen Downes shows in Chapter 27, Mahler's name was by no means unknown in the first half of the 1900s. Performances of his music occurred, albeit infrequently; most works had been recorded; editions had been published and were still available; and the composer had been the subject of several biographies.

Among the latter was a dual study of Mahler and Bruckner by Hans F. Redlich that was sufficiently popular when it first appeared in 1955 to warrant a new edition in 1963.[1] Introducing the revision, Redlich noted signs of increasing popularity: wide release of LP recordings, a higher number of live performances and broadcasts, a "spate of new editions" prompted by the 1961 expiry of copyright on Mahler's music, and the publication of books and articles in recognition of the overlapping anniversaries of his birth and death (the fiftieth of the latter occurring in 1961).[2] Among recent monographs, Redlich singled out E. Doernberg's *The Life and Symphonies of Anton Bruckner* (1960) and Donald Mitchell's *Gustav Mahler: The Early Years* (1958) as "books of scholarly pretensions, as conspicuous by the incompleteness of their information as by the debatable value of their argument" – qualities that he seemed to hope would stimulate further work.

---

[1] H. F. [Hans Ferdinand] Redlich, *Bruckner and Mahler*, 2nd ed. (London: J. M. Dent and Sons, 1963), vii–viii. The first edition was published in 1955.

[2] A list of commemorative articles appears in Michael Simon Namenwirth, *Gustav Mahler: A Critical Bibliography*, 3 vols. (Wiesbaden: Otto Harrassowitz, 1987), 3: 306–8.

Redlich's list, compiled by a scholar who was actively involved in research prior to the Revival, provides an organizational framework conveniently adaptable for a survey of the various components of the movement, from the distance of a half-century: (1) recordings (especially cycles), (2) lectures and published research, and (3) the Mahler *Gesamtausgabe* (Complete Edition), inaugurated in 1959.

Mahler Discography

It was apt for Redlich to call attention to the increased recordings of Mahler's music, as these would become an important measure of the composer's engagement with the public sphere, along with documenting the performance tradition for future generations of listeners. For some works, like the performing editions of Mahler's unfinished Tenth Symphony, the discography has become a crucial barometer of the reception[3] by reflecting dimensions of the historical record not necessarily captured in criticism or other secondary literature. The discography of this work, for example, shows the various versions that were performed, as well as the frequency of recordings, and these data can substantiate the recorded legacy, rather than perpetuate assumptions about the popularity of specific performing editions of the Tenth. At the same time, the Mahler discography[4] discloses the spotty history of recorded performances prior to 1960. Releases occurred infrequently, and Mahler's music was (with a few notable exceptions) typically not associated with specific conductors; rather, conductors would record individual works and combine them with pieces by other composers. The relatively recent phenomenon of the cycle, a series of recordings offering a comprehensive view of Mahler, began only with the Revival, aided substantially by the advent of the long-playing disc in 1948. As more conductors took interest in this music, their performances added to the legacy of Mahler's music in recordings, with the tendency to release individual works gradually shifting to cycles of the composer's works (see Chapter 33).

Most prominent among the achievements in Mahler discography post-1960 is the release of entire cycles of the composer's symphonies. Leonard Bernstein stands apart for his role in producing the first complete set of Mahler's symphonies as a multi-disc set (1968, based on recordings

[3] James L. Zychowicz, "Mahler's Unfinished Legacy: Exploring the Discography of the Tenth Symphony," *ARSC Journal* 43, no. 2 (2012): 197–223.
[4] Péter Fülöp, *Mahler Discography* (New York: Kaplan Foundation, 1995).

made between 1960 and 1967 and released individually between 1965 and 1968), so that listeners could hear those works in a single collection and benefit from the interpretation of the same conductor, the evenness (for the most part) of a single orchestra, and the sound quality that came from one recording company, the internationally prominent Columbia label.

Bernstein's approach to Mahler's music has elicited strong responses for its vivid interpretations of the scores, a dimension enhanced by the recording techniques used to capture the performances. Details in the supporting lines emerged more readily in Bernstein's recordings, such that some would hear the style as nervous or agitated. While none would question Bernstein's general affinity for the music, his interpretation of the scores resulted, at times, in excessive or exaggerated tempos that do not always match Mahler's meticulous directives. The interpretations also draw on the virtuosic quality of the New York Philharmonic, which Bernstein used to elicit full-bodied sonorities and tight ensemble-playing. While such an approach might have been found earlier in isolated recordings of individual works, the result is estimable when applied to a complete set of the composer's nine numbered symphonies.

This event distinguished Bernstein's efforts from competitors' (e.g., the earlier and first comprehensive cycle of recordings that the conductor Maurice Abravanel had recorded with the Utah Symphony Orchestra on the Vox label), so that for many listeners Mahler's music would be associated with the conductor's name and the New York Philharmonic. The set also included a bonus feature that connected modern listeners with the composer's lifetime through interviews with members of the New York Philharmonic who played under Mahler.

After the success of Bernstein's set, other conductors followed suit, most notably Sir Georg Solti and Herbert von Karajan, but also cycles by Haitink, Inbal, Chailly, and others. These modern sets reflect a comprehensive approach to Mahler's music that has a counterpart in the musicological investigation of the composer's body of work. Individual releases likewise have proliferated, allowing new generations of conductors and performers to explore the music one work at a time. Later recordings by Bernstein offered alternate versions of some music, for example, with tenor/baritone voices for *Das Lied von der Erde* (in contrast to the high/low vocal distinction in some versions of Mahler's score) and the admittedly idiosyncratic use of a boy soprano for the Finale of the Fourth Symphony. Some conductors made their mark with recordings of alternate or obscure pieces, enriching the body of available performances.

Centenary Lectures and Publications

Of the talks given on the centenary of Mahler's birth, Theodor Adorno's "Wiener Gedenkrede" stands out for its complexity and seriousness of intellectual purpose, developed substantially in the author's groundbreaking monograph on the composer.[5] Taken together, the monograph and the two essays on Mahler represent perhaps the strongest single influence on the perception of Mahler's works in the second half of the twentieth century.[6] Through his topical approach to Mahler's music, Adorno drew connections among works, and especially among the music and broader philosophical and social issues, that would have been theoretically impossible for commentators in previous generations (see Chapter 31). As a result, the critical and scholarly interest in Mahler's music found not just renewal but a new level of erudition, through an innovative approach that remains part of the composer's legacy. Adorno's critical profundity had a more traditional scholarly counterpart in emergence of biographical works dedicated to the composer alone. Of particular note are the expansive documentary studies published by Henry-Louis de La Grange, who in 1973 offered the first part of a planned two-volume chronicle that eventually grew into three lengthy tomes in French and ended with a 1,758-page fourth volume when revised for publication by Oxford University Press in 2008.

Among the various critical tributes paid to Mahler, Bernstein again made perhaps the most distinguished contribution, with a personal memoir explaining his determination to serve as champion.[7] Bernstein's perspectives eventually made their way from this brief essay into his 1972–73 Charles Eliot Norton lectures on modern music, a prominent series of public talks at Harvard University that became an international event in their broadcast on television.[8] Linking modern innovation to nineteenth-century precedents, Bernstein discussed the influence of Mahler as if it were a cosmic revelation. He began by invoking his acquaintance with Alban Berg's widow, Helene:

---

[5] Theodor W. Adorno, "Mahler Centenary Address," in *Quasi una Fantasia*, trans. Rodney Livingstone (London: Verso, 1998), 81–110. The article continues in the "Epilogomena" that follows (97–110). Neither essay is part of Adorno's monograph on Mahler (see Further Reading).

[6] John Williamson, "Adorno and the Mahler 'Revival,'" *The Musical Times* 131 (1990): 405.

[7] Leonard Bernstein, "Mahler: His Time Has Come," in *Findings* (New York: Simon & Schuster, 1982), 255–64. A version of the article was first published in *High Fidelity* 17, no. 4 (April 1967).

[8] Leonard Bernstein, *The Unanswered Question: Six Talks at Harvard* (Cambridge, MA: Harvard University Press, 1973), 12–21.

[Frau Berg] became my living link back to the death-ridden intercrossing of Berg, Schoenberg, and Mahler ... I began to feel myself in direct contact with Mahler's message. Today we know what that message was: and it was the Ninth Symphony that spread the news. But it was bad news, and the world did not care to hear it. That's the real reason for the fifty years of neglect that Mahler's music suffered after his death – not the usual excuses we always hear: that the music is too long, too difficult, too bombastic. It was simply too true, telling something too dreadful to hear. What exactly was this news? What was it that Mahler saw? Three kinds of death. First, his own imminent death of which he was acutely aware. (The opening bars of this Ninth Symphony are an imitation of the arrhythmia of his failing heartbeat.) And second, the death of tonality, which for him meant the death of music itself as he knew it and loved it ... And finally, his third and most important vision: the death of society, of our Faustian culture. Now, if Mahler knew this, and his message is so clear, how do we, knowing it too, manage to survive?[9]

Mahler has become the message, Bernstein his prophet. Certainly, questionable inferences emerge (the "heartbeat" rhythm), and even errors: "fifty years of neglect" overstates the case when we consider that the posthumous premieres of *Das Lied von der Erde* and the Ninth Symphony were reviewed prominently, with both scores subsequently published. Moreover, Mahler's music remained in print through the 1930s, and even when Universal moved to England after the Nazi Anschluss in 1938, the scores remained available, albeit from London rather than Vienna. And yet advocacy of the music by America's best-known conductor, who led one of the world's most famous orchestras, won for it a degree of popularity that otherwise might well have been impossible, vindicating Mahler's prediction vis-à-vis Richard Strauss: "when his time has passed, my day will come."[10] If Mahler's Revival is defined by the achievement of genuine fame, and indeed a degree of celebrity, Bernstein was indeed responsible for it.

The Mahler *Gesamtausgabe*

Concurrent with Bernstein's promotion of Mahler's music in the concert hall, the Internationale Gustav Mahler Gesellschaft commemorated the

[9] Ibid., 313–17.
[10] Gustav Mahler to Alma Mahler, January 31, 1902; *Gustav Mahler: Letters to His Wife*, ed. Henry-Louis de La Grange and Günther Weiss, in collaboration with Knud Martner, trans. and rev. Antony Beaumont (Ithaca: Cornell University Press, 1995), 100.

centenary of the composer's birth by inaugurating the publication of his collected works.[11] This vital scholarly undertaking was hardly incidental to the renewed interest in Mahler; besides making the works available in authoritative versions, it validated his presence in the musical world by placing the corpus of works alongside those of canonical figures such as Bach, Beethoven, and Wagner.

It must be said, unfortunately, that while the Mahler *Gesamtausgabe* resembles some of the others in presentation, it falls short by the critical standards of the twenty-first century. While some of the volumes were subsequently updated, the critical apparatus of the early releases is sparse and does not reflect the level of detail associated with the critical editing of music in recent decades. For many of the volumes, the Mahler Gesellschaft essentially reprinted previously published scores with some line corrections, without undertaking a newly typeset uniform edition and applying a set of editorial guidelines applied to all the works consistently, for example, with the systematic presentation of all variants. Rather, the edition has followed the principle of the *Ausgabe letzter Hand*, offering the last known version of the music as the composer left it. Such an approach would be satisfactory if it were limited to works that the composer saw into print. In Mahler's case, however, late works as well as youthful ones remained unpublished during his lifetime. Unfamiliar works – for example, the original first movement of the 1880 cantata *Das klagende Lied*, a substantial piece of music excised when Mahler published the work with Universal in 1899 – required significant editorial attention to be rendered performable. Likewise, the basis for the editions of *Das Lied von der Erde* and the Ninth Symphony was the composer's fair copy, which did not show important revisions; many earlier works likewise underwent substantial alteration after performances under Mahler. But these complaints aside, it must be said that by making the scores accessible from a single source, the *Gesamtausgabe* has performed an important service. If the editorial standards have met with an uneven reception among scholars and musicians, the publication of a collected-works edition nonetheless represents an important step forward.

---

[11] The *Sämtliche Werke/Kritische Gesamtausgabe* began in 1959 with the release of Symphony no. 7, ed. Erwin Ratz (Berlin: Bote & Bock, 1959). For an account of the project's background, see Reinhold Kubik, "The History of the International Gustav Mahler Society and the Complete Critical Edition," in *The Cambridge Companion to Mahler*, ed. Jeremy Barham (Cambridge: Cambridge University Press, 2007), 217–25.

Conclusion

Defining the Mahler Revival as a set of interrelated developments, rather than a monolithic event precipitated by a musical centenary, clarifies the tangible factors that increased the composer's public visibility. New recording techniques in the 1960s, for example, had a considerable impact, by making Mahler's lengthy compositions available on fewer discs than was possible with 78-rpm recordings. And beyond the advantage of mere accessibility, the improved reproduction quality captured performance details with a new and advantageous level of nuance. Bernstein's passionate support for the music at the podium, and his positioning of Mahler as a seminal force in fin-de-siècle European culture, certainly revealed the composer's achievements to the broader public. This linkage in turn was facilitated by the work of musicologists, writing about Mahler, editing his music, and trusting that in the long term an outsider of sorts could make his way into the canon. Mahler's music remains relatively new in the larger scheme of music history, but the last fifty years offer hope that in the hands of twenty-first-century musicians his legacy will continue to grow.

CHAPTER 30

Broader Musical Influence

Thomas Peattie

For a composer often said to lack direct compositional heirs, Gustav Mahler has exerted a wide-ranging influence on the history of twentieth and early twenty-first century music. During his lifetime, Mahler was held in particular esteem by Arnold Schoenberg, Alban Berg, and Anton Webern, each of whom engaged with his music in ways that left an important mark on their own compositional practice. Within the Austro-German orbit, interest among composers only intensified over the course of the twentieth century, something evident in the music of figures as varied as Kurt Weill, Hans Werner Henze, and Dieter Schnebel. Further afield, by the mid-1920s a distinguished array of composers including Aaron Copland and Dmitri Shostakovich had begun to engage seriously with Mahler's music. This trend would continue in the second half of the twentieth century, with the renewed attention paid to Mahler outside central Europe giving rise to an even more diverse group of followers, including those eager to find emancipation from some of the more influential strands of postwar modernism.

Copland

Outside continental Europe, Aaron Copland holds a distinguished place among Mahler's earliest defenders. Copland's initial encounter with Mahler's music came during his studies with Nadia Boulanger (1920–24), and his emerging enthusiasm for the composer only grew in the summer of 1922 when he heard *Das Lied von der Erde* in Berlin conducted by Bruno Walter. But it was the critical reception of a 1925 performance of the Second Symphony at Carnegie Hall that compelled Copland to public advocacy. In a letter to the *New York Times*, Copland praised qualities that he felt critics had long overlooked – Mahler's strength as an orchestrator, and his contrapuntal mastery – before hailing the first movement of the Seventh Symphony, the scherzo of the Ninth, the last movement of the

Fourth, and *Das Lied von der Erde* as "the stuff of living music." Copland was hardly unequivocal in his praise, pointing out that Mahler had also written music that was at times "bombastic, long-winded, banal." But while in the years that followed Copland often repeated these sentiments, dwelling in particular on what he took to be Mahler's weaknesses, he nonetheless acknowledged that "whatever we may think of [Mahler] as a composer in his own right, it is impossible to deny his influence, direct or indirect, on many of our present-day composers."[1]

The question of Mahler's impact on Copland had been broached as early as 1931, albeit in disparaging terms, by Virgil Thomson, who referred to the presence in Copland's music of "irrelevant memories of Nadia Boulanger's lessons, of the scores of Stravinsky, Mahler, and perhaps Strauss."[2] Later commentators would offer a more generous assessment, including Arthur Berger, who described the Third Symphony's "Romantic element" as Mahlerian rather than Wagnerian even as he wondered why Mahler would be a favorite composer of someone "so thoroughly oriented toward the incisive, economical, and athletic idioms of our time."[3] Yet with the exception of this important work – one whose orchestration certainly demonstrates Copland's familiarity with Mahler's scores – the older composer's direct technical influence on Copland was, in the end, relatively modest.

Britten

Benjamin Britten's debt to Mahler is more immediately audible, perhaps because his initial encounter with Mahler's music was such a formative experience. In 1942 – the same year in which he transcribed the second movement of Mahler's Third Symphony for reduced orchestra – Britten published "On Behalf of Gustav Mahler," a brief but enthusiastic tribute to the composer that recalls his Mahlerian awakening during a 1930 performance of the Fourth Symphony at the Royal College of Music in London. Having been advised by teachers to disregard Mahler, whose music they found to be long-winded, formless, self-indulgent, and, perhaps most damning, unoriginal, Britten (like Copland before him) recalls being struck by the clarity and transparency of Mahler's scoring.

---

[1] Aaron Copland, "Defends the Music of Mahler," *New York Times* (April 5, 1925), sec. IX, p. 6; Copland, *Our New Music: Leading Composers in Europe and America* (New York: McGraw-Hill, 1941), 34.

[2] Virgil Thomson, "American Composers. VII: Aaron Copland," *Modern Music* 10, no. 2 (1932): 71.

[3] Arthur Berger, *Aaron Copland* (New York: Oxford University Press, 1953), 40.

Furthermore, he lavished praise on the music's "cunningly contrived" form and its highly original melodic shapes, characterized in his view by a sustained rhythmic and harmonic tension.[4]

Britten soon began to study Mahler's symphonies, developing a particular attachment to the Fourth and later to *Das Lied von der Erde*. In connection with the latter, he wrote to Henry Boys: "It is cruel, you know, that music should be so beautiful. It has the beauty of loneliness & of pain: of strength & freedom. The beauty of disappointment & never-satisfied love. The cruel beauty of nature, and everlasting beauty of monotony."[5] At the same time, Britten hesitated to acknowledge Mahler's influence on his own works, even if he did admit that the composer's ear for sound, and his sense of form, were audible in the *War Requiem* (1961–62) and the *Spring Symphony* (1948–49). Critics, by contrast, have more readily pointed out Mahlerian traits in Britten's compositions, drawing particular attention to the influence of opera on his instrumental works, the use of popular tunes, and to an often "soloistic" style of orchestration that privileges both clarity of line and transparency of texture. Among Britten's symphonic works it is perhaps the *Sinfonia da Requiem* (1939–40) that contains the clearest Mahlerian echoes, particularly the allusions to the Ninth Symphony in the closing movement. Britten's later works, too, have often called Mahler to mind, including, above all, the *Cello Symphony* (1963), *Death in Venice* (1973), and the Third Quartet (1975–76).

Shostakovich, Schnittke, and Silvestrov

Dmitri Shostakovich offers another early example of a composer decisively influenced by Mahler, at least in his fifteen numbered symphonies. Shostakovich's evident familiarity with Mahler's music can already be felt in the First Symphony (1924–25), above all the biting irony of the work's scherzo. Yet it was during the course of Shostakovich's budding friendship with Ivan Sollertinsky – Mahler's most tireless Russian advocate – that his symphonies began to exhibit identifiably Mahlerian traits. This is particularly evident in the Fourth Symphony (1935–36), a work whose massive structure and grand narrative arc stand in stark contrast to the compact neoclassical symphonies of Prokofiev. A surviving page of extracts that

---

[4] Benjamin Britten, "On Behalf of Gustav Mahler," *Tempo* (American edition) 2, no. 2 (February 1942): 5.

[5] Britten to Henry Boys, postmarked June 29, 1937; *Letters from a Life: The Selected Letters and Diaries of Benjamin Britten 1913–1976*, ed. Donald Mitchell, vol. 1 (Berkeley: University of California Press, 1991), 493.

Shostakovich copied from Mahler's Third Symphony around this time, labelled "rare cases in orchestration," confirms Shostakovich's debt.[6] The Fourth Symphony's epic narrative sweep also characterizes the Fifth (1937), a work culminating in an apotheosis clearly modeled on similar passages in the closing movements of Mahler's First and Third Symphonies. But what truly distinguishes these works is the appropriation of Mahler's ironic voice, a gift he would pass on to his most distinguished successor, Alfred Schnittke.

Whereas the sheer expressive force of Schnittke's music has often been said to derive from both Shostakovich and Mahler, it would perhaps be more accurate to say that it comes from Mahler *by way of* Shostakovich. Even if Schnittke's musical "world" is less all-embracing than Mahler's, the "polystylism" of Schnittke's First Symphony (1972), in particular, shares important similarities with the heterogeneous and multivocal nature of Mahler's early symphonies. A more direct engagement with Mahler's music is reflected above all in Schnittke's Piano Quartet (1988), a compact work that serves in part as a commentary on the thematic and motivic content of a twenty-six-bar fragment for piano quartet by Mahler that dates from his youth. Schnittke's homage concludes by quoting Maher's fragmentary sketch, more or less directly, but with the final sonority altered. In the context of Schnittke's transcription of the Quartet in the second movement of his Concerto Grosso no. 4/Symphony no. 5 (1988), this fragment seems to emerge "as if from a distance," a gesture that returns the movement to its origins as a piece of chamber music. In the orchestral version, however, Schnittke heightens the unsettling nonresolution of the concluding polytonal chord with the performance instruction, *vibrato lento, quasi glissando.*

Mahler's position as a reference point among Soviet composers during the 1970s and '80s is also evident in the music of Valentin Silvestrov. Whereas allusions to Mahler are already present in some of his earliest works, including *Quiet Songs* (1974–84) and *Kitsch-Music* (1977), echoes of Mahler's late scores, above all the Ninth Symphony and *Das Lied von der Erde,* can be found in Silvestrov's own later works, especially the Fifth Symphony (1982), where Silvestrov treats the massive orchestra with chamber-like restraint. Yet in a work that Silvestrov himself referred to as a "post-symphony," the composer seems to hold its late romantic harmonic language at a distance, suggesting at best a melancholy embrace of that tradition.

[6] Laurel E. Fay, *Shostakovich: A Life* (Oxford: Oxford University Press, 2000), 306, n. 30.

After Copland

Given Leonard Bernstein's prominent role in popularizing Mahler's music in the United States, it is perhaps surprising that Mahler did not exert a more substantial influence on American composers. While it goes without saying that Mahler's presence can be felt in many of Bernstein's compositions (particularly in his three numbered symphonies, as well as in parts of the *Mass*), among those composers working in the second half of the twentieth century, only George Crumb and George Rochberg offer any kind of direct engagement with his music. Crumb's *Ancient Voices of Children* (1970), for example, presents a succession of gestural and sonic allusions to "Der Abschied" from *Das Lied von der Erde* while also engaging with the classic Mahlerian trope of "music from afar." *Black Angels* (1970) also features a number of obvious Mahlerian references, including instruments imitating other instruments (as in the *Pavana Lachrymae*, which features the marking "like a consort of viols," while the cello in the final movement is instructed to play "as from afar").

Rochberg's sustained engagement with Mahler's music is particularly evident in *Music for the Magic Theater* (1965) and the Third String Quartet (1971). Rochberg's writings from the late 1960s and early 1970s illuminate the stylistic pluralism of these works, an aesthetic in which the porous boundary between past and present allowed Rochberg to draw freely on compositional techniques and musical styles from a range of historical periods (here primarily the eighteenth and nineteenth centuries), an approach that the composer referred to as *ars combinatoria*. Whereas in *Music for the Magic Theater* (1965) Mahler's music emerges only in fragments (fleeting allusions to the first and last movements of the Ninth Symphony), in the Third Quartet (1971) Rochberg revisits this music in a more sustained fashion. In the quartet's fifth and final movement we encounter music that not only speaks in a Mahlerian voice but on more than more occasion *appears* to quote the Ninth Symphony's closing Adagio, albeit with substantial differences.

Berio and Nono

Luciano Berio's engagement with the music of Gustav Mahler began in 1968 with his elaborate reworking of the scherzo of Mahler's Second Symphony in the third movement of his own *Sinfonia* (1968–69). If Berio described this movement as a form of commentary, he also made clear that his ultimate aim was to produce an analysis of Mahler's scherzo. This analytical impulse extends to the bulk of Berio's transcriptions, a substantial body of work that includes ten early songs by Mahler that were published as *Fünf frühe Lieder* (*Five Early Songs*, 1986) and *Sechs frühe Lieder* (*Six Early Songs*, 1987) – the latter featuring a retranscription of "Erinnerung" ("Memory") from the first set. Here Berio's motivation was a desire to "bring to light the undercurrents of the original piano part: Wagner, Brahms, the adult Mahler, and the modes of orchestration that came after him."[7] Whereas Berio's interventions in these two sets are for the most part relatively modest, they nevertheless provide evidence of the composer's own listening habits, as well as those of the protagonists populating these early songs. Berio's attentive ears also revealed Mahlerian resonances in the music of other composers. In the preface to *Rendering* (1988–90), Berio's reworking of Schubert's fragmentary sketches for a presumed Tenth Symphony, he offers the bold claim that its second movement is "inhabited by Mahler's spirit." Berio further emphasized this connection by incorporating fragmentary quotations from the Finale of Mahler's Ninth Symphony in the newly composed "musical cement" that holds together Schubert's fragmentary materials.

Whereas Berio found in Mahler a kindred spirit, Berio's contemporary Luigi Nono expressed his admiration in more specific terms, drawing attention to the spatial qualities of the opening tableau of Mahler's First Symphony. Nono was particularly interested in the sound world evoked by Mahler's quasi-programmatic marking "*wie ein Naturlaut*" (like a sound of nature). Nono's engagement with this passage can be heard most clearly in *Prometeo* (1981–84; rev. 1985), where a Mahlerian "sound space" recurs at several key moments, including the Prologue – where the opening fifth "is diffused microtonally and used to branch out into ever higher and lower octaves, gradually seeping into all registers and the entire performance space" – and in the Third Island, where "the orchestras begin on the fundamental pitch C, spaced out in truly Mahlerian fashion: a 'sudden opening' spanning five octaves and rendered by violins and trombones in anti-clockwise motion from opposite poles in space (orchestras I/II – IV/III – II/I)."[8]

---

[7] Luciano Berio, *Remembering the Future* (Cambridge, MA: Harvard University Press, 2006), 41.
[8] Carola Nielinger-Vakil, *Luigi Nono: A Composer in Context* (Cambridge: Cambridge University Press, 2015), 228, 232.

Boulez

Pierre Boulez's complex relationship with Mahler's music revealed itself in characteristically polemical essays on the composer and in a succession of refreshingly unsentimental and frequently revelatory accounts of the symphonies recorded over some forty years. In addition to incisive liner notes for his 1970 *Das klagende Lied*, Boulez also wrote a number of more substantial essays, including "Mahler Now." Here Boulez acknowledges the continuing relevance of Mahler's music in spite of modern compositional trends favoring the economical use of musical materials, while also pointing to the "breadth and complexity of Mahler's gestures as well as the variety and intensity of the steps in his invention," characteristics that "make him essential for today's thinking about the future of music."[9] This was followed in 1979 by "Why Biography?," which appeared as the preface to the first volume of the French edition of Henry-Louis de La Grange's biography of Mahler. As for the connection between Boulez's own music and his deep knowledge of Mahler's scores from his experience as a conductor, Erling E. Guldbrandsen has argued that this experience exerted a considerable impact on his compositional practice not only in works like *Répons* (1981) and *explosante-fixe* (1991–93) but also in revisions of works like *Pli selon pli* (1980–89).[10]

Davies, Finnissy, and Harvey

Throughout the second half of the twentieth century Mahler's music has remained an important source of inspiration for a wide range of British composers, including Peter Maxwell Davies, Michael Finnissy, and Jonathan Harvey. In the case of Davies, the presence of Mahler is already evident in the *Second Fantasia on John Taverner's "In Nomine"* (1964), both in the work's Scherzo and in the closing Adagio that follows. (The Finale in particular has inspired comparisons with the Adagio movements in Mahler's Ninth and Tenth Symphonies.) More recently, Davies's Third Symphony (1984) has been heard to be in dialogue with Mahler (the Ninth), both gesturally and in terms of the work's larger formal plan. The work's scherzo, for example, is notable for the way in which it introduces

---

[9] Pierre Boulez, "Mahler Now," *New York Review of Books* (October 28, 1976), 40.
[10] Erling E. Guldbrandsen, "Modernist Composer and Mahler Conductor: Changing Conceptions of Performativity in Boulez," *Studia Musicologica Norvegica* 32 (2006): 140–68.

material that functions both as a conventional trio and as a window on the slow movement that serves as the symphony's finale.

Mahler's Ninth Symphony plays an even more important role in Michael Finnissy's String Trio (1986). Here not only does the work's twenty-eight-part structure follow Mahler's tempo markings for the Ninth's first movement (translated by Finnissy from German into Italian), but its basic materials are derived from the symphony's opening horn melody. For Jonathan Harvey – a composer who expressed particular admiration for Mahler's late scores, including the Ninth Symphony and *Das Lied von der Erde* – the so-called *Leb' wohl* (farewell) motive shared by both these works served as a particular source of fascination for its suggestion of an "oceanic whole" that is "gravity-defying, static, and timeless."[11] But if the extent to which Mahler's example left a mark on Harvey's scores is not always easy to parse, in the case of . . . *towards a pure land* (2005), the composer's late style is subtly inflected in the work's "ensemble of eternal sound," a small string ensemble that is "hidden on the stage," producing music seemingly distant but for the listener ever present.

---

[11] Jonathan Harvey, *In Quest of Spirit: Thoughts on Music* (Berkeley: University of California Press, 1999), 30.

CHAPTER 31

Adorno

Roger Allen

Vision and form determine each other.[1]

Theodor Ludwig Wiesengrund Adorno (born Frankfurt am Main, September 11, 1903; died Visp, Switzerland, August 6, 1969) was the most erudite and remains the most challenging of Mahler's critical apologists. Adorno came from a cultured background: his father, Oskar Wiesengrund (1870–1946), was an assimilated Jewish wine merchant who converted to Christianity; his mother, Maria Calvelli-Adorno (1865–1952), was a devout Catholic of Italian origin who insisted on the young Theodor being baptized a Catholic. Maria's unmarried sister, the pianist Agathe Calvelli-Adorno (1867–1935), lived with the family and was to be a decisive influence on the young "Teddie's" development. Adorno's family background thus represented a coming together of the twin poles of German rationalism and Italian lyricism, so perceptively interrogated by Thomas Mann (1875–1955) in *The Magic Mountain* (1929), that Adorno was later to critique as the foundation of the Viennese tradition extending from Mozart to his teacher Alban Berg (1885–1935). It was this tension, together with a Jewish view of history inherited from his father, that drove Adorno's critical engagement with the music of Gustav Mahler.

Adorno studied piano, violin, and viola, and, as was common at the time, acquired his wide knowledge of music through the playing of piano duets. "There was little in the symphonic and chamber music repertory that did not find its way into our domestic lives with the help of large oblong volumes bound in uniform green."[2] The breadth and depth of Adorno's musical knowledge was later attested by Thomas Mann, who at

---

[1] Theodor W. Adorno, *Mahler: A Musical Physiognomy*, trans. Edmund Jephcott (Chicago: Chicago University Press, 1992), 11.
[2] Theodor W. Adorno, *Gesammelte Schriften*, vol. xvii: *Musikalische Schriften IV*, ed. Rolf Tiedemann (Franfurt am Main: Suhrkamp, 1997), 303; cited in Lorenz Jäger, *Adorno: A Political Biography*, trans. Stewart Spencer (New Haven: Yale University Press, 2004), 3.

the time of their collaboration on the novel *Doctor Faustus* wrote, "But his knowledge of tradition, his mastery of the whole historical body of music, is enormous. An American singer who works with him said to me: 'It is incredible. He knows every note in the world.'"[3] The playing of the symphonic repertoire in four-handed arrangements was a practice Adorno evidently continued into adulthood. In the early years of his exile, when it was still possible for Jewish refugees to return to Germany, there is an account by his friend Peter Haselberg of playing a transcription for piano duet of Mahler's Seventh Symphony with Adorno. "Somehow or other I had managed to track down a transcription of Mahler's Seventh Symphony for piano four hands ... We played it several times."[4]

Adorno came to maturity during the political chaos of the immediate aftermath of World War I and the intellectual chaos of the Weimar Republic (1919–33). His philosophy was primarily shaped by critical engagement with the immediate challenges of the time. It seemed to Adorno that one layer above all in the social hierarchy had been compromised by the ideological storms that engulfed Europe in the early years of the twentieth century: that of the so-called liberal bourgeoisie of the prewar period. The establishment of communism in post-revolutionary Russia, with its promises of equality and social justice, encouraged this view and exercised considerable influence on intellectual radicals in Central and Western Europe. These included the Marxist philosopher Ernst Bloch (1885–1977). In 1921, at the age of just seventeen, the impressionable Adorno read Bloch's influential book *The Spirit of Utopia*, which put forward the then-unfashionable view that the medium of music culminated via Wagner and Bruckner in the symphonies of Gustav Mahler.

Adorno's composition teacher at the Frankfurt Conservatory was Bernhard Sekles (1872–1934). It was Sekles (whose other pupils included Paul Hindemith) who directed Adorno down the path of musical modernism that eventually led him to Vienna. After hearing a performance of three fragments from *Wozzeck*, Adorno decided to seek composition lessons from Berg. Although composer and philosopher formed an enduring association that was to last until Berg's death, initial encounters were not encouraging. Berg's wife Helene wrote, "A Jewish youth from Frankfurt am Main has arrived. He wants to have composition lessons from Alban ... We couldn't get rid of him."[5] Nevertheless, Adorno's persistence

[3] Thomas Mann, *The Genesis of a Novel*, trans. Richard and Clara Winston (London: Secker and Warburg, 1961), 39.
[4] Jäger, *Adorno*, 90.   [5] Ibid., 35.

paid off: direct contact between established composer and aspirant philosopher happened between January and August 1925 and continued on a less regular basis for the next three years. Adorno clearly showed some talent as a composer; most of his limited output dates from his years in Vienna before he decided to abandon composition and dedicate himself to philosophy. It was also during his time in Vienna that Adorno encountered the influential commentator and satirist Karl Kraus (1874–1936), whose political and social ideas helped the young Adorno reappraise the idea of decadence as an expression of humanity.

It was the sense of being an outsider, together with a growing attraction to Marxist ideology, that drove Adorno to join Max Horkheimer (1895–1973) in the Institute of Social Research. Founded in 1923 and run on Marxist lines, the so-called Frankfurt School developed a form of critical theory that advocated radical change in theory and practice as a cure for the ills of modern society. The activities of the School were, however, abruptly curtailed by the rise of fascism. In common with other intellectuals of Jewish origin, Adorno was displaced by the resulting general purge of left-wing intelligentsia. "No one," he wrote, "who observed the first months of National Socialism in Berlin in 1933 could fail to perceive the moment of mortal sadness, of half-knowing self-surrender to perdition, that accompanied the manipulated intoxication, the torchlight processions and the drum-beating." Adorno went into exile, first to England where he began but did not complete a doctorate at Merton College, Oxford (1934–37), then to New York to rejoin Horkheimer. He eventually migrated to California, where he lived in close proximity to Arnold Schoenberg and Thomas Mann. Adorno collaborated closely with Mann on the novel *Doctor Faustus* (1947). He not only provided a good deal of the musical input but appears, thinly disguised, as one of the manifestations of the Devil in the central chapter. "[He] has a white collar and bow tie, spectacles rimmed in horn atop his hooked nose, behind which somewhat reddened eyes shine moist and dark." Thus, as seen through the ironic eyes of Thomas Mann, the devil's features are a composite of those of Mahler and Adorno. Adorno's most important work written during his period of exile was *Philosophy of Modern Music*, which makes scant reference to Mahler but, rather, explores the dialectical tension between Schoenberg and Stravinsky.[6] After the defeat of Nazism

---

[6] Ibid., 76; Thomas Mann, *Doctor Faustus*, trans. John E. Woods (New York: Vintage International edition, 1999), 253; Theodor W. Adorno, *Philosophy of Modern Music*, trans. Anne G. Mitchell and Wesley V. Blomster (New York: Continuum, 2007).

and the collapse of the Third Reich, Adorno gradually came to terms with the emerging Federal Republic of Germany, and in late 1949 returned to the Institute of Social Research, now reestablished in Frankfurt as part of the university. In 1958 he became director of the Institute, and, although something of a target for the student protest movements of the 1960s, remained in post until his death in 1969 at the age of sixty-five.

Adorno first set out his approach to music criticism in the influential essay "On the Social Situation of Music" (1932). In this seminal work, which appeared in the first issue of the primary organ of the Frankfurt Institute, the *Journal for Social Research*, Adorno directly associates music with the class struggle recently energized by the rise of communism and the decline of the bourgeoisie. According to Adorno, there are two types of music: that which strives for commercial success (e.g., the Richard Strauss of *Der Rosenkavalier*) and the progressive music typified by Schoenberg. It is the dialectical tension generated between these twin poles of music as commodity and music as art that provides the critical oxygen for Adorno's writings on Mahler. Adorno was from the outset culturally and temperamentally disposed toward Mahler. Composer and philosopher had a good deal in common in their shared Jewish/Catholic heritage and sense of cultural alienation. Both were outsiders looking in, as is evident in Adorno's early forays into Mahler criticism. "Mahler Today" (1930) is a concise but wide-ranging essay challenging the prevailing view that Mahler was a late Romantic who had been superseded by the modernist trends of the 1920s. Adorno adroitly negotiates the dialectical space between music past and music present in which Mahler is situated. "The genuine significance of Mahler that can be discovered for today lies in the very violence with which he broke out of the same musical space that today wants to forget him." "Mahler Today" was followed by "Marginalia on Mahler" (1936), written to mark the twenty-fifth anniversary of the composer's death.[7] It is essentially a meditation on Mahler's approach to the subject of death (e.g., in *Kindertotenlieder* and *Das Lied von der Erde*) but at the same time critiques Mahler's use of kitsch and his exploitation of the banal. As the commentator Richard Leppert puts it, in Adorno's view "Mahler is a dealer in detritus, one who picks up from the scrap-heap of the present ... He finds new uses for the junk so that it gains a new essence, often profound and invariably meaningful."[8]

---

[7] Theodor W. Adorno, *Essays on Music*, ed. Richard Leppert, trans. Susan H. Gillespie (Berkeley: University of California Press, 2002), 391–436, 603–11, 604, 612–18.

[8] Ibid., 545.

In many ways the two early essays "Mahler Today" and "Marginalia on Mahler" can be seen as preparatory studies for Adorno's most important work on the composer, the book-length *Mahler: A Musical Physiognomy* (1960). This powerfully argued study is the culmination of Adorno's lifelong fascination with the problems and challenges presented by Mahler's music. In the course of eight brief but highly concentrated chapters, Adorno considers Mahler's works under the following headings: Curtain and Fanfare, Tone, Characters, Novel, Variant – Form, Dimensions of Technique, Decay and Affirmation, and The Long Gaze. Adorno's agenda is to relate Mahler's works to social and political reality. He sees Mahler above all as undermining the status quo: Mahler's symphonies are a challenge to the accepted rationality of the nineteenth-century German symphony as bourgeois artifact. In terms of accent, Mahler's music is inflected throughout with the dialect of a Bohemian Jew. It is the language of the outsider. "Through the contrast between the disruptive intention and the musical language, the latter is transformed unobserved from an *a priori* convention into an expressive means ... The energising antagonism between music and its language reveals a rift within society. The irreconcilability of the inward and outward can no longer be harmonised spiritually as in the classical age."[9] In his use of genres such as march, landler, and waltz, not to mention resonances of Jewish klezmer music, Mahler explores the potential of the banal as an expressive device in tension with the prevailing cultural norms and expectations of the symphonic genre. Mahler's "deconstruction" of the symphony and the quixotic character of his musical processes gives Adorno ample material for the development of his theory of musical form, or "the deduction of formal categories from their meaning [within the context of the work]." This represents a direct challenge to conventional *Formenlehre* analysis (which in Adorno's view misses the music's substance in its preoccupation with procedure), or Schenker's notion of fundamental structure and overarching line. For Adorno a work by Mahler generates its own form and meaning through its treatment of the musical material – unsophisticated and commonplace though it may be. Or, as Peter Franklin puts it, "Form becomes a goal, a quest after some initially inconceivable, perhaps utopian balance between details and whole." Adorno qualifies this argument by exploring a suggested analogy between Mahler's symphonies and the literary form of the novel, where the unexpected may occur at any time without being governed by the demands of the whole. In Mahler's symphonies musical

[9] Adorno, *Mahler*, 16.

events proceed rather like the characters in a novel: "Marches and Ländler in his [Mahler's] work correspond to the heritage of adventure stories and penny dreadfuls [*Kolportage*] in the bourgeois novel."[10]

Whether read in Adorno's German original or in Edmund Jephcott's English translation, *Mahler: A Musical Physiognomy* represents a formidable challenge. For one thing, Adorno's paragraphs are inordinately long and it is easy to lose a foothold. A further difficulty is that although Adorno makes frequent reference throughout to specific instances in the works themselves, there is (with the single exception of the title page in the German edition, which quotes a phrase from the song "Liebst du um Schönheit" ["If You Love for Beauty"]) a complete absence in the text of musical examples. Adorno thus optimistically presupposes on the part of the reader a detailed knowledge of Mahler's scores to equal his own (although both the German original and English translation do provide footnoted references to rehearsal numbers for many of the passages discussed). Yet for all (and perhaps even because of) its difficulties, what makes *Mahler: A Musical Physiognomy* such a compelling read is that the author is culturally and intellectually very close to his subject. Adorno's *Mahler* stands alongside his equally demanding *In Search of Wagner* as a landmark of musical criticism.

Adorno regarded the "Mahler Centenary Address," first published in July 1960 and included in the collection of essays published as *Quasi una Fantasia* (1963), as a "kind of synopsis of *Mahler: A Musical Physiognomy*." It is perhaps for this reason that it is the most immediately accessible of Adorno's writings on Mahler.[11] Many of the ideas of the earlier book appear here in a more concise form. Take, for example, the comparison of the symphony to the novel. "It has rightly been observed that the first thing that impresses the listener to Mahler's music is that it always develops in an unexpected way. But by the same token, his novelistic, unschematic approach is far removed from the merely episodic or arbitrary."[12] Writing of *Das Lied von der Erde*, Adorno uncharacteristically drops his guard and throws all critical caution to the wind in an eloquent and deeply felt encomium:

---

[10] Max Paddison, *Adorno's Aesthetics of Music* (Cambridge: Cambridge University Press, 1993), 175; Peter Franklin, "'... his fractures are the script of truth.' – Adorno's Mahler," in *Mahler Studies*, ed. Stephen E. Hefling (Cambridge: Cambridge University Press, 1997), 291; Adorno, *Mahler*, 62.

[11] Theodor W. Adorno, *Quasi una Fantasia*, trans. Rodney Livingstone (London: Verso, 1998); also Franklin, "Adorno's Mahler," 289. For comments on Livingstone's translation of *Quasi una Fantasia*, see ibid., 294.

[12] Adorno, *Quasi una Fantasia*, 94.

> Written by a man not yet fifty, this work, despite its fragmented form, is one of the greatest achievements of late musical style since [Beethoven's] late quartets. It is surpassed, if at all, only by the first movement of [Mahler's] Ninth Symphony. It lingers on the same Chinese Dolomite landscape of streams and pines, but frames the compressed fulness of the vocal part within a wide-ranging symphonic objectivity which represents a final leave-taking from the Sonata form ... The last work that Mahler completed ... is the first work of the new music.[13]

There can be no doubt whatsoever that Mahler's music mattered, and mattered deeply, to Adorno. Here, if anywhere, we can identify the irreconcilable tension that pervades all Adorno's critical engagement with the composer: what Peter Franklin aptly describes in the context of Adorno's response to Mahler's Eighth Symphony as "a critic struggling against his own experience of being swept away."[14]

Those willing to pick up the critical gauntlet thrown down by Adorno should not be discouraged: help is at hand in the form of two supporting texts, both already referenced. Max Paddison's *Adorno's Aesthetics of Music* (1993) wears its years lightly and remains the best single-volume exegesis of Adorno's aesthetics and sociology of music. Paddison interrogates the conceptual context within which Adorno's writings on music may be situated and how they interlock with his broader philosophical project. He is particularly helpful on Mahler as the ideal subject matter for Adorno's "material theory of musical form," his idea of Mahler as "survival of the expressive subject," and for a full bibliographic list of Adorno's writings on Mahler. Peter Franklin's article, "'. . . his fractures are the script of truth.' – Adorno's Mahler," deftly identifies and negotiates the pitfalls and problems of *Mahler: A Musical Physiognomy*, while eloquently extracting the critical marrow from Adorno's often dogmatic assertions and seeming abstractions. Both texts are indispensable aids to understanding Adorno's writings on music in general and Mahler in particular within the context of his overall philosophical enterprise. Moreover, the premise of Franklin's argument remains as valid today as when first formulated in 1997: "The threat posed by Adorno to conventional musicology ... can be directly equated with Adorno's interpretation of the threat often posed by Mahler to the aesthetic norms of his culture. That threat manifests itself in Adorno as an implicit challenge to those who support less disturbing, more straightforwardly affirmative or spiritually transcendent readings of

---

[13] Ibid., 92.   [14] Franklin, "Adorno's Mahler," 285.

Mahler's music."[15] The musicological landscape has changed considerably since 1997 when Franklin made that observation; yet, inflected though it may be with time-specific ideologies and agendas, Adorno's laser-like critical acumen remains a powerful tool of musical criticism. Adorno's writings on Mahler, and in particular his book *Mahler: A Musical Physiognomy*, present a profound understanding of his subject matter seen from the shared historical perspective of the "outsider" shaped by the political, cultural, and ideological paradigm shifts of the first half of the twentieth century. Adorno's enduring legacy and ongoing challenge is to suggest methodologies for further inquiry and models for critical response.

[15] Paddison, *Adorno's Aesthetics of Music*, 174–75; 258–60, 317, n. 46; Franklin, "Adorno's Mahler," 282–83.

CHAPTER 32

Influences in Literature

Matthew Werley

The absolute (genuine) musical composer = unliterary.
—Thomas Mann (1909)

Almschi forbade me to read.[1]

—Walter Kappacher (2012)

It is hardly surprising, given Gustav Mahler's lifelong disposition toward literature, that studies of his reception among writers have only marginally featured in an otherwise remarkably wide and sophisticated spectrum of critical engagements with the composer. Mahler harbored astonishingly conservative tastes in poetry, a frustrating choice considering that he built his early reputation as a symphonic composer upon reworkings of his own Lied settings. His gravitation toward *volkstümlich* (folkish) texts by social "outsiders," mainly men named Friedrich (Klopstock, Nietzsche, and Rückert), suggests an astute philosophical sensibility but not a voracious or internationally oriented literary appetite.[2] His self-authored poems, especially *Das klagende Lied* (1880), strike twentieth-century readers as dilettantish in tone and expression, and his music seldom sparked poetic responses from literary contemporaries.

Even more remarkable than these aesthetic proclivities is the personal dimension. Mahler not only gave fin-de-siècle Vienna's vibrant literary scene of coffeehouse intellectuals and salonnières a comfortably wide berth, but his actions and attitudes at times alienated prominent members of its inner circle. As early as September 1901, he ostracized Hugo von

---

[1] Thomas Mann, "Zum Literatur-Essay," in *Pro und Contra Wagner*, trans. Allan Blunden (London: Faber and Faber, 1985), 38–39; Walter Kappacher, *Trakls letzte Tage & Mahlers Heimkehr* (Salzburg: Müry Salzmann, 2014), 93.

[2] See Jeremy Barham's recent "'The Ghost in the Machine': Thomas Koschat and the *volkstümlich* in Mahler's Fifth Symphony," *Nineteenth-Century Music Review* 15 (2018): 353–90. My gratitude belongs to Karl Müller (Universität Salzburg) and Manfred Mittermayer (Literaturarchiv Salzburg), whose passion for Mahler equals their knowledge of Austrian literature.

Hofmannsthal by high-handedly rejecting his proposed ballet project with Alexander Zemlinsky, *Triumph der Zeit*. That only a month later Mahler would meet and fall in love with the latter's composition student, Alma Schindler – a woman whose intellectual standing and privileged upbringing could have easily facilitated the necessary social introductions – merely underscores to what extent he felt content contributing to Viennese culture solely from the orchestral podium. The names of his illustrious literary contemporaries rarely appear in Mahler's correspondence, and neither does his in theirs. If Alma was careful to note in her autobiography that she had already compiled her own private library by the precocious age of fifteen (seven years before meeting Mahler), then her marriage to Franz Werfel suggests that her previous two husbands constituted something of a literary interregnum.[3] That Mahler's other Viennese lover, Anna von Mildenburg, also married a major literary figure (Hermann Bahr) further serves to contrast the composer's profile against the dominant cultural backdrop of his age. Mahler emerges as the unmistakable embodiment of peripheral Habsburgian sensibilities rather than urban Viennese ones; little wonder that he provocatively hailed the immensely popular arch-outsider Peter Rosegger (1843–1918), "the little Parsifal in Lederhosen" from the Styrian countryside (to use Stefan Zweig's endearing phrase), as the greatest living author of his generation.

Composers in Literature around 1900

Mahler's career traversed a period of European cultural history when musicians and literary figures regarded their artistic aims as more conceptually unified than ever before. Novelists increasingly sought to "compose" novels, and composers conceived of music in terms of literature's narrative power. If Richard Wagner was the paradigm-changing colossus behind this aesthetic, it was arguably Ludwig van Beethoven who appeared more frequently and most decisively as the archetypal musical subject in fictional works around 1900.[4]

Embodying *bürgerlich* (middle-class) values, the "heroic" Beethoven served as the ideal myth-making figure for ascendant middle-class readers faced with upheavals in gender politics, rapid infusions of technological innovations into daily life, and ideologically charged nationalist movements that hurtled European societies forward at a vertigo-inducing pace

---

[3] Alma Mahler, *Mein Leben* (Frankfurt am Main: S. Fischer, 1999), 21.
[4] The standard overview is Angelika Corbineau-Hoffmann, *Testament und Totenmaske. Der literarische Mythos des Ludwig van Beethoven* (Weidmann: Hildesheim, 2000).

in the years leading up to 1914. Beethoven's influence on literature spread across national boundaries, from Leo Tolstoy's *The Kreutzer Sonata* (1889), which features the violin sonata at the center of a tragic affair, to Gerhart Hauptmann, whose second act of *Michael Kramer* (1900) transpires under the ominous shadow of the composer's death mask, and Romain Rolland, who placed the hybrid Belgium-German composer (a fusion of Beethoven and Richard Strauss) at the center of his Nobel Prize–winning musical novel, *Jean-Christophe* (1904–12).

Nowhere was Beethoven's presence in the cultural firmament more palpable than in Mahler's Vienna. Here the composer represented the ideal creative figure: a pure artistic genius who boldly stood naked (or sat, as in Max Klinger's 1902 statue) before the unforgivingly critical eye of the public. If Mahler's profile secretly served as the model for the gilded knight in Gustav Klimt's 1901 *Beethoven Frieze*, the allusion nevertheless sat within a larger homage to the German composer and his artistic potency for Secessionist aesthetics. Contemporary responses to Mahler in literature were not markedly different. Arthur Schnitzler was certainly the most sympathetic to Mahler among the fin-de-siècle Viennese establishment – indeed, he relished playing four-hand piano versions of his symphonies with his mother and hailed him as the greatest composer of his generation – but the central hero of his first major novel, Georg von Wergenthin in *Der Weg ins Freie* (*The Road into the Open*, 1908), released the year Mahler left for New York, is an unmistakably (flawed) German composer in the Beethovenian-Wagnerian mold, even if he is placed in the context of Mahler's Vienna.

It was only with Mahler's untimely death in 1911 that his influence on literature began to take shape. Briefly sketched, two thematic-historical patterns emerge in his literary reception. Authors writing around the First World War typically focused on Mahler's personality and aura as a performer. As a public figure he presented a seemingly irreconcilable set of elements: the Bohemian background, the assimilated Jew and victim of anti-Semitism, the ardent Wagnerian, husband of Alma, and charismatic leader of one of Europe's most important cultural institutions. After the Second World War, and corresponding with what one might label "the long Mahler Renaissance," authors began to respond more directly to his music as a source of poetic inspiration.

Death Maketh the Mann

The most famous evocation of Mahler's personality in literature is simultaneously one of the earliest examples of his poetic reception overall.

Thomas Mann based the name and physical description of the central character of his 1912 novella *Death in Venice*, Gustav von Aschenbach, on the Austrian conductor/composer. Prior to this, however, the author of *Buddenbrooks* had been only cursorily acquainted with Mahler's music and personality. In February 1904, he attended a concert of the Third Symphony in Munich, and in October 1908 fleetingly met the composer following the German premiere of the Seventh. In November 1906, about the time when his brother-in-law Klaus Pringsheim served as Mahler's assistant, Mann witnessed the composer rehearse his Sixth Symphony. Yet none of these impressions prompted the Munich-based author to take particular interest in either Mahler's conducting activities in Vienna or, more importantly, his stage reforms with Alfred Roller in the area of Wagner's operas. By 1909 he perfunctorily listed Mahler and Strauss as the most important representatives of Modernism, but by the end of the First World War his enthusiasm for Hans Pfitzner had eclipsed all other musical interests (Wagner aside).

This changed with the much-anticipated world premiere of the Eighth Symphony in Munich on September 12, 1910. Mann attended the concert and reception afterward, where he and Max Reinhardt spoke at length with the composer. Years later he confessed that it was not so much Mahler's music and the overwhelming success of the monumental "symphony of a thousand" but "his burningly intense personality [that] had made the strongest impression on me."[5] The focus of Mann's recollection is understandable. By this stage in his career Mahler was well on his way to becoming a living legend, and the biographical dimension of his art attracted wide interest, with the Munich-based Piper Verlag publishing not one but two character studies of Mahler by Paul Stefan in early September.

Although their encounter initially prompted a single exchange of letters, Mann's fascination with Mahler lay dormant for eight months until he travelled along the Istrian peninsula from Pula (now Croatia) up to Venice in mid-May 1911 – just as von Aschenbach does in the novella. It was during this coastal traverse that Mann first learned of Mahler's return to Vienna and his tragic death a few days later. Once in Venice, Mann drafted an article on Wagner for the June issue of *Der Merker*, and the following month (July) began fusing these personal, contemporary, and

[5] Thomas Mann, *Gesammelte Werke, vol. 12: Reden und Aufsätze* (Frankfurt am Main: Fischer, 1960), 367.

historical events together into the core themes and characters of *Death in Venice*.

In the second chapter of the novella, Mann unmistakably evoked Mahler's features – the thin brushed-back hair, lofty knotty brow, rimless gold spectacles, aristocratically hooked nose, furrowed cheeks – to create a mask-like cipher for his essentially Wagnerian character. Aschenbach's name is a metonym for Wolfram von Eschenbach, the historical Minnesinger and author of *Parzival*, who in Wagner's *Tannhäuser* represents one of the spiritually bleakest characters in his entire oeuvre. Venice, the setting where Wagner composed the second act of *Tristan und Isolde* in the spring of 1859, and later died in February 1883, helped Mann align his novella with the fateful trajectory of nineteenth-century German art music. But the anachronistic intermingling of such elements, including the Apollonian layer, also gave Mann space to dress his Mahlerian figure in a costume vaguely familiar to contemporary readers. His Faustian description of the artist, which captures Mahler's social withdrawal in Vienna, seems both vague and highly apt: "'You see, Aschenbach has always lived like this' – here the speaker closed the fingers of his left hand to a fist [*Faust*] – 'never like this' – and he let his open hand hang relaxed from the back of his chair."

For Mann, the affinity between Aschenbach and the deceased composer was private and had no immediate impact on Mahler's posthumous literary reception. Although this became public knowledge with the release of Wolfgang Born's illustrated edition of the novella in 1921, it was not until Luchino Visconti's 1971 Warner Brothers film, *Death in Venice*, which used Mahler in the soundtrack and turned Aschenbach into a composer (rather than an author), that the connection became cemented in the public imagination. Anna Mahler called it a "cheap publicity" tactic, and scholars have since labelled it "the most regrettable" deficiency of an otherwise compelling film.

A Demonic Aura

Chronologically, the first poetic response to Mahler was likely by Stefan Zweig. In 1910, the twenty-eight-year-old Viennese journalist, translator, and aspiring author contributed the poem *Der Dirigent* (*The Conductor*) to a collection in celebration of Mahler's fiftieth birthday, edited by his university friend Paul Stefan.[6] From the first line to the last, Zweig sought

---

[6] Paul Stefan, ed., *Gustav Mahler: Ein Bild seiner Persönlichkeit in Widmungen* (Munich: Piper Verlag, 1910), 58–61.

to replicate for the reader the sheer excitement of experiencing the conductor in performance. He sketched the Vienna Opera as a "beehive" of "countless human expectations" and described Mahler's presence over the music, musicians, and audience in oceanic terms. Like a ship cut adrift in rough seas, Mahler's podium gestures are elemental and generate uncontrollable "floods," "waves," "storms," "currents," and "foams" of sound. Audiences drift along until stirred into a restless dream-like state, "intoxicated by the sweet poison of *Klang* [sound]." Zweig's poem merits closer analysis, but its imagery bears the faint imprint of Mahler's last new production with Roller, Gluck's *Iphigenie in Aulis*, which the author attended in 1907 and praised lavishly in a letter to Bruno Walter years later. Not only do the symbols of Gluck's opera appear in the poem's metaphoric language (Classical references, seafaring images, stark contrasts of light and darkness), but its subject matter of return and personal sacrifice also blurs the lines between art and the biographical circumstances of Mahler's life around 1910. (Incidentally, Zweig was also a fellow passenger on the SS *Amerika* that carried Mahler home on April 8, 1911.)

Zweig then produced another, far more substantial piece on Mahler for the *Neue Freie Presse* on April 25, 1915. Titled "Gustav Mahler's Return" and written during the early phase of the First World War, the essay provided readers with a semi-fictional portrait of the artist. In a myth-building exercise of the first order, Zweig ratcheted up the cultural stakes by strategically deploying two highly charged terms, one of which would later feature prominently in Mahler's literary reception. The first is *Amokläufer*, referring to the Malaysian word *amok* that originally described a war cry, but since the early 1920s has exclusively denoted perpetrators of senseless mass-shootings. Zweig used the term to describe the correlation between the conductor's wild podium movements and his single-minded resolve to attain an ultimate state of musical consummation in performance. Such a goal was not merely aesthetic for Zweig but cultural on a generation-defining scale: "From his baton the rhythm of our blood quivers: just as a lightning rod binds the tensions of the entire atmosphere, so he brings our entire congested feelings into a single point" (2).

The second loaded word Zweig used – eight times, in fact – is *Dämon*, a slippery term that denotes genius, the demonic, and the artistically possessed, with precedents in the works of Goethe, Schiller, and E. T. A. Hoffmann (*Kreisleriana*, 1814). It was first applied to Mahler by Hauptmann, who after meeting the composer in Vienna on February 5, 1904, noted in his diary: "Distinguished head. Demonic natural power. Unmistakable stamp of a great genius." Bahr also used the term twice for a short article in the April 1920 issue of *Musikblätter des Anbruch*, no doubt gleaning it from Zweig, his friend and Salzburg neighbor. But whereas in Zweig's imagination the *dämonisch* denoted the volatile core of the artistic Will, for Bahr the "transfigured, inebriated look" represented the flip side of the Baroque, characterized by "technical perfection and incomparable precision." (Before 1909, Bahr had toyed with the idea of a novel about Mahler, but quickly abandoned the idea given his marriage to Anna von Mildenburg that year.) For Zweig, evoking the *dämonisch* was a way of vividly preserving the legacy of Mahler's aura for Viennese culture: "for our generation he was more than a musician, master, conductor, even artist, but that which is unforgettable from our youth."

Zweig's contemporary Kurt Frieberger (1883–1970), the Viennese civil servant, poet, and recipient of the 1908 Raimund Prize, saw in Mahler's personality and art the embodiment of Baroque theatricality. Frieberger's postwar collection *Barocke Balladen* (1919) opens with a poem, *Of the Solitary Face of the Heart*, dedicated "to the memory of Gustav Mahler." Structured in five parts, it takes up the imagery of a tired wanderer and his encounters with nature. Its penultimate section, *Memory (Vienna Opera, fin de siècle)*, is a cultural flashback to Mahler's charismatic conducting style: "where his eye blitzed hither / his baton stretched wildly / protruding a powerful shadow / against the velvet curtain folds / thus becoming Lord and Sovereign / of all carnal forces" (13). Even though Frieberger's Expressionist-tinged poem, which grasps at familiar tropes, has not weathered well, his evocation of the Eighth Symphony as a Baroque High Mass, with its "fervent cry of the martyr, *Veni, creator spiritus!*" (14), is perspicacious and hints at Mahler's synthesis of the artist and nature. For his readers, the at-times kitschy poetic recollections served as a welcome relief to the bleak realities of postwar Austrian life

Mahler's Eleventh

The end of the Second World War signaled a new phase in Mahler's literary reception. A younger generation of intellectuals, prompted by the rebuilding of Europe's cultural institutions after six years of war, sought to reevaluate Mahler's personality and music. By far the most important figure in this project was the Austrian author Ingeborg Bachmann. Born in Klagenfurt in 1926 to a father with a Nazi background, Bachmann was highly attuned to the political stakes of Austria's cultural rebuilding. She fell naturally into the activities of the Gruppe 47 and became the fourth recipient of its annual prize. Originally studying music and philosophy,

Bachmann wanted most of all to become a composer. Indeed, music, more so than any of her contemporaries, played a central role in her works: metaphorical and historical references to Mozart, Schubert, Wagner, and Schoenberg (among others) abound throughout her oeuvre, and she authored two important essays on the topic – "Die wunderliche Musik" ("Fantastical Music," 1956) and "Musik und Dichtung" ("Music and Poetry," 1959) – as well as three libretti for Hans Werner Henze (*Der Prinz von Homburg, Der junge Lord*, and *Ein Monolog des Fürsten Mysch-kin*). Although it is impossible to reduce her musical aesthetic into a pithy summary, music clearly signified a contested utopia in the postwar land-scape, one that nevertheless retained its status as the highest expression of the human spirit.

Bachmann's interest in Mahler's music stemmed from hearing Leonard Bernstein in concert, on the radio, and on recordings, and through discussions with friends such as Henze and Karl Amadeus Hartmann. For example, Henze mentioned hearing Mahler's Third Symphony in his letter to Bachmann of July 19, 1964, only weeks before the world premiere of his *Ariosi for Soprano, Violin and Orchestra*. Three years later, she dedicated to him the short poem *Enigma* (1967), which quotes from *Des Knaben Wunderhorn* in Mahler's Third Symphony, "And should I not weep, O bounteous God?" ("Und sollt' ich nicht weinen, du gütiger Gott?"), transforming it into "You should not weep, said the music" ("Du sollst ja nicht weinen, sagt eine Musik"). Five years later, in her short story, *Ihr glücklichen Augen* (*Eyes to Wonder*, 1972), the visually impaired Miranda attends a concert of Mahler's Sixth Symphony, having mistaken it for his more popular Fourth. In the early drafts, Bachmann had considered featuring Brahms and Schubert on the concert, but regarded the "Tragic" as a far more potent symbol for her character's misreadings of societal conventions.

The most important contribution of Bachmann to Mahler reception occurred in her major novel *Malina* (1971), conceived as the first in a planned trilogy titled *Todesarten* (*Ways of Dying*). Critics and contempor-aries have consistently described it as Mahlerian in tone and structure. On March 26, 1971, Henze famously sent her a telegram from Rome: "FIN-ISHED READING MALINA[.] VERY STIRRED BY ABUNDANCE OF IMMENSE SADNESS AND DESPERATION[.] YOUR FIRST SYMPHONY IS MAHLER'S ELEVENTH." It was the highest compli-ment the composer could pay. Bachmann claims to have "composed" rather than "written" its final section. Although references to modern music, especially Schoenberg, abound, the sudden dissonant crash of

memories into scenes evokes the grotesques that unexpectedly interrupt
Mahler's symphonies. As a structural model, his acoustic landscapes provided the catalyst for a novel that, as one critic has summarized, ranks as
the "most jagged renderings of female consciousness European literature
has produced. In its torrent of language, paralyzing lassitude, and relentless
constriction of expectation and escape, *Malina* condenses – and then
detonates – the neurasthenic legacy of the interwar Austrian novel."[7]
In the hands of Bachmann, Mahler's time had indeed finally come in
postwar fiction.

Musical-Literary Parallels?

Mahler's influence in literature, particularly regarding any substructural
parallels, remains an elusive line of inquiry. Arguably the literary Ur-
parallel to Mahler's music was the *echter*-than-all-the-rest Peter Rosegger,
whose best-selling novels never presented readers with an ambivalence-free
portrait of the pastoral life. A critic of globalism that gobbles up the little
things, Rosegger presented characters – in works such as *Jakob der Letzte*
(*Jakob the Last*, 1887), with its flawed hero rooted in earth and mud, pine
and schnaps, rain and moss, roots and limestone – who prompted Mahler
to sense the pre-tremors of a terrible cultural earthquake that would later
tear apart the old world. Such resonances with Mahler's situated worldview
can be detected in the Nigerian American Teju Cole, whose debut novel
Open City (2011) views the Ninth Symphony and *Das Lied von der Erde*
through the eyes of an immigrant-turned-urban flâneur in Manhattan.
Likewise, the Irish author Thomas Kinsella and Austrian playwright
Marlene Streeruwitz have also turned to Mahler on such terms. While
Mahlers Taktstock (*Mahler's Baton*, 2019), by the Graz-based Günther
Freitag, may also prove a continuation of this legacy, a new trend comes
from the Salzburg-born Walter Kappacher, whose *Mahlers Heimkehr*
(*Mahler's Return Home*, 2014), commissioned by the Salzburg Festival in
2012 (as *Mahlerlieder*), represents a tour de force of Mahler scholarship
woven into a poetic fantasy.

---

[7] Dustin Illingworth, "Detonating the Container of Consciousness: On Ingeborg Bachmann's
Incendiary Modernism," *The Nation* (June 18, 2019).

CHAPTER 33

Mahler on Disc

Richard Wattenbarger

Introduction

In the April 1960 issue of *Music and Letters*, Donald Mitchell offered a survey of Mahler recordings then available in Great Britain: "[W]e have in the current catalogue recordings of the first, second, fourth, fifth, sixth, eighth and ninth symphonies, 'Das Lied von der Erde,' 'Kindertotenlieder' and 'Lieder eines fahrenden Gesellen,' and a selection of songs. Riches indeed."[1] Mitchell contrasted this bounty with the paucity of recordings before World War II. At that time "there were available only the second and ninth symphonies, the Adagietto from the fifth, 'Das Lied von der Erde,' and an odd song or two." The Mahler centenary, however, found record collectors obliged to choose among duplicates of many works, including five "rival versions" of the First. In what followed, Mitchell sought to evaluate the existing recordings and to recommend the best reading of each piece.

Twenty-first-century collectors, faced with a surfeit of Mahler recordings, will find Mitchell's account quaint. In the decades since Mitchell's survey, Mahler recording has become an industry within an industry. For any given work, dozens of recordings, each characterized by a level of technical proficiency unimaginable in 1960, compete for the attention of consumers. No longer do the major labels of the eras of 78s and LPs have a corner on the market: newer labels such as Channel Classics, Oehms Classics, and Signum Classics, alongside labels of orchestras such as the London Symphony, the Philharmonia, the New York Philharmonic, and the San Francisco Symphony, have contributed complete cycles to this crowded field. Production of recordings and, indeed, of cycles shows no signs of abating: Ívan Fischer's cycle with the Budapest Festival Orchestra

---

[1] Donald Mitchell, "Mahler on the Gramophone," *Music & Letters* 41 (1960): 156.

will soon be complete, and others under Ádám Fischer (Ívan's older brother), Daniel Harding, and Osmo Vänskä are ongoing.

Formulating a comprehensive critical assessment of this array proves a daunting task. The last edition of Lewis M. Smoley's discography, a game attempt, appeared in 1996.[2] Publications such as *American Record Guide*, *Fanfare*, and *Gramophone* and websites such as Classics Today and Music-Web International continue to offer reviews and surveys of recordings, but a comprehensive overview of the field is no longer tenable. Over the past half-century, however, a consensus has emerged on canonical recordings for given works, and each new release becomes a candidate for inclusion. This development invites contemplation of crucial questions yet to be addressed among reviewers and reviews: What kind of document is a recording of a work by Mahler? Whose interpretation does it capture? The conductor's? The producer's? Does the recording merely embody an acoustic interpretation of a printed score or is it something more?

In this essay, I will sketch a history of Mahler on record that is more than a chronological account of documented sound. The dates on which a recording was made are less important to me than when it became available to the public in a durable form. Thus, while a recording such as Willem Mengelberg's 1939 version of the Fourth Symphony remains an indispensable document for the study of Mahler interpretation, for my purposes its significance begins with its 1962 release by Philips, when stereo recording began familiarizing a broader public with Mahler's oeuvre. (We might even suggest that the Mengelberg Fourth never existed except as a "historical recording.") For a history of recording, performance practice is less significant than the ways in which record production and marketing have shaped Mahler reception and enhanced the reputations of conductors, orchestras, and labels.

At the center of these developments has been the evolution of the recorded Mahler cycle, the first appearance of which, over half a century ago, transformed the ways in which audiences, collectors, and commentators came to view the composer. Through much of this period, the figure (or *a* figure) of Mahler and competing understandings of the composer's intentions have loomed large, providing criteria for interpretation and criticism as well as narratives for unifying recorded presentations of his symphonic oeuvre.

[2] Lewis M. Smoley, *Gustav Mahler's Symphonies: Critical Commentary on Recordings since 1986* (Westport, CT: Greenwood Press, 1996). See also Smoley, *The Symphonies of Gustav Mahler: A Critical Discography* (Westport, CT: Greenwood Press, 1986).

The "Second Nature" of the Recorded Work

The reception of a recording of a work from the long nineteenth century differs in fundamental respects from the work's place in the concert culture in which it originated. Mahler wrote his symphonies for performance in a public space; given the technologies of sound reproduction available during his time, private consumption would have been, if not unimaginable, inferior to the public experience. Even the best private experiences available at the turn of the century, the realization of four-hand piano transcriptions, could provide a real-time experience only of the music's harmonic and melodic contours. Not only was the timbral dimension absent from these realizations but, just as crucially, they were incapable of capturing the extent to which Mahler's music draws attention to the event and space of the public performance of a symphony through devices such as off-stage brass and instruments like the guitar, mandolin, and cowbell, normally out of place in a symphony concert.

From a historical perspective, then, hearing the orchestral works in private contexts threatens to dull the listener's sense of the high-stakes game Mahler was playing (along with modernist colleagues such as Richard Strauss) with the secular public liturgy of the symphony concert. The mass distribution of recordings not only has privatized the reception of the music but also has obscured that music's historical relation to the ceremonial aspects of public performance: the assembling of the audience members, the entrance of the concertmaster (to applause), the tuning of the orchestra, the entrance of the conductor and any soloists (again to applause), the silence in the hall before the first beat, and the reverent hush during the performance itself.

Hearing Mahler on recordings is certainly more than a two-dimensional representation of experiencing them in the concert hall. But a recording and a live performance do differ ontologically: the very being, say, of the Sixth as performed before a concert-hall audience differs from the being or "thing" that is the realization of the same score as heard in a home through a set of loudspeakers or headphones. We might even suggest that, divorced from the contexts of public performance and reception, the recorded work has acquired a "second nature."

The 78s

In the June 1936 issue of *The Gramophone*, Robert W. F. Potter wrote that "the permanent value of [Mahler's] symphonic works is a much-debated

point, but there can be no doubt that his songs will live."[3] Notwithstanding performances of complete cycles of the symphonies in the early 1920s
by Willem Mengelberg and Oskar Fried (in Amsterdam and Vienna,
respectively), the reservations noted by Potter show that many collectors
still did not entertain a strong concept of a Mahlerian oeuvre; that is, the
conviction that was to emerge in the 1960s and 1970s that any given
work required the context of the composer's full output in order to be
more fully understood had not become widespread. The reasons for this
were in part economic: while one could obtain a single record of a Lied or
the Adagietto from the Fifth at a reasonable price, the cost of an entire
symphony was prohibitive for many collectors. (In 1937, Compton
Mackenzie, writing in *Gramophone*, observed that the cost of Eugene
Ormandy's 1935 fifteen-disc recording of the Bruckner Seventh was
45s., more than £160 in 2017 currency.) By 1948, when Columbia
introduced the LP in the United States, it had become possible to
obtain recordings of the First, Second, Fourth, Fifth, and Ninth Symphonies as well as *Das Lied von der Erde*, but the recording of an entire work
ranged from twelve sides (in the case of the Fourth) to twenty-two (the
Second and the Ninth). Nor were performances of the symphonies,
and possibly radio broadcasts, frequent outside Central Europe and
the Netherlands.

In fact, the physical constraints of 78s probably did not significantly
influence the decisions of record companies on Mahler releases. A market
did exist, albeit a high-end one, for recordings of complete or near-
complete operas (such as the 1935 Covent Garden *Tristan* with only the
standard stage cuts). As unwieldy as a set of one or two dozen shellac discs
might have been, record changers, commercially available since the late
1920s, relieved the nuisance of changing discs every four and a half
minutes, thus enabling listeners to approximate the continuity of an act
of a Wagner opera – or a long movement of a Mahler symphony. Further,
with the exception of Oskar Fried's 1925 acoustic recording of the Second,
the sound of the pre-1950s recordings is remarkably clear, due in part to
the transparency of Mahler's orchestral textures. In retrospect, then, it
appears that the economics of the LP may have played a greater role in the
Mahler boom of the 1960s and 1970s than did the accuracy of sound
reproduction.

---

[3] Robert W. F. Potter, "A Plea for the Recording of the Songs of Gustav Mahler," *The Gramophone*
(June 1936): 8.

The 1950s: New Economics, New Recordings

The advent of the LP reduced the costs of producing recordings of Mahler symphonies, as is evident in the proliferation of recordings of the First. In 1949, Columbia Records reissued on LP Dimitri Mitropoulos's 1940 recording with the Minneapolis Symphony. By 1958, the year in which Sir Adrian Boult's account with the London Philharmonic appeared on the Everest label, eleven commercial recordings of the work had become available. This attests to the popularity of the First, a work that, not incidentally, fell well within the technical capabilities of the major professional orchestras of the time. It appears, then, that recording the symphony posed relatively little economic risk.

The same, however, cannot be said of the remaining symphonies or *Das Lied von der Erde*. Even the Fourth, a work whose technical demands were on par with the First, had received only one LP recording by the mid-1950s, and only two more before 1960. The period saw no more than three recordings of *Das Lied von der Erde* or of any symphony after the First; the Third received but one recording, and that on the somewhat obscure SPA label. Further, with the exception of the First, labels seem to have been unwilling to pay for more expensive orchestras and conductors. (Otto Klemperer, for example, led the Vienna Symphony in a recording of the Second, which Vox released in 1951. His decision, upon forging a relationship with Walter Legge, to record for EMI was informed partly by the promise of a degree of financial security that had eluded the conductor since 1939.)

Still, the LP did give rise to premiere recordings of the Third, Sixth, Seventh, and Eighth Symphonies as well as the Adagio and *Purgatorio* of the Tenth. By the mid-1950s, it was possible, at least in principle, for the most zealous and resourceful of collectors to assemble a complete Mahler cycle from commercially available recordings. In retrospect, however, one must ask, did a market exist to justify a complete cycle on record led by a single conductor?

The Birth of the Recorded Mahler Cycle

Cycles of the works of a composer – usually a collection of all the composer's works in a single genre – were not new in the LP era. Cycles of Beethoven string quartets and symphonies had existed since the 1920s, and Schnabel's recordings of the complete piano sonatas appeared in the 1930s. The appeal of Beethoven cycles may have lain in their capacity for tracing in music a narrative spanning a composer's career. Put bluntly, a widespread interest in the persona and life of a composer provided a motive – perhaps the crucial one – for undertaking the recording of a cycle.

Another precondition for recording a cycle was a broad enough base of customers who believed in the overall quality of the composer's oeuvre to make the recording commercially successful. Although Fried and Mengelberg had performed complete cycles of the symphonies in the early 1920s – early exhibitions of Mahler's oeuvre – many decades were to pass before the symphonies were sufficiently well known and regarded to justify recording a complete cycle. Further, such an ambitious effort may have been within the scope only of major labels having international distribution capabilities.

Yet the circumstances surrounding the release of the first recorded Mahler cycle also reflect the extent to which recordings are not transparent vehicles for historical and aesthetic experiences; they are, rather, commodities that offer similar experiences in the context not of the public concert but of the consumer's privatized, individuated reception. Packaging and presentation each play a role both in selling a product and in framing the customer's experience, thereby supplanting the ceremonial functions of the concert, one of the most important of which had been the symbolic enactment of a universal humanity. Two great recording projects of the 1960s, both appearing in 1967, threw this aspect of cultural consumption into high relief.

That year saw the release of two compilations of what their companies cast as monumental achievements of the stereo era: Decca's complete recording of Wagner's *Ring* under Georg Solti and Columbia Records's complete set of Mahler symphonies under Leonard Bernstein. The Solti set had appeared earlier in 1967; the nineteen LPs were packaged in separate boxes for each opera, and the entire set was contained in a cardboard slipcover. Further, Decca used glossy paper for the covers of the individual boxes and the slipcover, a design that, at the time, likely contributed to a sense of novelty surrounding the set.

Wittingly or not, Columbia, in its packaging of the Mahler, threw down a marketing gauntlet. As with the Decca *Ring* cycle, all the recordings in the Columbia Mahler cycle had been available separately, so Columbia shifted some of its focus toward packaging the set and presenting it to the world. Preceding the release, the company undertook an advertising campaign calculated to generate anticipation. Their full-page ad in the September 1967 issue of *High Fidelity* featured a calligraphically rendered invitation:

On October the twenty-third
Nineteen hundred and sixty-seven
Columbia Records [logo]
proudly invites you to participate
in the history-making premiere of
The Nine Symphonies of Gustav Mahler
available for the first time
in a magnificent 14-record set.

Leonard Bernstein
R.S.V.P.   The New York Philharmonic
Your record dealer   The London Symphony Orchestra

Beneath this invitation, the ad continued by describing the product as an

> elegant collector's item, a milestone of the stereo decade, ... an elaborate
> limited edition which includes a 36-page booklet ... This deluxe set also
> includes an actual reproduction of the Gustav Mahler Medal received by
> Leonard Bernstein ... for his outstanding contribution to Mahler's music.
> Also, as a bonus, you will receive a 12" LP, "Gustav Mahler Remembered,"
> containing reminiscences by the composer's daughter, Anna, and by musi-
> cians who knew and worked with him.

High Fidelity was in on the buildup to the release, carrying as the cover
story of the issue Bernstein's essay, "Mahler: His Time Has Come" and
including "an analysis" by Bernard Jacobson "of the sixty-odd recorded
versions available." Perhaps in response, Decca one-upped Columbia in
1970 by rereleasing its *Ring* in a new, deluxe edition including not only the
four operas of the cycle but Deryck Cooke's three-LP introduction, all
contained within a heavy, leather-covered wooden box with a gilded cover.
(Decca's initial compilation of Solti's Mahler cycle in 1972 would come in
a more modest but still deluxe package.)

Yet the Columbia set, like the Decca, was more than a mere technical
and marketing achievement. It also elevated the status of Mahler's symphonic output to that of an oeuvre, a collection of similar works that its
champions deemed capable of conveying essentials of a composer's persona
(already a some-time reality for the subset of the public attending the live
cycles led by Mengelberg and Fried in the 1920s). The collection of
Mahler's nine symphonies into a single package obviously echoed
Beethoven, the Great Man of nineteenth-century Central European art
music: Mahler was to be Beethoven's twentieth-century counterpart.
Further, if any doubts persisted that an aim of the package was to present
the Mahler persona as fully as possible, Columbia dispelled them by

including an LP containing both personal reminiscences of the composer and a recording of Mahler's Welte-Mignon roll of the Fourth Symphony finale. The package placed the collector in a position to feel directly connected with the music's creator.

The Columbia cycle had at least two significant ramifications. First, it represented not only the composer's oeuvre but the conductor's as well, insofar as collectors regarded the conductor as interpreter, that is, a figure who also brought his own ego to the product. Further, like the Decca *Ring*, a new compilation of Mahler symphonies by a single conductor transformed the recorded cycle into one of the 8,000-meter peaks of elite musical accomplishment. It was also to no small degree a feat of recording technology and marketing prowess, especially to the extent that these aspects became transparent to the consumer.

Columbia's cycle may have persuaded other labels that a larger market existed for Mahler recordings than previously imagined. Solti had recorded the Fourth for Decca in 1961, but only in 1964 did the label decide to embark on a cycle. Vanguard, likewise, began its cycle with Maurice Abravanel conducting the Utah Symphony in 1964. Then, in May 1967, six months before the Columbia release, the first installment appeared in Philips's new cycle in which Bernard Haitink led the Amsterdam Concertgebouw. A month after the Columbia cycle hit the shelves, Deutsche Grammophon kicked off its cycle by Rafael Kubelik and the Bavarian Radio Symphony with a recording of the Ninth. Further, the latter two labels seemed to have perceived some degree of urgency in getting a cycle before the world: while the Columbia cycle had taken seven years to complete, Deutsche Grammophon had completed theirs by September 1971, less than four years from its start; and Philips had released their cycle by the end of 1972, a little more than five years after its inception.

The legacy of these early cycles remains with us in the twenty-first century. The works are so familiar to listeners, and orchestras have become so proficient in performing them, that a new cycle must supply unique interpretive insights of an elite conductor. On record, the symphonies today are at least as much about Mahler as they are about the performers, producers, and their record labels.

CHAPTER 34

Film and Recent Popular Culture

Peter Franklin

Mahler, who had mobilized the youth of his day against slovenly Tradition, reerupted into a newly youthful popular culture in the 1960s thanks to both the centenary of his birth and the advent of the long-playing record. Conductors who had known him, like Otto Klemperer and Bruno Walter, were still (just) around, and their remembered performances and recordings inspired younger conductors like Leonard Bernstein and his many contemporaries, who were eager to present the composer's rediscovered musical energies in their own way. But not only musicians were touched by the wave of new recordings or intrigued by the dream-like collages of images and landscapes that adorned their covers – some anticipating the pop-art style of the famous Peter Blake and Jann Haworth LP sleeve of the Beatles' *Sergeant Pepper's Lonely Hearts Club Band* that came out in 1967 (see Figure 34.1).

A popularly modern and youthful "avant-garde" now blithely bridged the once opposed realms of "high" and "low" culture. Having skipped the Second Viennese School, it opted for a more experimental and visionary one drawing on experiences of Zen, magic mushrooms, and LSD. In 1964 the American poet Jonathan Williams (1929–2008) produced a sequence of short poems (one for each movement of all ten Mahler symphonies), written strictly while listening to the relevant movement with headphones on, sometimes writing as if automatically, "with eyes shut." Williams elaborated somewhat, in a note added in December 1967, to a new Cape Goliard edition of the poems: "The message appears to be coming in louder and clearer, what with this Christmas's package of nine symphonies and *Das Lied* by Bernstein; and the likelihood of similar collections from DGG and Victor within another year or two. I hope not to be put off by these astonishing populist developments."[1] The volume (internally simply titled *Mahler*) bore a cover by R. B. Kitaj,

---

[1] Jonathan Williams, *Mahler* (London: Cape Goliard Press, 1969).

Figure 34.1   *Mahler: Symphony No. 3 in D Minor*, Leonard Bernstein, New York
Philharmonic, Martha Lipton, mezzo-soprano (CBS, 1962).

who in 1965 had made a series of prints inspired by the poems in their first
edition. The new cover carried Jonathan Williams's name, top left,
dwarfed by two centrally crayoned words (thrice underlined in strident
scarlet): "Mahler grooves" (Figure 34.2). That unofficial title eloquently
testified to the youthful appropriation of Mahler across genre and
taste boundaries.

The significant point is that Mahler's initial emergence into post–
Second World War popular culture was in no way nostalgic. It was marked
instead by the discovery of a richness and vitality that testified to a
newfound directness of communicated experience, like that evoked in
Williams's response to the Rondo-Burleske of the Ninth Symphony:

Figure 34.2   Cover to Jonathan Williams, *Mahler*.
Cover design by R. B. Kitaj

what's red, bleeds
and runs in circles?

the miracle
of the art of
the human
heart

in a sweat

Cross-media appropriation of Mahler continued with John Cranko's 1965 ballet to *Das Lied von der Erde*,[2] but the "miracle" was surely

---

[2] Other Mahler ballets have followed. On more recent balletic and cinematic appropriations, see Jeremy Barham, "Dismembering the Musical Voice: Mahler, Melodrama and Dracula from Stage to

monumentalized in 1974 in Ken Russell's *Mahler* – a film (part bio-pic, part comic-strip) both celebrated and notorious. From the opening *coup-de-cinéma*, where a version of the composer's Attersee composing hut bursts into engulfing flames in precise coordination with the first of the violent outbursts that rend the Tenth Symphony's first movement, we are in a cinematic world where what is seen and what is heard are combined in ever bolder and sometimes surreally imaginative ways. There is the comic-strip-style satire of Cosima Wagner (Antonia Ellis) as an anti-Semitic cabaret Nazi, who whips Mahler (literally) into shape for conversion to Catholicism and access to the anti-Semitic Vienna Court Opera. There is the astonishing nightmare/dream in which Mahler "wakes" to find himself being marched to the crematorium in a glass-windowed coffin, to the strains of the funeral marches from the Fifth and First Symphonies; Alma (Georgina Hale) will shortly dance seductively on the coffin for her lover Max (standing in for Walter Gropius) to music from the first movement of the Ninth and the Seventh's Scherzo. Vulgar, shocking? Yes, in a way; but was not Mahler's music heard by many of his contemporaries as no less so? Some of Russell's implied visual and narrative interpretations of it are also tender, visionary, and even ecstatic – as when Mahler is seen explaining God and the soul to his two small daughters as they ponder Doré's illustrations to Dante (moments from the finales of the First and Second Symphonies) or where the young Mahler, walking in a wood at night, has a vision of the natural world when the moon shines forth in time with the transformative "dream" sequence marking the climax of the development of the first movement of the Seventh Symphony; it gives way to the "Panic" close of the Third's "animals" Scherzo, as a white stallion appears and carries the boy off at a thrillingly liberating gallop.[3]

A high point of the celebratory appropriation of Mahler by popular culture, if still on the boundary between the adventurously experimental and the esoteric-elitist, was as remarkable as it was largely unregistered by the many thousands of people who may have watched the spectacular opening ceremony of the Athens Olympics on television, on August 13, 2004. Directed by avant-garde choreographer Dimitrius Papaioannou and produced by Jack Morton Worldwide (project director David Zolkwer), the parade of the national teams was preceded by the customary symbolic

Screen," in *Melodramatic Voices: Understanding Music Drama*, ed. Sarah Hibberd, 237–62 (Farnham: Ashgate, 2011).
[3] On this film, see Ben Winters, *Music, Performance and the Realities of Film: Shared Concert Experiences in Screen Fiction* (New York: Routledge, 2014), 119–26.

spectacle depicting the host nation, on this occasion involving bouzouki players and drummers (with one of the latter relayed on screen from the original Olympic Games site to the modern stadium in Maroussi, a suburb of Athens). The fragmentation of the gigantic head of a cycladic figurine (the fragments representing the many Greek islands) alluded to the discovery and representation of the human form – optimistically presaging humanistic sympathy and understanding across national boundaries, where Greek culture permeated. This extended, densely symbolic pantomime concluded with a single male acrobat suspended above the arena, walking carefully forward on a large, slowly-revolving cube. The music that emerged to accompany the entire sequence was nothing other than an extended version of the final peroration of the concluding movement ("What Love Tells Me") of the Third Symphony, from reh. 28. (The sequence can be viewed on a currently available YouTube video from just over nineteen minutes into the ceremony.)[4] The few who realized what they were seeing and hearing (and why) in this extraordinary balletic pageant were appropriately moved. It deserves to be recognized as one of the most striking utilizations of Mahler's symphonic music in a modern mass-cultural event.

The positive response of both audience and critics, whether or not they knew anything about Mahler or his Third Symphony, could be explained by the readymade cultural and stylistic integration of this kind of musical testimony from the Austro-German 1890s into the lingua franca of mass-culture cinema, through the work of émigrés like Max Steiner, Erich Wolfgang Korngold, and Franz Waxman. They, in their turn, communicated much of the expressive manner and aesthetic technology of European late romantic music (from Wagner through to Richard Strauss and Puccini) to Americans like Alfred Newman, Hugo Friedhofer, and then later to Bernard Herrmann and John Williams, in whose big-orchestral, "new Hollywood" revival scores for blockbusters like the first *Star Wars* and *Close Encounters of the Third Kind* (both 1977) many features of Mahler's style and symphonic strategies were engaged.

Mahler, the historical conductor – known in the popular Viennese press of his day as the subject of endless anti-Semitic caricatures and a decidedly contentious contender for inclusion in the category of Great Composers[5] – figured not at all

[4] A video recording is currently (August 2019) available at www.youtube.com/watch?v=Y7xiDxt7kVk (see 19:12–25:22), accessed September 18, 2019. See also *Aohna 2004: The Opening & Closing Ceremonies of the Athens 2004 Olympic Games*, DVD (Beijing: China International TV Corp., 2004).

[5] See K. M. Knittel, *Seeing Mahler: Music and the Language of Antisemitism in Fin-de-Siècle Vienna* (Farnham: Ashgate, 2010).

in the kinds of cultural appropriation so far considered. It was rather that his
proto-cinematic music was a newly discovered source of intense and often
thrillingly overwhelming musical experiences that felt contemporary, relevant,
and "alive" in a way that educationally sanctioned Great Composers of the past
seemed, fairly or otherwise, not to be – unless you were "a musician," a Classical
Music initiate who knew "what to listen for." In her way, the arty, suicidal Trish
(Maureen Lipman), who opens the door to flat-searching Rita in the 1983 British
film *Educating Rita* (the Finale of the Sixth Symphony playing upstairs), and
who immediately ventures the unprompted question, "Wouldn't you just *die*
without Mahler?," is both such an enthusiast and an emblematic caricature. Her
role might equally be to make us laugh at the ways of the arty "music lover,"
while being inspired perhaps to find out more, to find out why she relied so on
this composer. The film helped, in its way, to objectify Mahler as modish, a posh
fad.[6] Thanks to the post-1960 Mahler boom, more books on him had become
available, as he slowly turned back into a Great Composer heading for
the pantheon of the dusty, and mostly male, dead. This art-lover's Mahler also
played his part in popular culture, alongside Mozart, Beethoven, Wagner, and
so on – composers whose complex and singular life histories were often found
more readily intriguing and consumable than their long, "heavy" symphonies
and operas.

The Mahler of myth was coming into being: the consulter of Freud, the
husband of the celebratedly notorious Alma – a famous "case" whose
idiosyncrasies probably explained his often violent, "schizophrenic" music
(as it came to be described, often by direct association with his Viennese
contemporaries, like Freud, Klimt, and Schoenberg). As a colorful biographical subject, he now suffered "contextualization" as a precursor of the
Second Viennese School and anticipator of Expressionism, of film and
stream-of-consciousness literature, but, more importantly, perhaps, as a
representative of the pre–First World War golden age of an Austro-
Hungarian Empire always "in decline." In this way his music became a
focus of nostalgia for a lost age of "decadent" luxury and indulgence in
things that modernity had now rendered more commonplace than dan-
gerous. No item of his musical output so succinctly represented this
Mahler as the Adagietto of the Fifth Symphony, popularized primarily
by a film that was already gently mocked in Ken Russell's *Mahler*, when
the composer looks out of his train carriage as it passes slowly through a
station on whose platform a boy in a kind of sailor suit is seen idly

[6] The style had perhaps been set in Sondheim's "The Ladies Who Lunch," from *Company* (1970): "A
matinee, a Pinter play / Perhaps a piece of Mahler's / I'll drink to that / And one for Mahler!"

swinging round the station roof's support poles, in sight of a Dirk Bogarde look-alike. The allusion (with the music) was recognizable by many in 1974 as referring to Visconti's 1971 film version of Thomas Mann's 1911 novella *Death in Venice*.

Laboriously overplayed by Visconti, the Adagietto nevertheless proves deliciously evocative of the Venice in which Wagner had died, a lost world of privileged luxury and introverted perversion that undermined Gustav von Aschenbach in Mann's novella exploring The Truth Behind a Great Novelist's Death (as the tabloids might put it). His stated facial and first-name resemblance to Mahler (whom Mann knew slightly) encouraged Visconti to turn Aschenbach *into* a composer, whose resemblance to the historical Mahler is emphasized by various details, like the use of the Welte-Mignon piano-roll "recording" of Mahler's playing of the last movement of his Fourth Symphony, which Aschenbach performs for a friend.

Mahler the unlikely decadent, the "troubled Artist," the Jewish ventriloquist of long-gone imperial Viennese sensibility and Secessionist luxuriance was thus born – and simultaneously prepared for the popular-cultural dustbin of dead male composers over whom one might shed a confusedly nostalgic tear. The confusion came from the music, which could still shock and excite, for all that it was apparently born (as the story ran) of psychosexual problems that explained it away as a symptom, appearing inconsistently to save us from worrying too much about our own readiness to identify with it.

The most recent cinematic exploration of this "symptomatically" contextualized and historicized Mahler appeared in 2010, marking the centenary of Mahler's notorious walking consultation with Sigmund Freud in Leyden. The consultation had been prompted and encouraged by Alma at a point of crisis in their marriage (the famous couch was never involved, but Mahler *had* serially cancelled appointments with the psychoanalyst). Written and directed by father-and-son team Percy and Felix Adlon, this striking, if problematic, German-language film (with English subtitles) – blithely titled *Mahler auf der Couch* (*Mahler on the Couch*) – relies primarily on Alma Mahler's own celebrated account of her first marriage. Appearing during the Second World War (in 1940; a second edition came out in 1949; both were published in the Netherlands), her *Gustav Mahler: Erinnerungen und Briefe* soon appeared in an inadequate but easy-to-read translation (*Gustav Mahler: Memories and Letters*, trans. Basil Creighton, 1946). Various subsequent editions of that translation, with notes and editorial commentary by Donald Mitchell and others, must be credited with having played a significant part in the popularization of Mahler as a biographical subject. Alma, mercilessly castigated and demonized by many Mahler devotees, was hardly indulging in the posthumous devotional eulogizing of a man by whom she had been fascinated, overwhelmed, but ultimately stifled – not least given the almost inevitable tensions related to their age difference of nearly twenty years. There is no spousal account of a famous husband quite like it, and the Adlons' film is in a sense best read as a portrait of and tribute to *her*, as much as to Mahler, the first movement of whose unfinished Tenth Symphony nevertheless supplies most of the underscore, in a specially recorded performance by Esa-Pekka Salonen with the Swedish Radio Symphony Orchestra.

Barbara Romaner's realization of Alma takes us well beyond Georgina Hale's nevertheless unforgettably constrained public manner (in both speech and dress) in Ken Russell's *Mahler*. Romaner gives us a full-on portrait of a young woman, intensely alive and intelligent, as she comes to terms with her sexuality in a pre–First World War Vienna that is as faithfully and lavishly reproduced as was Visconti's Venice. Secessionist costumes and period Viennese interiors provide the background to a self-consciously twenty-first-century depiction of Alma's relationship to her mother, to the film's rather startlingly reimagined Alexander Zemlinsky, and, passionately and problematically, to both Mahler and Gropius. Unfortunately, the depiction of Mahler by actor Johannes Silberschneider as a rather fussy and decidedly old German schoolmaster, with little outward evidence of any creative flair or passion, only highlights the power of Romaner's performance as Alma. Still more problematic, in this evidently serious and rather beautifully produced film, is the odd and uncertainly humorous way in which the central meeting between Mahler and Freud seems to be written for laughs (Freud played by Karl Markoviks) as a well-nigh offensive caricature of two comic-opera Viennese Jews trying to understand each other. The climactic scenes derived from Alma's account of Walter Gropius's misaddressed love letter (to Mahler rather than to her) and his appearance in the vicinity of Mahler's Toblach retreat are powerfully enough played by all concerned, although the Adlons, like Ken Russell before them, inexplicably overlook Alma's cinematically inviting account of Mahler having gone off across the fields to find him and bring him back for the cards-on-the-table showdown between the three of them: "It was night by this time, and in silence they walked all the way back up to our house, Mahler in front with a lantern and X [Gropius] following on behind. It was pitch dark. I was waiting in my room" (*ML*, 174). The climactic scene that follows (conflating more than one episode in Alma's account) ends with Mahler collapsing on the landing of their rented farmhouse with a heart seizure. It is the very stuff of operatic melodrama, but in the end it is perhaps difficult to be sure whether one's reaction is to the film or to Salonen's performance of the Tenth's opening Adagio, of which this representation of the composer seems to have little or no convincing knowledge. Indeed, it is difficult to decide whether the film provides a context for the music or the music for the film.

Mahler's music as performed often proves resistant or even threatening to the contexts in which attempts are made to represent, explain, or account for it. Perhaps it is just this that keeps Mahler current, alive, and still situated as somehow apart from the now institutionalized, yet effectively meaningless category of "Classical Music." In mass-cultural terms to be "classical" is generally assumed to mean conservative, probably boring and associated with class and/or money – with the suspicion of "decadence" always lurking in the wings. One episode of the American TV series *NCIS: Los Angeles* opened with an agent, shortly to be blown up for reasons the team must discover, whose overelaborate furnishings, expensively stylish dress, and lack of a wife, coupled with the background presence of Mahler's Fifth Symphony (albeit in *Sturm und Drang* rather than Ada-gietto mode) seemed deliberately to characterize and "place" him as a decadent aesthete. Reflecting on Mahler in a relevantly different manner was the Charles Schultz 1994 "Peanuts" cartoon in which Charlie Brown is confronted by two of his girlfriends, the first of whom tells him, "We've just been to a long symphony concert." Charlie looks behind her at the second girl, who appears disheveled and wrung out: "What's wrong with Patty?" Answer: "She was Mahlered!" When recently citing that cartoon, Paul André Bempéchat went on to quote Mikhail Gorbachev, interviewed in *Time* in May 1992 as having observed, "In life, there is always conflict and contradiction, but without those – there is no life. Mahler was able to capture that aspect of the human condition."[7] Perhaps that enabled him to speak to us all, regardless of racial or cultural identity.

---

[7] Both the cartoon and the Gorbachev quotation appear in Paul-André Bempéchat's introductory essay, "Why This Book?," to his edited volume *Naturlauf: Scholarly Journeys toward Gustav Mahler. Essays in Honour of Henry-Louis de La Grange for His 90th Birthday* (New York: Peter Lang, 2016), xiii.

Further Reading

1 FAMILY LIFE

Banks, Paul. "The Early Social and Cultural Environment of Gustav Mahler." PhD diss., Oxford University, 1980.

Feder, Stuart. *Gustav Mahler: A Life in Crisis*. New Haven: Yale University Press, 2004.

Haber, Michael. *Das Jüdische bei Gustav Mahler*. Frankfurt am Main: Peter Lang, 2009.

2 A CHILDHOOD IN BOHEMIA

Barham, Jeremy. "Juvenilia and Early Works: From the First Song Fragments to *Das klagende Lied*." In *The Cambridge Companion to Mahler*, ed. Jeremy Barham, 51–71. Cambridge: Cambridge University Press, 2007.

Fischer, Jens Malte. "Small Steps: Kalischt and Iglau." In *Gustav Mahler*, trans. Stewart Spencer, 12–41. New Haven: Yale University Press, 2011.

La Grange, Henry-Louis de. "Childhood: In Search of Himself and of the World." In *HLG1*, 13–26.

3 MUSIC IN IGLAU, 1860–1875

Achatzi, Johann, ed. *Iglauer Heimatbuch*. Heidelberg: Iglauer Sprachinsel e. V., 1962.

Fischer, Theodor. "Das Musikleben Iglaus im 19. Jahrhundert." *Zeitschrift des Deutschen Vereins für die Geschichte Mährens und Schlesiens* 36 (1934): 105–17.

Freeze, Timothy. "The Public Concert Life of Mahler's Youth: Iglau, 1866–75." *Naturlaut* 7 (2010): 2–8.

Karbusicky, Vladimir. *Gustav Mahler und seine Umwelt*. Darmstadt: Wissenschaftliche Buchgesellschaft, 1978.

Sonntags-Blatt, 1860–69; *Der Vermittler*, 1870–71; *Mährischer Grenzbote*, 1872–75 [digitized on books.google.com].

4 STUDENT CULTURE IN 1870S VIENNA

Blaukopf, Herta. "Mahler an der Universität: Versuch eine biographische Lücke zu schließen." In *Neue Mahleriana. Essays in Honour of Henry-Louis de La Grange on His Seventieth Birthday*, ed. Günter Weiß, 1–16. Berlin: Peter Lang, 1997.

Floros, Constantin. *Gustav Mahler's Mental World: A Systematic Representation.* Trans. Ernest Bernhadt-Kabisch. Berlin: Peter Lang, 2016.

McGrath, William J. *Dionysian Art and Populist Politics in Austria.* New Haven: Yale University Press, 1974.

5 VIENNESE MUSICAL ASSOCIATES, 1875–1883

McClatchie, Stephen. "Hans Rott, Gustav Mahler and the 'New Symphony': New Evidence for a Pressing Question." *Music and Letters* 81(2000): 392–401.

McColl, Sandra. *Music Criticis in Vienna, 1896–1897: Critically Moving Forms.* Oxford: Clarendon Press, 1996.

Wyn Jones, David. *Music in Vienna: 1700, 1800, 1900* (Woodbridge: Boydell Press, 2016).

Youens, Susan. *Hugo Wolf: The Vocal Music.* Princeton: Princeton University Press, 1992.

6 BECOMING A CONDUCTOR

Grassner, Helmut. "Kurorchester und Kurtheater Bad Hall – Wo Gustav Mahler seine ersten Sporen verdiente." *Oberösterreich. Kulturzeitschrift* 3 (1981): 57–62.

Kuret, Primož. *Mahler in Laibach.* Wiener Schriften zur Stilkunde und Aufführungspraxis, Sonderband 3. Vienna: Böhlau, 2001.

Schaefer, Hans Joachim. *Gustav Mahler – Jahre der Entscheidung in Kassel 1883–1885.* Kassel: Weber & Weidermeyer, 1990.

Willnauer, Franz. "Gustav Mahler und Oberösterreich." *Nachrichten zur Mahler-Forschung* 73 (June 2019): 53–84.

7 BETWEEN "THRICE HOMELESS" AND "TO THE GERMANS IN AUSTRIA"

Glettler, Monika. *Die Wiener Tschechen um 1900: Strukturanalyse einer nationalen Minderheit in der Großstadt.* Munich: R. Oldenbourg Verlag, 1972.

Krieger, Karsten. *Der "Berliner Antisemitismusstreit" 1879–1881: Eine Kontroverse um die Zugehörigkeit der deutschen Juden zur Nation*, 2 vols. Munich: K. G. Saur, 2003.

Malitz, Jürgen. "'Ich wünschte ein Bürger zu sein': Theodor Mommsen im wilhelminischen Reich." In *Die Antike im 19. Jahrhundert in Italien und Deutschland*, ed. Karl Christ, 321–59. Berlin: Duncker & Humblot, 1988.

Rozenblit, Marsha L. *The Jews of Vienna, 1867–1914: Assimilation and Identity*. Albany: State University of New York Press, 1983.

Sutter, Berthold. "Theodor Mommsens Brief 'An die Deutschen in Österreich.'" *Ostdeutsche Wissenschaft: Jahrbuch des Ostdeutschen Kulturrates* 10 (1965): 152–225.

8   OPERATIC AND ORCHESTRAL REPERTOIRE

Chevalley, Heinrich. *Hundert Jahre Hamburger Stadt-theater*. Hamburg: Broschek, 1927.

Martner, Knud. *Mahler's Concerts*. New York: Kaplan Foundation, Overlook Press, 2010.

Schabbing, Bernd. *Gustav Mahler als Konzert- und Operndirigent in Hamburg*. Berlin: Ernst Kuhn, 2002.

Willnauer, Franz. *Gustav Mahler und die Wiener Oper*. Vienna: Löcker, 1993.

9   COLLABORATORS

Bahr-Mildenburg, Anna. *Darstellung der Werke Richard Wagners aus dem Geiste der Dichtung und Musik: Tristan und Isolde*. Leipzig: Musikwissenschaftlicher Verlag, 1936.

Celenza, Anna Harwell. "Darwinian Visions: Beethoven Reception in Mahler's Vienna." *The Musical Quarterly* 93 (2010): 514–59.

Mahler, Gustav. *"Mein lieber Trotzkopf, meine süße Mohnblume": Briefe an Anna von Mildenburg*. Ed. Franz Willnauer. Vienna: Paul Zsolnay Verlag, 2006.

Thursby, Stephen Carlton. "Gustav Mahler, Alfred Roller, and the Wagnerian Gesamtkunstwerk: 'Tristan' and Affinities between the Arts at the Vienna Court Opera." PhD diss., Florida State University, 2009.

10   A PERFECT STORM

Horowitz, Joseph. "'The Imp of the Perverse' – The Mahler Broadcasts." *The Times Literary Supplement*, January 8, 1999.

Classical Music in America: A History of Its Rise and Fall. New York: Norton, 2005.

Review of Henry-Louis de La Grange, *Gustav Mahler*, vol. 4, *A New Life Cut Short*. *The Journal of the Society of American Music* 3, no. 1 (February 2009): 104–10.

"Henry Krehbiel: The German-American Transaction." In *Moral Fire: Musical Portraits from America's Fin-de-Siecle*. Berkeley: University of California Press, 2012.

11 CELEBRITY

Applegate, Celia. *The Necessity of Music: Variations on a German Theme*. Toronto: University of Toronto Press, 2017.

Berenson, Edward, and Eva Giloi, eds. *Constructing Charisma: Celebrity, Fame, and Power in Nineteenth-Century Europe*. New York: Berghahn Books, 2010.

Braudy, Leo. *The Frenzy of Renown: Fame and Its History*. Oxford: Oxford University Press, 1986.

Giloi, Eva. *Monarchy, Myth, and Material Culture in Germany, 1750–1950*. Cambridge: Cambridge University Press, 2011.

Rehding, Alexander. *Music and Monumentality: Commemoration and Wonderment in Nineteenth-Century Germany*. Oxford: Oxford University Press, 2009.

12 THE COMPOSER "GOES TO PRESS"

Banks, Paul. "Mahler and 'The Newspaper Company.'" *Nineteenth Century Music Review* 15, no. 3 (December 2018): 329–52.

Heinsheimer, Hans. *UE – Die ersten 37 ½ Jahre*. Vienna: Universal Edition, 2017.

Willnauer, Franz, ed. *Gustav Mahler. Briefe an seine Verleger*. Vienna: Universal Edition, 2012.

13 MAHLER AND PROGRAM MUSIC

Floros, Constantin. *Gustav Mahler: The Symphonies*. Trans. Reinhard G. Pauly. Portland, OR: Amadeus Press, 1993.

Gustav Mahler and the Symphony of the 19th Century. Trans. Neil K. Moran. Frankfurt am Main: Peter Lang, 2013.

Gustav Mahler's Mental World: A Systematic Representation. Trans. Ernest Bernhardt-Kabisch. Frankfurt am Main: Peter Lang, 2016.

Music as Message: An Introduction to Musical Semantics. Trans. Ernest Bernhardt-Kabisch. Frankfurt am Main: Peter Lang, 2016.

Listening and Understanding: The Language of Music and How to Interpret It. Trans. Ernst Bernhardt-Kabisch. Frankfurt am Main: Peter Lang, 2017.

14 INTERTEXTUALITY IN MAHLER

Almén, Byron, and Edward Pearsall, eds. *Approaches to Meaning in Music*. Bloomington: Indiana University Press, 2006.

Klein, Michael L. *Intertextuality in Western Art Music*. Bloomington: Indiana University Press, 2005.

Riffaterre, Michael. "Intertextuality vs. Hypertextuality." *New Literary History* 25, no. 4 (1994): 779–88.

Worton, Michael, and Judith Still, eds. *Intertextuality: Theories and Practices*. Manchester: Manchester University Press, 1990.

15 THE SYMPHONY, 1870–1911

Bonds, Mark Evan. *After Beethoven: Imperatives of Originality in the Symphony.* Cambridge, MA: Harvard University Press, 1996.

Brown, A Peter. *The Symphonic Repertoire, vol. III, part A: The European Symphony from c. 1800 to c. 1930: Germany and the Nordic Countries.* Bloomington: Indiana University Press, 2007.

with Brian Hart. *The Symphonic Repertoire, vol. III, part B: The European Symphony from c. 1800 to c. 1930: Great Britain, Russia, and France.* Bloomington: Indiana University Press, 2008.

The Symphonic Repertoire, vol. IV: The Second Golden Age of the Viennese Symphony: Brahms, Bruckner, Dvořák, Mahler, and Selected Contemporaries. Bloomington: Indiana University Press, 2003.

Deruchie, Andrew. *The French Symphony at the Fin de Siècle: Style, Culture, and the Symphonic Tradition.* Rochester, NY: University of Rochester Press, 2013.

Hepokoski, James. "Beethoven Reception: The Symphonic Tradition." In *The Cambridge History of Nineteenth-Century Music*, ed. Jim Samson, 424–59. Cambridge: Cambridge University Press, 2002.

Holoman, D. Kern, ed. *The Nineteenth-Century Symphony.* New York: Schirmer, 1997.

Horton, Julian, ed. *The Cambridge Companion to the Symphony.* Cambridge: Cambridge University Press, 2013.

16 MAHLER AND THE VISUAL ARTS OF HIS TIME

Carl, Klaus H. *The Viennese Secession.* New York: Partstone, 2011.

Glanz, Christian. "Gustav Mahlers politischen Umfeld." In *Mahler im Kontext/ Contextualizing Mahler*, ed. Erich Wolfgang Partsch and Morten Solvik, 20–31. Vienna: Böhlau, 2011.

Shapira, Elana. *Style and Seduction: Jewish Patrons, Architecture, and Design in Fin de Siècle Vienna.* Waltham, MA: Brandeis University Press, 2016.

Vergo, Peter. *Art in Vienna 1898-1918: Klimt, Kokoschka, Schiele and Their Contemporaries*, 4th ed. London: Phaidon, 2015.

17 MAHLER AND MODERNISM

Frisch, Walter. *German Modernism: Music and the Arts.* Berkeley: University of California Press, 2005.

Hefling, Stephen E. *Mahler: Das Lied von der Erde (The Song of the Earth).* Cambridge: Cambridge University Press, 2000.

Morgan, Robert P. "Ives and Mahler: Mutual Responses at the End of an Era." *19th-Century Music* 2 (1978): 72–81.

Youmans, Charles. *Mahler and Strauss: In Dialogue.* Bloomington: Indiana University Press, 2016.

18 RECEPTION IN VIENNA

Auner, Joseph. *A Schoenberg Reader: Documents of a Life.* New Haven: Yale University Press, 2003.

Bohlman, Philip V. *Jewish Music and Modernity.* Oxford: Oxford University Press, 2008.

Karnes, Kevin C. *A Kingdom Not of This World: Wagner, the Arts, and Utopian Visions in Fin-de-Siècle Vienna.* Oxford: Oxford University Press, 2013.

Koja, Stephan, ed. *Gustav Klimt: The Beethoven Frieze and the Controversy over the Freedom of Art.* Trans. Paul Aston, Robert McInnes, and Bronwen Saunders. Munich: Prestel, 2006.

Reilly, Edward R. *Gustav Mahler and Guido Adler: Records of a Friendship.* Cambridge: Cambridge University Press, 1982.

19 MAHLER'S PRESS FROM LONDON TO LOS ANGELES

Horowitz, Joseph. *Classical Music in America: A History of Its Rise and Fall.* New York: Norton, 2005.

Roman, Zoltan, ed. *Gustav Mahler's American Years, 1907–1911: A Documentary History.* Stuyvesant, NY: Pendragon Press, 1989.

Wagner, Mary H. *Gustav Mahler and the New York Philharmonic Orchestra Tour America.* Lanham, MD: Scarecrow Press, 2006.

20 ORGANIZED RELIGION

Beller, Steven. *Vienna and the Jews 1867–1938: A Cultural History.* Cambridge: Cambridge University Press, 1989.

Haber, Michael. *Das Jüdische bei Gustav Mahler.* Frankfurt am Main: Peter Lang, 2009.

Howard, Thomas Albert. *Religion and the Rise of Historicism: W. M. L. de Wette, Jacob Burckhardt, and the Theological Origins of Nineteenth-Century Historical Consciousness.* Cambridge: Cambridge University Press, 2000.

McGrath, William J. *Dionysian Art and Populist Politics in Austria.* New Haven: Yale University Press, 1974

Niekerk, Carl. *Reading Mahler: German Culture and Jewish Identity in Fin-de-Siècle Vienna.* Rochester: Camden House, 2010.

21 GERMAN IDEALISM

Ameriks, Karl, ed. *The Cambridge Companion to German Idealism,* 2nd ed. Cambridge: Cambridge University Press, 2017.

Hefling, Stephen E. "Siegfried Lipiner's *On the Elements of a Renewal of Religious Ideas in the Present.*" In *Mahler im Kontext/Contextualizing Mahler,* ed. Erich Partsch and Morten Solvik, 91–114. Vienna: Böhlau, 2011.

Lipiner, Siegfried. "Über die Elemente einer Erneuerung religiöser Ideen in der Gegenwart/On the Elements of a Renewal of Religious Ideas in the Present" (1878). In *Mahler im Kontext/Contextualizing Mahler*, ed. Erich Partsch and Morten Solvik, 115–52. Vienna: Böhlau, 2011.

Solvik, Morten. "Mahler's Untimely Modernism." In *Perspectives on Gustav Mahler*, ed. Jeremy Barham, 153–71. Hants: Ashgate Press, 2005.

"The Literary and Philosophical Worlds of Gustav Mahler." In *The Cambridge Companion to Mahler*, ed. Jeremy Barham, 21–34. Cambridge: Cambridge University Press, 2007.

22 NIETZSCHE

Aschheim, Steven E. *The Nietzsche Legacy in Germany 1890–1990*. Berkeley: University of California Press, 1992.

Gartenberg, Egon. *Mahler: The Man and His Music*. New York: Schirmer, 1978.

Ingleby, Melvyn. "Nietzsche's Vienna: The Reception of Nietzsche's Philosophy in 19th Century Vienna, 1870–1900." PhD diss., University College London, 2014.

McGrath, William J. *Dionysian Art and Populist Politics in Austria*. New Haven: Yale University Press, 1974.

Niekerk, Carl. *Reading Mahler, German Culture and Jewish Identity in Fin-de-Siècle Vienna*. Rochester, NY: Camden House, 2010.

23 FECHNER

Heidelberger, Michael. *Die innere Seite der Natur: Gustav Theodor Fechners wissenschaftlich-philosophische Weltauffassung*. Frankfurt am Main: Klostermann, 1993.

Nature from Within: Gustav Theodor Fechner's Psychophysical Worldview. Trans. Cynthia Klohr. Pittsburgh, PA: University of Pittsburgh Press, 2004. (Includes a chapter not found in the German edition.)

24 LITERARY ENTHUSIASMS

Barham, Jeremy. "Mahler the Thinker: The Books of the Alma Mahler-Werfel Collection." In *Perspectives on Gustav Mahler*, ed. Jeremy Barham, 37–151. Aldershot: Ashgate, 2005.

Fischer, Jens Malte. "The Avid Reader: Mahler and Literature." In *Gustav Mahler*, trans. Stewart Spencer, 125–39. New Haven: Yale University Press, 2011.

Floros, Constantin. *Gustav Mahler's Mental World: A Systematic Representation*. Trans. Ernest Bernhardt-Kabisch. Frankfurt am Main: Peter Lang, 2016.

Niekerk, Carl, *Reading Mahler: German Culture and Jewish Identity in Fin-de-Siècle Vienna*. Rochester, NY: Camden House, 2010.

Solvik, Morten. "The Literary and Philosophical Worlds of Gustav Mahler." In *The Cambridge Companion to Mahler*, ed. Jeremy Barham, 21–34. Cambridge: Cambridge University Press, 2007.

25 ROMANTIC RELATIONSHIPS

Feder, Stuart. "Before Alma: Gustav Mahler and 'Das Ewig-Weibliche.'" In *Mahler Studies*, ed. Stephen E. Hefling, 78–109. Cambridge: Cambridge University Press, 1997.

La Grange, Henry-Louis de, and Günther Weiss, eds., in collaboration with Knud Martner. *Gustav Mahler: Letters to His Wife*. Ed., revised, and trans. Antony Beaumont. Ithaca: Cornell University Press, 2004.

Mahler-Werfel, Alma. *Diaries 1898–1902*. Selected and trans. Antony Beaumont. Ithaca: Cornell University Press, 1999.

Solvik, Morten, and Stephen E. Hefling. "Natalie Bauer-Lechner on Mahler and Women: A Newly Discovered Document." *The Musical Quarterly* 97 (2014): 12–65.

26 MAHLER AND DEATH

Cacciari, Massimo. *Posthumous People: Vienna at the Turning Point*. Trans. Roger Friedman. Stanford: Stanford University Press, 1996.

Gay, Peter. *Schnitzler's Century: The Making of Middle-Class Culture 1815–1914*. New York: Norton, 2002.

Kitcher, Philip. *Deaths in Venice: The Cases of Gustav von Aschenbach*. New York: Columbia University Press, 2013.

Mitchell, Donald. *Gustav Mahler: Songs and Symphonies of Life and Death. Interpretations and Annotations*. Woodbridge: Boydell Press, 2002.

Niekerk, Carl. "Vienna around 1900 and the Crisis of Public Art (Klimt, Mahler, Schnitzler)," *Neophilologus* 95, no. 1 (2011): 95–107.

27 POSTHUMOUS REPUTATION, 1911 TO WORLD WAR II

Botstein, Leon. "Whose Gustav Mahler? Reception, Interpretation, and History." In *Mahler and His World*, ed. Karen Painter, 1–53. Princeton: Princeton University Press, 2002.

Downes, Stephen. *After Mahler: Britten, Weill, Henze and Romantic Redemption*. Cambridge: Cambridge University Press, 2013.

Mugmon, Matthew. "Beyond the Composer–Conductor Dichotomy: Bernstein's Copland-Inspired Mahler Advocacy." *Music & Letters* 94 (2014): 606–27.

"An Imperfect Mahlerite: Nadia Boulanger and the Reception of Gustav Mahler." *The Journal of Musicology* 35 (2018): 76–103.

Weiner, Marc. "Mahler and America: A Paradigm of Cultural Reception." *Modern Austrian Literature* 20 (1987): 155–69.

28 MAHLER AND THE SECOND VIENNESE SCHOOL

Budde, Elmar. "Bemerkungen zum Verhältnis Mahler-Webern." *Archiv für Musikwissenschaft* 33 (1976): 159–73.

Danuser, Hermann. "Karl Horwitz' 'Vom Tode' – Ein Dokument der Mahler-Verehrung aus der Schönberg-Schule." In *Mahler-Interpretation. Aspekte zum Werk und Wirken von Gustav Mahler*, ed. Rudolf Stephan, 177–90. Mainz: Schott, 1985.

Jacob, Andreas. "Ein sachlicher Heiliger? Schönbergs Mahler." In *Gustav Mahler und die musikalische Moderne*, ed. A. Jacobshagen, 145–56. Stuttgart: Steiner, 2011.

Puffett, Dereck. "Berg, Mahler and the Three Orchestral Pieces Op. 6." In *The Cambridge Companion to Berg*, ed. Anthony Pople, 111–44. Cambridge: Cambridge University Press, 1997.

Rexroth, Dieter. "Mahler und Schönberg." In *Gustav Mahler. Sinfonie und Wirklichkeit*, ed. O. Kolleritsch, 68–80. Vienna: Universal Edition, 1977.

Roman, Zoltan. "Decadent Transitions. Mahler, Modernism and the Viennese Fin de Siècle." In *Rethinking Mahler*, ed. Jeremy Barham, 253–70. New York: Oxford University Press, 2017.

29 THE MAHLER REVIVAL

Adorno, Theodor W. *Mahler: A Musical Physiognomy*. Trans. Edmund Jephcott. Chicago: University of Chicago Press, 1992.

Bernstein, Leonard. *The Unanswered Question: Six Talks at Harvard*. Cambridge, MA: Harvard University Press, 1973.

"Mahler: His Time Has Come." In *Findings*, 255–64. New York: Simon & Schuster, 1982. A version of the essay was first published in *High Fidelity* 17, no. 4 (April 1967).

Metzger, Christoph. "Issues in Mahler Reception: Historicism and Misreadings after 1960." In *The Cambridge Companion to Mahler*, ed. Jeremy Barham, 203–16. Cambridge: Cambridge University Press, 2007.

Williamson, John. "Adorno and the Mahler 'Revival.'" *The Musical Times* 131 (1990): 405.

30 BROADER MUSICAL INFLUENCE

Downes, Stephen. *After Mahler: Britten, Weill, Henze and Romantic Redemption*. Cambridge: Cambridge University Press, 2013.

Fanning, David. "The Symphony since Mahler: National and International Trends." In *The Cambridge Companion to the Symphony*, ed. Julian Horton, 96–129. Cambridge: Cambridge University Press, 2013.

Guldbrandsen, Erling E. "Modernist Composer and Mahler Conductor: Changing Conceptions of Performativity in Boulez." *Studia Musicologica Norvegica* 32 (2006): 140–68.

Keller, Hans. "The Unpopularity of Mahler's Popularity." *The Listener* 85, no. 2194 (April 5, 1971): 491.

Mugmon, Matthew. *Aaron Copland and the American Legacy of Gustav Mahler.* Rochester, NY: University of Rochester Press, 2019.

Whittall, Arnold. "'A dark voice from within': Peter Maxwell Davies and Modern Times.' In *Peter Maxwell Davies Studies,* ed. Kenneth Gloag and Nicholas Jones, 1–20. Cambridge: Cambridge University Press, 2009.

31 ADORNO

Franklin, Peter. "'. . . his fractures are the script of truth.' – Adorno's Mahler." In *Mahler Studies,* ed. Stephen E. Hefling, 271–94. Cambridge: Cambridge University Press, 1997.

Jäger, Lorenz. *Adorno: A Political Biography.* Trans. Stewart Spencer. New Haven: Yale University Press, 2004.

Paddison, Max. *Adorno's Aesthetics of Music.* Cambridge: Cambridge University Press, 1993.

Witkin, Robert W. *Adorno on Music.* London: Routledge, 1998.

32 INFLUENCES IN LITERATURE

Kogler, Susanne, and Andreas Dorschel, eds. *Die Saite des Schweigens: Ingeborg Bachmann und die Musik.* Vienna: Edition Steinbauer, 2006.

Mertens, Volker. *Gross ist das Geheimnis: Thomas Mann und die Musik.* Leipzig: Militzke, 2006.

Wagner, Margarete. "Mahlers Verhältnis zur zeitgenössischen Literatur." In *Mahler im Kontext/Contextualizing Mahler,* ed. Erich Wolfgang Partsch and Morten Solvik, 291–335. Vienna: Böhlau, 2011.

33 MAHLER ON DISC

Fülöp, Péter. *Mahler Discography.* New York: Kaplan Foundation, 1995.

La Grange, Henry-Louis de. "Appendix 2B: Mahler as a Performer of His Own Works (The Piano Rolls and Their Transfer to Disk)." In *HLG4,* 1619–35.

Smoley, Lewis M. *The Symphonies of Gustav Mahler: A Critical Discography.* New York: Greenwood Press, 1986.

Gustav Mahler's Symphonies: Critical Commentary on Recordings since 1986. Westport, CT: Greenwood Press, 1996.

Werner, Sybille, and Gene Gaudette. "The Dawn of Recording: Business and Art Collide." Booklet notes to Gustav Mahler, "The Music of Gustav Mahler: Issued 78s, 1903–1940." New York: Urlicht AudioVisual collector's edition, 2013.

34   FILM AND RECENT POPULAR CULTURE

Barham, Jeremy. "Dismembering the Musical Voice: Mahler, Melodrama and Dracula from Stage to Screen." In *Melodramatic Voices: Understanding Music Drama*, ed. Sarah Hibberd, 237–62. Farnham: Ashgate, 2011.

Williams, Jonathan. *Mahler*. London: Cape Goliard, 1967.

Winters, Ben. *Music, Performance and the Realities of Film: Shared Concert Experiences in Screen Fiction*. New York: Routledge, 2014.

Index

Abravanel, Maurice, 253, 290
Adler, Guido, 5, 11–12, 14–15, 37, 44, 103–4,
  158–61, 207, 235, 237, 247
Adler, Sigmund, 36
Adler, Victor, 11, 36–37, 39, 43, 141, 190
Adlon, Felix, 297
Adlon, Percy, 297
Adorno, Theodor, 3, 131, 194–96, 209, 236–37,
  243–44, 246–47, 254, 266
  Kindertotenlieder, 269
  Mahler Centenary Address, 271
  Mahler: A Musical Physiognomy, 270–72
  Mahler Today, 269
  Marginalia on Mahler, 269
  Philosophy of Modern Music, 268
  Quasi una Fantasia, 271
  On the Social Situation of Music, 269
Alighieri, Dante, 294
Appia, Adolphe, 74
Arnim, Ludwig Achim von, 210
Arp, Hans, 229
Auber, Daniel, 29, 67
Aue, Hartmann von, 213

Bach, J. S., xxi, 122–23, 125, 236, 239, 256
  *Capriccio sopra la lontananza del suo fratello
    dilettissimo*, 110
  St. Matthew Passion, 251
  Well-Tempered Clavier, Book I, Prelude and
    Fugue in F Minor, 124
Bachmann, Ingeborg, 280–82
Badeni, Count Kasimir, 57–59
Bahr, Hermann, 43, 192, 211, 275, 280
Bakhtin, Mikhail, 118
Balakirev, Mily, 132
Balfe, Michael, 26, 30
Barthes, Roland, 118–19, 122, 126
Bartók, Béla, 86
Bauer-Lechner, Natalie, xxii, 4, 6, 9, 48, 117,
  191, 221
Bauernfeld, Eduard von, 50

Baumann, Ludwig, 145
Baur, Ferdinand Christian, 177
Bayreuth Festival, 68, 79, 81, 98
Beach, Amy
  Gaelic Symphony, 86
Beatles
  Sergeant Pepper's Lonely Hearts Club Band, 291
Bechstein, Ludwig, 209
Beckett, Samuel, 122
Beethoven, Ludwig van, 13, 26–27, 66, 69, 71,
  82, 88, 91, 112, 114, 127–29, 134, 143,
  154, 194, 230, 239, 243, 247, 256, 272,
  275, 287, 289, 296
  Egmont Overture, 50
  Fidelio, 55, 67–68, 76, 162
  Symphony no. 6, "Pastoral", 111, 131
  Symphony no. 9, xxi, 71, 74, 116, 129, 144,
    154, 168
Behn, Hermann, 103–4
Bekker, Paul, 240, 244
Bella, Johann Leopold, 112
Bellini, Vincenzo, 29–30
Benjamin, Walter, 243
Berg, Alban, 109, 115, 235, 242–45, 249, 254,
  258, 266–67
  Lulu, 236
  Three Orchestral Pieces, op. 6, 245
  Violin Concerto, 236, 245
  Wozzeck, 236, 267
Berg, Helene, 254, 267
Berger, Arthur, 259
Berio, Luciano, 122, 262–63
  Rendering, 263
  Sinfonia, 122, 262
Berkeley, George, 183
Berkhan, Wilhelm, 103
Berlioz, Hector, 110–11, 149
  Le carnaval romain, 72
  Rob Roy, 72
  Roméo et Juliette, 111
  Symphonie fantastique, 70, 72, 111, 131, 133

CPSIA information can be obtained
at www.ICGtesting.com
Printed in the USA
LVHW080557260423
745306LV00004B/648

9 781108 438353